Teaching in the
Elementary School

Planning for Competence

Teaching in the Elementary School

Joseph F. Callahan

Leonard H. Clark

Jersey City State College

Macmillan Publishing Co., Inc.
New York

Collier Macmillan Publishers
London

87291

Macmillan Publishing Co., Inc.
866 Third Avenue, New York, New York 10022

Collier Macmillan Canada, Ltd.

ISBN   0–02–318070–6

Printing: 2 3 4 5 6 7 8   Year: 8 9 0 1 2 3

To Jane E. Callahan *and* Maria A. Clark

Preface

In this volume, Module 1 attempts to bring you up to date along a historical time line by briefly recapitulating significant happenings that affected the evolution of the elementary school. The discussion of colonial beginnings is followed by a focus on growth during the development of the young republic, by an examination of later nineteenth-century happenings, and then by a glimpse of education after World War II. Reforms in education in each of these periods are presented to prepare you for an understanding of how teaching is done today.

Modules 2 and 4 are devoted to an examination of the child. The former focuses upon growth and development in general, and the latter upon the individual differences that result during this development.

Module 3 is devoted to the basic goals of an elementary education program and the general methods that can be used to achieve curricular goals.

Modules 5 and 6 focus on the act of teaching. Securing the support of each student and his active pursuit of learning through positive and humanistic discipline is the thrust of Module 5. Module 6 investigates the ways in which a prepared teacher can orchestrate the operation of the entire class to achieve effective and efficient results.

Modules 7 through 10 suggest specific methods that have been found effective in teaching each of the subject fields. Module 7 suggests methods to use in language arts and reading classes; Module 8, methods for science class; Modules 9 and 10, methods for social studies and arithmetic classes, respectively.

The remaining two modules are general in nature and cover the entire curriculum. Module 11 encourages creativity in all endeavors in the elementary school and Module 12 cites illustrations of how values can be cultivated no matter what subject is being taught.

J. F. C.
L. H. C.

Contents

Teaching in the Elementary School

To the Student

Welcome to an adventure in learning.

Now that you have begun to think seriously about a career in teaching, it is our guess that you will find adventures of this sort very helpful in planning to meet the challenges that await you in the classroom. It seems safe to predict that not only will you increase your background in educational theory and methodology as you work your way through these modules, but also you will improve your chances of becoming an effective teacher when the time arrives to put theory learned into practice.

Probably you have not encountered many books organized as this one, calling for such active participation on your part. From this point forward, you are expected to become a sensitive, self-motivated learner engaged in making frequent and sound judgments about your learning. You will be the one to control the rate of progress through the various modules and you will decide when you have mastered the knowledge presented in each. We have tried to help by (1) listing the objectives of each module, (2) providing a comprehensive set of questions to test your mastery at the end of each module, and (3) providing an answer key for your use in evaluating progress. Those with little time to spend on study can move through the various modules and finish quickly so long as they study attentively and demonstrate the mastery called for on each test. Slower-paced individuals, who wish to ponder and probe various areas and who decide to read extensively from the selected readings listed in each module, can establish a pace that suits their purposes.

It is not intended that any student will be able to prepare himself for a teaching career solely by completion of this kind of study program. Teaching is a human activity. It deals with people, with children, parents, and fellow professionals. It involves various kinds of knowledge, judgments, and decision making; it requires communications skills, human relations techniques, and a host of other attributes for the cultivation of which human interaction and professional expertise are necessary. But faithful and zealous use of this learning tool will add depth and meaning to your classroom sessions in education courses. Mastery of these modules will carry you beyond the initial steps of preparation so that you may place into context more of the campus lectures about education which you hear, and ask questions about schools and students that go beyond the layman's level of significance.

The sections of the book are called modules, for essentially they are self-contained units that have cognitive values by themselves. Each module contains a rationale, a list of objectives, a post test, an answer key, and a list of selected readings. The rationale attempts to establish the purpose of each module and, in some cases, the link with other aspects of pedagogical knowledge. The objectives inform you very specifically what you should know and be able to do as a consequence of your study of the module. The test and the key inform you of your progress toward module mastery. The general study plan recommended is as follows:

1. Read the rationale to acquaint yourself with the task you are addressing and, if possible, with how this module fits among the others that you will study.
2. Examine carefully the module objectives. Find out what will be expected of you upon completion of your study.
3. Read through the module, checking back from time to time to see how well you are mastering the objectives. Review what you do not understand.
4. Take the Post Test. Evaluate your success by using the answer key. Where your answer differs from that of the author, search out the sentence or paragraph in the text that confirms your answer or his.
5. If you score less than 85 per cent on any test, reread and retake the test until your mastery improves.
6. Try out your knowledge by exposing yourself to some of the suggested reading. Your progress should accelerate as you bring more and more knowledge to each book that you read.
7. Engage in interaction with fellow students, professors, and members of your family on the topics studied, whenever possible.
8. Enjoy the experience. The profession needs zealous seekers of knowledge who enjoy learning and who, in the process, develop a capacity for infecting other people with the same "felicitous virus."

The Elementary School in the United States: Present and Past

Janet M. Leonard

Jersey City State College

module 1

State and Local Powers / Decentralization / Colonial Beginnings / Education in the Young Republic / Later Nineteenth Century Education / Reform in Elementary Education / Education and the Depression of the 1930s / Education and World War II

RATIONALE

The elementary school in the United States is a myriad of social forces which reflect the cultural life of the people. Elementary schools throughout the nation vary in many aspects, such as staff, curriculum, student population, financing, means, and goals. A rural, midwestern school may contrast sharply with a school in inner-city New York, both in the strengths each possesses and in the problems each encounters. However varied the schools may be, there is a generally accepted belief that all children should have an educational experience that at least includes elementary and secondary training.

When one attempts to view the elementary school structure, it is evident that, in spite of geographic, fiscal, or ethnic differences, certain assumptions are commonly held by most Americans. Four of these assumptions reflect value choices which Americans believe to be a part of the fabric of their lives.[1] The first belief is that of democracy as a working way of life. The executive, legislative, and judicial branches of the United States government are based on the shared participatory actions of its citizens who, through their constitutional rights, vest powers in and limitations upon their elected representatives. Although the Constitution has been expanded and reinterpreted during its almost two-hundred-year existence, the belief that the people do participate in government and do control its functions is a basic premise for the understanding of democracy.

Closely allied to the concept of the democratic way of life is the belief in the equality of every individual. If each person is held to have the same intrinsic worth, then equality of opportunity must be provided. Such commitment to equality means that each person's opinion must be respected, that the majority must reckon with the minority, and that conflicting ideas must be given an audience.

The third value that has traditional roots in America is the belief in material progress. The "land of opportunity" for the earlier immigrants embodied the assumption that the wealth and prosperity of this nation would advance and that the individual could share in that prosperity. Closely joined to the belief in material progress is the American success in science and technology. This success, underpinning the country's national and international image, has been viewed as proof that material progress is both an ideal and a reality.

The belief in democracy, equality, and national progress is linked to a fourth belief, the value of education. To prepare a person to participate in national life and to share in its richness requires a proper educational environment. The role of education, whether it is to be a reflection of society's values or a catalyst for changing those values, may be disputed; however, the belief that education is essential for an individual's fulfillment and for a nation's development has been traditionally accepted.

To cite certain values as basic ingredients of American life does not mean that they have been, or are, uniformly understood and accepted. In fact, the dissent concerning these values and about how values are to be incorporated has resulted

---

[1] Daniel Selakovich, *The Schools and American Society,* 2nd ed. (New York: John Wiley & Sons, Inc., 1973), p. 30.

in forces for change at every level of American society, including education. To help you understand the role of education in American life today, this module examines the structure and function of the elementary school, focusing on its present mode in the light of its historic past, and points toward some of those areas in which future changes may occur.

SPECIFIC OBJECTIVES

When you have completed the study of this module, you should be able to do the following:

1. Cite four of the basic beliefs held by Americans in common, reflecting their value choices pertaining to democratic living.
2. Identify the source of greatest control over the daily functioning of the elementary school.
3. Identify the source of power for local boards of education.
4. Describe the source of financial support for local schools.
5. Define decentralization.
6. Explain the main purpose of New England colonial schools.
7. Explain the main purpose of New England grammar schools.
8. Cite the percentage of blacks estimated to have been literate in 1863 and 1910.
9. Identify Rousseau and explain briefly his foundation for Emile's education.
10. Explain how Rousseau's plan for Sophie differed from his plan for Emile.
11. Identify the founder of the first kindergarten.
12. Identify the person recognized as the "father of the American Common School."
13. Identify Joseph Rice.
14. Specify the four main problems which Dewey attempted to solve through his laboratory school.
15. Identify the main purpose of the Science of Education movement.
16. Explain the function which the Reconstructionists wanted the schools to perform.
17. Identify the stereotypes in three major areas which schools have been accused of perpetuating in the 1970s.
18. Describe the role played in elementary education by the local school district, the state legislature, and the federal government.
19. Identify the "Massachusetts Law of 1642" regarding education.
20. Explain the derivation of the name "Old Deluder Act" and specify its major provision.
21. Describe briefly the "Dame Schools."
22. Explain the major difference between schools in the Middle Colonies, in New England, and in the Southern Colonies.
23. Identify Pestalozzi and Herbart.

24. Describe the impact of the Irish immigrations of the 1830s and 1840s upon the common school movement.
25. List some of the reforms which educators in the Progressive Education movement wished to effect.
26. Describe the divisions of elementary school life as viewed by Dewey.
27. Contrast Dewey's position regarding the mind with the position commonly held earlier about the "little man."
28. Identify Edward Lee Thorndike and contrast his position with that of the Progressive Education movement.
29. Describe the impact of Sputnik upon American education.

MODULE TEXT

State and Local Powers

Although education in the United States is a prerogative of the states, the functioning of the elementary school is carried out by local government, which, through either elected or appointed boards of education, administers the educational program. It is the local school district that has traditionally been strong in American elementary education. The local district is governed by a board of education which represents the citizens who reside in the geographical area. The local board of education receives its powers from state statutes. These statutes delineate the procedures to be used for selection of board members, length of office, and duties and rights of members. Usually, members of local boards are citizens who have shown interest in the community's schools. It is through them that communities can improve and enhance their schools. Although all districts must comply with minimum state regulations, local control allows residents of the area to raise their schools' standards and offerings beyond those required by the state.

Essentially, the policy-making responsibility for education resides in state legislatures which grant powers to various state and local boards. The powers of the various boards differ according to the laws of each state. The basic powers of state boards of education involve the rights to issue and to revoke teaching certificates, to establishd accreditation standards, and to systematize educational data. State boards of education prepare both long- and short-range educational goals, and advise the governor and legislature concerning recommended goals. To provide necessary information, state boards of education often appoint commissions to study problems involving curriculum, teacher certification, textbooks, school district reorganization, finance, building standards, and other matters.

Every state has a chief school officer, either elected or appointed, under whose direction the state department of education functions. State departments of education, however, have not exhibited strong leadership in the past.

It is important to realize that American education is essentially public. The fact that it is financed by the taxpayers, many of whom enroll their children in the local school, means that the school is visible, nearby, and of immediate concern to the citizens. The public nature of the school has many political implications, especially in regard to societal values, social class, and community power. Although the federal government has established various educational agencies and has allocated money for specific educational purposes, the Constitution reserves to the states inherent control of education. The public nature of the schools is, therefore, an essentially state and local matter. Local control of schools is often the most immediate way citizens have of exercising their authority. It is among state, cities, other intermediate levels, and local districts that conflicts usually arise.[2]

Much disparity in quality and services has resulted from local funding of schools. Some state monies have usually been available to all districts; yet, most of the money used for locals schools is raised through community taxes. Recently, the State Supreme Court of New Jersey struck down the practice of reliance on local taxation for education as unconstitutional. Stating that all children have a right to a "thorough and efficient" education, the Court decreed that a new way to finance public schools must be found.[3] More centralization of education, with the state supervising an equitable distribution of money to school districts, appears possible. Such redistribution will guarantee more money to financially pressured, urban, inner-city schools, and less fiscal aid to more affluent, suburban ones. It should be noted that revised fiscal allocation may serve to equalize educational opportunities within a state; however, the fact remains that many differences in school services and quality exist among the fifty states. Statistical evidence shows that there is great disparity in the quality of education on a national level.

Decentralization

The decade of the sixties witnessed a dramatic effort, mainly by urban minorities, to decentralize the schools. Desiring to have more direct control over school administration, curriculum, and teaching, urban minorities demanded that smaller geographic areas replace large, urban school districts. Such smaller districts would enable citizens to elect their own school boards, to have real power in the selection of school personnel, and to have fiscal control. Such demand for decentralization reflects the shifting of the white, middle-class from the cities to the suburbs. The newer urban populace is frequently economically poor and made up chiefly of racial minorities. These urban minorities, often outside the mainstream of social mobility and economic opportunity afforded to earlier American immigrants, realize that their children's schools reflect a society whose values and structures do not seem to be relevant to their needs and aspirations.

It is true that for three decades, from the 1930s through the 1950s, large cities had attempted to centralize all their governmental functions, including education. Elected school boards, chosen from a city-wide slate, often had no inner-city minority representation. The middle-class, white values, which were accepted as educational norms, were not perceived as discriminatory educational goals. The city school board hired teachers and other school personnel who often neither lived in nor understood the ghetto area to which they were assigned. Eventually, urban minorities demanded changes not only in the appointment of personnel, but also in the school curriculum which, they insisted, should better reflect their own mores.

---

[2] For further readings on state and local powers in education, see Robert Bendiner, *The Politics of Schools: A Crisis in Self-Government* (New York: The New American Library, 1970).

[3] *The New York Times,* May 24, 1972.

A third target for change was that of fiscal control. Advocates of decentralization viewed fiscal control as one way of achieving equitable distribution of monies.

The issue of decentralization confronted many cities during the 1960s. The fight for control in New York City between proponents of centralization and of decentralization resulted in Mayor John V. Lindsay's bringing in McGeorge Bundy of the Ford Foundation to arbitrate the issue.[4] The decentralization conflict was not confined to New York City; similar struggles occurred in many other American cities. The pressure for decentralization has been moderately successful in Detroit, Seattle, and St. Louis, but has met with less success in Boston and Philadelphia. In New York City the issue was fraught with confusion and hostility. Positions polarized, and the problems were compounded because of the American Federation of Teachers' strike in 1968 after nineteen teachers were dismissed. Decentralization efforts in New York City, however, have met with moderate success since separate school districts, each of which has its own governing board and administrative staff, were established. Difficulties continue, nevertheless, as evidenced in the school board elections of the early 1970s.[5]

Much of the thrust for decentralization has involved black people whose consciousness of their racial identity is linked to their awareness of the need for political power. Elected black mayors represent only one aspect of the expanding political power of the black community. With regard to American education, blacks reflect the traditional evolution of earlier American minorities who eventually achieved their goals by means of acquiring political power.

In spite of some implementation of school decentralization, there remain major obstacles to overcome. In no case in which decentralization has occurred has the legislature of any state provided a solution to the fiscal problem.[6] If school funding continues to reside in the local district, the economic inequity separating poor ghetto schools from more affluent suburban schools will continue. Such economic differences will be reflected in all parts of the educational system, from the hiring of personnel to the purchase of equipment and maintenance of buildings. The result of such fiscal discrepancy could be greater segregation and deterioration of inner-city schools. Only when state or national economic aid is fairly distributed can there be a solution to the financial hardship of the ghetto schools.

To better understand present, complex, educational issues, among which are control, funding, and administration, it is necessary to trace the general outline of the development of the elementary school in the United States. Basic values, such as democracy, equality, and opportunity, all considered as inherent in the American ethos, have traditional roots. How much influence have these values had on education in this country, and how much impact will they have in the future? To answer these questions, one must study the beginnings and evolution of the elementary school in the United States.

Colonial Beginnings

It was logical that New Englanders, who had come to the New World so as to freely pursue their religious beliefs, wanted to educate their children in those be-

4 Op. cit., p. 89.
5 *The New York Times,* May 12, 1975.
6 D. Selakovich, op. cit., p. 90.

liefs. The "Massachusetts Law of 1642," passed only twelve years after Boston was settled, empowered the selectman of every town to require that all parents and masters provide for the education and employment of their charges. Each selectman had to make sure that children learned to read, to understand their religion and the laws of the country, and to be able to find useful employment. The 1642 law allowed parents latitude in how they were to educate their children; they could teach them at home or they could arrange for group instruction. The purpose of the 1642 law was, however, designed to remedy "the great neglect of many parents and guardians in training their children in learning and for labor which may be profitable to the commonwealth."[7]

Five years after Massachusetts passed its initial legislation concerning education, it passed the "Old Deluder Act." This law received its name from the preamble's statement that "It being one chief project of ye ould deluder, Sathan, to keepe men from the knowledge of ye Scriptures."[8] In order to thwart Satan's attack, the state fathers required that public elementary education be established. The "Old Deluder Act" required towns of fifty families to provide the basic skills of reading and writing. Towns of one hundred families had to have grammar schools. Despite the fact that not all communities fully complied with the law, the fundamental concept of the "public school" was established.

The education laws of 1642 and 1647 reflected Puritan theology. Based on Calvinist theology, Puritanism viewed human nature as basically corrupt and evil. Salvation was only given to those chosen people whom God had predestined. Although such predestination was beyond any individual's merit, it was each person's responsibility to conform his life to God's law as revealed in Scripture. If there was any hope for redirecting the evil inclinations of perverse human nature, it was to be realized through the reading of God's word, the memorizing of Scripture, the careful scrutiny of one's actions, the care taken to safeguard the religious practices of the community. The "godly life" was the goal of the Puritan. Early education in New England reflected this religious orientation.[9] Such religious emphasis gave girls, as well as boys, the opportunity and obligation to learn at least the rudiments of reading and writing.

In practice, compliance with the laws often meant that children's initiation to education was at a "dame school," where they were taught by a woman who supervised their learning in her home. In return for small payment, the woman would listen to the children recite the alphabet, read from their primers, and master basic spelling and writing skills. The hornbook—not a book at all, but a piece of printed paper about four inches long and fastened to a board—provided the letters of the alphabet, the vowels, letter blends, and religious prayers.

Grammar schools, established by the 1647 law, were attended by boys of seven or eight years of age, who had mastered the basic skills provided either at home or at the dame school. Feminists who are interested in tracing sexist roots in American education may learn cogent lessons from the colonial period. Higher education was not open to women; even the Latin grammar schools were male

---

[7] Clifton Johnson, *Old Time Schools and School Books* (New York: Dover Publications, Inc., 1963), p. 1.

[8] Ibid., p. 2.

[9] Bernard Bailyn, *Education in the Forming of American Society* (New York: W. W. Norton & Company, Inc., 1972), p. 27.

enclaves. Women's role in education was relegated to the training of very young girls in domesticity and housekeeping.

New England adapted the English concept that a grammar school was one in which Latin was the basic language taught as preparation for entrance to Harvard and higher studies. In practice, the grammar schools of New England combined a study of Latin and English. The grammar schools were supported variously by grants, by land rentals, by tuition, and by taxes. There was no uniform way of financing the schools, and each town could devise its own means. Although poor people advocated free education, the wealthy opposed the idea. It was not until 1827 that Massachusetts made school support by taxation compulsory.

One of the most commonly used textbooks, the *New England Primer,* provided many opportunities for reading and memorization, and at the same time combined religious instruction. For example, in learning the use of *A,* children would read

> In Adam's Fall,[10]
> We sinned all.

Aspects of life other than the religious were included in the primer. For instance, a reference to a monarch in an early edition introduced the letter *K* with this rhyme:

> King Charles the Good
> No man of blood.

The rhyme was altered by the time of the American Revolution to read

> Kings should be good
> No men of blood.[11]

Although the religious impetus of Puritanism waned as the new land evolved, the emphasis on education as a vital force for the betterment of the individual and of society continued to flourish. The New Englanders who established the first public schools made such an impact on American society that the belief that all people should be literate remained a societal value even after the religious impetus of Puritanism diminished.

Education in the Middle Colonies was more diverse, mainly because of the variety of religious beliefs held by the settlers of that region. Education in the Middle States was, therefore, parochial because it reflected the dominant religious belief of the people of the area. New Amsterdam established a public school in 1633, but its use was reserved only to members of the Dutch Reform Church.

Unlike the New England colonies' public education and the Middle Colonies' parochial thrust, the South developed private education for the wealthy and missionary education for the poor. Although some public and some parochial education existed in the South, neither form was characteristic of the area. The large land holdings mitigated against the close township structure found in the North.

[10] Johnson, op. cit., p. 80.
[11] Ibid., p. 82.

Geographically isolated, a wealthy farmer found it more advantageous to employ a tutor for his children. The tutor would impart basic skills and also develop the talents of an elite class in dance, music, and art.

The Southern poor were educated by the Society of the Propagation of the Gospel in Foreign Parts, a missionary branch of the Episcopal Church. Such education consisted of the rudiments of learning, combined with hymns and prayers. The term *old field schools* was often applied to this form of missionary education because the school was often an abandoned building situated on a piece of worn-out land.

Education for blacks was generally nonexistent. Southern laws later made it a crime to educate blacks. To cite only one instance, anyone who taught a black person to read in South Carolina was subject to a $100 fine.[12]

The Society for the Propagation of the Gospel in Foreign Parts opened a school for blacks in New York City in 1714 in which 200 children were enrolled. The Society continued to found schools for blacks in various parts of the country. Such educational efforts were rare and affected only a small percentage of the black population. White slave owners generally feared that education would make the black more aware of his plight, and would lead to discontent and even rebellion. A few black people did attain education, and contributed much to the nation's intellectual growth. It is impossible in a module of this scope to cite all black intellectuals, but among them are Phyllis Wheatley, a poet; Benjamin Banniker, astronomer and clock manufacturer; John Chavis, teacher of aristocratic whites; and Frederick Douglass, advocate of vocational education for blacks. Most blacks, however, remained academically uneducated. It must be realized that the moral strain of slavery affected the social fabric of the country in such a way as to hinder any really strong effort to educate its black people. In 1863 when Lincoln issued the Emancipation Proclamation, it is estimated that only 5 per cent of the black population was literate. By 1890, the figure was estimated to be at 40 per cent, and by 1910 the literacy rate had risen to 70 per cent.[13]

In summary, the founding of American schools, whether in New England, the Middle Colonies, or the South, had religious connotations. Essentially, the public schools, established by the Puritans, had as their basic aim the education of a person who could better understand his religious beliefs. The schools of New England differed not so much in purpose from those established in the Middle and Southern colonies; rather, it was the way the people financed their schools and in their insistence on compulsory schooling that made them different.

All the colonies accepted the fact that the responsibility to educate was a function of the church. Whether or not the particular denomination could acquire state help in maintaining schools was another question. It is not to the colonial period but rather to the post-revolutionary time that the concept of public education, free of denominational control, is to be applied. The shift from denominational to public education involved transitional stages, as evidenced by the Ordinance of 1787. Although the Ordinance required that land in the new Northwest Territory

[12] S. Samuel Shermis, "A Brief Survey of American Education," *The Pursuit of Excellence,* ed. by Donald C. Orlich and S. Samuel Shermis (New York: American Book Company, 1965), p. 16.

[13] James A. Johnson, Harold W. Collins, Victor L. Dupuis, John H. Johnson, *Introduction to the Foundations of American Education,* 2nd ed. (Boston: Allyn & Bacon, Inc., 1973), p. 321.

should be set aside for schools, the provision was not really implemented until fifty years later.[14]

The beginnings of American education, as already noted, were for religious rather than for democratic purposes. In order that education should become democratic, basic societal changes had to occur and influence the changing American scene. The founders of the American republic were men whose intellectual formation owed much to their European heritage; therefore, it was logical that the political and social thinking prevalent during the eighteenth century Enlightenment period would affect the thinking of American leaders in education as well as in politics.[15] As early as 1750, Franklin proposed education for American youth as a way of strengthening the country: "Nothing is of more importance for the public weal than to form and train youth in wisdom and virtue."[16] Viewing education as a primary function of the state, Franklin proposed that its goals center on broad-based, enlightened citizenry. Such a goal offered a wider alternative than the rather narrow, religious purposes of the New England schools. Jefferson believed that democracy could succeed only through education and that an uneducated populace could easily be seduced by tyrants. Advocating equal education for all, Jefferson proposed that states finance school funding. Although Jefferson's proposal, made in 1779, was not immediately implemented, it provided the philosophical groundwork for the idea of public education in the United States.[17] George Washington wanted public education as a way to promote nationalism and as a means by which the young could assimilate the "principles, opinions, and manners of our countrymen."[18] In his opinion, education would assist and strengthen the nation, but would not replace morality: "Whatever may be conceded to the influence of refined education . . . reason and experience both forbid us to expect that National morality can prevail in exclusion of religious principles."[19]

Although the founding fathers spoke highly of public education, their words must be read in the broader context of their political views. Not even liberal Federalists advocated public education of such a broad-based nature as to make all the masses enlightened citizens. The narrow franchise of the day, with qualifications mainly based on being male, white, free, and a property owner, reflected the Federalists' view about who should rule the country and, by implication, who should receive much education. The values of equality, democracy, and opportunity were not granted unreservedly to all. Women, slaves, and white, nonpropertied males were not the focus of the founding fathers' thrust for education and an enlightened citizenry.

Education in the Young Republic

The period of Jackson's presidency is often heralded as the coming of age of the common man. The belief that people were capable of making decisions that

[14] For further discussion of the relationship of denominational financing and public taxation, see B. Bailyn, op. cit., pp. 40–49.

[15] Ibid., p. 73.

[16] Jared Sparks, ed., *The Works of Benjamin Franklin* (Boston: Whitmore, Niles, and Hall, 1856) **7**: 47.

[17] D. Selakovich, op. cit., p. 54.

[18] Ibid p. 54.

[19] John C. Fitzpatrick, ed. *Writings of Washington* (Washington, D.C.: United States Government Printing Office, 1940) **35**: 229.

were reflected in their lives and in the welfare of the entire nation influenced attitudes regarding education. In actuality, a more democratizing process had emerged earlier; the election of Jackson was as much a result of as it was a catalyst for the age of the "common man." Many states provided in their original constitutions for the establishment of public schools. It was generally accepted, though not by all, that some amount of education was desirable for the general well-being.

The European intellectual heritage remained a force. One of the most important European writers who influenced American education was Jean-Jacques Rousseau. In his work, *Emile*, Rousseau described what he believed to be a boy's ideal education. Freed from the discipline of punishment for failing to master abstract material learned by rote, Rousseau's Emile would learn from nature. Observation of the world around him, coupled with insightful questioning and careful tutoring, would produce an integrated man whose education would be based on the reality of human nature and natural law. Such an approach would have teachers "respect childhood . . . let nature act a long time, before intervening to act in its place, for fear of counteracting its operations."[20]

As an addition or appendage to his work *Emile*, Rousseau also wrote a treatise on the education of girls. This treatise, entitled *Sophie*, in no way approaches the importance of the four books involving Emile's education. Stating that woman is made especially to please man, Rousseau envisages her education as a means of preparation as Emile's future wife. Each sex must be trained for its natural instincts: "The one must be active and strong, the other passive and weak."[21] Sophie will learn to read and write so as to be a good household manager; she will become adept at sewing, weaving, music, and dance so as to use effectively her natural gifts and charm. To cultivate in the woman manly qualities is a severe detriment to women, because they lose their feminine graces and still remain inferior to men. Rather, because it is their nature to obey men, women must cultivate docility and submissiveness. Such cultivation of moral qualities, proper to their sex, when joined in learning of domestic skills, were in Rousseau's opinion the way to harmony and happiness: "Indeed, nearly all little girls learn to read and write with repugnance; but they always learn willingly to ply the needle."[22]

It should be remembered that Rousseau was not an educator. His ideas on education were basically theoretical, and were written as recommendations to be followed by tutors of the aristocratic class, working with individuals only or with very small numbers of children.[23] It was Heinrich Pestalozzi who attempted to implement many of Rousseau's ideas.[24] A Swiss schoolteacher who opened schools for orphans, Pestalozzi modified Rousseau's theoretical ideas and formulated what became known as *objective teaching*. His methods emphasized that children should be taught from concrete experiences and objects by teachers who showed love and patience. Followers of Pestalozzi enthusiastically spread his pedagogical methods throughout teacher-training institutions.

Two other European educators, directly influenced by Pestalozzi, were Herbart

[20] Jean-Jacques Rousseau, *Emile, ou de l'éducation* (Paris: Editions Garnier Frères, 1964), p. 102. The author of this module is grateful to C. Barry for translating the cited passages.

[21] Ibid., p. 446.

[22] Ibid., p. 459.

[23] For further reading on Rousseau and education, see Mabel L. Sahakian and William S. Sahakian, *Rousseau as Educator* (New York: Twayne Publications, Inc., 1974).

[24] See Johann Heinrich Pestalozzi, *How Gertrude Teaches Her Children* (London: George Allen & Unwin, Ltd., 1924).

and Froebel. Herbart organized Rousseau's educational views into a formalized psychology of education which stressed learning by association. Froebel established the first kindergarten, putting an emphasis on creativity and social development. It was Froebel who originated the idea that young children are best educated by women. It should be noted that the contributions of Rousseau, Pestalozzi, Herbart, and Froebel did not come to real fruition in the United States until the latter part of the nineteenth century;[25] however, their work and the European intellectual climate of the time did affect earlier American thinkers.

The Common School movement of the early nineteenth century owed its genesis to an American, Horace Mann. Mann led the way to the establishment of the public school idea in Massachusetts and strongly influenced the rest of the nation. He believed that religion should be taught in the public schools, but that religious teaching should be confined to the basic tenets of belief which all Christians affirmed. The schools would, therefore, be nonsectarian and teach only those "common truths" held by all American religious sects. He promised that such teaching would "not encroach one hair's breadth upon the peculiar province of any party or any denomination."[26] Urging his fellow citizens to accept the Common School as a vehicle for educating a strong citizenry, Mann assured them that education in a "Protestant and a Republican county" would "give to all so much religious instruction as is compatible with the rights of others and with the genius of our government, leaving to parents and guardians the direction . . . respecting politics and theology."[27]

Many churches assailed Mann's ideas. Especially critical were the Lutherans, who had established more than 400 schools during the colonial period. In Pennsylvania alone, there were approximately 240 Lutheran schools by 1820. It is not surprising then that Pennsylvania Lutherans called for a repeal of the free school law of 1934.[28]

The Presbyterian Church also opposed the establishment of public schools; its General Assembly expressed strong support for parochial education. In 1845, the New Jersey Synod approved a resolution calling for state support of denominational schools.[29] It is difficult to speculate on the outcome of the school controversy because the combatants and the issues altered quickly and radically because of the ensuing massive immigration of the Irish.

If the United States had remained basically Protestant in its religious orientation, the outcome of the Common School movement might have been very different from what actually transpired. The influx of new immigrants in the 1830s and 1840s altered the course of popular education and polarized Protestant reaction. The deep-rooted fear that many Protestants had of Catholicism was epitomized by the Nativist movement which swept many sections of the country. Anti-Catholic sentiment helped unite educators and religious leaders who now agreed that the Bible should be read in schools, and that parochial education should not receive public funding.

[25] Dewey often cites his indebtedness to these Europeans. See John Dewey and Evelyn Dewey, *Schools of Tomorrow* (New York: E. P. Dutton & Co., Inc., 1929).
[26] Horace Mann, *Lectures on Education* (Boston: Lemuel N. Ide, 1850), p. 262.
[27] Ibid., p. 263.
[28] J. P. Wickersham, *A History of Education in Pennsylvania* (Lancaster, Pa.: J. P. Lippincott Co., 1886), pp. 320–331.
[29] Lewis J. Sherrill, *Presbyterian Parochial Schools, 1846–1870* (New Haven, Conn.: Yale University Press, 1932), p. 2.

Many Protestant denominations that had originally argued for state support of church schools changed their position. The "common truths" that Mann advocated reflected those basic tenets which Protestants could accept. The King James version of the Bible, unacceptable to Catholics, was read in the classroom. The religious instruction, prayers, and hymns were of Protestant origin; textbooks often included derogatory remarks concerning Catholics, and the Pope was referred to as a sinful man in league with the powers of evil.[30]

As Irish immigration increased, Catholic requests for their parochial schools engendered much opposition. Hostility and suspicion characterized many of the debates that ensued. Finally, Bishop Hughes, leader of the Catholic position, advocated a completely secularized form of public schooling in New York. The state legislature adopted the law, but much bitterness and hostility remained.[31]

Most Protestant denominations that originally had been critical of the Common School plan began to support it. They now viewed public schools as Protestant institutions which carried on the Puritan legacy of true Christianity. Congregationalists, Methodists, and Baptists were strong in identifying the public school with the Protestant ethos; furthermore, it was generally believed that such education was a defense against Catholicism. Many Protestant spokesmen urged state, not church, control of elementary schools, and wanted to make attendance in a public elementary school compulsory for all. Public schools were regarded as "American" and, thus, were the essential means to make worthy citizens of the entire republic.[32]

The Nativist and Know-Nothing movements, which had far-reaching impact on public education, openly attacked Catholic immigrants. By the time of the Civil War, the crucial issues, centering on funding and Bible reading, reached a climax. Laws which stipulated that public monies would be given only to public schools were passed in many states.[33] These states also enacted laws which made daily Bible reading of the King James version compulsory.

Later generations would view the public school as an institution inherently founded in the Constitution. Nineteenth-century educators saw it as a vehicle for transmitting a predominantly Protestant society's values. Religious instruction in public schools, cherished by Protestant groups and upheld by law, would in the future come under strong attack. Eventually, the nonsectarian position required a reformulation of the public school's position concerning the viability of transmitting "common truths" of religion that were not commonly held by all the people.

Reading of the Bible and the recitation of the Lord's Prayer in public schools was declared unconstitutional by the Supreme Court in 1963. The court emphasized that government must remain neutral on religious matters, and that Bible reading and obligatory prayer violated the First and Fourteenth amendments of the Constitution. Even though various efforts have been made in the past decade to reintroduce some form of prayer into the schools, such efforts have not met with much success.

It has been noted that during the nineteenth and early twentieth centuries the

---

[30] Ray A. Billington, *The Protestant Crusade, 1800–1860: A Study of the Origins of American Nativism* (New York: Macmillan Publishing Co., Inc., 1938), pp. 142–145.

[31] Ibid., pp. 148–157.

[32] Lloyd P. Jorgenson, "The Birth of a Tradition," *The Pursuit of Excellence,* ed. by D. Orlich and S. Shermis, p. 56.

[33] Ibid., pp. 59–60.

vast numbers of immigrants helped to change what had been a basically Protestant, Anglo-Saxon society into a pluralistic one. The problem of teaching value choices became difficult. The texture of American life altered from that of a rural, agricultural society to that of an urbanized, industrial nation. As a result of the complexity of modern life and of the pluralistic nature of American society, issues of race, religion, nationality, and patriotism have come to the forefront.

It was Horace Mann who, in spite of innumerable obstacles, successfully launched the public school in the United States. In addition to his battle for the common school, Mann also was responsible for increased appropriations for education; improved training of teachers; increased school attendance; and acceptance of the idea that education is free, universal, and nonsectarian. He well deserves to be called "Father of the American Common School."[34]

Later Nineteenth Century Education

Coming to a new world which held out the promise of a better livelihood, Irish and other northern Europeans, who had come in the earlier part of the nineteenth century, were followed by Italians, Russians, Lithuanians, Yugoslavians and many other groups as the century ended. There had been only 2,000 to 3,000 Jews in the United States in 1800. After 1881, large numbers of Jews emigrated from East Europe.[35] They established Talmud Torah institutions, and were initially fearful that their religious and cultural heritage might suffer from "Americanization." Gradually, the Jewish community became socially and economically assimilated, and its leaders realized that integration in American life need not threaten their mores. While guarding their traditions, Jews, by the early part of the twentieth century, had incorporated themselves into the cultural and educational pattern of the larger democratic American society.

One of the salient reasons for immigration was the growth of industrialization. The development of manufacturing was a key factor in the North's winning of the Civil War, and by the beginning of the twentieth century the United States was already launched as an industrial nation. Such industrial growth required many workers who, as industrialization advanced, needed more specific skills and training. The resultant emphasis on occupational training directly affected higher education and influenced elementary schools.[36]

Since most immigrants settled in cities where employment was available, it was up to urban schools to accommodate to their needs. It was mainly in the school that the immigrant's child learned the basic academic skills and some occupational skills, developed an understanding of American government, and learned the ways of American society. For these immigrants and their children, education was essential for their personal lives and for the nation's growth.

The latter part of the nineteenth century witnessed growing criticism of American society. Social critics, termed "muckrakers," exposed the tactics of large

---

[34] J. Johnson, et al. *Introduction to the Foundations of American Education*, p. 259.

[35] Sydney E. Ahlstrom, *A Religious History of the American People* (New Haven, Conn.: Yale University Press, 1972), p. 573.

[36] Lawrence A. Cremin, *The Transformation of the School: Progressivism in American Education* 1876–1957 (New York: Vintage Books, 1964), p. 33.

corporations and the deficiencies of American life.[37] Crime, corruption, and exploitation were themes which social evangelists described in moving terms to effect necessary changes. Education also came under heavy criticism.

One of the first attacks that gained national attention came from a physician, Joseph Rice.[38] He visited many classrooms and was shocked by the conditions he found. Overcrowded classrooms, regimented children, unrealistic curriculum, tyrannical administrators, and unqualified teachers were only part of Rice's indictment against education. In his opinion, such conditions, coupled with beatings and whippings administered to children of both sexes, reflected cruelty and sadism.

In such a sterile educational atmosphere as that which Rice was attacking, it is no wonder that children left school at an early age. The dropout is not a modern phenomenon. The stultifying environment of the late nineteenth-century schools, plus pressing economic need, caused many children to leave school before finishing even elementary education. Rice realized that the poor immigrants and the minority students left school earlier than did the wealthy; therefore, he concluded that public education fell far short of attaining the democratic ideal.

Reforms in Elementary Education

The works of Rice and other critics resulted in a reform movement that incorporated many and diverse groups.[39] Shocked parents banded together to investigate classes their children attended; state legislatures passed laws relating to teacher preparation; state commissions were delegated to do depth studies of school systems. Educators themselves sought ways to achieve reform. One of their most notable attempts became known as "Progressive Education." Progressive educators stressed spontaneity, self-expression, and interest in the natural world and in the arts. The curriculum they advocated emphasized student interest and placed the teacher in a guidance role. "Experience" was an essential word in a progressive classroom. For example, a learning experience might begin with children's desire to study animals. They would read about various animals, make reports and drawings, and visit a zoo. The teacher would act as a guide and resource person. Testing procedures would be devised cooperatively by students and teacher to ascertain what learning had been accomplished through the experience. Once the reform movement gained momentum, the legacy of Rousseau, Pestalozzi, Herbart, and Froebel could be more broadly implemented.

One of the most important educational reformers was John Dewey who established a Laboratory School at the University of Chicago in 1896.[40] He believed that ordinary schools, with their traditional emphasis on book-centered curriculum, had been adequate for an agricultural country but were deficient in providing for the industrial, urban nation that the United States had become. Dewey emphasized

[37] For a discussion of the "muckrakers," see Samuel Eliot Morison and Henry Steele Commager, *The Growth of the American Republic*, 5th ed. (New York: Oxford University Press, Inc., 1962), pp. 440–475.

[38] Rice's articles were printed in *The Forum* from October 1892 through June 1893.

[39] For in-depth reading on progressivism and its impact on education, see Cremin, *The Transformation of the School.*

[40] John Dewey, *The School and Society,* 2nd ed. (Chicago: University of Chicago Press, 1929), p. 7.

the fact that the modern city child lives surrounded by manufactured goods, but has no idea of their origin. In his view, children of an earlier time had usually lived on a farm and had been intimately involved in the total process of harvesting produce or making objects from raw materials. Dewey believed that such sharing of work on home and farm had built up the child's mind and character naturally without great conscious effort.[41] It was such harmonious blending of intellectual and moral development that Dewey believed traditional school methods lacked. His Laboratory School was conceived to be a means of adjusting the balance by subordinating abstract, intellectual development to growth oriented toward practical ends that involved the child's real world.

It is true that the traditional classroom which Dewey criticized was structured for lecturing and listening. Instruction focused on book subjects. Children sat at fixed desks listening to the teacher's lecture. Such a structure was based on group instruction, not individual learning. Its classroom arrangement militated against any learning-by-doing approach. If children were not allowed to get out of their seats, how could they truly individualize themselves? Dewey considered such traditional methods both intellectually disastrous and morally bankrupt.

Until recently school education has met the needs of only one class of people, those who are interested in knowledge for its own sake, teachers, scholars and research workers. . . . the growth of democratic ideals demands a change in education.[42]

In trying to create a new learning atmosphere, Dewey presented four problems that his Laboratory School tried to solve: (1) How can the school get closer relations with the home and community? (2) How can history, science, and art be taught so as to have true relevance for the child? (3) How can the formal subjects of reading, arithmetic, and spelling be integrated with other subjects and linked to the child's daily experiences? (4) How can adequate attention be given to the child's individual needs and abilities?[43]

In trying to answer these four problems, Dewey attempted to model his school on the ideal home.[44] Concurring with the philosophy earlier advocated by Pestalozzi, Dewey believed that in an ideal home parents know what is best for their children and supply those needs. Through daily conversation and household chores in such a home the child acquires knowledge and good working habits. He learns industry, order, cooperation, sharing, and respect for the rights of others. He also learns to respect his own worth, realizing that he is an integral part of a group. Dewey's conception of the school as an enlarged family meant that the school could provide opportunities for learning which most families lacked, such as better equipment and scientific training. The child would then view school not as something apart from but, rather, as an extension of his regular family life. Similar to the home, the school would also be a genuine community, extending the child's interests and providing him opportunities to work with others for common goals.

Implementation of Dewey's beliefs was achieved at the Laboratory School by

[41] The many early educational reformers before Dewey include Bronson Alcott, Stanley Hall, and Francis W. Parker.

[42] J. Dewey and E. Dewey, *Schools of Tomorrow*, p. 306.

[43] For further development of Dewey's thought, see William Boyd and Edmund J. King, *The History of Western Education*, 10th ed. (London: A. & C. Black, Ltd., 1972), pp. 399–407.

[44] Dewey, *School and Society*, p. 3.

centering activities on shopwork in which children used tools and wood, participated in cooking lessons, and did weaving and sewing in textile work. Both boys
and girls were involved in all three activities. The activities became a springboard
for achieving integrated learning. For instance, ten-year-olds, studying the invention of cloth, were given raw cotton, wool, and flax. With the help of the
teacher, the children decided how to turn the wool into cloth, and reinvented the
first frame for carding wool and the simple tool for spinning it. The children
continued to experiment with fibers until they understood the structure and use of
the modern loom. These activities, coupled with investigations into the history and
science of cloth-making, provided integrated learning experiences.

Dewey believed that learning developed in stages according to the mental
growth of the child. He divided elementary school life into three parts: (1) play
period, ages four to eight; (2) spontaneous attention period, ages eight to twelve;
and (3) reflective attention period, which begins at the age of twelve. His development of these stages emphasized the first two growth periods. He never fully
developed the third, reflective stage.

The play period is characterized by directness of social and personal relations.
The child of four to eight years centers his interest on his home and immediate
surroundings. These interests gradually expand to other areas, such as the study of
prehistoric life. In the last year of the play period, the child was introduced to
reading, writing, and the rudiments of geography.

Dewey viewed the child between the ages of eight and twelve as a person who
is rapidly acquiring skills. Unlike the younger child, the child in the spontaneous
attention period can distinguish between means and ends; he can analyze details
and can understand regulations required for the solution of problems. American
history was introduced during this period to show children how people secure their
goods under various conditions of climate and locale. Geography and science
were also taught with the same emphasis on adaptation of means to end. All the
subjects were designed to be directly practical for the child's life.

When methods of thought, inquiry, and activity are adequately mastered, the
child is in the third period, that of reflective attention. At this stage the child is
capable of asking his own questions and finding answers independently. As indicated earlier, Dewey never completely developed this third stage.

It should be remembered that Dewey's educational philosophy was not unique
to him. Essentially, his beliefs reflected the contemporary psychology which applied
evolutionary concepts to mental development. Dewey succeeded in bringing current
psychological study into concrete educational practice. He shared his contempo-
raries' belief that the mind was a process of growth rather than an unchanging
entity. Earlier views had conceived the mind of the child to be the same as that
of an adult, only smaller in size. The boy was thought to be a little man, and his
mind, although it developed powers of memory earlier than powers of judgment,
lacked only the range of an adult. Dewey disagreed with such a concept, and
contended that the mind was always growing, thus reflecting different phases of
interest and ability. He also believed that a social environment was essential for
the development of the mind. Earlier, education was thought to be the result of
bringing children into contact with masses of facts relating to various subjects.
No attempt was made to connect these facts with the child's life. Dewey believed
that it was society's use of such facts that made them of importance to education.
For example, a child studying heat and light needs to understand how people have

used heat and light in fulfilling their individual and societal needs. Science, history, and art were studied in the context of the social situation from which they had arisen.

In shifting from the idea that learning consisted of a static and ready-made use of material outside the child's experience, educators began to view learning as intrinsically linked with the child's present experiences. Attempts were made to establish an organic wholeness between the child's interests and the school curriculum. It was believed that such merging would result in real motivation for learning, and reason would replace much of the memory work that had relied on rote method. The immense success Dewey achieved in education drastically changed schools and curriculum throughout the country.

Coinciding with the rise of Progressive Education was the Science of Education movement which attempted to apply scientific methods to the study of human behavior. Through formulating hypotheses and gathering data, educators acquired statistical analyses which, based on the experimental method, enabled them to devise suitable curriculum. The Science of Education promoters scrutinized all aspects of education. They designed tests to measure intelligence, aptitude, and personality, and reading comprehension.

The most important person connected with the Science of Education movement was Edward Lee Thorndike. For more than forty years, he did extensive research on the nature of learning, on testing, curriculum planning, and teacher training. This research, in addition to his theory of stimulus-response psychology, greatly influenced educational development. In the view of recent critics, educators such as Thorndike did much harm because they based tests, including those for intelligence, on white, middle-class values. Such values do not necessarily reflect minority and cultural differences. Critics contend that the result of such tests is the replacement of the American ideal that the masses are capable of self-government by the belief that only a few should lead the country. "The definition of democracy had changed. It no longer meant rule by the people. It meant rule by the intelligent."[45]

Essentially, Progressive Education and the Science of Education movement were very different from each other. As noted earlier, progressive educators believed that people learn as they grow and develop, and that it is natural for persons to develop in stage-by-stage growth. Promulgators such as Thorndike believed that learning was the result of outside influences. The teacher must know what ought to be taught, proceed to teach the material, and then test for mastery. The result was that teaching was blocked into units of work with emphasis on drill until the children gave the correct responses. The proof of learning was in the giving of correct responses. Such learning techniques were in sharp contrast with those held by the proponents of Progressive Education.

Implementation of the Science of Education theory in classroom teaching meant, for instance, that the teacher would emphasize a topic, such as farm products of the United States, which would be valuable for children to know as adults. A pretest would be given to ascertain what they already knew; the unit on farm products would then be taught, and would culminate with an objective test on the unit.

The Progressive Education and the Science of Education movements greatly

[45] Clarence J. Karier, Paul C. Violas, Joel Spring, *Roots of Crisis: American Education in the Twentieth Century* (Chicago: Rand McNally & Co., 1973), p. 122.

influenced teaching and, in practice, the two theories were often used together in classroom instruction and in curriculum planning. Although the mixing of the two has been done on a wide range, such combining has caused rather serious problems for teachers since the 1920s. Some of these problems may be discerned in curriculum still prevalent in many elementary schools. In the primary grades, the child's interests are often the catalyst for learning activities. Music, drama, and art are integrated into the curriculum, and children are given much freedom to initiate and execute learning experiences. However, by grade four, units of work, workbooks, drill, and testing for mastery begin to dominate many classrooms. The Progressive methods used in primary grades are replaced by the more structured, Science of Education approach.

Because Dewey's impact on American education had been so great, many years passed before any of his detractors gained much attention. Not until Russia launched the first satellite in 1957 did a massive attack against Progressive Education occur. Critics believed that American education had not provided enough hard-core study, especially in mathematics and science. Progressive schools were criticized for discouraging an individual child's initiative and ability in favor of adaptation to social rules and behavior. Critics also noted that such rules were not formulated by the children, but were made for them by doctrinaire professional educators and overprotective parents.[46] Demands were made that more attention be given to the individual child's potential, that challenge to existing environment rather than adaptation to it be emphasized, and that training for global responsibility which results from environmental change be taught.

Education and the Depression of the 1930s

The societal and political upheaval that resulted from the stock market crash and the Depression of the 1930s obviously affected educational thinkers. Many believed that schools could be the instrument for achieving a new social order, one based on cooperation rather than on competition. Such advocates of social reform through education were known as the Social Reconstructionists. *Dare the Schools Build a New Social Order?* was the title of an important book by George Counts in this view. *The Social Frontier,* a magazine published by the Social Reconstructionists, disseminated the views of the movement during the 1930s.

The essential idea of the Social Reconstructionists was that the task of the school was to change society's values, not merely to transmit those values as it had in the past.[47] Teachers would encourage the importance of cooperation, equality, and concern for helping the less fortunate. Through critical evaluation of American society, children would reaffirm democracy as a cooperative endeavor. It was believed that such restructuring of values, taught by means of the scientific method, would replace the earlier emphasis on capitalism and the "Protestant ethic."

The Social Reconstructionists were criticized for attempting to indoctrinate children with left-wing, liberal beliefs. A follower of Dewey, Boyd Bode, asserted that any form of indoctrination, liberal or conservative, was to be avoided. Actu-

[46] Boyd and King, *The History of Western Education,* p. 406.
[47] For further reading on Reconstructionism today, see Theodore Brameld, *Patterns of Educational Philosophy* (New York: Holt, Rinehart, & Winston, Inc., 1971).

87291

ally, the ideas of the Social Reconstructionists were not broadly implemented. People were reluctant to put such ideas into practice, and by the time America entered World War II the movement had waned. However, the Social Reconstructionist movement was important because it convinced people that schools, far from being neutral concerning controversial issues, could become pivotal points in many disputes.

Education and World War II

After World War II, the question of providing quality education for all children became a goal in American society. This industrial, democratic nation had provided the impetus for winning the war; it was logical for Americans to believe that their country could surmount existing domestic problems, including those posed by education. Another key reason that the United States was concerned about education was the development of the Cold War, the ideological struggle which arose between the United States and the Soviet Union. As a result of this struggle, much of the curriculum, especially in the social studies, became propagandistic in attempting to prove that the American way of life was superior to that of Russia.

Population continued to rise. In 1930, there had been 123 million Americans; by 1950, there were 151 million; by the 1960s, there were 200 million. Such growth put tremendous pressure on school facilities, resulting in emergency certification of teachers and increased production of buildings. One of the outcomes of the population explosion was the development of various machines to aid the teacher in classroom instruction. A wide spectrum of audio-visual materials became accepted as valuable tools and have continued to be utilized. American technology found a rich market in classrooms since educators realized the assistance such equipment could give in the child's learning process.

As noted previously, the Russian orbiting of the first satellite, Sputnik, in 1957, ushered in a period of criticism and demand for change in American education. During the decade of the 1960s, elementary education witnessed sweeping changes in curriculum, teaching materials, methods of instruction, and teacher preparation. Innovative techniques and developments became a part of many schools, as evidenced by new mathematics programs, educational television, team teaching, and individualized instruction. Such changes were viewed as ways of encouraging the child's intellectual abilities, and were often rebuttals to the earlier child-centered approach that had stressed personal-social development.

In spite of changes in curriculum, teacher preparation, and deployment of materials and personnel, schools continue to be assailed. Beatrice and Ronald Gross state that many schools are not even decent places for children because "they damage, they thwart, they stifle children's natural capacity to learn and grow healthily."[48] Critics contend that the innovations of the late 1950s and early 1960s had focused on the mastery of basic skills and subject matter, but had failed to confront the basic questions concerning the nature of the child, the function of education, and the place of culture in a democracy. Although all agree that the federal

---

[48] Beatrice and Ronald Gross, eds., *Radical School Reform* (New York: Simon & Schuster, Inc., 1969), p. 13.

funding of programs through the Elementary and Secondary Act of 1965 resulted in richer programs and more creative teaching, some critics still contend that these efforts were essentially impotent, because they did not address themselves to the larger social forces which question the relevance and very existence of formal education.

The new phalanx of educational reformers include theorists such as Kenneth Clark and Paul Goodman, and teachers such as John Holt, Sylvia Aston-Warner, Jonathan Kozol, and a host of others. Essentially, they all agree that America is a sick society and that American schools reflect that sickness.[49] Their opinions are derived from various perspectives of America as being inherently racist, imperialistic, wedded to the competitive ethos, suppressive of minorities, and lacking compassion for the unfortunate at home and abroad. The radical reformers believe that schools mirror society's ills, thus forcing children into classrooms that are intellectually stifling, irrelevant to life, degrading, and oppressive of humanity.

Many critics advocate that public education be abandoned, to be replaced by private and public schools which would compete for the student population. The voucher plan, by which parents in an area may select a school for their child rather than sending him or her to the nearby school, has been tried in a few regions.

Blacks view schools as essential elements in their fight for equality. The deprived child and the dropout are important realities for black people. They are highly aware of the need to bring the deprived child and the youngster who has left school back into the educational mainstream. The raising of black consciousness has greatly affected the teaching of values because people are now cognizant of the fact that much of society's values reflect a white racial bias.

Although blacks attained freedom after the Civil War, their education was usually in segregated schools. In 1896 (*Plessy* v. *Ferguson*), the United States Supreme Court upheld the concept of separate but equal public accommodations for the black and white races. This doctrine, which included school facilities, existed until 1954 when the Supreme Court (*Brown* v. *Board of Education of Topeka*) overturned the decision. This later decision, forbidding states to segregate by law or official action, did not solve the problem of segregated schools. Local housing patterns continue to contribute much to segregated schooling insofar as neighborhoods that have a predominantly black population result in predominantly black local schools. In addition to this de facto segregation resulting from the location of neighborhood schools, the Supreme Court decision of 1954 met with much recalcitrance. States were so slow to implement the Brown decision that the Civil Rights Act of 1964 was passed to give the federal government power to withhold money from those states that did not comply with the court decision.

Supreme Court rulings for school desegregation have been coupled with United States District Court mandates that require extensive busing of pupils to achieve integration. Busing has been successful in some areas; it has been a grave point of conflict in others. In 1975 and 1976, the city of Boston was the focus of national attention because of friction and violence arising from the busing of students into school districts outside their neighborhoods. If Americans truly believe that all citizens have an inherent right to equal opportunity, they must resolve the inequities resulting from both *de facto* and *de jure* segregated education. A pluralistic

---

[49] Ibid., p. 15.

ties resulting from both *de facto* and *de jure* segregated education. A pluralistic society is an essentially integrated one and cannot achieve its desired unity by tolerating segregated schools. Whether busing is the most judicious mode for achieving integrated schools may be debated. What cannot be argued, however, is that the moral responsibility of this country requires that all its people receive a quality education.

Children spend much of their lives in elementary schools. Most states require six hours a day for 180 days which totals more than 1,000 hours a year at the elementary level. It is apparent that this length of time is significant not only for intellectual growth, but also for societal and attitudinal development. Recently critics of curriculum have been concerned by the racial, ethnic, and sexual stereotyping found in various learning materials, including textbooks, films, supplementary readers, and informational guides.[50] Black and ethnic consciousness has demanded revisionist writing in history and other academic disciplines so as to include the achievements of minority groups which were often overlooked in the past. The women's liberation movement has resulted in a review of school materials that often promote sex stereotypes. For instance, a recent study has revealed that most reading books used in elementary schools portray girls as dependent, passive, inclined to domesticity, and lacking in strong intellectual and moral stamina; boys, on the other hand, are depicted as independent, active, and capable of high intellectual and moral attainment.[51] Many subject area materials, including those of mathematics and science, are filled with examples that encourage such stereotypes. Countless illustrations could be cited in which a boy experiments with a chemistry set while his sister looks on or, at best, bakes cookies. History books, biographies, and fiction have a predominance of male models and give scant attention to girls or women. Such neglect cannot help but teach and reinforce in girls' minds the belief that they are essentially inferior to their male counterparts. Boys are also affected in that their projected superiority has a high price tag in achievement, aggressiveness, and success.

The growing awareness of sexual prejudice has resulted in many school systems offering more varied activities to both boys and girls. Learning activities, such as weaving, cooking, carpentry, and home mechanics, are now offered more often to combined groups of both sexes. Some textbook publishers have issued guidelines for their authors so as to avoid sex-stereotyped vocabulary.[52] Extracurricular and intermural activities are becoming more evenly divided with less emphasis on separation of the sexes in games and athletics. However, prejudice of any kind, including that of race or sex, is not easily overcome. Continued efforts by enlightened educators will be necessary for the foreseeable future.

Possibly the ending years of the twentieth century are witnessing a new revitalization of the traditional American values of democracy, equality, liberty, and justice. There has developed a demand for concrete realization of these basic values rather than mere abstract affirmation of them. Such democratic values are now

---

[50] Judith Stacey, Susan Bereaud, Joan Daniels, eds., *And Jill Came Tumbling After: Sexism in American Education* (New York: Dell Publishing Co., 1974); see especially Chapters II and III.

[51] Nancy Frazier and Myra Sadker, *Sexism in School and Society* (New York: Harper and Row, Publishers, 1973), p. 103.

[52] "Guidelines for Equal Treatment of the Sexes in McGraw-Hill Book Company Publications" (New York: McGraw-Hill Book Company).

considered as working guidelines and platforms for action. American education has deep roots in the traditional development of this country; rapid changes in the political, social, and economic life of its people have acted as catalysts for educational change.

Education in the United States has always been closely related to the political development of the country. Broadly viewed, the history of American education may be divided into three periods: limited education of colonial days; broader-based education for enlightened citizenship during the early decades of the young republic; and participatory, grass-roots democracy involving compulsory, comprehensive, mass education. It is this last emphasis that has characterized American education for much of the twentieth century. The resultant pressure to apply democratic values to all the populace is a key to the confusion and challenge facing educators today.

SUGGESTED READING

Ahlstrom, Sydney E. *A Religious History of the American People*. New Haven, Conn.: Yale University Press, 1972.

Bailyn, Bernard. *Education in the Forming of American Society*. New York: W. W. Norton & Company, Inc., 1972.

Bendiner, Robert. *The Politics of Schools: A Crisis in Self-Government*. New York: The New American Library, 1970.

Boyd, William, and King, Edmund J. *The History of Western Education*. 10th ed. London: A. & C. Black, Ltd., 1972.

Cremin, Lawrence A. *The Transformation of the School: Progressivism in American Education 1876–1957*. New York: Vintage Books, 1964.

Dewey, John. *The School and Society*. 2nd ed. Chicago: The University of Chicago Press, 1929.

——— and Dewey, Evelyn. *Schools of Tomorrow*. New York: E. P. Dutton & Co., Inc., 1929.

Goodel, Carol, ed. *The Changing Classroom*. New York: Ballantine Books, 1973.

Gross, Beatrice and Ronald, eds. *Radical Social Reform*. New York: Simon & Schuster, Inc., 1969.

Karier, Clarence J., et al. *Roots of Crisis: American Education in the Twentieth Century*. Chicago: Rand McNally & Co., 1973.

Orlich, Donald C., and Shermis, S. Samuel. *The Pursuit of Excellence: Introductory Readings in Education*. New York: American Book Company, 1965.

Selakovich, Daniel. *The Schools and American Society*. 2nd ed. New York: John Wiley & Sons, Inc., 1973.

Silberman, Charles. *Crisis in the Classroom*. New York: Random House, In., 1970.

POST TEST

1. What are the four basic beliefs about a democratic society held by most Americans? _____

2. Does the local, state, or federal government have most control over the daily functioning of the elementary school? _____

3. From what main sources do local boards of education receive their powers?

_____

4. How do local schools get most of the money they need? _____

5. Has decentralization in the past decade been mainly an urban or a suburban problem? _____

6. What is a major obstacle to educational opportunity even when decentralization has occurred? _____

7. What was the main purpose of New England colonial schools? _____

8. What was the main purpose of the New England grammar school? _____

9. a. What percentage of blacks are estimated to have been literate in 1863? _____

    b. What percentage of blacks were literate by 1910? _____

10. On what foundation did Rousseau base Emile's education? _____

11. Did Rousseau advocate the same education for Sophie as he did for Emile? _____ Why, or why not? _____

12. Who established the first kindergarten? _____

13. Who is regarded, through his Common School movement, as the founder of the public school in the U.S.? _____

14. How did Joseph Rice contribute to educational reform in the late nineteenth century? _____

15. What four problems did Dewey attempt to solve through his Laboratory School?

_____

_____

_____

_____

16. What was the main purpose of the Science of Education movement? _____

17. When was a massive attack launched against Progressive Education? _____

18. What main function did the Social Reconstructionists want of the schools?

_____

19. What is the main criticism that is directed today against the educational innovations of the 1950s and 1960s? _____

20. School curriculum has recently been criticized for allowing stereotypes in what three major areas? _____

Child Growth and Development

Serafina F. Banich

Kean College of New Jersey

module 2

Physical Development / Social-Emotional Development / Intellectual Development / Moral Development

Rationale

Anyone who enters a school and looks at the children can't help but be impressed by a seeming paradox: the children are very much alike in their appearance and behavior; yet, at the same time, each one is unique and different in some ways from all the others. In Modules 2 and 4, we will consider the ramifications of this anamoly; Module 2 will consider patterns of human growth and development, and Module 4 will present individual traits and differences.

Curriculum choices are determined by a variety of wide-ranging factors; among them are the needs of society, the economic capabilities of the school district, the expectations of the local community, the goals of teachers and administrators, the output of huge educational industries, and the potentialities of children. It is the last dimension with which we are concerned in Modules 2 and 4.

The interplay among these forces is ultimately resolved in the kinds of curriculum choices teachers make. Teachers need beacons or guidelines that will assist them in making the most judicious choices. For decades one of these has been the knowledge of how human beings develop and grow.

Such information reduces costly trial and error and very often prevents failure. Recognizing the commonality of children at any particular age band enables teachers to deal with the numbers of pupils found in the classroom. Further, it encourages teachers to understand and to accept as normal the behavior of pupils at a particular developmental level, and to gear educational expectations so that they are neither too frustrating nor too unchallenging for pupils.

Just as in other disciplines, the body of knowledge in the area of human growth and development is constantly subject to redefinition, refinement, and elaboration, all of which filter into and affect the content and methodology of the school. Sometimes these changes are dramatic and imposing; other times they infiltrate so imperceptibly that they are manifest only to the trained, professional person.

SPECIFIC OBJECTIVES

The purpose of this module is to present the basic data that teachers need so as to understand the behavior of children and to relate this information to curriculum decisions. We shall focus on the various facets of human growth and development, and demonstrate how the physical, social-emotional, intellectual, motor, and moral dimensions are inextricably intertwined with each other. We will see how they are all integral components in the unraveling of life from birth to adulthood. The content will be organized around (1) general patterns or laws which govern the course of human development; (2) the theoretical extrapolations of eminent contributors to the field of human growth and development; and (3) educational implications of these data.

Your goals in studying the module, then, are to be able to name, define, and illustrate the components of human development, and to be able to state how this knowledge would influence your decisions as a teacher.

By the end of the module, you should be able to do the following:

1. Give five reasons why it is important to know about human growth and development.
2. Define and give an example of the laws of cephalocaudal and proximodistal development.
3. List and explain in a few sentences the five stages of development according to Freud.
4. List and explain in a few sentences the eight stages of development according to Erikson.
5. Compare and contrast in a one-page essay the theories of Freud and Erikson.
6. Draw a schema showing the time of development according to Freud, Erikson, Piaget and Kohlberg.
7. State two advantages and disadvantages in interpreting pupils' behavior from the perspective of developmental patterns.
8. List and define Piaget's stages of intellectual development.
9. List and define Kohlberg's stages of moral development.
10. In a one-page essay, show the relationship between Piaget's and Kohlberg's theory of development.
11. Name three principles of development and give an illustration of each.
12. Name, define, and illustrate three kinds of learning.
13. State the importance of peer relationships during the gang age.
14. Define readiness and give three reasons why it is important for teachers to know about it.
15. Define maturation and tell how it differs from readiness.
16. Explain in a one-page essay the effects of cultural forces on sex typing.
17. Name four factors that influence the development of intelligence.
18. Explain the difference between intrinsic and extrinsic motivation.
19. Tell in one paragraph how attention affects learning.

MODULE TEXT

Physical Development

Children grow and develop as total organisms. For the purposes of study, we separate various elements, but in reality they are interrelated and interdependent. Growth along any one of the elements may spurt ahead or reach its hegemony at a certain age, but invariably it hinges upon concomitant and concurrent growth of related, contributing dimensions.

Of these, the physical elements are most cogent, for they exist right before our eyes—palpable and unavoidable. We see the sizes of children, their heights and weights, their body structures and shapes, the color of the eyes and hair, their dexterity in holding a pencil or throwing a ball, their speed in running, and hundreds of other changes. Nor can we escape the vision of atypical children whose body structures or functions have been impaired by inheritance, birth, accident, or illness. For this reason, we are more inclined to accept the physical differences and capabilities of children, as compared to intellectual, moral, or social capacities.

Inheritance and Birth. The period of prenatal development is usually nine months in duration when the fetus is encased within the mother's womb. At this time, certain fundamental processes that are fairly predictable and universal occur. At conception, the cell from the ovum and sperm combine and reform into the zygote, which inherits 23 chromosomes from each parent for a total of 46. Within the chromosomes are smaller protein masses called genes, which serve as the transmitters of hereditary factors. As the original cell divides and redivides in the process called mitosis, it also becomes increasingly more complex and brings to light the hereditary program enveloped in the genes. Since no two people except monozygotic identical twins inherit the same set of genes, all humans are in some ways unlike all other human beings. Genes not only give us our uniqueness, but they also set the limits within which environmental factors affect attainment. For example, the best or the poorest diet and health regimen can influence the future height of a child only within the limits set by nature.

The progression from single cell to a completely formed human being, capable of existence outside the mother's womb, follows a very orderly, predictable sequence. Increase in size, specialization of function, and appearance of more complex tissue follow predictable patterns which enable scientists to estimate the time certain manifestations will occur and the sequence in which they will proceed.

The School Age Child. The occurrence of common patterns obtains also after birth. Most children will learn to walk between nine and fifteen months, and they will crawl before they walk. But we are most concerned here with the patterns that apply to the school-age child. Typically, they are between the ages of six and thirteen. The spectacular changes of size, appearance, and physical development that occur during early childhood slow down during these years. Children pretty much have their bodily functions and muscular development in hand; they grow larger and stronger, develop greater dexterity and control, and refine their coordination.

The most dramatic physical change in the elementary school child is at the onset of puberty, the shift from childhood to adolescence. Glandular changes occur, children begin to assume more of the physical characteristics of the adult appearance, and they lose their childlike physiognomy. Attendant upon these physical changes are a host of emotional and social changes, which will be discussed later. Because the onset of puberty can vary two or three years among children, by the time youngsters leave elementary school, they comprise a widely assorted lot, ranging from those who still resemble children to the muscle-bound, six-foot boy or the well-developed, mature-looking girl. The typical first grader is somewhere in the vicinity of forty-two inches tall, and by the time he or she is in the eighth grade, height will reach about five feet, but could range anywhere from under five feet to six feet. The attendant social and emotional factors which accompany puberty—the turmoil of new feelings and coping with a transformed body shape—influence school behavior more than the physiological changes themselves.

Of course, physical illness or impairment will have impact on children's growth and behavior. Generally, however, children have advanced to a sufficiently sophisticated level of physical development to manage the learning tasks the school sets for them. Unless a physical impairment or deficiency exists, teachers need not wait for physical processes to appear. The physical basis is there; it is rather in the other areas of development that they need to assess and determine the readiness of pupils.

Neuromotor Development. Nevertheless, two patterns of physiological development do in fact define and delimit curriculum choices, especially in activities requiring motor skills. These patterns are most marked after birth and during the preschool years, but they become refined during the elementary school years. One is the cephalocaudal law of development in the direction from the head to the toes, and the other is the proximodistal law of development from the center to the extremities. These laws mean simply that maturation occurs first in the areas of the head and the center of the body, and then downward and outward. These laws operate with regard to maturation in terms of speed, accuracy, steadiness, strength of muscular control, and motor movements. Thus, teachers notice that first-grade boys can easily throw a ball but have difficulty gripping a pencil and writing accurately. By sixth grade, they can throw the ball farther and with much greater precision, and will have no problem in staying within lines when cutting or coloring. Teachers can enhance maturation of motor skills by providing children with many opportunities and experiences that require use of neuromotor movements. As we noted earlier, these skills bear only peripherally on school achievement, but they are extremely important to the child's self-image and social acceptance. Children who are graceful and well-coordinated, who are adept in sports and other physical activities, will probably, although not necessarily, think well of themselves and be more accepted by their peers than will the gawky, clumsy, uncoordinated child.

Readiness and Maturation. Maturation refers to those phenomena that occur on their own when the body development is ripe enough to handle them so that certain tasks seemingly are managed spontaneously. Training has little or no effect; the maturation process takes over and manifests itself when the organism is ready. Attempts to accelerate mastery generally are fruitless and very often lead to failure and frustration. However, a deprived or extremely negative environment can inhibit and curb seemingly natural maturation processes. Some examples of maturation are the lifting of the head, rolling over, and sprouting of teeth, which occur on their own but need a support base of a favorable environment.

Beyond this basic level of self-initiating activities there exists in humans a higher domain of functioning that does not operate automatically when physiological maturation occurs. Mastery is essentially induced by the learning environment, building upon the physiological basis. Thus, a child can manage utterances only when his speech mechanism is mature enough, but to develop his language facility, he needs to hear language and to be spoken to.

Timing is a key factor in readiness. Training can foster readiness, but if started too soon it can result in frustration and failure. On the other hand, readiness for certain tasks peaks and then declines. Delay and postponement beyond the summit of readiness inhibits maximal and optimal learning. In addition, while the most propitious timing for the mastery of tasks can be predicted in a general way, individual readiness rates vary tremendously from child to child.

Readiness for a task is difficult to assess because all the contributing factors are unequally developed at any given time. Let us take the case of the first-grade teacher who usually makes the decision about when a particular pupil should start reading. The teacher must put together a composite picture of the child's development and, on that basis, decide if he is ready to read. In that composite picture, the teacher must assess the pupil's mental age, his visual and auditory acuity, his emotional maturity and attention span, and his familiarity with words and language. All too often children are far more advanced in one area as compared to the others; yet, the function of the teacher is to seize the most advantageous time for instruction.

In this context, the responsibility of the school is both vastly complicated and extremely significant; it must at the same time wait upon and induce readiness so that for each pupil optimal learning will result. The school must chart a course that challenges without frustrating and maintains without stagnating.

Social-Emotional Development

Research into the physical aspects of the human organism has been going on for centuries and continues today on a large scale. In the realm of social-emotional development our knowledge is more scant. Only within this century have social-emotional processes become the target of scientific, systematic investigation. Further, we can see and touch the body, but the origins of emotional-social behavior lie in processes not so easily manifest. Also, these processes often lie beyond the individual himself in his interaction with other people and with his environment. The substantiation and proof feasible in studying the physical aspects of the body are hard to come by in discovering those forces which produce negative or positive behavior, sound or unsatisfactory adjustment, happy or disturbed behavior. Lacking hard evidence, we rely on the insights and investigations of eminent theorists. We shall briefly consider two of them in this module, Sigmund Freud and Erik Erikson.[1]

Freudian Stages of Development. Freud attributed a dominant role to the sex drive in shaping human behavior. Early childhood experiences are of great importance because lack of gratification in these early interactions leaves the child fixated at one level, and impairs his ability to adapt to succeeding higher levels. He will fall back on earlier patterns of adjustment, and regress. In this sense, Freud's stages are developmental, a ladderlike sequence, one building upon the other.

Drives often remain at the subconscious or unconscious level so that the forces they exert are often undetected by the individual. The core of the personality consists of three parts: the id, ego, and superego. The id is present at birth, and is occupied with the satisfaction of needs and the avoidance of pain. It is referred to

[1] You will find references to Freud's work in all books on child development and many translations of his work. For a discussion of stages of development, see Sigmund Freud, *The Basic Writings of Sigmund Freud,* translated and edited (New York: The Modern Library, 1938). Eric Erikson, *Childhood and Society,* 2nd ed. (New York: W. W. Norton & Company, Inc., 1964).

as the pleasure-pain principle. The ego is the reality principle, and it serves to mediate the wants of the id with the demands of life and society. The ego develops as the child matures and increases his sense of responsibility. The third element is the superego or conscience, and it serves as a censor to the pleasure-seeking id. The superego develops early in life and usually represents those values imposed by the family or by society.

ORAL STAGE. The greatest sources of gratification and of learning about the outside world are in the physical act of sucking and the feeling of well-being that accompanies the soothing, fondling contact with the mother. This stage lasts from birth to about eighteen months. It represents the archetype of the taking or accepting relationship. Fixation at this stage manifests itself at the adult level in physical oral habits, such as nail-biting or gum-chewing and, symbolically, in dependent relationships with others.

ANAL STAGE. In the next stage, gratification shifts from the intaking mouth to the excreting or withholding anus. Through control over the processes of urination and defecation, the child realizes his growing power over himself and the outside world. This leads to conflict and negativism in his relationships with adults. This stage lasts from eighteen months to about three years of age. Fixation at this stage manifests itself in constipation, guardedness, orderliness, or the opposites of excessive sloppiness or disorderliness.

PHALLIC STAGE. The phallic stage lasts from age three to six. Children at this time become very much aware of genital differences, and a good deal of sex activity occurs. In this stage, the child becomes the rival of the parent of the same sex for the affection of the other parent. He realizes the hazard of competing with the powerful parent, so he develops ambivalent feelings of affection for and dislike of parents. This is known as the Oedipus or Elektra Complex. The contradiction is usually resolved in aligning oneself with the parent of the same sex, and inhibiting undesirable feelings. Failure to integrate the dilemma of the oedipal stage manifests itself in neurotic behavior.

LATENCY STAGE. From ages six to twelve, children go through the latency stage. This is the stage with which the elementary school is most concerned since during these ages children are attending elementary school. More to the point, however, is the fact that at this stage the child's sex drive remains quiescent or dormant between the openly sexual phallic stage and the later genital stage. The sublimation of sex is redirected toward vigorous intellectual curiosity and activity.

GENITAL STAGE. Finally, adult sexual awakening accompanies the biological maturation of the body. This genital stage commences at puberty and continues throughout life. The emotionally mature individual allies the gratification of physical sex urges to a person with whom there exists a loving relationship. Failure to achieve this stage results in a host of mildly to grossly deviant behaviors.

Educational Implications. Freud's theory suggests two significant consequences for the school. The children of elementary school age are at their peak of psychological readiness for intellectual advancement. It is a time of avid and insatiable intellectual curiosity—a time to learn about the world and to control it. Children's primary interests have shifted from the home to their peers, the school, and the outside world. Teachers, then, should move full speed ahead by providing pupils with the richest milieux for the flowering of intellectual capacity.

If motivation of behavior often remains below the conscious level for both teachers and pupils, then the teacher should exercise caution in ascribing reasons for the behavior of children. The overt behavior that teachers see tells them what children are doing, but knowing why may require the services of a professionally trained person to uncover. When they reward or punish children, teachers should keep in mind that they are treating symptoms or outward manifestations of behavior without having direct access to its causes.

Erikson's Stages of Development. Building upon Freud's theory, Erikson has broadened psychoanalytic perspective of human behavior to include not only individuals but cultures as well. Erikson believes that development is a universally lived process of biological, social, and psychological stages. These stages are marked by a fundamental dilemma or crisis, during which the individual is both biologically ready and impelled by cultural pressures. Development is a continuous, lifelong process, and failure to resolve the crisis at any one level stymies advancement to the next. Although Erikson puts more emphasis upon the interplay of societal forces and inner generative activity, you will see how Erikson's theory is related to Freud's. To illustrate the polarity of possible alternatives, Erikson states each crisis in terms of antithetical positions.

TRUST VERSUS MISTRUST. The needs of the newborn are primarily physical. He obtains oral gratification principally through the mother's loving care. As the infant's ego needs are satisfied, a sense of trust develops. Frustration of the biological needs and the attending emotional component leads to mistrust. The duration of this stage is from birth to about eighteen months.

AUTONOMY VERSUS DOUBT AND SHAME. In a stage similar to Freud's anal stage, the child struggles between the desire to prove his control and mobility and his reluctance to defy parental wishes. A sound, cooperative relationship with parents in toilet training and other areas of living builds self-esteem and autonomy. Shame and doubt, for instance, arise when the child is denied the support and guidance he needs from parents. This stage lasts from eighteen months to about three years old.

INITIATIVE VERSUS GUILT. This is the stage of play when play is the work of children. The crisis of this stage arises because the child's play intrudes upon the behavioral mode of others which very often is at variance with his own. On the other hand, there is the desire to curb his initiative because of the discomfort and guilt aroused by his contact with others. Sexual awareness leads to interest in and exploration of genitalia of both sexes, and the resolution of the oedipal complex by identification with the same sex parent. This stage lasts from ages three to seven.

INDUSTRY VERSUS INFERIORITY. This next stage, which occurs between the ages of seven and eleven is characterized by a struggle to utilize an abundance of energy towards the mastery of necessary societal skills against the fear of failure, of falling short of ambitions, and of retrogressing to a lower level of accomplishment. This is the time that peers replace adults in importance and as sources of identification. The child measures his own sense of worth and accomplishment against that of his peers, and it is upon them that he primarily depends for his social growth during these years.

EGO IDENTITY VERSUS DIFFUSION. This is the stage of the identity crisis for which Erikson is so well known. In chronological terms, it is the period of adolescence; in psychological terms, it is the holding period before adulthood, the time for integrating the past with the future. Childhood patterns are synthesized into present and future roles. The adolescent selects his future adult roles by an amalgam of his sense of personal worth with the world as he finds it. The society affirms the significance of this delay before the plunge into adulthood by supplying many opportunities for discovery and self-knowledge through prolonged education, or apprenticeships. The major decisions regarding the course of life begin their formulation and implementation at this time. The dilemma of this stage places the commitment of specific adult roles against the uncertainty of the adolescent's own capacities and of his place in society.

INTIMACY VERSUS ISOLATION. Childhood and adolescence are left behind, and the individual is ready now to select a partner with whom to share the intimacy of marriage without fear of ego loss. Integrating work choices into adult associations is also part of this challenge. The negative counterparts of this stage are feelings of ineptitude and social distance.

GENERATIVITY VERSUS SELF-ABSORPTION. Accepting or rejecting the challenge of creating and preparing the next generation for the society poses the crisis of this stage. It involves not only parental responsibility in passing on to their offspring their own ideals and wisdom, but also in supporting and maintaining a society that nourishes the flowering of human potential. It is expressed in giving and loving as a parent instead of taking and being loved.

INTEGRITY VERSUS DESPAIR. This final stage is characterized by a feeling of having lived a fulfilled existence within the perspective of the ideals of society and history. Its opposite modality fears death and despairs of life.

EDUCATIONAL IMPLICATIONS. Elementary school children are in the Freud's latency stage, and in the industry stage of Erikson. Both describe this stage as one of prodigious effort on the part of children to gain mastery over themselves and the environment. Competitiveness and the need to achieve prod them to explore new avenues of endeavor and to test their newly acquired skills in a world that increasingly yields to their control. The job of the school then is to make the most of this drive and to open up many opportunities for children to satisfy their intellectual curiosity, to acquire new skills, and to enhance their self-esteem. The school needs to provide a broad range of educational materials, activities, and methods into which this massive energy and driving ambition can be channeled. In addition, teachers need to keep in mind that, at this time when physical and sexual growth slow down and intellectual vigor is rampant, pupils vary markedly in their intellectual interests and growth rates. Teachers' expectations should be in harmony with the diversity of capacities.

Peer Relationships. The preschool child is an egocentric, self-oriented individual whose capacity for considering the feelings and wants of others is rather limited. His social structure is organized chiefly on the satisfaction of his own needs and desires, and he will often become enraged or throw temper tantrums if they are not quickly satisfied. One of the primary purposes of the nursery school or kindergarten is to move the child from his egocentric basis to the point of adaptation to other children, whose life styles may be very different from or even in conflict with his own. He needs to adjust to the more impersonal environment of the school, where the teachers and the other children may be strangers to him, and to develop the skills he needs to maintain harmonious social intercourse with other members of the school society. His world expands to include a host of unfamiliar people and places, whose motives, interests, and actions are strange to him, and to which he must respond. He relies upon the guidance of parents and teachers in charting this unknown course. He marvels at their worldly wisdom and admires and respects them. His awe of them at times almost seems blind adoration. His peers simply add another perspective to life as he relates to them mostly in play groups.

In later childhood, however, parents and teachers fade out as sources of behavioral standards, and it is the peer group to whom he seems to have an unquestioning attachment. This is known as the gang age, and it starts at about nine years of age. Children band together in ubiquitous, yet specific, gangs and cliques with their own elaborate rules, secret codes and oaths, and exclusive membership. The banding together creates a fortress against the adult world. They depend on the adult world for life's necessities; yet, they are struggling to attain independence from it. Caught in this anamolous position, individual members lose some of their uniqueness in almost slavish adherence to the tyrannical dictates of the gang, which serves as arbiter of appropriate modes of dress and behavior.

Sex Typing. The social sex role refers to the typical behaviors expected of male or female members of a society in terms of emotional responses, attitudes, and characteristics. Sex typing defines the essence of maleness and of femaleness. The manner by which this process occurs is of much current debate. At one extreme are those who believe that sex roles are biologically determined and immutable. This view holds that because women are the bearers of children, they are destined to be homemakers, and they are naturally more passive, docile, and receptive than men. Men, who are stronger, more aggressive, assertive, and less emotional than women, are committed by their inherent biological structure and emotional makeup to the role of provider for and protector of the family. At the other extreme are those who maintain that sex role typing is wholly culturally induced and that if these rigid casts of sex roles were eliminated, the biological differences of men and women would not block the expression of a wide range of behavior on the part of both sexes. Given the chance, they claim, both sexes would behave in ways that would be impossible to label as typically male or female.

What is certain, however, is that the society imposes upon the young certain behavioral modes according to sex. In our society, boys are permitted more open displays of aggression, hostility, and anger, and girls are allowed to weep, show hurt and fear, and act demurely. In terms of occupational and recreational choices, males play football and hunt, and become architects and pilots, and females play with dolls and sew, and become secretaries and stewardesses. Much of the efforts of the women's liberation movement has been to break down these stereotypes by opening up and equalizing the options available to both sexes. The movement has been especially critical of sexism in the schools, where children encounter these stereotypes so often in the books they read and in the teachers' expectations that they accept them as natural and normal.

Intellectual Development

The study of intellectual development as a systematically organized and researched discipline is of recent vintage and dates from only about the beginning of this century. Since that time, voluminous amounts have been amassed on the origins, nature, and measurement of intelligence. Yet, despite this, we find ourselves in the same quandary as with social-emotional development; we know that a combination of inherited and internal processes interact with external forces to produce behavior and learnings which we label as intelligent, but we are still searching for more precise indices for defining, nurturing, and measuring intelligence, especially with regard to the individual child.

Nature of Intelligence. Because thought processes are nonmaterial, and even the thinking mechanisms of the brain and nervous system are hidden from view, scientists have been stymied in their explorations of the mind and its thinking powers. The problem is further complicated by two factors: What is the role that heredity and environment play in mental development? How do we measure a quality whose nature is disputatious with instruments whose validity are problematic at best?

Alfred Binet,[2] a pioneer in testing intelligence, defined it as a cluster of capacities which included such dimensions as memory, attention, and recall. Lewis Terman,[3] who revised Binet's scale, identified intelligence as the power to engage in abstract thinking and to deal with abstract symbols. J. P. Guilford,[4] using factor analysis, defined intelligence according to three fundamental categories: process, content, and products.

Piaget's Theory. Many other theorists have conjectured about the nature of intelligence. Foremost among them is Jean Piaget,[5] who has studied the total development of children, and whose writings in the areas of moral and intellectual development have been particularly influential in today's schools. He maintains that intellectual or cognitive development is a continual process of unfolding. Each stage or level is rooted in a previous one and flows into the next. Each level repeats the level of cognition but at a higher level of organization and patterning so that a hierarchy of graded experiences results. Each child must go through one stage before he can move on to the next, and his movement from one level to the next hinges on his maturation and experience. Piaget's theory is complicated and his writings are voluminous. What follows is a very brief and sketchy summary.

SENSORIMOTER PHASE. The sensorimotor stage extends from birth until about two years of age. The chief developmental task at this stage is the integration of sensory perceptions with motor activities. The child augments his range of responses from his initial neonatal reflexes to trial- and-error learning and solving of simple problems.

PREOPERATIONAL PHASE. Language develops during the preoperational stage from ages two to seven. The chief modality of behavior is play, which the child uses

---

[2] Many sources discuss Binet's contribution to our understanding of intelligence. For one of the early writings, see R. Pinter, *Intelligence Testing: Methods and Results* (New York: Holt, Rinehart & Winston, Inc., 1923).

[3] Lewis M. Terman, *The Measurement of Intelligence* (Boston: Houghton Mifflin Company, 1916).

[4] J. P. Guilford, "Three Faces of Intellect," *The American Psychologist*, **14**: 469–479.

[5] If you want to read an original source, see Jean Piaget, *Judgment and Reasoning in the Child* (New York: Harcourt Brace & Jovanovich, Inc., 1928). If you want an updated and summarized discussion of Piaget's work, read: John L. Phillips, *The Origins of Intellect: Piaget's Theory* (San Francisco: W. H. Freeman & Co., Publishers, 1969).

as a vehicle for grasping meaning from his experiences and the world. The languages he uses are merely imitative with little regard for accuracy. His abilities are limited to concrete events and objectives; he may speak of abstractions such as time, but he lacks comprehension of them.

The child moves from an egocentric stance to that of social creature. He reacts more realistically to his environment, and commences to use words to express his thoughts. He has only a crude cognizance of relationships, and his thinking shifts from the particular to the particular. He judges by the external appearances of a situation, and cannot grasp intrinsic indices of experiences.

CONCRETE OPERATIONS PHASE. From ages seven to eleven, the concrete operations stage is distinguished by the child's ability to see relationships in his experiences and to order them into organized wholes. In the previous stage, thinking was delimited to and rigidified by intuitive thought; now he can discern relationships among parts and between parts and the whole. He develops thinking processes beyond the stimuli of immediate events and objects, and his thinking moves from the inductive to the deductive modality.

FORMAL OPERATIONS PHASE. In the final or formal operations stage, which lasts from about age eleven through adolescence, the child is no longer anchored to realistic events and objects, but he can move into the world of ideas. He can operate mentally at the purely symbolic level. He can reason hypothetically by unifying his experiences into a systematic, realistic whole. Additionally, he can project into the past or future, and can think by implication.

EDUCATIONAL IMPLICATIONS. Although Piaget did not start out to devise a theory of teaching, his work has had tremendous impact on curriculum decisions. His writings indicate that the passive child does not learn. The child must be actively involved if his cognitive skills are to grow. Further, the new learnings should be sufficiently consonant with previous inputs so the child can assimilate them into his present cognitive structure; yet they should be sufficiently dissimilar and complex to challenge the child to a more sophisticated organization of his thought processes. In short, if the child is to learn, he must be actively involved at a level that is suited to his stage of thought development. The function of the school then is to present to children a host of learning stimuli, which enable them to invent, so to speak, their own cognitive structures and to integrate the new learnings with previous ones. This would suggest a lush learning environment with many opportunities for children to experiment, probe, and explore without teachers imposing the answers to or the method of solving problems.

Factors Influencing Intelligence. Just as there is no consensus on the definition of intelligence, no common agreement exists on the part that heredity and environment play on mental development. Many studies have been conducted on the correlation of intelligence between parents and children, among children in the same family, and between fraternal and identical twins. Generally, these studies conclude that twins, especially identical twins, are more likely to have similar intelligence scores than are siblings, and that intelligent parents are more likely to have intelligent children than are duller parents. These results substantiate, if only in a minimal way, that heredity does affect intelligence.

Environmentalists challenge this conclusion on the basis that intelligent parents provide a culturally rich environment that stimulates the growth of intelligence and that it is this condition rather than heredity that accounts for intelligence in families. Studies in fact do indicate that a stimulating environment can raise the scores on intelligence tests. The opposite is also true. Children who live in institutions, homes, or other social settings that are extremely devoid of care, warmth, guidance, and stimulation score poorly on intelligence tests. Most psychologists eschew the extreme positions of the geneticists and the environmentalists, and acknowledge the impact of both. Within the limits set by heredity, there remains a wide area in which environmental and cultural factors can modify intelligence.

As mentioned earlier, developmental patterns hinge on physiological underpinnings. Children with inferior diets and poor nutrition or those stricken by diseases which affect the brain or nervous system very often manifest diminished intelligence. The health and nutrition of the mother during pregnancy is also vital because 70 per cent of the adult brain size is formed before birth.

Learning. KINDS OF LEARNING. Learning is a word that is common in our vocabulary, and it has any number of meanings. The term applies to a group of disparate but interrelated functions that can be organized into a hierarchical arrangement.

Sometimes we use the word *learning* to signify a process which results from maturation. As mentioned earlier, this occurs quite naturally, without the benefit of training, when the body is physiologically ready. This is what we mean when we say a baby learns to smile, learns to crawl or walk, and learns to control his bowels. Parents sometimes believe they have taught their children these skills. However, children master them quite spontaneously when their organisms are biologically ready unless some kind of damage or impairment intervenes.

Two simple kinds of learning are conditioning and trial and error. When a child develops a perfunctory, ingrained mode of response to a certain stimulus, this is called conditioning. For the condition to become established and maintained it must be reinforced over and over again by repetition. Usually immediate rewards and sometimes punishments are employed to maintain interest in the learning until it is overlearned and routine.

Conditioned learning is the approach that experimental psychologists use in discovering how and what animals learn. It is also the method employed by animal trainers in the circus and in other forms of entertainment. You notice that the trainer will throw a piece of meat or fish to the animal as a reward for his performance.

Some human habits learned through conditioning are unproductive or even destructive. A child may have formed the wrong response to reducing fractions to the lowest terms, or an adult may be killing himself by his smoking habit. These counterproductive responses need to be eliminated or extinguished. They are when, through lack of reinforcement, the conditioned responses break down and either cease to exist or no longer operate. Some psychologists believe conditioning is extremely pertinent to modifying or instilling responses in humans. This is called behavior modification.

Trial-and-error learning occurs when the method for solving a problem is unclear or unknown, such as in learning to ride a bike or putting together a disassembled cube. Uncertain of the appropriate responses, the learner randomly tries one solution after another until he hits upon the correct one by chance. The characteristic running down blind alleys is eliminated when the correct pattern or response is learned.

Animals, which are placed in a maze and need to find their way out, utilize trial-and-error learning. Similar to humans, they can discover the pattern that solves the problem, and employ it as a short cut when confronted with the maze in subsequent trials.

Higher types of learning distinguish human thinking from animal thinking. Animals are incapable of forming concepts, deriving generalizations, organizing theories, or thinking creatively. These higher modes require the ability to classify information into serviceable taxonomies, to interpret data in fresh and original ways, to abstract from facts laws that have predictive value, to see the relationship between cause and effect, and to solve difficult and complex problems. Schools attempt to nourish these advanced thinking modes, and intelligence tests attempt to measure them.

MOTIVATION. *Motivation* is defined as the propelling force that incites the individual to action so as to attain a goal. At the physical level, motivation impels a person to satisfy basic needs or drives such as hunger or thirst. At the psychological level, one's need for approval, for acceptance, or for love may spur him to prolonged and arduous attempts to attain his goals. Behavior is directed toward a goal that satisfies the physical or psychological impetus to action. Goal satisfaction can be immediate as in eating to satisfy hunger, delayed as in waiting until all are served to win social approval, or far distant as in dieting to lose fifty pounds to improve one's health and appearance.

Infants demand immediate saatisfaction of their needs which are primarily physiological. When frustrated, they become enraged, cry, and scream. As children get older, the satisfaction of social needs becomes as important to them as the basic drives, and they can defer immediate gratification for social approbation. By the time they reach puberty, children can set their sights on long-range goals and work towards their attainment for years and years.

Motivation is closely linked with maturation. The culture usually exerts the external pressure to goal attainment to mesh with the internal maturational urgings of children. This coinciding of inner and outer motivations smooths the learning process. If a person's motivation is out of sequence and occurs either earlier or later than for most other members of the society, he still can attain his goals, but he will experience more difficulty because the opportunities available to him in society are limited. For example, in our society most members attain the goal of a high school education between the ages of fourteen and eighteen. Individuals who are ready to attain this goal earlier or much later in life find their chances are considerably diminished as compared to those within the standard age bracket.

Motivation is intrinsic if the springboard to action arises from within the individual, or extrinsic if he is goaded to goal attainment by some external prompting. In school, children are intrinsically motivated if they engage in their learning tasks because they enjoy them and want to satisfy their intellectual curiosity. When they work for a reward, such as good grades or avoidance of the teacher's criticism or punishment, they are extrinsically motivated. Ideally, teachers want to motivate a child so he becomes excited about learning and eager to develop his intellectual capacity as its own reward. The challenge is indeed monumental because the motivational devices that teachers employ may stimulate some, discourage others, and be of no consequence to the rest.

ATTENTION. Attention involves the selective narrowing of and focusing on one set of stimuli to the exclusion of others. Attention is a very elusive quality and subject to many influences, such as the age of the learner, his work habits and motivations, his feelings about the subject, his relationship with the teacher, and whether the teaching techniques intrigue him or not. The length of time the learner can maintain attention to a task is called the attention span. As children get older, their attention span increases. Children can hold and even stretch their attention spans if they are challenged by the learning task and have had some voice in its selection. Children lose interest and become restive and inattentive when the schoolwork is too familiar, or too difficult, or has little relevance to their interests and maturity.

Moral Development

We call behavior moral when it coincides with what society dictates as ethically correct; that is, moral behavior concurs with culturally accepted standards of conduct. Behavior is considered immoral when the individual responds in ways that defy the standards of ethical conduct established by society. Societies control the violations of their moral codes by imposing sanctions or punishments that range from mild public rebukes to execution, depending on the severity of the transgression.

What is labeled immoral behavior varies according to the culture and to the sub-cultural groups of peers, family, caste, social status, and religious affiliation. For instance, whether premarital sex constitutes immoral behavior depends on the laws and customs of the particular society, and the values of the age group, the family, the socioeconomic level, and the dogma of religious orientation. Very often the moral codes of these groups are in conflict with one another, although most cultures and groups define immoral behavior as that which does harm to the individual or to other members of society.

The purpose of moral education is to help the child develop controls which enable him to curb behavior that is destructive to himself or to others. The epitome of moral conduct is to behave in ways that subordinate one's own immediate well-being to that of all humanity, and to internalize this standard as the steadfast guide to the solution of moral dilemmas. Very often, however, even adults behave morally for more pedestrian, selfish reasons. They are afraid of getting caught and want to avoid punishment, so they obey the moral code. Others are afraid of social disapproval or they seek to project an image of themselves as solid, law-abiding citizens.

Past and Present. At one time, moral development was the exclusive province of the home and the church, and the school shied away from overt, systematic instruction in this area. Today, however, character development is considered a very important component usually of the social studies curriculum, which seems more nearly attuned to the interactive processes than are other curriculum areas. Many schools exercise as much care in organizing their curriculum for moral development as they do for the teaching of the basic skills of reading and arithmetic.

In the past, teachers were often cautioned against intervention, so opportunities for character development were ignored, left to chance, or suppressed. If an unavoidable situation arose, teachers enforced a preconceived standard of behavior by preaching or punishing. This climate is slowly yielding to one in which children are free to talk more openly and honestly about justice, fairness, involvement, and other social ideals. Instead of imposing, teachers are encouraging pupils to explore alternative responses and to select from among those which are most creditable and estimable. Children are encouraged to explore the reasons for their choices and to build empathy for the other protagonists in the moral situations that confront them.

Many school supply companies are producing a vast amount of materials related to moral development. The advent of the new strategies has left many teachers confused and unsure. Not wishing merely to jump on the band wagon, they seek a solid basis upon which to proceed. Again, one of the sources they can tap is the discipline of human growth and development.

Kohlberg's Stages of Moral Development. Lawrence Kohlberg,[6] who has been investigating the origins of character development, has concluded that children's moral growth also follows a predictable pattern of movement from a lower stage to a higher one. Although all children follow this sequence, they don't all move to the highest level of moral reasoning, but may remain fixed at any one level. The purpose of instruction in character development is to move children from one level to the next higher one; in other words, it provides the cultural stimulus to improved moral reasoning. But the cultural stimulus is insufficient of itself; on the part of the children there must be a minimum level of cognitive development for the moral reasoning to flourish.

The stages of development according to Kohlberg include the following.

PRECONVENTIONAL LEVEL. The child regards right or wrong in terms of rewards or punishments in the preconventional level. In Stage 1, correct behavior is prompted by fear of punishment or blind allegiance to power figures. In Stage 2, correct behavior is prompted by pragmatic practical considerations. Individuals remain at this level usually until the end of childhood.

CONVENTIONAL LEVEL. The child regards right or wrong in terms of complying with the hopes and wishes of other people and of society in general at the conventional level. The prods to moral behavior are a need for conformity and a sense of loyalty. In Stage 3, correct behavior is prompted by a desire to please others and to be labeled a good person according to the society's definition of good. At Stage 4, correct behavior is prompted by a law-and-order mentality which values duty, authority, and respect for rules and laws. This level commences at about the age of puberty.

POSTCONVENTIONAL LEVEL. The individual regards right or wrong in terms of universally applicable precepts regardless of group affiliations at the postconventional level. At this point, the individual moves beyond the practical and expedient, beyond the pressures of his social groups to those moral values and judgments that transcend the immediate and simplistic solutions to ethical problems. In Stage 5, correct behavior is prompted by an individual set of values that have been carefully scrutinized in conjunction with regard for the rights of others. There exists a respect for laws, but a willingness to change them if needed. At Stage 6, correct behavior is prompted by abstract, universal, ethical principles, based on the inherent dignity of mankind. Adults are capable of achieving this level of moral development, although many of them do not.

---

[6] Lawrence Kohlberg, "The Claim to Moral Adequacy of a Highest Stage of Moral Development," *The Journal of Philosophy*, **52:** 630–646.

EDUCATIONAL IMPLICATIONS. As in other areas of development, the growth of moral cognition is subject to the influences of social institutions. It is incumbent upon the school, then, to assiduously nourish pupils' potential in this area and not leave it to happenstance or haphazard, impromptu instruction. It suggests the use of a broad spectrum of techniques and materials as part of an ongoing program to provide ample opportunity for frank discussion of ethical-moral problems.

For parents and teachers, it further suggests the importance of their roles as models of fairness, justice, and integrity for children to emulate until they reach the independence of the postconventional stage. At the time of children's developmental stage of wishing to please others and to conform, teachers should, as far as possible, exemplify in their personal behavior and classroom practices the advanced stage toward which children are striving.

Values of Studying Patterns. The importance of knowing about the progressive stages through which children pass as they grow and develop has been pointed out several times in this module. It enables teachers to better understand children's behavior at any particular age level, and it is a basic component in selecting appropriate content and instructional strategies. At this point, it seems fitting to indicate the advantages and disadvantages of using knowledge of patterns in understanding the behavior of the individual child.

ADVANTAGES. Among the advantages of knowing growth and development patterns are the following:

1. Knowing about patterns affords teachers a shorthand way of making decisions about what and how to teach. Rather than going through the costly process of trial and error, teachers can turn to the body of knowledge about human growth and development to understand their pupils' behavior and how to deal with it. It saves much time, frustration, and perhaps even failure to make fitting choices the first time around. Patterns are beneficial indicators of the most appropriate time to introduce certain concepts and skills and of the kinds of strategies to use to teach them successfully.

2. Knowledge of patterns enables teachers to pick up danger signals in their pupils' development. Because most children progress through each stage within a chronological age band, failure to achieve certain tasks when past the age band signals a possible defect or deficiency. This is especially true in cases of physiological development which appear spontaneously, but it is pertinent also to culturally induced tasks. For instance, most children learn to read between the ages of four or five and six or seven. If a particular pupil is still not reading as he approaches his eighth year, the teacher will look for an encumbrance, such as a visual defect, neurological impairment, or mental deficiency.

3. In a world that is accumulating knowledge and changing at accelerating rates, teachers know they can't teach all the skills and content their pupils need to master, so they need to make hard choices as to which content will yield the greatest educational benefits for the greatest number of pupils. Knowledge of patterns is useful in making these difficult decisions.

DISADVANTAGES. Among the disadvantages of adherence to fixed patterns are the following:

1. Certain pupils do not fit the age bands of development; they are early or late bloomers, and reach their readiness sooner or later than the prescribed time. Late bloomers are pressured by teachers to learn skills for which they are not ready, and

this leads to frustration or failure. Often they are labeled as impaired or deficient in some way when their need is for an extended period of time. In the case of early bloomers, teachers often forget that advanced development along one dimension does not necessarily mean equal attainment in other areas. For example, teachers often expect tall pupils to behave more maturely than small pupils of the same age, or they expect a gifted first grader, who is reading at the third-grade level, to be equally skilled in his peer relationships.

2. The possible range of normal human responses at any developmental stage is numberless. Pupils' cultural backgrounds may be so diverse that teachers may define as deviant some responses for which they are unprepared but which are perfectly normal for the pupil's milieux. In their own thinking, teachers may delimit what they define as normal patterns.

Further, the variety of responses points to the indirect connection between knowledge of human growth and development and curriculum choices. Patterns offer broad suggestions, but teachers must still decide what is the most appropriate learning environment for a particular group of pupils and for the individual children within that group.

3. The impact of our knowledge of human growth and development on curriculum constantly changes as new information about patterns develops. However, the conversion of new information into improved curriculum occurs only if teachers are willing to make the transition. Sometimes teachers are not informed or flexible enough to re-evaluate their curriculum choices in the light of new findings.

Principles of Moral Development. We have looked at the unfolding of the growth and development of the child from birth through adolescence. You may have noticed that certain ideas recur throughout the module. These are the principles of development that have applicability and that are relevant to how most people grow from childhood to adulthood. Parents and teachers need to keep these in mind in their daily interactions with children through their upsets, their joys, their frustrations, and their victories. We can therefore summarize the following conclusions:

1. The range of human behavior is extremely diverse and varied. The newborn child, already a distinctly unique creature by virtue of his inheritance, possesses potential which, unlike the animals, can respond in myriad ways to the environment. The newborn is the raw material, a bundle of possibilities, ready to respond to the endless variety of possible influences from the home, the peer group, the school, the society and culture, and the world.

Consider, for example, the range of possibilities just within the context of a single family. Often you have heard people express amazement that two siblings in the same family can be so different. But is it so amazing when you think about it? First of all, each child has inherited a unique set of genes; therefore, the potential to respond is different. The mother's pregnancies may have been somewhat different in terms of her diet, her care of herself, her health and, certainly, of her age. Upon the birth of the second child, the first-born ceases to be an only child. Now his parents cannot devote themselves exclusively to him. He has a sibling to contend with, and his role shifts to that of older brother.

The parents are older now and experienced in caring for a child, an experience they may have found pleasant or otherwise, which conditions their attitude towards raising another child. Perhaps the family scene has changed to include a grandparent or a maiden aunt. Perhaps their fortune may have improved so that they now live in a better neighborhood and they can afford to provide the children with many stimulating opportunities, or perhaps their fortunes have reversed and the opposite conditions obtain. Perhaps a great misfortune that involves serious damage to or even the loss of life or property has struck. The changing society and world culture may have altered the parents' goals, attitudes, feelings, interests, and values. If we extend these permutations to all environmental forces, we begin to envision the broad range of possible human behavior.

2. Development is the product of interaction between the human organism and the environment or, stated another way, development is the result of maturation and learning in response to stimulation from the environment. Although development is limited by the maturational possibilities of the individual, evidence seems to indicate that very few people ever reach their limits for growth. This being the case, it would seem that the intervention of the environment is crucial for the fullest flowering to take place.

Even in those cases of spontaneous maturational phenomena, which are common to all mankind, the stimulation of the environment provides an incentive to respond. For example, an infant will learn to walk on his own when his body is physiologically ready. However, the joy and laughter of his parents at his first steps, their rewarding kisses and embraces convey to him their approval and become a source of encouragement to him.

Much potential is latent, however, and doesn't materialize spontaneously. It must be nurtured by an atmosphere that enhances its growth and gives full vent to its expression. If not, it fades and wilts much as a seed that is planted in poor soil. You may have heard the expression of a born musician or a natural pitcher. These persons from the beginning of their careers show talent far superior to that of most others, but require years of rigorous and determined training before they become truly expert.

Another aspect of training, whether of the mind, of the body, or of the social-emotional processes, regards the appropriateness of the stimulation. When it is improper, incorrect, or defective, then much time is wasted, and failure or frustration may result. Correcting the responses, if that is at all possible, may require years of retraining and re-education and, perhaps, also restoring the individual's faith in himself and his self-esteem.

Consider, for example, a pupil who has learned an incorrect method of regrouping numbers in addition, or a singer whose vocal training was faulty. Both may go a long time before the flaws are discovered. In the meantime, the child is having trouble with not only addition but also subtraction, multiplication, and division, and he hates mathematics because it is not one of his good subjects. The singer seems to be making no headway in her career and in her vocal maturity. Fortunately, some types of faulty responses such as the mathematics pupils's are easily corrected once they are detected; but others, such as the singer's may require years of retraining. It is therefore a responsibility of the home and the school to monitor the initial responses of children, and to ferret out poor responses or habits, if failure and frustration are to be avoided.

3. Developmental patterns proceed in an orderly, sequential, and predictable fashion. The universality of their existence applies to all persons, no matter where or when they were born. We see this in the life cycle as the glandular, reproductive, skeletal, and other body systems follow a hierarchal plan of growth and develop-

ment common to all mankind. Further, the evidence seems to be mounting that the social-emotional, intellectual, and moral aspects likewise pertain to all of mankind. They also follow a ladderlike arrangement of one sequence building upon and forming the foundation for the next. The knowledge of this phenomenon is extremely useful in refining our understanding of the mechanism of human life, and in excising and in preventing maladaptive form and function.

4. Growth and development are continuous but never uniform in their rates. The capacities of the human organism never cease to grow and develop until they reach maturity, but they proceed at different rates and reach their peaks of maturity at different ages of life. The period from conception through the first two years of life, of course, is one of rapid development for the entire organism. The prenatal, microscopic zygote, containing the whole spectrum of human potential, increases billions of times its size by the time its cell differentiation and specialization are manifest in the completely albeit rudimentary, functioning of the two-year-old child.

Uneven development rates are exemplified in the spurt of growth of sexual organs at the age of puberty, the rapid swell of speech facility at about age two, and the surge of ability for abstract thinking in early adolescence. Development was going on prior to and will continue after these spurts, but at a much slower pace.

The school should take advantage of these peaks and spurts of growth when the learner is most motivated and ready to learn.

5. All aspects of development are interrelated and interdependent. Because development is an integrative process of maturation, learning, and environmental stimulation operating as a totality, failure of any of the parts to function properly will of necessity affect all the other parts as well as the whole.

Let us take the example of the child whose speech is defective or damaged in some way either through inheritance, disease, or accident. The chances are that when he learns to talk, he may have a speech impairment, and there may be a delay in the age at which speech starts. His social-emotional adjustment could be affected, because if he has difficulty in making himself understood, he may become tense when interacting with others. He may withdraw from contact with other people or try to avoid speaking, if possible. His parents may openly or subtly communicate their anxiety about the problem, push him to speak, or even unconsciously reject him. By the time he is in first grade, the school expects him to learn to read. One of the requisites for smooth and successful mastery of reading is an extensive use of language and manipulation of words which this youngster might lack. He may be further hampered by the fact that the way he pronounces words doesn't agree with the way they are written, so he may have difficulty with phonetic analysis in reading and in spelling. Thus, the totality of development could be affected by any one of its aspects.

6. Growth rates vary from person to person although they tend to remain constant for the individual. This principle seems in conflict with previous ones. But you must remember that while all children proceed through the life cycle which has spurts of growth, the differences in their potentials and environments will make the timing very specific for each individual. Further, given the wide variety of possible responses, children will develop some choices extensively and ignore or only minimally deal with others. Some may select artistic expression, while others may prefer sports or scientific endeavors.

For example, most children learn to talk at about two years of age, but some will start at eighteen months, and others at two and one half or even as late as three. Serious harm can result if parents and teachers fail to recognize the wide time span of normal development, and if they set rigid time schedules for children. The early-speaking child, who delights in the use of speech and in the manipulation of words may go on to become a linguist or an expert in language. Others may choose only to master the native language at the simplest level of functioning.

The constancy of development is illustrated by the fact that the adult height of a female child can be predicted by doubling her height at age two, and at age two and one half for a male child. The tall child at this age will tend to become a tall adult because growth patterns over the years are likely to remain stable for the individual person. This does not mean that growth rates do not vary at different times in life, but that rate indicators in childhood are somewhat predictive of an adult.

Studies show that young children with weight problems will be overweight in adulthood. Teachers have been notably accurate in picking out potential delinquents from the social maladjustment these children exhibited in elementary school. Longitudinal studies of children indicate that the personality characteristics they possess in early childhood—whether pensive or impulsive, quiet or exuberant, happy or cheerless—tend to be the same qualities they possess as adults. Children who score well on intelligence test scores are likely to maintain this advantage on subsequent testings throughout the years.

These tendencies do not signify that changes do not occur or are not possible; we have already discussed the impact of a deprived or a rich environment on one's potential. Rather, they suggest that inheritance does play some part in growth and development. More importantly, however, they suggest that nurturing in the first few years of life is of critical importance, and that throughout the years from infancy to adolescence parents and teachers have a tremendous responsibility in affording children a rich supportive environment.

SUGGESTED READING

General Texts

The books listed are general texts on the subject of human growth and development. They concern all the topics presented in this module, but in much greater detail. If you want to increase your background, read any one or several of them. They are all excellent, up-to-date books. You will notice that some of them are already in their third or fourth editions.

Baller, Warren R., and Don C. Charles. *The Psychology of Human Growth and Development*. 2nd. Ed. New York: Holt, Rinehart & Winston, Inc., 1968.

Bee, Helen. *The Developing Child*. New York: Harper and Row, Publishers, 1975.

Bernard, Harold W. *Human Development in Western Culture*. 4th Ed. Boston: Allyn & Bacon, Inc., 1975.

Hurlock, Elizabeth B. *Child Development*. 4th Ed. New York: McGraw-Hill Book Company, 1964.

Johnson, Ronald C., and Gene R. Medinnus. *Child Psychology: Behavior and Development*. 3rd. Ed. New York: John Wiley & Sons, Inc., 1974.

Kennedy, Wallace A. *Child Psychology.* Englewood Cliffs, N.J.: Prentice-Hall Inc., 1971.

Papalia, Diane E., and Sally Wendkos Olds. *A Child's World: Infancy Through Adolescence.* New York: McGraw-Hill Book Company, 1975.

Piaget, Jean. *The Origins of Intelligence in Children.* New York: International Universities Press, 1952.

Stone, L. Joseph, and Joseph Church. *Childhood and Adolescence.* 3rd. Ed. New York: Random House, Inc., 1975.

POST TEST

DIRECTIONS: *Circle the letter choice which best completes each statement.*

1. Billy tried to decode a cryptogram. He substituted an *a,* then a *b,* then a *c* for each cipher until he had broken the code. This is an example of
   a. trial-and-error learning.
   b. conditioning.
   c. ability to see cause and effect.
   d. theorizing.
   e. creative thinking.

2. Jimmy sees ten discs stacked in a pile and ten others scattered across the table. When asked which is the greater number, he designates the scattered discs. This is an example of Piaget's
   a. sensory motor phase.
   b. preconceptual phase.
   c. concrete operations phase.
   d. formal operations phase.

3. Eight-year-old Johnny can catch balls in centerfield, but his teacher says he has trouble following an outline when he cuts with scissors. This is an example of
   a. oral fixation.
   b. identity crisis.
   c. proximodistal development.
   d. lack of attention span.
   e. social-emotional immaturity.

4. Susie wept openly, but her brother, Keith, fought back the tears when his team lost the school championship playoffs. Robert noticed Keith's tears and called him a crybaby sissy. This is an example of
   a. neurotic behavior.
   b. inherent biological sex differences.
   c. male superiority.
   d. social sex typing.
   e. poor sportsmanship.

5. Marilyn cried and screamed when her nursery school companion refused to give her the doll she wanted. Her teacher directed Marilyn to another doll and didn't punish her because
   a. the teacher was too permissive.
   b. Marilyn might cry harder.
   c. the teacher was afraid of hurting Marilyn' feelings.
   d. the teacher understood that Marilyn's behavior was typical of four-year-olds.
   e. the teacher feared what Marilyn's parents might think if they found out she had punished Marilyn.

6. Puberty is often a time of turmoil and difficult adjustment because
   a. boys and girls are attracted to each other.
   b. the shift from childhood towards adulthood brings on many changes.
   c. parents and teachers don't understand children at this age.
   d. the schools are little concerned with the problems of this age and do little to help.
   e. girls are more mature at this age than boys.

7. The study of human growth and development is important to teachers because it enables them to
   a. construct better tests to use in the classroom.
   b. make wiser decisions about curriculum matters.
   c. have a friendlier relationship with children.
   d. keep up with the younger generation.
   e. make a good impression on the principal and parents.

8. An example of maturation is when a child learns to
   a. talk.
   b. read.
   c. ride a bicycle.
   d. do a headstand.
   e. walk.

9. Peer relationships are uppermost during the gang age because
   a. the adult world is out of step with the younger generation.
   b. children have discovered by this age that most adults are hypocrites.
   c. friends know more about the world than parents or teachers.
   d. children at this age are striving for independence from adults.
   e. having friends wasn't important before this age.

10. Mrs. Martin's first child walked at ten months. Her second child is now twelve months old and still not walking. She is not upset or alarmed because
    a. she is a more relaxed mother the second time around.
    b. her husband says he didn't start walking until he was fourteen months old.
    c. she knows that the longer he waits, the stronger his legs will be for walking.
    d. a neighbor boy is eighteen months old and he is still not walking.
    e. she knows that he is within the normal time band for the development of walking.

11. Readiness is a key factor for teachers to understand and implement because
    a. it gives them more free time during class hours.
    b. it makes them sound educated when they have conferences with parents.
    c. ignoring it makes learning more difficult for children.
    d. teachers should operate from a theoretical base.
    e. children will sense that they are better teachers for it.

12. The large-size brain of a newborn infant compared to the rest of his body is an example of
    a. cephalocaudal development.
    b. the moro reflex.
    c. a hereditary factor.
    d. a congenital defect.
    e. a poor maternal diet during pregnancy.

13. According to Freudian theory, if a pupil vows he doesn't know why he suddenly flew into a rage, it is because
    a. he is trying to avoid punishment.
    b. he is afraid of telling the teacher the truth.
    c. his motivation was subconscious.
    d. it is typical of children during the latency stage.
    e. he is fixated at the oral stage.

14. One of the major differences between Freudian theory and Erikson's theory is that
    a. Freud has fewer developmental stages.
    b. Freud's theory ends with the adolescent stage.
    c. Freud gives greater importance to the sex drive.
    d. Erikson builds on Freudian theory.
    e. Erikson doesn't deal with the Oedipus Complex.

15. Mr. Canfield wants Bryan to do as well in school as his older brother, Fred, despite the fact that Bryan is trying his best. Mr. Canfield is ignoring the causative factor that
    a. intelligence runs in families.
    b. Fred probably had better teachers.
    c. his sons' inherited potentials are different and unique.
    d. as an only son, Fred probably received more time and attention.
    e. Bryan does much better in sports.

16. When Frank was in kindergarten, he labored over spelling his name. Now in first grade he does it without thinking about it. This kind of learning is
    a. trial and error.
    b. cause and effect.
    c. extinction.
    d. generalizing.
    e. conditioning.

17. It is important for teachers to reckon with the motivation of learning because
    a. it is part of the lesson plan format.
    b. school should be fun for children, and learning, easy.

    c. it is the driving force that moves children to learn.
    d. it increases the popularity of those teachers who plan for it.
    e. it is the fashionable thing to do in educational circles.

18. Intrinsic motivation is considered superior to extrinsic motivation because
    a. teachers can then avoid the use of punishment when children become bored.
    b. teachers will run out of rewards to give children.
    c. when children learn of their own volition, they learn more and better.
    d. when children learn on their own, the teacher's job is easier.
    e. it eases the pressure put on children to get into the right schools and colleges.

19. Rachel returned the pencil she took from Marie's desk because she was afraid of the punishment if she got caught. This illustrates Kohlberg's
    a. preconventional level.
    b. conventional level.
    c. postconventional level.

20. It is difficult for teachers to assess pupil's readiness for a learning task because
    a. all the elements of readiness do not mature at the same time.
    b. many elements of readiness are not outwardly visible.
    c. parents push their children to achieve.
    d. many schools don't have the tests to give.
    e. teachers are poor at judging from pupil's overt behavior.

21. The knowledge we have of child growth and development helps in curriculum decisions by
    a. providing the theoretical and practical framework for knowing what to teach and when.
    b. freeing teachers for the more important tasks of marking papers and tests.
    c. telling teachers what content should be taught at every grade level.
    d. freeing teachers of the responsibility of deciding what to teach.
    e. giving teachers an escape when they make the wrong choices.

22. Schools that are organized according to our knowledge of human growth and development would be those in which
    a. children in the same class are all assigned the same learning tasks.
    b. children have a wide variety and a large number of learning opportunities.
    c. teachers keep the noise level in their classroom low so children can learn.
    d. children learn principally by trial and error.
    e. interfering parents are discouraged from visiting the school.

23. If fourteen-year-old Paul is small for his age and always has been, then his mother is probably wrong in telling him that he will grow up to be the tallest one of his group because
    a. Paul didn't inherit tallness as one of his attributes.
    b. the growth pattern for Paul is a constant one.
    c. Paul's diet is lacking in sufficient protein.
    d. it's too late for Paul to start growing now.
    e. the growth pattern is related to Paul's social-emotional development.

24. Mrs. Gimes is going to give her three-year-old son, Scott, a head start for school by teaching him to read. This is probably an unwise decision because
   a. she is only doing it so she can brag about her son.
   b. Scott would rather play with his friends.
   c. all the readiness factors for reading do not appear at this age.
   d. she is not a teacher and she won't do a good job with it.
   e. Scott is at the phallic stage, and he needs to resolve his Oedipus complex first.

25. Mr. Foxx was told at school that his only son, Richard, had only an average intelligence, according to the school test. If Mr. Foxx wants to improve his son's intelligence, probably the best thing he can do is
   a. feed him a lot of fish because it is brain food.
   b. prepare his son for taking the tests by drilling him in the same kind of exercises as found on the tests.
   c. provide him with many stimulating cultural experiences.
   d. check every night to see that Richard does his homework.
   e. insist that Richard be retested on a different test to see if he gets a higher score.

General Methods

J. Glorianne Rice

George H. Rice, Jr.

Bryan, Texas

module 3

Lecture / Demonstrations, Field Trips, and Films / Recitation and Questioning / Discussion / Games / Simultation / Role Playing / Independent Study / Textbooks / Practice / Inquiry

RATIONALE

One of the first things a college student learns when starting on an elementary education program is that the field is filled with controversy. Even so, most educators agree that the three basic goals of an elementary education program are to provide each student with (1) basic technical (intellectual) skills in reading, writing, and arithmetic; (2) social skills that enable him to establish meaningful, interpersonal relationships and to integrate himself into society; and (3) physical skills and acuity. Curriculum content and methods for teaching skills will, of course, vary from time to time and from school to school.

Function of the School

To plan a teaching program, it is necessary to consider the basic function of a school. Most of the time, teachers are much more concerned with the day-to-day process of accomplishing the teaching function than they are in contemplating the philosophical arguments of "Why are we here?" Nevertheless, a teacher can do a much better job of designing her program if she knows the purpose of her efforts, and why the elementary education program is considered to be so important in our society.

One concept of the function of schools emphasizes that schools should preserve and transmit our cultural heritage. Proponents of this function place most emphasis on intellectual development. They believe that students should be trained primarily in the liberal arts, with little or no emphasis on any specific profession. In the lower grades of the elementary school, the emphasis would be centered upon reading, writing, and arithmetic, according to this concept. Logic, mathematics, history, science, art, and philosophy would be taught more in the upper elementary grades. Basic education would be just that—basic. Such phrases as "education of the complete child," or "education for democratic citizenship" would have no place in such a school system. Under this concept, the intellectually competent student is much more highly valued than is his less competent peer, and a disproportionate amount of time and attention are devoted to the competent student's education.

An alternative concept of the function of schools is that schools act as instruments for cultural change. This has been a popular concept for many years, dating since the time of Horace Mann. Under this concept, schools provide a country with the skills necessary for social progress on the national level, and for social mobility on the individual level. So, an underdeveloped country, in starting its effort toward modernization, starts by teaching its people to read and to write. Or, a government might offer scholarships in medicine, or in engineering, or in whatever field the nation needs. From this concept have come many changes, both in curriculum and in special programs for disadvantaged children. Integration and busing are the most publicized social missions, and the United States space program has been one of the most active physical science missions.

The third and last concept of the function of the school stems from John

Dewey's philosophy that the appropriate function of education is the development of each individual student, or development of the "whole child" to his maximum potential. This concept has been far-reaching. Grade placement of subject matter has been influenced by the emphasis on child development. Learning theory and motivation are now a part of every teacher's training. The nongraded school, the open classroom school, special education, vocational education, exceptional children programs, kindergarten, head start, and day care centers are all based on Dewey's philosophy. Even the growing emphasis on emotional development, counseling, and guidance owes its start to the philosophy that a child should be helped in every way needed to maximize his particular intellectual, social, and physical growth.

TEACHING METHODS

There are probably as many approaches, interpretations, and definitions of how to teach as there are elementary school teachers. Each person learns to use a style suited to her individual skills, her students' capabilities, and the expectations of her principal and parents. Some states have set up general guidelines on curricula and methods, then have permitted each school district to adjust to fit its own needs. Some states have left the entire responsibility for devising the school program with the individual districts. Emerging patterns seem the result of two influences: (1) colleges have placed greater emphasis on innovative methods; and (2) larger, consolidated school districts, regarded by professional educators as leaders, have tended to develop programs and methods which are copied, adapted, and adopted by smaller districts.

The methods of teaching discussed in this module include both older and newer methods that can be used in the elementary classroom. Perhaps they will be mentioned in the teaching material issued to a teacher, but given little emphasis. Perhaps a beginning teacher will be able to consult with a more experienced teacher as to how each method might be best used. But more likely, the new classroom teacher will find it necessary to experiment in the classroom, to develop techniques that work, and to try out various approaches. The different methods give different results, of course, and the selection of a particular method should be based on the educational objective which the teacher is pursuing.

SPECIFIC OBJECTIVES

The importance of having a variety of methods is that a teacher may change her teaching style to reach each child in the room, and to develop the child's knowledge and understanding to the maximum.

Your goal in studying this module is twofold: to identify the methods of teaching, and to determine when to use each method.

When this module is completed, you should be able to perform the following:

1. Write a purpose for the study of methods of teaching.
2. Describe the nature of a lecture and when to use the lecture method.
3. List the qualities that make the lecture an effective teaching method.
4. List three concrete experiences that a teacher can provide for pupils in the classroom.
5. Write an explanation of the differences between demonstrations, field trips, and films.
6. List the steps for effective questioning.
7. Outline the planning needed to achieve a successful field trip.
8. Write a definition of the methods of teaching described in this module.
9. Answer at least seventeen of the twenty questions on the Post Test without error.
10. Write a paragraph describing the advantages and disadvantages of using recitation as a method of teaching.
11. List the steps that lead to good questions.
12. Write a paragraph on the reasons for using discussion as a method of teaching.
13. Write a description in paragraph form of the development of games for the elementary classroom.
14. List the contributions and limitations of games in the classroom.
15. Interact with a group of peers in a short, role-playing situation.
16. List a hierarchy of role-playing situations, from those that are low to those that are high in emotional value.
17. List in order the components of inquiry.
18. Write a paragraph defending the use of textbooks in the classroom.
19. Develop a list of ideas for independent study to be used in the classroom, and also note the approximate grade level for each.
20. Write a paragraph discussing why a teacher should be extremely careful when using simulation, games, role playing, or inquiry in the classroom.

MODULE TEXT

In a general sense, all teaching methods are used to implant and develop ideas and conceptual skills in the child. Since they must all deal with the child's mind, they must all address themselves to the nature of the mind, and conform to the routine that the mind uses to learn. This is why so much of a teacher's education is devoted to the study of maturation, growth, behavior, socialization, and other aspects of educational psychology. But all teaching methods are different in that they involve different experience bases in the child, and address different skills and fields of knowledge.

The methods discussed in this module are not the only methods that can be used to teach in the elementary school. Also, methods overlap to a great degree. Nevertheless, the various methods are discussed separately to emphasize certain aspects of each approach.

Lecture

Teaching by lectures is probably one of the oldest methods used by classroom teachers. Most student teachers feel comfortable with this method because their teachers used lectures. It is a very traditional method of teaching and, therefore, has received a great deal of criticism in a time when educational methods and curriculum content have been undergoing extensive examination and reform.

To use the lecture method most effectively, a teacher needs to know the basic nature of a lecture, when it can best be used, and some of the techniques to make a lecture more efficient.

The basic underlying assumptions of the lecture are that the teacher has knowledge, or can acquire knowledge, and that the teacher can give this knowledge to students.

No matter how easy this method of teaching may appear to an observer, the real key to success is the same as with any other teaching effort—organization and planning. The planning must cover both the subject matter to be presented and the manner in which it will be presented. Unless the lecture is planned very carefully, it will probably not result in a very effective learning experience for the student.

Organization of the Lecture. The organization of a lecture follows the form of an information paper. There should be an introduction in which the teacher identifies the subject of the lecture, fits this subject in with past lessons, and generally tries to stimulate interest in the subject matter. Usually, interest is generated by helping a student identify with the subject and recognize how he might need to use the knowledge at some future date.

The body of the lecture presents the subject in a logical order, building from what the student already knows toward new knowledge that the teacher wants the student to absorb. Knowledge is presented in small enough increments that the student can absorb the material, and at a slow enough pace that he can assimilate it with his past knowledge. The pace should not, however, be so slow that the student becomes bored. Both the level of vocabulary used and the technical nature of the subject must correspond to the capability of the students.

The conclusion of a lecture should sum up what has been presented, emphasize what the teacher considers to be the important points (which the student is expected to remember), and point to future studies that will depend on this knowledge for successful learning.

Audience Size. It is difficult to define the optimal size audience for a lecture. One teacher might lecture to fifty students and hold their attention. Another might lecture to 200 students and make each of them feel a personal and individual bond with the lecturer. Probably, the minimum number of students for a suitable audience is from fifteen to twenty. With any smaller group, it is difficult to give a formal presentation.

Theoretically, there is no maximum limit to the size of an audience. Formal speeches by famous people on television are heard by millions of listeners at a time. For practical purposes, though, audience size is usually limited by the capacity of the room available and by the number of people interested in the subject.

Maintaining Student Interest. In an elementary school setting, a maximum time or duration of the lecture becomes very important. The younger the child, the shorter is his interest span, and the more limited is his ability to retain points given in the lecture. Adults usually can sit for an hour's lecture, but younger elementary students can sit for only about twenty minutes, and older elementary school students can sit for no more than forty minutes.

There are two ways to keep students interested in a lecture presentation. The first is to keep them amused, and the second is to keep them involved or identified with the subject. Although there is a great deal of merit in keeping them amused, the second approach is usually considered more intellectually productive. Involvement of students in the lecture is most desirable; the most common criticism of the lecture method is that students are often passive participants. Involvement comes about when students recognize the importance of the subject matter as knowledge they may need at some time in the future.

A primary advantage of a lecture is its ability to present a large number of facts in a short period of time, but it is necessary that the student be conditioned to accept and understand the subject matter to be presented. It is desirable, therefore, that the lecture not concentrate exclusively on the presentation of raw facts. Concepts, generalizations, principles, interpretations, and evaluations of the topic should also be included.

A lecture must be presented in an enthusiastic manner, with vocal inflection, gestures, and emotion. Nothing will kill the enthusiasm of an audience more quickly than a lecture given in a monotone by a speaker who shows no enthusiasm for the subject. Such a lecture is almost as deadly as having a teacher read to his students from the textbook.

Instructional Aids. The purpose of a lecture is to draw a word picture of the subject. But words are effective only if the student has the concept to which a word applies. Some things cannot be conveyed by words alone, and at such times a teacher must illustrate what is being said by the use of some physical object. For example, in teaching colors to a young child, it does no good to explain the wave length of a color. It is necessary, instead, to hold up a card and say, "This card is red." Nor is it possible to lecture on the alphabet without physically illustrating the letters. A chalkboard is indispensable in teaching mathematics, and natural sciences are much more understandable if the lecturer uses pictures of animals and plants.

In addition to illustrating the speaker's points, instructional aids serve to focus a listener's attention by utilizing his visual sense, thus reinforcing the message received by his ears.

The use of instructional aids, or props, requires careful planning. To introduce such an aid too early or too late in the lecture can reduce its effectiveness as much as to use one that the audience cannot see well. A good picture, diagram, or model can improve a lecture immensely, but an inept illustration or a poorly used visual aid can weaken a lecture. Lecture time is much too valuable to spend it trying to get a slide projector to work.

Other Hints. There are several general rules that should be observed to make a lecture effective.

Seat the audience in comfortable chairs, facing away from windows to avoid light glare in their eyes. If a glare is unavoidable, let it be in the speaker's eyes, and not in the eyes of his audience.

Keep distracting noise to a minimum. Outside noise prevents listeners from hearing the lecturer and distracts their attention.

The room should be neither too hot nor too cold. If the listeners are uncomfortable, they will be irritated and will not be able to concentrate on what the speaker is saying.

Movement attracts attention. Although it is possible for a speaker to move around too much when lecturing, the opposite is probably more common. This is one reason that a speaker should use a training aid: it helps him to move around the stage to a certain degree. But a warning should be noted here. Members of the audience must be able to see and hear the speaker at all times. If he is using a microphone, he must stay by the microphone so as to be heard. If he is using an instructional aid, he must not get between the aid and the audience, or he will block visibility.

Finally, no single teaching method should be used exclusively. To maximize learning, a lecture should be followed by discussion, testing, practice, or some other method. Very rarely can a lecture, by itself, accomplish a teaching objective.

Demonstrations, Field Trips, and Films

Schools traditionally have used verbal tools as the major, or primary, form of instruction. As learning theory has had more influence upon practices in the classroom, however, teachers have started making deliberate efforts to provide children with enriching experiences. These experiences have their beginnings in a concrete or real world. To a child, the things that are real are those that relate to the five senses, can be taken apart, put together, labeled, given names, seen, touched, and used.

Three types of concrete experiences that a teacher can provide for students are demonstrations, field trips, and films.

Demonstrations. A demonstration resembles a lecture in that the teacher is the doer and the students are passive observers. The demonstration has many of the same advantages and disadvantages as the lecture as a teaching method. It can be presented to a large audience, it can cover a great number of points quickly, and it requires planning and a skilled teacher to be effective. Usually, it is much easier to command the attention of an audience with a demonstration than with a lecture.

Demonstrations answer the questions, "What is it?" and "How does it work?" They apply to physical things, rather than to abstract ideas or values. Demonstrations are particularly useful in showing activities that require a high level of skill or that might be dangerous, such as a chemical laboratory experiment.

There are several things that a teacher can do to increase the effectiveness of a demonstration. Students must be able to see and sometimes hear that which is being demonstrated. It is also important that students be prepared for the demonstration in advance so they know its significance and what to look for.

There should be a postdemonstration discussion or practice period to permit students to understand and to apply what they have seen. This further illustrates that teaching methods must be combined to be truly effective.

Use of a demonstration requires that a teacher practice before presenting it to the pupils. The rehearsal should include a complete presentation, using all props, models, speeches, manipulations, drawings, and results achieved. This does several things for a teacher. It tells her how long a period the demonstration will require. It assures her that all equipment and parts are on hand and can be used. It insures that the results which the teacher wants will be obtained during the demonstration session. A demonstration loses its effect if the teacher fails to get the results which she has told students to expect.

Field Trips. Field trips are very popular because they provide students with real experiences in the community outside the classroom. They allow students to expand their horizons beyond the limits of family and school classroom. The community becomes a laboratory, and students often become more interested in schoolwork when they see a relationship between what they are studying and the real world.

The first thing a teacher needs to consider when thinking of a field trip is how the trip fits in with subjects being studied in classwork. Will the trip be valuable enough to justify the time used? Just what, specifically, is the field trip supposed to accomplish?

After a decision has been made to take a field trip, much preparation is required of the teacher. It must be fitted into the school schedule, and this usually means that student absences from other classes must be cleared with other teachers. Permission must be obtained from the places to be visited, and this often requires that the teacher make an advance visit. Transportation must be scheduled, either by private automobile, school bus, or commercial transportation.

The teacher will also have to do some student preparation for the trip. The purpose of the trip should be explained, and students should be asked to look for specific things, and told what they will be expected to learn.

A strict time schedule should be observed for the convenience of parents, bus drivers, cooperating teachers, and hosts of the visit. Adequate rest stops should be scheduled, and enough slack built in to accommodate the unanticipated.

Discipline is a must. There should be an adequate number of supervising teachers, parents, chaperones, and others to make sure that no one gets lost or injured. This aspect of the field trip should probably get a bit of extra attention. If the class creates a good impression with its host, a teacher will find it much easier to get permission to come back next year. So, count the students onto the bus, check off their names, put name tags on them, count them off the bus, count them into and out of each rest stop, set up a "buddy system," make older students responsible for younger ones, get a whistle, and always have someone watching throughout the entire visit.

The problem of liability should be mentioned, and it is unfortunate that a teacher must pay attention to it. Schools have traditionally been held harmless for accidents that occur on school property if a normal amount of supervision is provided. But as soon as students are taken away from the school, the proof of "adequate" supervision becomes a problem. Automobile accidents, falls, illness, and other dangers become increasingly menacing. To offset law suits, it is common, good sense to require any student who goes on a field trip to give a release before going. This usually takes the form of a "parent's permission slip." A teacher should check with the school principal to be sure that liability insurance is adequate to cover the trip.

Films. Events in 1941 gave impetus to an innovation in teaching methods that has had a profound effect on education. World War II came at a time when the motion picture industry was at its peak. Vaudeville had faded, the common man had little access to live theater productions, but what he had was the "picture show." When it became necessary to train millions of men in the shortest possible time to fight in the armed forces or to work in defense plants, there was a highly skilled and prolific movie industry to do the teaching. It was very successful.

There are not as many films for use in the elementary school as there are for use in the armed forces, but the field of audiovisual aids has made significant contributions to public school education.

Films are similar to lectures, demonstrations, and field trips in that students are passive observers rather than active participants. Films are, however, able to generate a larger degree of interest, to be more entertaining, and to pack more instruction into a small time period than any of the other three methods. Because they can use professional actors and lots of action to illustrate their teaching points, films are very effective in getting their message across. The problem is finding a film that contains what a teacher wants to teach.

A film should always be previewed by the teacher before it is shown to a class. This insures that the film is in good condition, not broken or scratched, and that it covers the desired subject matter. It may be necessary, for example, for a teacher to change the sequence of the lesson to accommodate the film, or to teach something that had not been planned originally.

Films are sometimes so impressive that they overwhelm a teacher. It should always be remembered that the film is there to assist the teacher, and not vice versa. She should feel free to use parts of it, disagree with it, or even ignore it.

Recitation and Questioning

Another method of teaching that is commonly used in the elementary school is recitation. It is a term that is old-fashioned and rarely heard in college these days. Basically, it includes both verbal testing of the student, and training him in the ability to express himself.

Although "show and tell," oral book reports, speeches, debates, and formal presentations by students can all be classed as recitations, by far the most common is the "question and answer" session in the classroom.

It does not take much of an extention to broaden the concept of recitation as a teaching method to include written tests as well. Testing serves several useful purposes. It gives a teacher feedback on how well she is accomplishing her teaching objective. How well do the students understand the subject matter? What do they remember of the facts involved? It establishes a level of present knowledge so that instruction can be planned to take the class forward.

Testing emphasizes to a student what is important in the subject to be learned, and sets forth a logic to explain its value. It also serves as an extrinsic, motivating device for the student, offering reward to those who learn, and punishment to those who fail to learn.

Since in recitation the teacher is checking on what the student knows, recitation poses a threat to the student, who must prove that he knows certain things. Some students find this situation very unpleasant, even if they give the correct answers. Although a teacher praises a correct answer, the reward gained from praise does not match the sense of ridicule or shame the student feels when he gives an incorrect answer.

Recitation is performed by a student, but the student does not act without the teacher asking a question or posing a problem to which he is expected to respond. So, the success of recitation depends on the skill with which the teacher asks the questions.

Questioning Techniques. The first study of questions used in the classroom was published by Romiett Stevens in 1912. The findings of the study seem very contemporary. One significant finding was that teachers asked many questions, as many as 100 to 200 in a 45-minute high school period. Such a pace was described as deadly for the students.

When a teacher fires questions at students at a rapid pace, it is the teacher that is doing the classroom work. The student, in turn, is unable to draw upon his experiences or make generalizations about the subject matter under question. Usually, the students have only a brief time in which to answer, so expression is not emphasized.

The needs of the individual are usually overlooked when a teacher uses a large number of questions. The student who becomes interested in an area has little time to explore on his own, or even to have his own questions answered.

Questioning of this type emphasizes memory work. The classroom becomes an arena in which students can show off their knowledge, instead of being a place where the student can gain understanding. There is very little analysis or creative thinking involved in such a situation.

When a teacher uses questions in the classroom, there are ways to improve their effectiveness as a teaching method.

Stop. Cut down on the actual number of questions used in the classroom.

Pause. After asking a question, the teacher should allow time for students to answer. The length of time will be determined by the type of question asked. The teacher needs to develop a feeling for the timing of questions. Make it a habit to repeat or restate the question as well as the student's response. Expect the students to use the period of silence to think about the question.

Think. Think about the questions you ask. Intellectual skills have been divided into five categories by Bloom and others. This taxonomy classifies intellectual skills as comprehension, application, analysis, synthesis, and evaluation. Most teachers question at the memory level with little thought given to the higher intellectual skills, such as synthesis and evaluation. N. M. Sanders, for example, suggests that teachers use at least one third of their class time asking questions that are above the memory level.[1]

---

[1] Norris M. Sanders, *Classroom Questions: What Kinds?* (New York: Harper and Row, Publishers, 1966).

Using higher level questions requires that the teacher be well versed in the subject matter being presented. If the teacher requires only memory from the students, then she needs to know only the facts. But if she is going to ask for concepts and generalizations, she must know the concepts and generalizations.

Shift Gears. It does not do much good to ask questions and expect responses when students do not possess the knowledge or information required to answer. Therefore, the teacher needs to take into account what the student already knows, and shift questions as needed.

As the level of questioning progresses from memory to evaluation, there is a change in student responses. The higher the level of questioning the more diverse are the responses. Students will not all give the same answers, and evaluation of answers by a teacher also shifts from a "right or wrong" to a "good or better" judgment. Also, if a teacher asks a student for his ideas or his opinion, it is not possible for the student to be wrong. It is also a good idea to be prepared for the unexpected, because students often give answers that the teacher does not expect.

Draw Them Out. One valuable use of the recitation method is to draw out a reluctant student, make him a more active participant in classroom activity, and less passive in his learning effort. There are several techniques that can be used to accomplish this, and there are some dangers to guard against.

The first technique is to always ask the question before designating a student to answer it. Otherwise, all students except the one who is required to answer will relax, and not formulate a response for themselves. If the question is asked first, all students will try to think of an answer in the event they are called on to respond.

Second, do not play games with students. Do not change the answers, argue at a level above their comprehension, disagree with the textbook, or use illogical reasoning with them.

Third, and perhaps the most important thing to remember about the entire recitation method, *never humiliate a student!* Students are emotionally vulnerable during a recitation session. A teacher can use this situation to strengthen a child's self-confidence, or she can humiliate him to the point that he has no further will to learn. Therefore, address each question to a class member who can be expected to answer it correctly. An incorrect answer does no one any good, and is especially damaging to the student who responds incorrectly.

Used correctly by a skilled teacher, the recitation method of instruction is a very useful educational tool. Used incorrectly, it is potentially the most dangerous of all methods for possible damage to the student. A teacher should use it very carefully.

Discussion

In the recitation method of teaching, the teacher asks questions and the student answers them. In the discussion method of teaching, the student asks many or most of the questions, and other students or the teacher answer them. This is one of the most widely used and most popular methods of teaching in the modern school. It is a very old method, dating at least since the time of Socrates.

Teachers who use and prefer the discussion method of teaching believe that understanding comes from within the individual, and not from outside sources, such as the teacher. The teacher in this case does not transmit knowledge to the student; the student learns through an active effort on his own part. Emphasis is not on the teacher's teaching, but on the student's learning.

A teacher who uses this method usually sees himself as a facilitator, who encourages his students to discover things for themselves. Students gain knowledge and understanding as they see relationships among their learning experiences. This development of generalizations has several names in education, such as insight, inquiry, and discovery.

The discussion method teaches on two levels at the same time. The first is the learning of subject matter, and the second is the development of a skill in the student to learn on his own without constant help from a teacher.

Students easily become actively involved in the learning process through discussions. They become interested in the subject studied, and progress at a rate that maintains their interest. Interest promotes study, and study promotes learning. Proponents of the discussion method, therefore, argue that the learning, or the gaining of knowledge and understanding, is its own reward.

Because students are so involved, feedback to the teacher is rapid and accurate. The teacher can quickly and easily adjust her teaching effort to the needs of the class. Also, feedback is gained with much less threat than is present in the recitation method.

There is an obvious trade-off when using the discussion method of teaching. Because discussion involves more time, less subject matter can be presented than by the lecture method. But students learn more of what is presented. The trade-off is between getting "a part of a lot," or getting "a lot of a part."

Discussion in the classroom requires the teacher to organize the room for best results. A good discussion requires that a number of students participate. Most teachers like to have twelve to twenty students in a group. Usually, some form of a circle arrangement will permit them to be close enough to hear each other when speaking in a normal voice. Eye contact among the students is also very important.

Training aids, such as recording and video equipment, are sometimes useful in a discussion. If laboratory equipment, maps, or other props are to be used, they should be readily available. Library and other resources that students can use for references should be accessible to them quickly. The whole focus is on permitting the student to explore a subject easily. The teacher needs to be flexible, therefore, in both subject coverage and in time scheduling when using this method.

One of the most desirable aspects of the discussion method is that it helps a student develop logic through comparison of his own ideas with those of his peers. By expressing his concepts, asking for clarification, and engaging in argumentation, his understanding becomes sharper and more accurate. This is the real value of discussion.

Games

Games as a teaching method are receiving a great deal of attention at the present time. Attempts to introduce gaming into the classroom also involve a certain degree of controversy.

Games, as such, have been with mankind for a long time. Chess, for example, has been played in its present form for well over 2,000 years. Sports have been used to train a student not only physically, but also to instill in him such social traits as cooperation, respect for law, planning and strategy, interpersonal (inter-action) skills, self-discipline, and self-confidence.

Training exercises are used by the military forces to teach troops to perform their duties under natural conditions. But officers play another type of game called a "war game." These games, of which there are many variations, involve the simu-lated movement of opposing military forces, subject to the limitations of time, in-formation, and assets available to a commander in terms of men, artillery, ammuni-tion and supplies, and terrain in which he is operating. Many war games involve the use of electronic computers to keep track of all the factors involved.

A similar type of game is played by business students in college, and is ap-propriately called a "business game." Business students buy and sell, hire em-ployees, invest in new machinery, advertise and make product improvements, add or subtract inventory, and compete with others in the market place. Many of these games are also computer-assisted.

A third type of games is the "case study" which is used to train doctors, law-yers, and business students, as well as educators. In a case study, a situation is presented to the student, who is then asked, "Now, what would you do, or suggest, in this situation?"

In all of these games, a student is able to identify with the situation, analyze it on the basis of his skill and knowledge, and make a decision, all without the danger that would be present in a real-life situation in which the stakes are high and poor judgment is disastrous.

But what does all this have to do with teaching in the elementary classroom? To bring it down from graduate school to elementary school, it is necessary to take a closer look at the basic nature of games.

Modern game theory owes its heritage to the work of two mathematicians, John von Neumann and Oscar Morganstern, who wrote in the early part of this century. They divided all games into two categories, games against nature, and games against persons. They further divided the second category into person-to-person games and person-to-group games, but they concluded that person-to-group games always deteriorate into person-to-person games, so the first category is the only one of importance.

When a game theorist talks about games of man-against-nature, he is not talk-ing about birds, bees, grass, and trees. To him, the term *nature* involves all the *givens* of a situation, or all of the factors in the environment, both physical and social, over which the player has no control. Nature is the true world. Nature in-volves the facts of the situation. Nature is a body of knowledge that a student is trying to learn. Nature is the community, or the school system, or the policy man-ual, or the laws of chemistry, or the fact that there are thirty-nine children in the classroom. Games against nature are such things as spelling bees, or mathematics problems, or multiple-choice tests, or foot races against the stop watch. They pit a student against a body of knowledge, or against the physics of gravity, or against some other inanimate phenomenon.

Games against persons, on the other hand, involve competition against an ad-versary—an active, thinking, calculating opponent. Chess is a person-against-person game. War games and business games are person-against-person games. Whereas the solution to most games against nature involves cooperation among players, games against persons involve competition.

Games of chance or luck are not really games at all, since a player does not exercise any decision making, other than the decision to participate or not to participate. However, at the lower grades of the elementary school, games are apt to have a high element of chance and a low element of discretion. Much of the time, the discretion will involve physical skills, such as counting, or color recognition, or accuracy in identifying various objects and situations. Therefore, board games may be very popular among younger children. Most students will be familiar with simple board games, and will have played them before they were old enough to attend school.

When a teacher decides to use games in the classroom, thought should be given to the question, "Why do I want my students to play games?" The answer will often be that students are motivated by them. They enjoy playing games and, by using this method, a teacher can often break down resistance to learning. Much of what passes for education in the classroom involves the student only passively. But games involve the student in active participation. Games resemble packages that are eagerly opened. The actual subject or issue of the game is of secondary importance; the game itself is primary as a motivating factor. So as to win the game, a student will gather and use the information, knowledge, and skill necessary. This often causes the student to become familiar with the subject matter involved, to delve into it with enthusiasm, and to learn—which is what it is all about.

Student involvement has many remarkable side effects. The control and influence that a child exercises in a game gives him feedback approaching that of a teaching machine. He does not have to depend on feedback from his teacher. The results of the game are usually quick, and thus reinforce learning. A game often offers the child an opportunity to use skills that are not rewarded in the usual classroom situation. Such skills might include creative ideas, social interaction, or strategy.

Games can be used to force students to interact with other students in the classroom. They learn from each other, and they develop skills of coordination and cooperation.

One valuable contribution that games can make in the classroom is the involvement of those students who are not scholastically skilled. There are those in every classroom who do not excel in intellectual activity, but often they are good at sports, interpersonal relationships, or other activities. and are capable of making valuable contributions to society. The use of games can permit these students, through the use of their own personal skills, to obtain a sense of confidence and self-worth that can carry them through some very difficult schoolroom experiences.

In selecting a game, the teacher should recognise that it will have both cognitive and affective results. Perhaps the game will be selected primarily for the cognitive skills it professes to teach. Generally, these will include comprehension, analysis, synthesis, judgment, and often verbal ability.

There are some limitations to the use of games, and the teacher should be aware of them. The first danger involves what was mentioned as the game's chief advantage—motivation. It is possible that students will become so excited they have trouble settling down to other activity. If there is a high chance content and a high reward for winning, a game can become addictive.

Another limitation is that games for the lower elementary grades must be quite simple, and may not be as useful in teaching skills as are other methods. Couple this with the fact that games require a great amount of time, and they become a very expensive form of instruction.

The third limitation is that the chief value of the game lies in its ability to require a student to use his existing knowledge to solve a problem. There is no new knowledge in the game itself. A student must bring his knowledge to the game. In the course of playing the game, he may become aware of a need for additional skill or knowledge, and may then seek it if he plans to play the game again, but rarely does he have a chance to learn new facts while playing the game. This means that games can only be used to reinforce other teaching methods. They cannot be used as the sole or primary teaching method in the classroom.

Simulation

One of the first learning routines in which a child engages is the act of simulation. Pretending is apparently a natural approach to his modeling experience. Little girls play with dolls and pretend to be mothers. Little boys play with trucks and pretend to be fathers. By the time a child reaches school age, he is very familiar with this type of learning experience.

Attempts to use simulation in teaching have resulted in designing play areas or study areas to resemble adult, or real situations. On the playground, the child may find a tree house or a model airplane, and in the schoolroom he may find a model kitchen. At the upper-grade level, these models can become more elaborate, and become real kitchens, real woodworking shops, and real cars for driver education.

Perhaps the most familiar use of simulation at the elementary school level is the class play or program. These can be formal and elaborate, or informal, simple classroom experiences. The application of the teaching method is limited only by the teacher's imagination.

Simulation, then, insofar as this module is concerned, involves the participation of a child in a simplified representation of a real-life situation. It might involve symbolic models of social situations, physical models, field trips (particularly if the child is permitted to actually sit in the fire truck and wear the fireman's hat), and participation in such civic programs as "youth city council," or "mayor for a day."

Role Playing

The definition of role playing is a bit difficult, because the term is used both to describe a type of game and a type of attitudinal, conditioning experience. It has both educational and therapeutic overtones. But for the purpose of this module, role playing is defined as the acting out of structured or designed situations.

The key words are *acting out* and *situations*. There are no models of society in role-playing activity. Its purpose is to permit students to be problem solvers, particularly in the area of interpersonal relationships. Role playing has been used by teachers for many years to help students develop their attitudes, values, and interaction skills.

A teacher, in trying role playing with a class for the first time, will probably find that it takes several sessions for her and the pupils to feel at ease with this tactic for handling social issues. Students who have had no experience with role playing are reluctant to permit themselves to become so deeply involved in an issue that their personal values come to the surface.

Role playing also requires a warm-up period, or preparation of the class, before it can be successfully conducted. Warm-ups are recognized as necessary for physical games, but they are sometimes not recognized as necessary for an intellectual or emotional (and role playing is intensely emotional) experience. Usually, one or more students are selected as role players, and the rest of the class acts as the audience, or as observers. The teacher must work with the class to create the proper atmosphere for the role-playing issue. Then the students act out a situation. But the lesson does not end at this point. Follow-up is essential.

Follow-up can take the form of a class discussion which evaluates the behavior of the role players. Sometimes it is desirable to replay the situation, using different behaviors, and recognizing a deeper awareness of the personal feelings involved.

Sometimes, students want to continue the exercise until a solution has been reached, but most of the time, this is not possible. If role playing is continued, however, follow-up should also be continued.

Although there are instructional resources that provide issues for a teacher to use in the classroom, many teachers prefer to develop their own issues. There are a few general guidelines or assumptions, which can help to make the role-playing method more effective. The issue chosen for the role play should be a practical one, and students' feelings should be a major part of the issue. These permit the action-consequence relationship to be developed and the resulting personal and societal consequences to be taken into account.

Decisions that involve values should be made in an agreeable, or cooperative, manner. This may require the teacher's firm, guiding hand, as well as her sympathetic ear, and sensitivity to hidden issues.

Generalizations can occasionally be accepted. Students at the elementary school level cannot be expected to get as deep into a subject as can students at the secondary level or at the college level.

Independent Study and Practice

Teachers do not often think of independent study on the part of a student as a teaching method, but it is. Perhaps a more accurate description would be to call it a learning method, since its emphasis is not so much on the teacher's behavior as it is on the student's behavior. Such terms as *learning skills, independent work, study habits,* and *maturity* are common in connection with the use of this method.

Seatwork. Perhaps the first encounter that a student will have with independent study will be when he first gets seatwork in the first grade. Usually, he enjoys the experience. Seatwork can be used to train the child in color discrimination, manual dexterity, word recognition, and a great many of the physical and intellectual skills learned in the lower elementary grades. The purpose of seatwork is not just to keep the students busy while the teacher prepares for the next lesson!

Although seatwork can be used to introduce new material, its best use is probably to reinforce what the teacher has already covered in the classroom. It gives the child a chance to try what the teacher has told him, and this often makes the subject take on meaning, or become real to him.

Another benefit of seatwork is the feedback it gives a teacher. If a teacher handles it correctly, seatwork need not carry the threat that is usually associated with a test or evaluation. If she teaches a child to enjoy seatwork, he will approach testing as a challenge, rather than as a fearful experience. It can become a game.

To be effective, seatwork must tie in with other lessons on the same subject. A student should know both what is expected and why it is important that he do the seatwork. What is the teacher trying to teach him?

Of course, accuracy and neatness are paramount. These apply to both the student's work and to the teacher's preparation of seatwork materials. Students cannot be expected to be more accurate or neater than the teacher has demonstrated as adequate for her own work.

Homework and Research. Homework and research have always been considered as the realm of independent study. They require an active learning effort on the part of a student.

In the upper grades, homework can be used to introduce a student to a new study area. But in the lower grades, it is probably better used to reinforce, or to practice, that which has already been taught in the classroom.

In the upper elementary grades, homework can take the form of preparation for formal presentations by a student, or even study for a test. But in any case, the homework should be carefully planned by a teacher to accomplish what she wants the student to learn from the effort. Also, a teacher must always keep in mind that she shares the student's study time with other teachers. She cannot give so much homework that a student does not have time to do all of his work adequately.

Research starts in the lower elementary grades with very simple tasks, such as looking up words in the dictionary. From there it is a short step to encyclopedias, or a simple series such as *I Want To Know About,* published by Children's Press, Chicago. This series has an index, and a very elementary reading level, suitable for second-grade students. Books of this type are often very useful in the study of science.

The purpose of research is discovery, which is both exciting and broadening. It not only generates interest in subject matter, but also develops ability in a child to grow in depth and maturity, to be self-directing, and self-sustaining. It reduces his dependency. No longer is he a passive receiver of someone else's knowledge; he is a generator of his own knowledge, and an interpreter of that which he has generated. Now his mind has wings, and he is not confined to the beaten path of a predetermined classroom experience.

Textbooks

Textbooks have been the backbone of the classroom for many years. Often they comprise the largest portion of the learning bundle. A teacher will refer to the textbook to organize the presentation of subject matter, using it as a guide both for sequence and for content. When used this way, students know what to expect, and can prepare themselves.

Selection of a textbook series often locks an elementary school into a curriculum and into a teaching philosophy, and therefore its selection is not to be taken lightly. Usually, the selection is made by school administrators, rather than by the classroom teacher.

To make a textbook effective, the teacher should take a look at how the author intended the book to be used, what its aims are, and how they will be accomplished. The teacher should then put her own ingenuity to work. The textbook can give the general course outline and its organization. It can also give instructional language and classroom activities. But the teacher must provide for individual differences and for the use of local resources to the best advantage. The teacher uses the textbook, and not the other way around. She should recognize it for what it is, a tool to be used to help accomplish the teaching mission.

Practice

Just as we have come to think that a person cannot learn to drive a car without actually driving the vehicle, so it is that students must practice in order to learn. This is obvious when speaking of muscle skills or coordination, such as penmanship or sports, but it may not be so obvious when speaking of spelling, writing complete sentences, or other intellectual skills.

Practice comes after initial instruction in a subject. This prevents learning the wrong way as much as possible. Instruct, practice, inspect, correct, and more practice make up the sequence.

Practice is particularly important in learning mathematics. One old mathematics professor was very fond of saying, "You learn mathematics by working mathematics problems." He was right.

Another area in which practice is important is in self-direction and decision making. A child learns to make good decisions by making bad decisions. If he is never permitted to make bad decisions, he probably will never make good decisions, or any decisions for that matter.

The amount of time spent on practice varies with the age of students. Usually, shorter and more frequent practice sessions are more useful than one long session. Some students need more practice than do others.

Normally, students enjoy practice. They easily become involved, and since they are actively engaged personally, they become engrossed in the subject. Teachers need only to define the skill level that they are seeking, and schedule practice sessions until the skill is achieved. Practice sessions must be interspersed with additional instruction to reinforce both the subject and the need for the skill level sought.

Inquiry

Inquiry is controversial because it teaches students to do things that many people think children should not do. It teaches students to question, to analyze, to disagree with and, occasionally, to depart from what others (parents or teachers) think is true, good, best, or appropriate. Inquiry teaches a child to think for himself, and many adults find this both disconcerting and dangerous.

Inquiry as a teaching method is not new. Its history dates from Aristotle, and through John Dewey to modern times. Its various components are problem identification, student self-awareness, reasoning, method of seeking evidence, and deliberation.

It is not necessary for students to learn labels for the phases through which they pass in their individual search for truth. The teacher, however, should understand the progression to better guide a child's search.

Most students are comfortable and familiar with the traditional roles of the teacher as one who asks questions and of the student as one who gives answers. This is true even of very young children. They are also familiar with the reverse situation, in which the child asks questions, and the teacher, parent, or friend gives answers. He is probably aware, also, that the second situation does not result in satisfaction very often. Sometimes there just are not any good answers. Unfortunately, when he leaves school, his life will be characterized by the second situation rather than by the first. He should, therefore, learn how to ask questions.

If a teacher is considering this technique for teaching, she should first consider herself. How does she see her role relationship with the student? Is she able to handle open inquiry? Does she have the emotional strength and self-confidence to permit students to disagree with her? If she is comfortable in lecturing or questioning for 50 to 75 per cent of the class day, it is not likely that inquiry will be successful. The atmosphere in the classroom would need a radical change. The atmosphere must be open so that a student can learn to think for himself, and to seek resources other than the teacher for information.

Consider the statements a teacher makes in the classroom. Do they have a tendency to stop the thinking or questioning of students? Do the teachers' statements include such approaches as "We all know . . . ," or "Be sure you are right," or "This is all we need to know," or "The author of the book knows more than we know"? Such statements as these establish an atmosphere indicating that a student is expected to memorize certain information, and if he gets enough of it, he will know the answer to all of the presumed important questions. Inquiry, then, is not appropriate in this classroom situation.

To implement an inquiry lesson, a teacher can plan topics, generalizations, and ideas that will be of interest to the class. The planning also includes the organizing, timing, spacing, and sequencing of material. The teacher often needs to introduce the initial reference material or source documents to which the students will turn for information. Once students have identified the problem, become aware, and applied reasoning, the teacher needs to challenge and to continually encourage them to explore and to test new alternatives. As the students reach the methodology stage, the teacher must insist that they share beliefs in public, and have a defense or basis for their beliefs. The teacher must then recapitulate, summarize, and seek clarification of points. Usually, it is the teacher who raises additional questions. The teacher is the one who, during deliberation, legitimizes creative expression. Throughout the inquiry process, the teacher maintains control of the class, recognizes students, and makes announcements.

Children not used to using the inquiry method will need to have issues and ideas presented that have a low emotional impact. Age, in this instance, is not the key factor. Even if students are in the upper elementary grades, when their inquiry skill is low, problems should be simple.

As students begin to work with the inquiry process, some changes in their attitudes will develop, especially their attitude toward knowledge. Knowledge will become tentative and approximate, rather than absolute. Students will be willing to review and to confirm knowledge claims presented to them. The inquiry process helps students organize their own learning.

The inquiry method can be used in classes that have a wide spread of abilities among students. Its use results in a high level of motivation for learning. The only limit to its successful use is the emotional health of the teacher.

A Final Comment. This module started with a statement that the goals of education are to provide a child with intellectual skills, social skills, and physical skills. All of these skills involve the acquisition and utilization of knowledge. Teaching involves not merely the transmission of raw facts from a teacher to a child, but the development of skills within the child to utilize or exercise knowledge, so that he knows how to solve problems in his future life.

The degree of sophistication or depth of knowledge acquisition and utilization may be described as follows:

1. Description: the acquisition of factual knowledge, or basic skills (reading, writing, mathematics).
2. Analysis: the evaluation of knowledge, or the exercise of value judgments.
3. Problem solving: the actual participation in constructive activity, projects, exercising initiative, synthesizing knowledge, writing, art work, field trips, and athletic competition.

Each of these degrees of sophistication applies to each of the three types of skill —intellectual, social, and physical. Perhaps the emphasis will be different from school to school, or from class to class within a school. For example, one school might emphasize intellectual skills and carry a student through all three phases, and yet not emphasize athletic skills beyond teaching basic rules of the game and informal practice on the playground. Another school might organize a formal program of competitive athletics, but would not ask elementary school children to plan their own end-of-semester school picnic, or publish their own school newspaper.

The type of skill the teacher is trying to develop in the students will determine to a great degree the type of method that she uses. For example, if she is in the descriptive phase, she would probably find it advantageous to use one of the more teacher-controlled methods, rather than one of the more student-controlled methods. But if she were trying to develop analytical or problem-solving skills, she would probably find it advantageous to use one of the more student-controlled methods.

The methods discussed in this module can be distributed ordinarily along a teacher-controlled and student-controlled continuum, with lecture at one end and inquiry at the other end. Such a distribution is shown in Figure 3-1. Professional educators might disagree on the order in which the various methods are listed, and might argue that one method belongs farther to the left or farther to the right on the continuum, but they would all agree that the various methods include various mixes of teacher and student participation.

A teacher uses many teaching methods. A good teacher is able to use a wider variety of teaching methods than is a less skilled teacher, and can use them more appropriately. A good teacher gets results with less pain and more enthusiasm in her students than can a poor teacher. The mark of a good teacher is not that

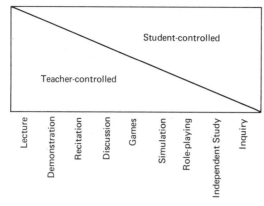

Figure 3-1 *A Continuum of Teaching Methods.*

she uses all of the newer techniques, but that she uses the right method to get the job done.

Some of the newer teaching methods, such as games, role playing, and inquiry, are powerful emotional tools, and must be used with extreme care to avoid damaging a child. Emotional cripples are just as helpless as physical cripples. A classroom teacher in the elementary grades has a greater responsibility than does any other teacher, and as great as almost any other member of our society.

SUGGESTED READING

Anderson, Robert H. *Teaching in a World of Change*. New York: Harcourt, Brace Jovanovich, Inc., 1966.

Beauchamp, George A. *Basic Dimensions of Elementary Method*. Boston: Allyn & Bacon, Inc., 1965.

Berman, Louise M. *New Priorities in the Curriculum*. Columbus, Ohio: Charles E. Merrill Publishers, 1968.

Collier, Calhoun C., Robert W. Houston, and Robert R. Schmatz. *Modern Elementary Education: Teaching and Learning*. New York: Macmillan Publishing Co., Inc., 1976.

Cutts, Norma E., and Nicholas Moseley. *Providing for Individual Differences in the Elementary School*. Englewood Cliffs, N.J.: Prentice-Hall, Inc., 1960.

Frazier, Alexander. *New Directions in Elementary Education*. Champaign, Ill.: National Council of Teachers of English, 1967.

Goodlad, John I. *School Curriculum and the Individual*. Waltham, Mass.: Ginn/Blaisdell, 1966.

Jarolimek, John, and Clifford D. Foster. *Teaching and Learning in the Elementary School*. New York: Macmillan Publishing Co., Inc., 1976.

Jarvis, Oscar, and Marion Rice. *An Introduction to Teaching in the Elementary School*. Dubuque, Iowa: William C. Brown Company, Publishers, 1972.

McDonald, Blanche, Leslie Nelson, Mary Louise Reilly, and Ronald L. Brown. *Methods That Teach*. Dubuque, Iowa: William C. Brown Company, Publishers, 1972.

Margolin, Edythe. *Young Children: Their Curriculum and Learning Processes*. New York: Macmillan Publishing Co., Inc., 1976.

Rogers, Frederick A. *Curriculum and Instruction in the Elementary School.* New York: Macmillan Publishing Co., Inc., 1975.

Schuster, Albert H., and Milton E. Ploghoft. *The Emerging Elementary Curriculum: Methods and Procedures.* Columbus, Ohio: Charles E. Merrill Publishers, 1970.

POST TEST

DIRECTIONS *Circle the letter choice which best completes each statement.*

1. Which of the following is *not* a basic function of the school?
   a. Schools provide students with intellectual skills.
   b. Schools preserve and transmit our cultural heritage.
   c. Schools act as instruments for cultural change.
   d. Schools develop the "whole child" to his maximum potential.

2. The most basic underlying assumption of the lecture is that
   a. it is probably one of the oldest methods of teaching.
   b. most teachers feel comfortable using this method.
   c. it is easy to organize.
   d. the teacher has knowledge that can be given to students.

3. The most common criticism of the lecture is that
   a. too many facts are presented.
   b. it is difficult to identify the subject.
   c. students are often passive participants.
   d. the capacity of students to listen is limited.

4. The use of demonstration as a method of teaching most resembles
   a. a field trip.
   b. a lecture.
   c. an instructional film.
   d. a discussion.

5. The most difficult problem a teacher has in using an instructional film as a method of teaching is to
   a. preview the film.
   b. have students become active participants.
   c. find a film that teaches the subject matter being studied.
   d. find a film that is impressive.

6. Recitation as a method of teaching is most commonly used to
   a. give students real experiences.
   b. teach a wide variety of subjects.
   c. draw a "word picture" of the subject being presented.
   d. give the teacher immediate feedback on her teaching.

7. Field trips are popular methods of teaching because
   a. students can do most of the planning.
   b. students can expand their life space.
   c. students can easily be disciplined.
   d. students can easily be impressed.

8. The most important thing for a teacher to remember about recitation is to
   a. never humiliate a student.
   b. never ask questions students cannot answer.
   c. never designate a student to answer the question.
   d. never draw out a reluctant student.

9. The level of questioning that emphasizes memory work is classified as
   a. analysis.
   b. evaluation.
   c. comprehension.
   d. application.

10. When discussion is used as a method of teaching, emphasis is
   a. upon the teacher's teaching.
   b. upon the questions asked.
   c. upon outside sources.
   d. upon the student's learning.

11. Simulation, games, role playing, and inquiry are important because each child can
   a. determine what he wants to learn.
   b. actively participate in learning.
   c. easily learn the social values of adult society.
   d. become skilled in a variety of games.

12. Simulation as used in this module means
   a. an attitudinal conditioning experience.
   b. a simulation game.
   c. a simplified representation of a real-life situation.
   d. a problem situation.

13. The most common use of simulation in the elementary classroom is a
   a. class play.
   b. car for driver education.
   c. trip to the firehouse.
   d. student designated as mayor for a day.

14. The game which is *not* a man-against-nature game is a
   a. spelling bee.
   b. war game.
   c. multiple-choice test.
   d. foot race.

15. Students entering school will be most familiar with
   a. board games.
   b. role playing.
   c. races.
   d. person-to-person games.

16. Role playing in this module can be defined as
   a. a model of society.
   b. an approach to inquiry.
   c. acting out designed or structured situations.
   d. deep personal values.

17. Of the methods discussed in this module, the one surrounded by the most controversy is
    a. simulation.
    b. recitation.
    c. role playing.
    d. inquiry.

18. The learning bundle or backbone of a classroom is
    a. the teacher.
    b. the textbook.
    c. the seatwork.
    d. the tests.

19. The main purpose of seatwork is to
    a. teach students to work independently.
    b. teach students to follow directions.
    c. reinforce material already studied.
    d. check student's knowledge.

20. The purpose for using research in the elementary school is for
    a. follow-up.
    b. discovery.
    c. preparation for upper grades.
    d. independent learning.

Individual Traits and Differences

Serafina F. Banich

Kean College of New Jersey

module 4

Intellectual Differences / Personal and Social Traits / Physical Traits / Atypical Development / Providing for Differences / Cumulative Records

RATIONALE

In every classroom the teacher encounters and must resolve a fundamental dilemma. Aware that most pupils in his class follow similar patterns of development and are at comparable points along the growth continuum, he recognizes the advantages of gearing the curriculum and instruction to this segment of his class population. On the other hand, even a casual observer can perceive that some of the pupils fall at the extremities beyond the wide middle range, and that even within this middle range, there exist many gradations of capacity and performance. Does the teacher tailor instruction to this vast middle range or does he attempt to accommodate all levels of ability? The former sacrifices individual needs of all the pupils, especially those at the extremities, but serves the majority efficiently. The latter proliferates the curriculum content and materials almost to the point where the teacher's task becomes hopelessly detailed and overextended. Then the question becomes: Should the teacher devote as much time and effort to the few at the extremities when most pupils fit in the middle range? Basically, the question boils down to one of whether to teach to the similarities or to the differences in children. In either case, the teacher needs to be guided by the knowledge of how pupils grow and develop in similar and disparate ways. Module 2 considered the similarities among children. But even in the most homogeneous class, pupils vary somewhat in their potential, achievement, and behavior. This module considers the tools and information teachers need so as to understand and deal with the individual differences among pupils.

Because of the limitations on teachers' time and on availability of school equipment, the most efficient curriculum design was thought to be that which focused on the wide middle range. While this type of organization had its advantages, it also rigidified the curriculum in terms of content, materials, methods, and pacing of instruction. Pupils mastered educational tasks within a time frame predetermined by the school. If they happened to learn more rapidly, they had to wait for others to catch up. Conversely, slow learners fell more and more behind or had to repeat a grade. Teachers assumed, when pupils entered their classes, that they had mastered the content of the previous year and it was not their responsibility to teach it again unless the curriculum guide so indicated. If it existed at all, differentiation of instruction occurred in the form of mathematics or reading groups, or allowing rapid learners some measure of independence.

Children of limited capacity lost more and more on the route from kindergarten through high school. In addition, the seriously handicapped—the blind, deaf, retarded, and palsied—were siphoned off from the regular school population; they were either ignored completely as their family's responsibility, or they received home tutoring, or they were placed in special schools or classes.

This notion of education was based upon and justified by the fact that children are more alike than unlike. But in the course of time, many parents, administrators, and teachers became disgruntled with this arrangement. They observed that there were simply too many instances wherein not only the exceptional pupil but also the average child, at some time or other, experienced difficulty in adjusting to and profiting from the inflexible curriculum. They also observed the frustration and damaged self-image that resulted from failure to learn. Further, these observations were substantiated by the findings in the area of the psychology of learning. Many differences of learning modalities, intelligence components, adjustment mechanisms, and personality factors exist even between two pupils who are matched as nearly as possible in terms of age, I.Q. scores, health, achievement level, and social adjustment.

Also, certain events and conditions after World War II prepared the climate for experimentation and change in the elementary schools. One was the emergence of the United States as the richest and most powerful country in the world, with the resources to mount an educational system to match its prestige. The money and resources that poured into the schools at this time were previously unheard of, and technological growth and improvement made possible a wealth of materials and equipment whose costs were formerly prohibitive.

Also, the accelerating rate of change made it patently clear that the school curriculum was not enabling pupils to adjust and to meet the demands of this onrush of change. Supported by the financial backing and motivation for revision, the curriculum in the past two or three decades has shifted in its orientation from emphasizing the similarities of children to stressing their uniqueness. Individualization of instruction became the hallmark of the modern, up-to-date curriculum.

As the curriculum organization changed, so did the roles of teachers and pupils. Teachers moved from the role as dispensers of information to that of facilitators of learning, and pupils shifted from roles as receptors of knowledge to initiators and conductors of their own learning. Teachers explored ways to provide invigorating learning climates for pupils individually or in groups. To do this they needed to know the ways in which pupils are unique and how to apply this knowledge to the various learning styles of the pupils in their classes. The focus of this module is on the uniqueness of and the dissimilarities among pupils.

Specific Objectives

The primary thrust of this module is the study of the ways in which pupils are more unlike than like each other, what specifically causes differences in pupils to develop, how differences manifest themselves in classroom behavior and how schools attempt to accommodate these differences. The content of the module is organized around (1) the range and kind of traits that are observable in human behavior; (2) the forces of the culture and society that evoke the qualities of humanness within its members; and (3) how these traits and individual differences are managed by the school.

Your goal in studying the module is to discern and explain how human traits evolve and to know how this background of information should influence your teaching behavior. By the end of the module you should be able to do the following:

1. Give three reasons for the shift towards the individualization of instruction.
2. Write a one-page essay comparing and contrasting individualized instruction and whole class teaching.

3. Define what is meant by the term *trait,* and give an example of an intellectual, personal, social, and physical trait.
4. Give the generally accepted definition of intelligence.
5. Describe in one paragraph the contributions of Binet to the testing of intelligence.
6. Name three objections to the use of I.Q. tests in schools.
7. Define C.A., M.A., and I.Q., and explain their relationship.
8. List three ways in which the I.Q. score is helpful to teachers and administrators.
9. Define the curve of normal distribution, and explain the range of I.Q. scores that fall within it.
10. Define the validity of a test and tell how it is measured.
11. Give three reasons why it is difficult to establish the validity of an I.Q. test.
12. Name two hereditary and two environmental factors that affect the development of intelligence.
13. Explain in one paragraph what is meant by the range of a trait.
14. Explain how the peer group and family help to shape traits.
15. List five ways in which culture and society influence trait development.
16. Explain three ways in which school performance is affected by middle- or lower-class orientation.
17. Define and give two illustrations of a primary group.
18. Define identification and give an example of it.
19. In a one-page essay, explain how the teacher manages the group dynamics in the classroom.
20. Define sociometric device and give three examples of it.
21. In a one-page essay, describe how sociometric devices are used in the classroom.
22. Tell what kinds of information are found on a cumulative record.
23. Explain how anecdotal records are kept and used.
24. Explain the relationship between perceptual skills and learning.
25. Name five instances of atypical development.
26. List three advantages and three disadvantages of homogeneous and heterogeneous grouping.
27. In a one-page essay, describe four ways in which the schools adjust their curriculums to the differences in trait development.
28. Take the Post Test and score no more than three errors.

MODULE TEXT

Intellectual Differences

Because learning is primarily an intellectual process, teachers need to be concerned with differences of intellectual capacity among pupils. The nature of intelligence has been a matter of intense study and research, especially within the past fifty years, and yet a precise definition of it has eluded psychologists. A broad definition generally accepted is that intelligence is wise and fruitful adaptation to the environment. When one considers how amorphous and ambiguous this description is, one can appreciate the monumental task of measuring intelligence. It also raises some very serious questions: How can we be sure that the test samples do, in fact, measure intelligence? Is the kind of intelligence we measure to predict success in school equally useful in estimating intelligent behavior in everyday life? What extraneous factors enter into the measurement of intelligence?

Intelligence Tests. Teachers and administrators, in attempting to devise a curriculum that would meet individual abilities, sensed a need for an index of pupils' intelligence. Simply observing pupils to discern intelligence proved inadequate because so much of intellectual prowess needs to be aroused and brought to fruition and because the seat of intelligence, the brain, is not directly observable. So despite the shortcomings of methods adopted for testing intelligence, teachers still need and use these measures of pupils' capacity to learn.

The first scientifically planned test of intelligence was developed by Alfred Binet, a French psychologist, at the beginning of this century. Binet observed that feeble-minded children were incapable of performing certain tasks compared to other children of similar chronological age. This led him to experiment with learning functions that appeared to affirm intelligence and to construct for each chronological age level a series of graduated tasks that made it possible to distinguish among retarded, average, and rapid learners. By establishing a hierarchy of tasks that many children in each age group could perform, but which were too easy for the next higher level and too difficult for the next lower level, he created norms or standards for judging the intelligence of pupils. Because there were no scientifically developed intelligence tests before his time, Binet entertained many notions regarding those factors that constitute intelligence before he was able to eliminate those that had no bearing on the level of mental capacity. Binet found that the qualities that proved most testworthy were the ability to remember, to do abstract thinking, and to see relationships and patterns.

Binet revised his test several times thereafter. The version which has gained the greatest acceptance in the United States is the Stanford Binet test, which is the revision of the Binet test by Lewis Terman, an American psychologist, who worked at Stanford University. The person who administers the Binet test, a psychometrician, must put in many months of study and practice before he is ready to give the test. The Binet is an individual test which means that because the testee must perform certain tasks under the observation of the tester, it can be given to only one individual at a time. The time and cost involved make it impractical to use with all pupils; instead, it is employed in special cases where a more trustworthy estimate of the individual is desired. Another individual intelligence test often used in the schools is the Wechsler Intelligence Scale for Children, also called the WISC. It was developed by David Wechsler, a clinical psychologist at Bellevue Hospital.

In most schools students are given a group intelligence test three or four times during the span of their school years. Group tests are paper and pencil tests designed so that many people can take them at the same time and so that they can be administered by teachers. Therefore, their results are less accurate indicators of true potential or capacity. Nonetheless, averaging out an individual's test scores over the years probably yields a fairly sound reading of intelligence. A large number of group intelligence tests are available today. Some of those used very often in the schools are the Otis Quickscoring Tests of Mental Ability, the California Test of Mental Maturity, and the Primary Mental Abilities Test.

The Intelligence Quotient. You have often heard the expression I.Q. It refers to the first letters of the term *intelligence quotient*. The intelligence quotient is arrived at by the formula $\dfrac{\text{Mental Age (M.A.)}}{\text{Chronological Age (C.A.)}} \times 100$. In short, it is the ratio between mental age and chronological age. The M.A. tells the mental age of an individual as obtained from the results of an intelligence test, and it is usually computed in terms of years and months. The M.A. is calculated apart from the C.A., so that an eight-year-old pupil could have an M.A. of seven, eight, or nine years, or any gradation in between or beyond.

Once the M.A. has been discovered, the I.Q. can be computed by using the formula given. An individual with an exact match of M.A. and C.A. would have a perfectly average I.Q.; that is, his I.Q. would be 100. In the previous example, the eight-year-old with an M.A. of 8 would score an I.Q. of 100 $(\frac{8}{8} \times 100 = 100)$.

Very few people score exactly at this point, but most scores hover within ten points above or below it. Scores within a range from 85 to 115 are considered average. Approximately 68 per cent of the population at large fall within this range.

Persons who are considered intelligent have M.A.'s that are higher than their C.A.'s, the brightest being those who have the greatest discrepancy between the M.A. and the C.A. An eight-year-old with an M.A. of 9 would have an I.Q. of 113 $(\frac{9}{8} \times 100 = 112.5)$. Persons whose I.Q. scores fall within the 115 to 130 range are considered bright, superior, or high average, depending on the classification system, and they comprise about 13 per cent of the population. Only 2 per cent have I.Q.'s between 130 and 145, and they are considered very superior, superior, very bright, or gifted. Some psychologists place an I.Q. of 145 or above as gifted, and only one half of 1 per cent of persons fall in this category. You will notice that the classification systems differ and overlap but, invariably, the higher the I.Q., the more intelligent the individual, and the higher one goes up the scale, the instances become rarer and rarer. The same conditions obtain for those whose scores fall below 100, except the implications are the opposite in that the lower the score, the less intelligent the individual is considered. The eight-year-old with an M.A. of 7 has an I.Q. of 88 $(\frac{7}{8} \times 100 = 87.5)$. Persons whose scores fall within the 70 to 85 range are considered slow learners, borderline mentally retarded, or slow average, and they comprise 13 per cent of the population. Only 2 per cent have I.Q. scores between 55 and 70, and they are labeled mentally retarded, mildly mentally retarded, or mentally deficient. Fewer than one half of 1 per cent have I.Q. scores that fall below 55, and they are thought to be feeble-minded, extremely mentally retarded, or mentally retarded.

If we were to plot the dimensions of I.Q. discussed, the result would be a bell-shaped curve, also called the *curve of normal distribution*. If we were to use a large enough sample, we would find that many traits or conditions, such as height or weight, would result in the same bell-shaped curve. You will notice that the right and left halves are exact duplicates of each other, and the bulk of the scores bunch up at the middle and taper off at the ends. An illustration of the bell-shaped curve appears as Figure 4-1.

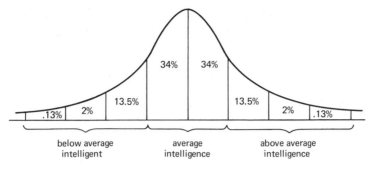

below average
intelligent

average
intelligence

above average
intelligence

Figure 4-1 *The Bell-shaped Curve.*

Causes of Differences in Intelligence. Why some children are more intelligent than others raises questions about the role of inheritance versus environment, how we define intelligence, and the instruments we use to measure it.

First of all, one of the ways in which very intelligent persons are distinguished from those who are less intelligent is whether they fit our description of intelligence. If we said, for instance, that the most intelligent persons are those with the sharpest memories, then those who are most able to remember are the smartest. But if we defined it another way, by success in school, then those with the greatest amount of school learning would be the most intelligent.

Binet defined intelligence as the ability for self-criticism, the ability to adapt to obtain a goal, and the ability to take and maintain a direction. An early psychologist, Charles E. Spearman, postulated intelligence as consisting of a general factor and of many specific factors in which general intelligence is manifest. Edward L. Thorndike, in contrast, defined three dimensions of intelligence: social, mechanical, and abstract. L. L. Thurstone presented intelligence as the primary verbal, spatial, reasoning, numerical, memory, perceptual, and motor abilities. Guilford carried this factor analysis further to include 120 elements under the three headings of operation, product, and content. Essentially these definitions fall into two categories: one defines intelligence as a composite general ability to learn, and the other, as multivaried learning factors. The core of agreement that runs through all of them is the facility with which learning occurs and the profiting from experience.

Having defined intelligence, we now must confront the problem of measuring it. Let us take as an example the definition of intelligence as memory. Would the test include remembering nonsense syllables, or a series of numbers, or the details of a story or picture, or the length of time from which an individual can recall information? The person who has a good memory for numbers but not for the other elements will do best if the test only contains the former items and omits the latter. His score will be lower if the test includes all the elements, and it will be lowest if numbers are excluded from the test. When we give an intelligence test, we assume that our test samples do measure intelligence, which may or may not be the case. This essential quality of a test is called *validity;* that is, it measures what it professes to measure. Many test makers measure the validity of their tests against that of the Binet. Finding how closely one test stacks up against another with regard to validity is measured by a statistical device called the *correlation coefficient.* But no matter how high the coefficient of correlation, the assumption is still made that the test against which validity was established does measure intelligence.

Whether this is the case or not is the subject of much debate today. The validity of the original tests was established with a white, middle-class, urban sampling. Many groups contend that this creates a bias in these and subsequent tests in favor of white, middle-class children because the tasks, the vocabulary, and other facets of the tests' contents are based on experiences that are familiar to this population but which may be somewhat or completely alien to other children. They contend that the emphasis on verbal ability favors middle-class children and militates against lower-class youngsters whose language experiences are quite different; that farm children score lower because the test items ignore rural life; and the standard American English used in the tests discriminates against children who speak a dialect.

HEREDITY AND ENVIRONMENTAL FACTORS. The essence of the critics' argument, then, is that the I.Q. tests measure environmental influences rather than native, inherent capacity. Probably both play a part, but to what extent is still undetermined. Nevertheless, certain genetic and environmental forces which affect intelligence have been ascertained, as follows:

1. The force of genetic inheritance is established by the fact that the I.Q. of identical twins is more alike than that of fraternal twins and by the fact that intelligent parents tend to have intelligent children.
2. A child's chromosomal inheritance may include an aberration that leaves him mentally defective. If a child inherits Down's syndrome, for instance, he will be born mongoloid, and he will fall in the category of mentally retarded.
3. Lack of maternal health and care during pregnancy can produce a mentally defective child. If the mother contracts rubella (German measles) in the early months of her pregnancy when the development of the brain takes place, it can result in a seriously brain-damaged child.

But even the richest inheritance requires stimulation and nurturing. That environmental forces affect intelligence is borne out by the following evidence:

1. Adopted children who are placed in the rich learning environment of well-educated middle-class parents score much higher on I.Q. tests than do their biological mothers.
2. Children with the same I.Q. scores at age two will have markedly different scores as they get older, depending on the environment in which they are raised. Those from families that have the opportunity, time, and resources to stimulate learning score higher than those brought up in poverty-stricken or working-class homes.
3. Family life affects I.Q. in that the oldest child in a family usually has the highest I.Q. of all the siblings, presumably because the parents can devote the most time and attention to the first-born. Also, studies show that children whose I.Q. score dropped consistently over the years came from home backgrounds that did not cherish intellectual endeavors, whereas those children whose I.Q. scores increased came from families that pushed their children to succeed and to learn rapidly.

EDUCATIONAL IMPLICATIONS OF I.Q. When so little can be incontrovertibly established about the I.Q. score, teachers need to be wary of labeling children and of having a rigid attitude toward their potential. The I.Q. is not a fixed and immutable score. All too often, when teachers know the I.Q. of some pupils, they give up on them instead of providing the very stimulation children need if they are to improve their I.Q. scores. Teachers should also be careful about categorizing pupils, especially on the basis of only one test score. They should keep in mind the variation of test content and the extraneous elements that can influence a test score, which often can make a difference of ten to twenty points or more from one test to another.

Considering the tenuous nature of the I.Q. score, one might ask what is the value in knowing it? Despite its shortcomings, the I.Q. score is a rather stable and accurate predictor of scholastic ability. Because both the school and the tests place such a heavy emphasis on the language of words and numbers, the I.Q. scores have been found to be fairly safe indicators to use in separating those who have the potential to succeed in school from those who do not. Realizing this, the teacher can then use the I.Q. score as one factor in deciding on appropriate learning tasks for pupils, in grouping them, in pacing instruction, in selecting apposite materials, and in guiding pupil choices. A wise teacher knows that pupils' interests and motivation, previous success, the self-image, the peer influence, and school environment are other factors which also influence the ability to learn.

The teacher can provide relevant learning modalities according to pupils' abilities. Slow-learning children need much more repetition and reinforcement than rapid learners. Slow learners have more difficulty in dealing with abstract concepts; they need many concrete learning activities, reinforced by a variety of interesting drills and practices, and supplemented by a gradual induction into the higher learning processes. Very bright children, on the other hand, can be let loose in an opulent learning milieu that allows free rein to their tremendous learning potential.

Personal and Social Traits

The brain and nervous system form the physiological bedrock upon which learning rests, but it is the personality of the learner that gives it impetus and energizes it. Every teacher has observed that some children are too fearful of failing to risk experimentation, some bask in the limelight but others wither under it, and some respond to reassurance but others easily become discouraged or distracted.

Range. Earlier in this module, it was stated that the quality of intelligence is measured along a continuum from those who possess this trait in the greatest amount to the least. This difference between the greatest and least values of an attribute is called the *range,* and it describes a difference in degree rather than in kind. The pupil who exhibits leadership qualities, or artistic tendencies, or pluck, or perspicacity exemplifies these characteristics often enough to be so designated. But he does not display them invariably and uniformly, for there are times when he is deficient in them. So it is with the child who possesses the opposite traits. It isn't that he doesn't possess leadership or pluck, but that he exhibits them so seldom he is labeled lacking in these characteristics. It is important for us to remember that the difference is not one of possessing a trait or lacking it, but one of the degree to which it manifests itself in behavior.

Causes of Differences in Traits. Why some individuals possess certain traits to a larger extent than do others has long been a source of perplexity to social scientists, psychologists, and philosophers. The role of heredity in the acquisition of human traits is undoubtedly present, but which traits are inherited and to what degree are the subject of some fascinating research and study. Some anthropologists, for instance, believe that the aggression trait in man is inherited, and some psychologists think the sense of attachment and curiosity are also genetically endowed. The fact that, except for monozygotic twins, all humans inherit a unique and unduplicative set of genes means that the potential for trait distinction exists right from the moment of birth. In fact, any pediatric nurse will attest that the newborn infants in the ward already display varying personality characteristics; some are placid and docile, and others are cross and unruly.

CULTURE AND SOCIETY. No matter what his inheritance, the newborn infant develops his sense of humanness as he associates with other human beings in the intimate circle of the home to the broad perspective of the culture and society. Feral children, who by some accident of fate were lost or abandoned by their parents and raised by animals, have displayed markedly animalistic behavior in their vocal sounds, posture, movements, and eating habits, and they lacked language, ethics, and other human qualities.

The culture, which comprises all of the artifacts and possessions, beliefs and values, and ways of behaving in a society, is the most pervasive of the environmental determinants in terms of its sphere of influence. A smaller unit of a larger society that has developed its own distinct cultural identity is called a subculture. From the culture the young pick up language, which is an abstract, shortcut manner of communicating about the reality of the world and which very much influences thinking and feeling. The folkways or mores, the ideals and values, and the institutions of a culture also help to shape personality. The religious beliefs of a culture, for instance, affect whether people develop traits of resignation, charity, materialistic acquisition, social activism, perserverance, or any number of other values.

The American culture, of course, is a mosaic of multireligious, multiethnic, and multiracial groups. Nonetheless, certain ideal personality traits, such as individualism, regard for the dignity of humans, and sense of accomplishment, are esteemed throughout the society, and our young are encouraged to strive toward the attainment of these ideals. Because of our pluralistic American society, we belong to various subcultures, based on ethnic origin, religious affiliation, social class orientation, age, or geographic location, all of which help to shape the totality of personality. How one spends one's spare time, food and clothing preferences, attitudes towards political issues and social problems, feelings about one's self-worth, choice of career and marriage partner, and many other factors are influenced to some extent by this subcultural diversity.

THE SCHOOL. The school, one of the most prominent of American institutions, has a telling effect on the personal and social traits of children. In school, children are constantly bombarded by the values it promulgates—maximizing one's potential, especially intellectual capacity, ambition and industry in attaining one's goals, resolution of conflict through reason rather than physical combat, and getting along with others. These are principally middle-class values, and most of the teachers are middle-class in their origin or orientation. Pupils, whose subcultural values are in conflict with these ideals, or who for whatever reason do not assimilate them, often experience some kind of difficulty in school. It may be they are unwittingly or deliberately rejected by their teachers as being inferior, or their teacher may term them lazy or slow learners and give up on them, or their classmates don't relate to them in positive ways. Soon these pupils feel less and less secure about themselves as learners in school; as a result, they may become hostile toward the school and drop out. In fact, consistently over the years, the highest dropout rates have occurred among lower-class children.

For the pupil, especially the bright one, who adopts the school's values, however, the picture is altogether different. He is constantly rewarded and praised for his ambition and success and, very often, is touted as an exemplar to the other children. In these ways, then, the school serves to reinforce certain values that affect pupils' self-image.

Classroom management and curriculum choices also bear upon trait development. If the teacher runs an open classroom with much pupil participation and self-direction, then pupils will have occasion to develop their potential for friendliness, leadership, and responsibility. If the teacher encourages open and honest discussion of issues and problems that arise in the class and works to resolve them fairly, then pupils will have opportunity to develop trust, honesty, fairness, and sensible resolution of conflict. On the other hand, if pupils are not allowed to make a choice or a move without the teacher's approval, then dependency, lack of initiative, and mistrust of one's own good judgment are encouraged. Or if the teacher ignores or arbitrarily resolves conflict, then pupils might become angry, sneaky, manipulative, apathetic, or frustrated.

SOCIOECONOMIC CLASS. For the purposes of describing the multifaceted dimensions of American society, social scientists have divided the American people into three classes—upper, middle, and lower—and sometimes these basic units are further subdivided. What social class a person belongs to is generally determined by a composite of wealth, education, position in the community, family background, occupation, kind of home and neighborhood one lives in, and values held. Putting together all of these factors into a whole sometimes results in discrepant interpretations, according to the weight given to each of the factors. Nonetheless, the American society is generally considered to be equally divided among the middle and lower class with only 1 to 3 per cent falling into the upper class, the one that carries the greatest prestige, wealth, power, and position. Although one is born into a socioeconomic class, one's position in it is not fixed or irreversible; by marriage, education, acquisition of wealth, or position, one can move into a higher class. This phenomenon, which is prevalent in American society, is called upward social mobility.

For our purposes, however, we are primarily concerned with the life styles that obtain for the various classes and how they affect trait development. Because the upper class is so small and its members usually send their children to private schools, we are concerned here with the middle and lower classes. The lower class has the least wealth and consists mostly of those who live in depressed, rural areas or blighted, urban slums. They are jobless or they hold factory or menial positions that require the least education and carry the least prestige. In times of recession or depression, these workers are the first to lose their jobs. They live in the shabbiest dwellings or in modest homes, often on the "wrong side of the tracks" or, in the case of migrant workers, in temporary shelters. The jobless are also called the disadvantaged, which often means they live on welfare in the inner city ghettos, are from a racial or ethnic minority, and suffer the most from the social problems of disease, unemployment, drugs, crime, and poor housing. They have the least education and are usually the first to drop out of school. In this milieu they often develop the posture of fatalism, defeatism, cynicism, hatred, and violence. They are often viewed by members of other social classes and former members of their own class as pathological, unambitious, and unstable.

As the poor flock to the cities, the urban middle class, which cannot insulate itself from them as readily as the upper class, moves out to the suburbs. Very often, mother must work or father holds down a second job to maintain their standard of living, which usually includes a home, car, vacations, and giving their children the opportunities they didn't have. Education is highly prized because middle-class parents see it as the stepping stone to upward mobility, so they support the schools and push their children to get a good education. If they can afford it, they may send their children to private school to obtain a better education. They encourage children to work hard, to try their best, to get ahead, and to sacrifice for the future. You can see that these values jibe more consistently with those of the school, and this accounts to some degree for the better fit between schools and middle-class children.

PEER GROUP. The influence of the peer group commences at about age eight and continues through adolescence. During the gang age, the groups are usually same-sexed cliques that slowly yield to the heterosexual groups during the adolescent years. The peer groups band together as they strive toward independence from adult domination. Acceptance by the peer group is extremely important to youngsters and to adolescents, for much of their social and individual worthiness hinges upon the group's approval. It is for this reason that the control of the group, to which its members willingly submit, can be almost tyrannical in its dictates about appropriate behavior, dress codes, and values. These dictates are often in conflict with those of the home, much to the consternation of parents who can't understand why their children have gone so awry. Among boys, those who are athletically inclined and athletically built seem to achieve the highest status in their groups. Also those individuals who are friendliest, most outgoing and, in some cases, the brightest seem to be the most popular.

The peer group, similar to the family, is also a primary group, a term sociologists use to describe those groups that are characterized by intimate, face-to-face contact and that have the power to shape and proscribe the behavior of its members. Further, it is a group with which the individual identifies. Identification is the process of close emotional association wherein the individual assumes some of the values, behaviors, and characteristics of the group of persons with whom he identifies. This great influence of the peer group is the cause for alarm among parents and teachers when children fall into what elders consider an undesirable group. To gain the group's approval, boys can be pushed to assume traits of daring and bravado to the detriment of their health, safety, talents, or position. Girls are less subject to these postures but can be pressured into a position of sexual accessibility and sophistication.

MASS MEDIA. Almost every day one hears about whether the mass media— newspapers, movies, television, books, and magazines—mold undesirable of favorable human behavior. Critics of the mass media point to the violence, the wanton disregard for human life and dignity, the stereotyping of certain roles and groups, and the degradation of females as sex objects. They contend that the innocent and unknowing young, bombarded daily by a diet of these ills, assume them to be normal modes of behavior and adopt them as their own. They cite as proof the nation's weakened moral fiber, the graft and corruption rampant in our society, the increase in crime and violence, and the upward turn of divorce and family disintegration.

Supporters of the mass media point out that what they report and publish and show reflects the realities of life. They claim they expose children to knowledge about many areas of the world and about conditions of life to which children otherwise might have little or no access. Listening to and reading standard American English increases children's vocabulary and exposes them to an educated level of written and spoken language. Even the violence serves as a catharsis, it is asserted, to relieve and release feelings of aggression and hostility.

Despite the protestations of either side, the evidence so far is contradictory and inconclusive, so that at this stage a determination about the effects of the mass media on behavior is tenuous at best.

FAMILY. The smallest cultural unit in size and still the most powerful in the view of some social scientists is the family. Countless studies and reports on the family's structure, variety, and influence have been conducted over the years. Although discrepancies exist from one study to another on particular aspects of family life, the overwhelming evidence points to the solid influence of the home on the development of children. This makes sense when one considers that family is a primary group and that its imprints commence from the outset of life. Further, parents tend to perpetuate the child-rearing attitudes and practices to which they were subject as children. A review of Module 2 will recall the positive and negative impact of the home on the development of personal and social traits.

In recent years, two studies in particular have had much to say about the organization and arrangement of schools and school districts. Both studies dealt in part with the influence of the family in preparing children for school.

The first was conducted by James S. Coleman, a sociologist, at the behest of the United States government to study the availability of educational opportunity in this country. It took two years to complete and covered all fifty states. It has come to be known as the Coleman Report.[1]

Two findings from the study relate directly to our discussion. Coleman found that the most telling factor in school achievement is how pupils feel about themselves. Pupils who hold a more favorable self-image and feel more in control of their environment achieve to a higher extent than those who manifest these traits to a lesser degree. This conclusion seems consistent with the psychology of learning that pupils who feel they will succeed are more likely to do so.

The conclusion that has generated the greatest controversy and discussion, however, is Coleman's finding that the pupils' home background and the social environment of the pupil population have more impact on the achievement of pupils than do the teachers, books, school building, and other educational resources. If Coleman's conclusion is valid, one cannot underestimate the power of the home on pupils' achievement levels.

---

[1] J. S. Coleman, et. al., "Equality of Educational Opportunity" (Washington, D.C.: United States Government Printing Office, 1966).

The other study was conducted by Christopher Jencks,[2] a professor at Harvard, and some of his colleagues. Its purpose was to discover the effects of schooling on equality of opportunity by examining the data already gathered on the topic, including the Coleman report. The research, started in 1968, took several years to amass for presentation of the findings.

Similar to Coleman, Jencks found that the school, its equipment, and the teachers had very little significance on pupils' achievement; that children are much more influenced by what happens at home as compared to what happens in school; and that the output of the school—the achievement of its pupils—can best be measured by the input of the traits pupils possess when they enter school. Jencks concludes, therefore, that a school should not be judged by its pupils' performance levels but, rather, on whether pupils feel it to be a satisfying place which enriches their lives. This conclusion would bear out the findings, previously mentioned, that students who feel less comfortable in school and believe that it has little to offer them are those who drop out the soonest and in greatest numbers. Both studies, therefore, attest to the tremendous significance of the home on pupils' feelings about and their attainment in school.

Recent research casts considerable doubt about the validity of Coleman's and Jencks' research techniques and findings. This does not diminish the findings concerning the significance of the home although it indicates that the school has more impact than the Coleman and Jencks' studies seem to indicate.

Educational Implications. Consideration of the host of forces that help to shape traits of pupils has two important implications for the school: teachers must keep an open mind about pupils and their backgrounds, and they should work to make the learning and social climate in the classroom as fruitful as possible for pupils.

Keeping an open mind entails freeing the mind of stereotypes which can be destructive of pupils' self-image and potential. A teacher should not make the unfounded judgment that the lower-class pupils in a class have little regard for education. Many of them, in fact, are prodded by their parents to get the best education possible. Nor should teachers judge the pupils according to the pejorative stereotypes of the groups to which they belong, because in any segment of the population the manifestation of a quality or trait will show a tremendous range. No one group has the corner on crime, stupidity, violence, indolence, or other depreciatory traits, but they are widespread among all groups. Therefore, teachers should hesitate to label a pupil as passive, unambitious, dirty, or uncouth because of the racial, ethnic, or any other group affiliation. Judgment of a pupil should be based on his observable behavior and not on the characteristics of his groups. Teachers should be wary of criticizing, condemning, or denigrating the homes, subcultures, and other group affiliations of pupils.

It has been pointed out several times that pupils' feelings about themselves and their adjustment to their peers and teachers are crucial to their success in school. Therefore, it behooves teachers to understand, assess, and arrange the social climate in the classroom.

GROUP DYNAMICS. As a teacher frees the learning environment in the classroom, he must of necessity cede some of his control over the interaction in the class-

---

[2] Christopher Jencks, et. al., *Inequality: A Reassessment of the Effects of Family and Schooling in America.* (New York, Basic Books, 1972).

room and allow more of it to flow into the hands of pupils. At one time, the teacher solely decided who would speak, when, and to whom, and if pupils could move about the classroom. Pupils who spoke or moved without the teacher's permission were considered disobedient and were often punished for their infractions. When curriculum revision allowed pupils to have more choice and responsibility, teachers had to permit more freedom in the classroom. With pupils engaged in many activities and with many groups functioning at the same time, the teacher was no longer expected to dominate and steer the forces of interaction almost single handedly. Now the teacher's function has shifted more to being observer and guide of interaction rather than its unequivocal leader. This means that teachers need to be informed about group dynamics, which is the study of interacting forces within a group. Because group interaction can be positive or negative, teachers who adopt the group dynamics approach study the way in which a group functions. They look for the answer to questions such as: Do the members pull together to accomplish their task or is the group's energy dissipated in haggling, dissension, or animosity? How does the group resolve conflict or differences of opinion when they arise? Which pupils serve as facilitators or leaders to draw the group into a cohesive working unit, and which obstruct it or sit by passively?

These teachers not only become skilled observers of group dynamics but also learn a new approach. Instead of telling pupils how they must manage conflict, when they can talk and move, and how they must respond to others, they begin to use a more indirect approach which puts more responsibility on pupils. Let's assume that a group of youngsters becomes involved in a name-calling and shouting match because they can't decide whose suggestion is the best for writing a report. Formerly, the teacher would have squelched the shouting, declared that name calling was objectionable behavior and not permissible, and might even have gone so far as to resolve the dispute by selecting the suggestion he considered the most propitious. Today, however, a teacher who is concerned about encouraging pupils' responsibility and independence and in fostering group dynamics would evoke from the group answers to questions such as: What is the problem that is causing all the shouting? Does name calling help to resolve the problem? How many suggestions do you have? Would it be worthwhile to list the advantages and disadvantages of each? Looking at your list, which one seems the best for your report?

You can see that operating in this manner requires much more time and skill compared to coming down hard on pupils and telling them what they should do and how they should do it. It also means that conflicts and differences will be inadequately resolved because sometimes pupils will make unsatisfactory choices. But over the years as pupils receive guidance from their teachers, they learn how to share in the group's work, sometimes as leaders and sometimes as followers. They also learn that denigrating others and obstructing action have deleterious effects on group functioning, and that the negative feelings which are sometimes aroused need to be handled in ways that are not damaging or harmful to themselves or others.

SOCIOMETRIC DEVICES. No matter how astute an observer the teacher may be, he often supplements his data by getting reactions to the social climate in the classroom from the pupils by the use of measuring instruments called sociometric devices. Very often the teacher's perception of the class can be slightly or grossly inaccurate, depending on how alert and objective he is in his observations. The teacher is inclined to view the stars of the class more from the standpoint of academic achievement whereas the pupils' scope may be altogether different. Further, the teacher observes pupils during a limited part of their lives, the school day. How pupils react in informal neighborhood groups, in clubs, and in play activities are experiences to which the teacher is seldom privy.

One of the most commonly used sociometric devices is the sociogram in which pupils make choices of partners for some school activity. The teacher might ask pupils to list first, second, and third choices for partners or groups on a field trip, project in the social studies, lunch tables, or spelling practice. After charting the results, the teacher would know who are the stars—those children most often selected—and who are the isolates—those least selected—and who form cliques—those who associate with each other to the exclusion of others. In the sociogram charted as Figure 4-2, at the extremes are the stars, Peggy and Bill, isolates, Joe and Susan, with all the other pupils falling in between. Mary, Beth, and Carla form a clique. Based on the information gleaned from the sociogram, the teacher attempts to draw out the sociability of the isolates, and also to analyze and to restructure the forces that lead to isolation in the first place, as far as that is possible. For instance, the teacher might put Joe in Peggy's group because she is one of Joe's choices and he would probably feel comfortable with her. Since she is a star, she may draw him out more so than if he were placed with another isolate.

Another sociometric technique is the Guess Who? device in which pupils name someone in the class who fits the description of the trait mentioned, such as "Guess who disturbs the class when pupils are trying to work?" or "Guess who has lots of friends in this class?" Answers to these questions enable the teacher to see how pupils perceive which children pull the class together into a cohesive social unit, which disrupt its unity, and which are ignored.

Whatever the sociometric device, the teacher needs to exercise caution in using it. The privacy of pupils' choices should be respected by teacher and pupils alike, and only revealed for professional reasons, if at all. Indiscriminately divulging such information can only serve to further damage the low status of the child who is

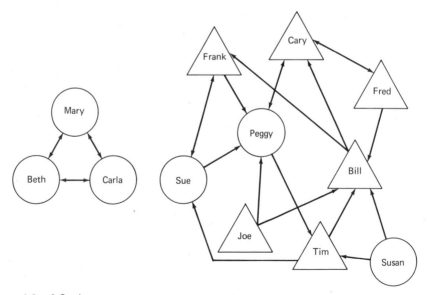

Figure 4-2 *A Sociogram.*

already a social pariah. In no case should the teacher use the results of sociometric devices in retribution against pupils who are disruptive or who misbehave in class.

ANECDOTAL RECORDS. Very often a teacher will observe a situation in a classroom and wish to keep a record of it. The situation can be indicative of the habitual or rarely seen work habits or behavior of the pupil. The record can be written in running narrative form or in a few summary phrases; in either case, the teacher needs to be careful to separate what he observes from his interpretation of it. Sometimes anecdotal records paint a composite picture of pupils' social and academic behavior. They are especially useful as aids to the teacher in planning for parent-teacher conferences and in filling out the nonacademic portion of report cards. The accuracy of anecdotal records, however, hinges on the observation skill and objectivity of the teacher.

Physical Traits

Although most physical traits are patently visible, others escape the attention of parents and teachers. Very often children are not aware that their learning mechanism is deficient or defective in some way; they simply assume that everyone experiences the same conditions that obtain for them. Until the source of the difficulty is discovered, these pupils are often labeled as lazy, stupid, or unmotivated, and sometimes they are even punished for their inability to learn.

Some types of disturbances are rather easily detected by the alert parent or teacher. For instance, the child who cocks his head to one side may suffer a hearing loss, and the one who squints or rubs his eyes may need glasses. The listless or flaccid child may be the victim of malnutrition or other health problem.

Perceptual difficulties, however, are of a different order because they are less easily detected and require diagnosis by a more highly trained person than the teacher or the school nurse. Perception is the process whereby stimulation of the senses sends nerve impulses to the brain for interpretation and back to the muscles for action. Sometimes a blockage or misconnection occurs along these pathways, which results in a dysfunction of some kind. Because so many perceptual skills, working in harmony with each other, are involved in the process of reading, their malfunction very often results in a reading problem which may go for a long time before being detected. For instance, a child with a reading problem may be sent to the school nurse for an eye test which he might pass. What the test may fail to reveal, however, are such perceptual shortcomings as seeing letters or words upside down, or in reverse, or in inverted order, or in misshapen form, or in many other distorted ways. It is important, then, that teachers not overlook the possibility of a physical disturbance or deficiency with pupils who have a learning problem. They should enlist the aid of the nurse, doctor, learning disability specialist, psychologist, or other appropriate diagnosticians in an effort to find the source of the difficulty.

Atypical Development

Earlier it was mentioned that traits manifest themselves in varying degrees among pupils and that most pupils fall within the vast middle range. Because there are so many of these students, the school gears its curriculum and instruction to pupils who are considered average. The school also attempts to accommodate in special ways those pupils who fall at the far ends of the range.

Underachievers. We have already alluded to the breadth of the range of intelligence from the retarded to the gifted. As if this array of ability were not enough, the school must also deal with another phenomenon, the underachiever or the pupil who for some reason or other reaches an achievement level which is in no way commensurate with his potential. The underachiever may be of any achievement level and, unfortunately, all too often he is intelligent. The reasons for underachievement vary: boredom with school, lack of interest in learning, poor self-image, dissension or mistreatment at home, poor study habits, or emotional disturbance.

Physically Disabled. In the realm of physical traits, pupils with a marked handicap require special instruction and materials for their schooling. Pupils with limited physical disabilities often go undetected when early diagnosis might alleviate the physical condition and prevent the accompanying learning problems.

Emotionally Disturbed. When children suffer the severe emotional disturbances of childhood schizophrenia or infantile autism, they are usually too psychotic to spend all or some time in a regular classroom. Less marked are minor behavioral disorders from which most pupils suffer at one time or other. Minor behavioral disorder is a grab bag term that includes a host of conditions such as the state of being overactive, overly tense or anxious, too fearful or too unhappy. Another kind of disorder occurs when pupils act out their negative feelings against society in acts of violence, vandalism, delinquency, and disobedience.

Providing for Differences

Handling such a range of pupils' needs taxes the school's ingenuity and resources. Basically, the school deals with the diversity of needs in the following ways:

Special Schools. Special schools or classes are organized for those pupils whose needs are so unique that they cannot be accommodated in the regular classroom. Such children are those of limited muscular movement, the blind and deaf, the mentally retarded, and the severely emotionally disturbed. Many educators feel, however, that since these pupils ultimately must adjust to the world, it is better to "mainstream" them into regular classrooms. If they continue to live in their hothouse environment of the special school or class, they will be unprepared for the challenges and realities of the world outside the classroom.

Those who favor these special environments point to the teachers' highly specialized training which the regular classroom teacher does not have. Placing a blind or deaf child in a regular class would take too much time and attention away from the rest of the pupils. Enrollments in special classes are very small compared to a regular classroom. Also, the classes and buildings are fitted with specialized equipment and material, the installation cost of which would be prohibitive in a regular classroom. Sometimes schools attempt to get the best of both worlds by having pupils spend part of their day in the special class and part in the regular classroom.

Homogeneous Grouping. In the schools today, probably the most extensive practice for accommodating differences among pupils is homogeneous grouping. Homogeneous groups are composed of pupils who resemble each other with regard to a particular trait or dimension. In a sense, special classes and schools are homogeneous groupings because they put together pupils who have the trait of blindness, or mental retardation, or deafness, or emotional disturbance. Homogeneous groups can be organized around similarity of interests, achievement levels, learning potential, or physical aptitude. Many kinds of grouping are possible within a school or classroom. The one most often employed is ability grouping wherein pupils are grouped according to scores on achievement or I.Q. tests. Because reading is the fundamental skill the school teaches, the reading level is usually the key factor for grouping on the basis of achievement. Some plans that have achieved national attention and implementation are the Dalton Plan, the Joplin Plan, and the Winnetka Plan.

Most elementary schools are self-contained; one teacher is responsible for instruction of most of the academic areas with perhaps the exception of music, art, or physical education. The class may be homogeneously grouped according to I.Q. or reading level, or it may be a heterogeneous group that represents a cross section of the school population without regard to similarity of traits. In such a class, one finds a melange of slow and rapid learners, mixed socioeconomic levels, and pupils of varying physical size and social adjustment. The only feature pupils have in common is that they are at the same grade level.

The self-contained class contains tremendously different learning abilities, usually a span of three or more years. This is especially true when a class is heterogeneous in its make-up. Faced with the impossibility of whole classroom instruction, the teacher usually groups pupils according to reading level. The wider the span of pupils' abilities, the more groups the teacher would need. If the teacher can also manage additional groupings, he then arranges pupils into arithmetic and, possibly, spelling groups. The other content areas, such as social studies and science, are taught by whole class instruction, or as individual projects of pupil-selected groups.

Because children who are superior in reading are usually, although not necessarily, also superior in the other subjects, the grouping by academic ability puts the same children together and isolates them somewhat from contact with the rest of the pupils. To overcome this, the teacher might employ other kinds of groups, according to pupil preference or interests. In social studies, the teacher might group those pupils who, according to the results of a sociogram, want to work together, or he might group them by their interest in working on a particular topic or project.

Although homogeneous grouping has been practiced for decades, many educators and psychologists are not in favor of it. They believe no class can be truly homogeneous and this designation only heightens false distinctions among pupils. They contend the variety of the heterogeneous class is more challenging to pupils and truer to life outside school. Social and emotional growth is hampered for academic advantage because those pupils placed in slow groups suffer damage to their self-image and those in the higher group take on a false sense of superiority. Further, the distinctions will fall along socioeconomic lines and segregate pupils on this basis.

Those who favor ability grouping point to the impossibility of the teacher's job in providing a good education to pupils of such a vast range. They say that pupils can discern who are the most able whether in groups or not, and the outside world makes these distinctions in sports, in the job market, and in social affiliations. If given the choice, they claim pupils associate with others who are like themselves, so the school is merely duplicating the realities of the outside world.

Differences in Pace. Accommodation of the differences in the pace of learning is accomplished by skipping those pupils who learn more rapidly than their peers and by retaining for another year those who need more time to learn. This practice was more widespread in the past than it is today. Many educators believe that adjusting only to the pace of learning is insufficient and that pupils placed in unlike peer groups suffer a social disadvantage. Further, the stigma of repeating a grade is too damaging to pupils' self-image and not worth the alleged gains.

Individualization. Many teachers and administrators became disenchanted with the retention or skipping and grouping policies because they believed these practices still violated the uniqueness of pupils and did not meet their individual needs. The solution seemed to be the individualization of instruction; that is, tailoring the curriculum to fit the academic needs of every pupil so that no matter what his unique features, he could fit into almost any classroom.

But implementing such a design involved many problems. It required a host of new materials geared to the many gradations of ability and interests in the class. In reading, for instance, instead of the usual three sets of basal readers, reading materials covering at least six grade levels of achievement and a range of interests from serious historiography to light fiction was mandatory. Then the teacher had to reorganize his reading program to include detailed assessment of pupils' reading skills, individual reading conferences, and grouping of pupils according to instructional needs. For many teachers it meant breaking loose from whole class instruction and the presentation of content to the new role of leading pupils to become self-directing and self-instructing. It entailed for teachers retooling and retraining by taking further course work, attending workshops, conferences and in-service programs. One teacher alone could not attend to the multitudinous needs of pupils, so aides had to be hired and trained to assist the teacher. Skyrocketing costs led to enlisting the services of unpaid aides, usually from the ranks of parents and future teachers.

Sometimes teachers combined two or more classes into one large group with each teacher developing a speciality in certain content areas. One teacher might teach the language arts and social studies, another might teach arithmetic and science, and the third might assume overall responsibility for the team and teach the rest of the subjects.

Along with team teaching there emerged the nongraded, continuous progress primary or intermediate unit. A primary unit usually consists of pupils from ages six to eight, and the intermediate unit from nine to eleven. Pupils are grouped into one large instructional unit and taught by a team of teachers. Pupils learn at their own rate and instruction is organized around pupils' needs, interests, or abilities without regard to pupils' ages or grade levels. This arrangement reduces the stigma attached to pupils who are atypical in their development, because in a group of such a wide range of age, ability, and size, no one pupil stands out for the particular traits he possesses or lacks.

The advantages of individualized instruction are obvious. Each pupil works and progresses at his own pace; failure and its attendant consequences are eliminated; pupils interact with others of varying backgrounds; pupils develop more responsibility for their own learning; and a sounder relationship develops between teachers and pupils. Its detractors state that pupils working individually are isolated from the intellectual stimulation of others; in trying to keep tabs on each pupil, the teacher's job is hopelessly proliferated; it has not been proven that its high cost is worth the benefits; too many aides are needed and many of them are not qualified or skilled in working with pupils; pupils have to relate to too many adults in the classroom; and it places too much freedom and responsibility on young pupils who often cannot make sensible choices.

Cumulative Records

With all the information the school garners year by year about each of its pupils, it needs some way of storing it efficiently. Most schools maintain cumulative records which contain information for all the years that pupils are enrolled in the school. Every teacher fills in the information on the progress of the pupils who are in his class each year. Such information would include report card grades, attendance records, standardized test scores, unusual achievements, and some details about study habits and social-emotional adjustment. Additional information might include pupils' family background and health and medical history.

The cumulative record is a short history of the pupil from kindergarten through sixth or eighth grade. If the school has done its job well, that history should be one of growth and learning, happily accomplished.

SUGGESTED READING

Frost, Joe L., and Thomas G. Rowland. *Curricula for the Seventies: Early Childhood through Early Adolescence.* Boston: Houghton Mifflin Company, 1969.

Hilgard, Ernest R., Richard C. Atkinson, and Rita L. Atkinson. *Introduction to Psychology.* 5th Ed. New York: Harcourt Brace Jovanovich, Inc., 1971.

Mussen, Paul, Mark R. Rosezweig, et. al. *Psychology—An Introduction.* Lexington, Mass.: D. C. Heath & Company, 1973.

Sartrain, Aaron Quinn, Alvin Jones North, Jack Roy Strange, and Harold Marin Chapman. 3rd Ed. *Psychology—Understanding Human Behavior.* New York: McGraw Hill Book Company, 1967.

Schell, Robert, Chief adviser and coordinator. *Developmental Psychology Today.* 2nd Ed. Random House, Inc., 1975.

Stott, Leland H. *Child Development: An Individual Longitudinal Approach.* New York: Holt, Rinehart & Winston, Inc., 1967.

Young, J. Z. *An Introduction to the Study of Man.* Oxford: The Clarendon Press, 1971.

POST TEST

Circle the choice which best completes the item.

1. Billy has an M.A. of 11 and a C.A. of 10. His I.Q. figures out to be
   a. 120.
   b. 91.
   c. 111.
   d. 101.
   e. 110.

2. Jane Dillard, the eldest of six children, has an I.Q. of 138. The chances are her siblings will not match her I.Q. because
   a. the first pregnancy drained Mrs. Dillard's brain-giving potential.
   b. an I.Q. that high comes only once in a family.
   c. the oldest child in the family usually has the highest I.Q.
   d. the older the parents are at the time of conception the less intelligent their children will be.
   e. her parents are probably not that intelligent.

3. When a test maker seeks to eliminate the extraneous elements that might distort what the test tries to measure, he is improving the test's
   a. reliability.
   b. correlation coefficient.
   c. validity.
   d. objectivity.
   e. scoreability.

4. If Jonathan has an I.Q. of 135, it means that about only the following proportion of the population is brighter than he is:
   a. 68%
   b. 82%
   c. 3%
   d. 15%
   e. 14%

5. The I.Q.'s of the pupils in Mrs. Costello's class go from a low of 84 to a high of 145. This is an example of the traits'
   a. uniformity.
   b. validity.
   c. variability.
   d. range.
   e. uniqueness.

6. The I.Q. score is most useful in predicting those pupils who
   a. will succeed in business and the professions.
   b. have the greatest potential scholastic ability.
   c. will get the highest grades in school.
   d. have the largest size brains.
   e. will have no learning difficulties.

7. When Mrs. Richards complains that her son is totally untidy, what she really means is that
   a. she hasn't trained him properly to keep things in order.
   b. tidiness is so seldom observed in his behavior that he seems completely deficient in it.
   c. there is little hope of changing him into a neat, orderly child.
   d. he picked up the habit from his father who likes to leave things around.
   e. the trait of tidiness was missing in his genetic inheritance.

8. Millicent refused to wear the expensive dress her aunt sent her for her birthday because her crowd said dresses were "out" for parties. This is an example of
   a. the power of a primary group to dictate to its members.
   b. disintegration of family unity.
   c. a cultural artifact.
   d. conflict resolution within a society.
   e. subcultural diversity of a racial or ethnic group.

9. Ronnie has learned to resolve his disputes by fisticuffs. When he does this in class, the best way for the teacher to handle it is to
   a. tell him only animals behave this way.
   b. write a note home to his parents about the poor upbringing their son has had.
   c. send him to the principal for punishment.
   d. elicit from him alternative ways of resolving conflict.
   e. use it as an illustration of the inferiority of certain ethnic and racial groups.

10. Priscilla admires her young, vivacious teacher and imitates her in many ways. This is an example of
    a. the influence of the mass media.
    b. middle-class competitiveness.
    c. upward social mobility.
    d. trait development.
    e. identification.

11. A sociogram will *not* tell
    a. who are the stars and who are the isolates.
    b. which pupils form cliques.
    c. changes in preferences since the last sociogram was administered.
    d. why pupils made the choices they did.
    e. the choices of partners made by the pupils for a school activity.

12. Grant is in fourth grade but reading only at the second grade level. He has an I.Q. of 109 and works very hard at his school tasks. He probably is having difficulty in reading because
    a. the teacher is giving him books that are too simple.
    b. he hasn't been checked for a perceptual problem.
    c. his previous teachers were too easy with him.
    d. he watches too much television.
    e. he isn't intelligent enough to advance that far in reading.

13. The fact that Georgette obtained an I.Q. score on the California Test of Mental Maturity when she was in fourth grade is most likely to appear on the
    a. cumulative record.
    b. report card.
    c. teacher's anecdotal record.
    d. health card.
    e. record of parent-teacher conferences.

14. The pupils in a multi-age primary unit would
    a. be at approximately the same level of social development.
    b. have comparable levels of reading ability.
    c. be grouped for instruction according to their ages.
    d. have little contact with pupils in the class of other age levels.
    e. be unlike in their ages and abilities.

15. The pupils in Mrs. Kelly's class test at five different reading levels. On that basis she organized them into five reading groups. This is an example of
    a. homogeneous grouping.
    b. heterogeneous grouping.
    c. individualization of instruction.
    d. multi-age grouping.
    e. interest grouping.

16. In the Guess Who? device administered by the teacher, Paul was selected most often as the pupil who disrupts the class. The best way for the teacher to use this information is to
    a. tell Paul how the other pupils perceive him the next time he is disruptive.
    b. observe Paul to discover when and why he is disruptive.
    c. keep a record of it in his cumulative folder.
    d. spread the word in the lounge so other teachers will be forewarned.
    e. ask his parents to do something about it.

17. At the final parent-teacher conference, Mr. Adams, a third-grade teacher, took the credit for the tremendous advancement in Lance's learning. According to Coleman and Jencks, the single most significant impetus to his achievement can be credited to
    a. Lance's M.A.
    b. Mr. Adam's teaching.
    c. the new school building.
    d. the influence of the home.
    e. the teaching materials and equipment Mr. Adams used.

18. Mr. Jenkins, a high school graduate, works in a factory and then pumps gas at night for extra money. He wants his son to go to college and join the ranks of professionals. This is an example of
    a. the generation gap.
    b. lower class fatalism.
    c. ethnic pride.
    d. the pluralistic American society.
    e. upward social mobility.

19. It is important for teachers to learn about the topic of individual traits and differences because
  a. the trend in curriculum organization today is moving towards this concept.
  b. it encourages pupils to be different.
  c. it enables teachers to be more scholarly in their approach to teaching.
  d. principals and parents have more confidence in a teacher with this knowledge.
  e. teachers are more capable of conducting parent-teacher conferences.

20. One of the disadvantages of individualizing instruction is that
  a. pupils' physical needs are not met.
  b. parents don't know how well their children are doing compared to other pupils.
  c. it eliminates the essential ingredient of competition among pupils.
  d. it requires more assistance and materials than many teachers have available to them.
  e. it causes confusion among the pupils.

21. Many educators object to homogeneous grouping because
  a. it makes teaching too easy and unchallenging.
  b. principals and parents expect teachers to get better results with pupils.
  c. it really doesn't take care of the individual differences among pupils.
  d. it groups pupils who may not get along with each other.
  e. minority groups in the community would charge discrimination.

22. In most schools today the primary consideration for homogeneous grouping is based on
  a. grade levels.
  b. age levels.
  c. ability levels.
  d. family background.
  e. pupil preferences.

23. One of the basic differences between whole class and individualized instruction is that
  a. parents work as aides in the individualized programs.
  b. teachers have less choice of curriculum materials with whole class instruction.
  c. the role of the teacher changes from presenter of information to facilitator of learning.
  d. curriculum decisions shift from the school personnel to members of the community.
  e. report cards are replaced by parent-teacher conferences.

24. A group in Mrs. Hill's class is working on a bulletin board and cannot agree on how to share the chores. If Mrs. Hill believes in group dynamics, she would
  a. ask them to go to their seats because they were noisy.
  b. tell them the best way to solve their problem.
  c. discontinue group work until pupils are mature enough to handle it.
  d. raise questions that will enable the group to reach their own solution.
  e. scold the pupils who are not in agreement with the rest of the group.

25. Mrs. Pierson teaches all the subjects in her class except for the art, music, and gym, which are taught by specialists. This is an example of
    a. ability grouping.
    b. self-contained classroom.
    c. individualized instruction.
    d. team teaching.
    e. nongraded primary unit.

Discipline

Marjorie Kingsley

Joseph F. Callahan

Jersey City State College

module 5

Nature of Discipline / Elements of Good Discipline / Factors to Consider in Handling Specific Situations / Some Tips and Techniques Related to Discipline

RATIONALE

If you were to ask any group of preservice teachers to tell you what area of teaching most worries them, the chances are that the unanimous answer would be "Discipline!" They may even report nightmares, populated by defiant pupils shouting, "I won't" or "I can't," and filled with chaotic classrooms in which the pupils are completely out of hand.

Apprehensions about one's ability to maintain discipline are more universal and more intense than about any other aspect of teaching. It makes little difference whether the cause for this anxiety is the memory of high school days past when mischievous classmates plotted to get to their teacher or more likely the substitute teacher to enliven a dull day in spring or when some particularly distressed youth created traumatic moments for an entire class by behaving in a raucous or uncontrolled fashion. The tension exists and must be faced.

In truth, there is really no need for such extreme anxiety. Most elementary school students want to like their teacher and want to be liked by him. Many of the things which together create "discipline problems" can be prevented, and the problems that occur can be handled in ways which make them local issues instead of federal cases. We hope that this module will help you to find ways to operate effectively with children and to minimize any apprehensions you may have concerning maintaining discipline in your classes.

Specific Objectives

After you complete the study of this module, you should be able to do the following:

1. Explain why it is necessary for you to be able to distinguish between acts of misbehavior that are manifestations of normal growth and those that are purely disruptive.
2. Write a paragraph in which you explain the statement, "the punishment must fit the crime."
3. List at least three possible causes for a pupil's failure to do his homework.
4. Describe at least three signals that can be used to attract the attention of the class, and explain when these signals might be used.
5. Explain how you can get a daydreamer back into the group without causing a fuss.
6. Name five variations on control by proximity.
7. Write a short paragraph about the wisdom and legality of "laying of hands on a child."
8. Identify as true or false the statements regarding the maintenance of good discipline in a classroom as developed from this module.
9. Explain the position suggested in this module for you to assume relative to cheating during a test.
10. Give the procedure you might follow in handling the class clown.

11. List at least three reasons why it is unwise to punish an entire group for the deviant behavior of one student.
12. Describe the initial response you might make to the student who says, "I won't" so as to prevent a traumatic confrontation.
13. Explain what position you should assume and what you should avoid when a student begins to debate any established rules or policies of the school or classroom.
14. Describe what your action should be when a student shows a need which is outside the range of your professional preparation or competence.
15. Justify your action in sending someone to the principal.
16. Explain psychological space as it relates to your responses to misbehavior and to your words in presenting a lesson.
17. State the reasons why a decision to change the time of an already scheduled test or activity should not be based upon shallow causes.
18. Specify why classroom rules and regulations should be kept to a minimum and should be well known and understood.
19. Explain why the variables pertaining to rules should be compiled with the cooperation and participation of the entire class.
20. Describe the compromise position you should assume according to this module between consistency and fairness.
21. Illustrate the value of using humor as well as the pitfalls to avoid in its application in the classroom.
22. Justify the use of the thunderstorm technique.
23. Describe the effects of too frequent use of the "big gun."
24. Describe how you will proceed to establish a "catch them being good" climate.
25. Explain why discipline by recipe is not possible.
26. Explain what research has shown about repressive action.
27. Describe the single best preventative to misbehavior in a classroom.
28. Write a short paragraph about the role of mutual respect and affection in the behavior of students.
29. Explain how the personal characteristics of some students or of some groups will force the adaptation of rules to make them fit changing situations.
30. Describe the influence that your values and your students' values will play in the behavior of the students in your classroom.

MODULE TEXT

Nature of Discipline

Although good control, like good art, may be basically very simple, it is not easy to master. The anxiety referred to earlier can be put to good use as you prepare yourself for your profession if it leads you to inquire, to observe, to research, and to learn the skills that may be utilized in the various classroom situations that will emerge. You should, however, remind yourself that there are no simple pre-packaged mixes or special recipes that can be whipped up on a moment's notice to solve every discipline problem that arises. In your search for a compendium of how to's, you will be well advised to gather from a variety of sources examples and illustrations, strategies, techniques, principles, and friendly tips on discipline so as to prepare yourself to draw upon your own accumulation of knowledge as the variables in each situation change. So many different types of teachers have been successful with so many different strategies for controlling so many different sorts of pupils that it is impossible to reduce the number of acceptable disciplinary procedures to a concise list. No one answer and no one form of teacher behavior will suffice for all varieties of people and all situations, and not even the powers of the all-mighty computer push button can be made sensitive enough to respond appropriately in every instance. In many situations, teachers who respond intuitively are very effective. They reach their goal successfully because by personality, temperament, experience, and previous study, the stimulus of the situation evokes a response from them which is truly artistic and appropriate. At the same time, there are other teachers who seemingly respond in exactly the same fashion but who are unsuccessful and who bungle many situations because some vital ingredient concerning human interaction has been left out of the process. The majority of teachers fall between these two extremes of artist and bungler. They are often successful and sometimes not, but always they strive for greater success by developing their repertoire of possible solutions and their capacity for sensitive response to fellow human beings.

As you begin here to compile your list of don'ts and dos, keep in mind that not every person can use each of these techniques successfully. Not every suggestion listed here will be compatible with your temperament or your style of teaching. Examine and respond intellectually to all that you read and select as many of those suggestions as seem to fit your style so that your future teaching behavior may be varied and serviceable. Above all, remember as you read and question that there are no *right* answers. Nevertheless, it will prove helpful if you keep the following basic generalizations in mind as you start your quest of mastery of the discipline function:

1. *Good discipline is necessary everywhere*—in the streets, in the home, in the classroom, and on the ball field. Rules and their enforcement are a vital part of efficient living as is apparent to anyone who will consider the confusion that would reign if they did not exist. The teacher in the classroom must help the child in the class to perceive rules and regulations not as taboos or as limitations placed upon his freedom but, rather, as facilitators of social interaction enabling people to realize their individual and collective goals with maximum efficiency.

2. *Rules are not good or bad* except in terms of purpose to be achieved at a particular time and of the stage of development of those involved. The rule of quiet in the classroom, for example, is sound but may actually interfere with efficient learning when the class is working on certain class projects. Generalizations about treating all students alike may not always be practicable because students within class groupings are so different in abilities and motivation as to constitute almost different populations.

3. *All misbehavior is an attempt to satisfy some need.* Many children who misbehave do so because they have learned to gratify their needs through misbehavior. They may have found, for instance, that they can satisfy their need for attention by disruptive behavior or their need for status by defying the teacher.

For pupils to find more suitable ways of satisfying their needs may become an exasperating problem when the curriculum is inadequate or the classroom is filled with tensions resulting from pupil–pupil conflicts. If the work assigned for a class is too easy or too hard or if the instructional goals are too remote from the students' objectives, the teacher will find it difficult to eliminate misbehavior.

Disciplinary measures that ignore pupils' needs are doomed to failure. In past years, when the primary emphasis was on suppressing misbehavior, educators discovered that the disciplinary processes used generated tensions that precipitated misbehavior. Consequently, modern discipline is based on the philosophy of helping children learn to satisfy their basic needs in socially acceptable ways by providing guidance in finding suitable outlets and practice in acceptable behavior.

4. *Much of misbehavior is simply the manifestation of normal growth.* When dealing with children, one must remember that no matter how annoying their behavior they need to have the opportunity to experiment with immaturity. As they experiment and try out new ways of conduct, it is quite normal for them to get into trouble. Sometimes, as a matter of fact, viewed from the vantage point of their overall development, pupils' misbehavior may be desirable. Children need opportunities to assert their initiative and to learn from accepting the consequences of their actions. If they are eventually to take their proper role in our democratic society, they must practice democratic living. For this reason, childhood should be, at least in part, an apprenticeship during which pupils can learn from their mistakes, trials, and errors until they become capable of self-direction.

Unfortunately, teacher behavior may inhibit pupils' optimum development. The marking and grading practices in some schools provide a case in point. Supposedly, marking and grading should both facilitate student personnel accounting and motivate students to high levels of achievement. Yet, often, the marking and grading practices used in the schools inhibit the realization of educational goals. Instead of being motivated by marks and grades, the pupils may be restrained by them. From their observation, pupils learn that errors are punishable and that mistakes are penalized. The fact that bad marks are awarded to those who don't get the right answer teaches students to repress their initiative, lest it not fit the right answer format. This contributes to the growth of counterproductive activities in the school as a whole.

5. *A diagnostic approach generally accomplishes more than do repressive and punitive measures.* The effective teacher realizes, for example, that some of his students would like to be cooperative but cannot because cooperation with the teacher would involve rejection of a friend or rejection by the group. He also knows that sex typing causes boys to react differently than girls on many occasions and that children from one cultural environment respond differently from those living in a different home environment. Consequently, he treats each case of misbehavior as a separate matter and applies his judgment to the causes behind the manifestation.

6. *Good discipline contributes cumulatively to the major educational goal: developing independent, sustained self-control in each child.* For this reason, as well as others, teacher response to misbehavior of students should be based upon the spirit of the law rather than upon the letter. Children who have been included in the planning and the formulating of regulations that will affect them generally respond by exerting their personal influence upon fellow students who deviate.

When the climate of their environment has been changed so that the classroom is looked upon as a place where one can work toward worthwhile goals instead of a place in which to wage perpetual warfare against an authoritative teacher, the classroom assumes a different aura and a positive atmosphere. The letter of the law can be used to support learning well only if it is filtered through the fine-meshed screen of sensitivity and good judgment. Without this screening, the letter of the law may kill rapport and profitable teacher–pupil interaction. Whereas the letter of the law calls for the ultimate penalty, the spirit of the law may inspire a solution which keeps alive a hope for success and a motivation to try again. Simply stated, "What does it profit a teacher to adminster the ultimate penalty in November or January if he still has to survive living with the culprit–pupil until June?"

7. *The purpose of discipline is to change behavior, not to punish.* As with all aspects of teaching, one must know his students well so as to handle problem situations in ways which fit each of those involved. What will change behavior in one child may not reach another. One also needs to keep in mind that similar misbehavior in five children can have five different causes. Failure to complete homework, for example, might mean a) no place to work at home for one; b) the work is too easy; c) the work is too difficult; d) the work seems ridiculous; e) the student is mad about something that has nothing to do with the assignment or with the school; f) a combination of these things; or g) something else. If teachers are to bring about effective and permanent changes in pupil behavior, the strategies they use must make sense to the pupils involved. Beware of the trap that says, "If it works, it must be good." If children are sufficiently threatened, they will comply and appear to have changed although nothing basic will have been altered. These students have simply learned how to survive.

8. *Real discipline comes from within the individual.* Our big goal in working with students is to make it possible for them to grow toward self-discipline. As is the case with all areas of learning, there must be readiness for self-control. Teacher expectation of this control before children are ready for it can be disastrous. External controls are absolutely necessary until children are ready to provide their own.

9. *The best preventative of problems is a productive, interesting classroom.* Students who are fruitfully occupied with tasks that they perceive as meaningful are not likely to become behavior problems. The important point here is that the students do the perceiving, not the teacher. The teacher may consider that what is going on is both productive and interesting but if the students do not think it is, it might just as well not be.

10. *If punishment is absolutely necessary, it must "fit the crime."* Sooner or later every teacher finds it necessary to punish someone. When this time comes, care should be exercised to keep the punishment positive, to avoid letting it be influenced by vindictive feelings, and to make it as appropriate as possible to the occasion. A great many meaningless and really stupid tasks have been assigned in the name of punishment. What on earth, for example, is the relationship between being noisy in the halls and copying a page of a dictionary? The problem begging for solution in this instance concerns learning why we need to be quiet in the halls during school hours and then to keep quiet for the right reasons.

One tendency that causes the punishment to be inconsistent with the offense, strangely enough, results from teachers' attempts to be patient. For one reason or another, these patient teachers hold off from taking action to punish misbehavior until a point when the proverbial "final straw breaks the camel's back." Then they crack down. Frequently, the final straw is really something very minor, but the total impact of the accumulated annoyances strike the teacher as very serious and perhaps also very irritating. As a consequence, the punishment meted out tends to be out of proportion and to be misinterpreted by the offender, who has a faulty recollection concerning past offenses. Not much can be done about this phenomenon except to urge cool thinking and sound judgment in passing sentence and to warn against succumbing to natural inclinations to include all past offenses in one's punishment.

11. *Timing is an important component of solutions to problems of discipline.* Small problems can become big ones if they are not nipped in the bud or not managed in accordance with recognized principles. As the defensive automobile driver is alert to happenings in the street hundreds of yards before his car approaches them, so the alert teacher can head off calamitous situations by remaining cognizant of developments at each stage in the evolution of trouble. The defensive driver does not necessarily stop his car when he views two small children tussling near the curb a block or more away. He does remain alert to developments though so that if the children should push each other into the road, he will be able to respond and avoid striking them. The teacher behaving in a similar fashion can let many things happen in expectation that the potential disruption to the classwork will cease before the critical moment arrives when incisive action becomes necessary. He holds himself in readiness, though, to take whatever action the developing situation dictates.

12. *Reward and approval are useful ingredients in maintaining proper discipline.* So are reproof and punishment. It is imperative for students to know what is acceptable behavior and just as necessary to know what is not acceptable. Extreme permissiveness is as out of place as extreme authoritarianism.

The advertising slogan that claims, "a little dab will do" might be changed in this instance to "much more might even do better." The truth of the matter is that those students about whom it is hardest to find something commendable have the greatest need for reward and approval. Students of this type have received so few pats that they desperately need to be made to feel worthy. The teacher need not resort to gushiness to achieve this goal. A smile, a wink, a nod, or a poke on the arm may be more effective. What is needed is optimistic, positive response that shows approval, cultivates some measure of self-pride, and helps build a degree of self-confidence.

13. *Some classroom misbehavior cases have their origin in the home, the neighborhood, or in the pupils' own aggressive tendencies.* There is no need for teachers to feel guilty or personally responsible for all cases of misconduct. In many instances, students' deviant action is generated by causes over which the teacher has no control; nothing he might have done would have been effective. Suffice it to feel blameworthy for those cases of misconduct which you have caused, which result from poor teaching or planning on your part, or which you made worse because you erred culpably in your application of a remedy. You need not feel guilty for misbehavior resulting from causes other than those for which you can be responsible.

Elements of Good Discipline

As you have seen, social control in the classroom is necessary to allow learners to achieve the objectives of the course. Too much control can be oppressive and can give students a lasting distaste for teachers, for school, and for learning; too little control may not give the students an adequate opportunity to achieve the course objectives and may well be disrupting to the school in general.

Each teacher gradually evolves his own system of techniques to prevent student behavior from getting out of control. No matter how many fine models he has observed nor how much sound theory he has studied, in the final analysis it is what he does that makes the difference. Either he learns how to cope and thus experiences his share of personal happiness and instructional efficiency or he comes up short and is forced out of the profession. Without an orderly classroom, he is assured of failure since effective instruction cannot take place amid disorder. Consequently, he strives to train his students in self-control. When the immaturity of some individual students retards this development toward personal inner control, the teacher brings external influences to bear upon those students so as to achieve the kind of conformity demanded for learning.

Without doubt, there would be differences in the lists submitted by groups of experienced teachers of points to consider in working toward personal mastery of the discipline function. On some lists, the respondents would stress mental hygiene considerations; on others, the stress would be on developmental psychology or cognitive structuring or other considerations. But overall, all the lists would include items that could be classified as elemental. What follows is the writer's list of elements, based upon a multitude of years of working in this field.

1. *Good discipline is based on mutual respect and liking.* If students and teacher respect and like each other, most discipline problems simply do not occur, and in the instances in which discipline does go away, resolution of the problem is fairly simple. People who respect and like each other can work out their difficulties. A teacher whose life is devoted to working with children should love and like his students and be successful in communicating his affection to his students. The most important factor in this relationship is that the students must be convinced in a number of ways of the genuineness of their teacher's affection and solicitude.

Positive feelings of mutual respect are as infectious in spreading a supportive esprit as are grumbling tones in the hatching of rebels. When the cheerful touch of affection is at work, teachers do not humiliate students nor do peers mock peers. They discuss standards, they respect opinions, and they support the search for self-control.

2. *Good discipline is possible when the teacher's "essentials" are made known, are understood, and are kept to a minimum.* Again, "essentials" vary with the individual teacher. They might include such things as required behavior on fire drills, or the need for work to be in on time and the student's responsibility for making suitable arrangements when such is not possible. Classroom regulations such as, "When others are talking to the class, the rest of us listen," leave little room for doubt about acceptable classroom performance.

3. *Good discipline includes the working out of "variables" with students as*

situations arise. Working out the variables with students does two things: it provides understanding for all of what is involved, and it makes the "rule" when adopted the rule of the students rather than solely the teacher's rule. The process is time-consuming but the benefits far outweigh that expense. In one first-grade class, children resolved the problem of the rapid depletion of the year's supply of drawing paper. They decided that there should be three "piles": one of completed pictures, one of incomplete pictures, and one of new paper. No child was to take a new piece until he had finished the one in the incomplete pile. The consensus decision required no outside authority for implementation.

4. *Good discipline means that rules which have been set are carried out.* Students need a reasonable framework within which to operate, and following "our rules" is one thing that makes for reason. It behooves one to be exceedingly careful about the rules that are set. When students are involved in making those rules, it is important that the limitations within which those decisions are made are clear to the students.

5. *Good discipline encompasses consistency and fairness.* It looks and sounds simple, but it is difficult to be both consistent and fair. What if, because of a large class in a too small area, it were necessary to restrict children's movement within a classroom? There are two children, one lethargic and imperturbable, the other bouncy and wiggly. The lethargic child might cope fairly easily with some restriction of movement whereas the wiggler could come unglued. The teacher has to find a way to provide some flexibility within the consistency element so as to cope with the fairness element. Children are generally very understanding and accepting of such flexibility when there is a need for it.

6. *Good discipline includes an explanation when a stated plan has to be changed.* It is important not to change plans unless it is really necessary. If at all possible, the change should be made and announced in time to prevent hardship for the students. In an emergency situation, this may not always be possible, of course. But the avoidance of post hoc penalties nearly always is preventable. It is possible, for example, that you have a test planned, but some school problem has occurred and the principal calls an all-school assembly. This is quite different from the situation of deciding "that morning" for no reason in particular that you won't have the test after all. It could also happen that in checking the previous night's homework you discover some major misunderstandings and it might well be wise to postpone the scheduled test until the items are clarified. Once the students really understand that the teacher has good reasons for his behavior, or understand the nature of the situation, it won't be necessary for the teacher to belabor the "why." He will have established trust with the students. Especially will this be true if students are never penalized for infractions committed before the rule was made.

7. *Good discipline is generally helped by a light touch* (*humor*). Many, many things can be handled with humor in a way that makes for good learning and that keeps minor infractions from becoming federal cases. One of the best things a teacher can do is to learn how to laugh at himself. He sets the example for the youngsters that enables them to laugh at themselves.

Teachers need to encourage some children to look for the humorous side of those experiences in life that they appear to be taking too seriously. They need to urge students to laugh with them at other traumatic incidents over which everyone will cry unless they can find the aspect which justifies laughter. The intense, serious, sober-sided child will naturally need more attention and more assistance than his frivolous, jolly, or more carefree companions.

An important caution must accompany this element of discipline: never use humor tinged with sarcasm to achieve your purpose. The temptation appears great for some nimble-tongued teachers to create situations for laughter at the expense of the children in their classroom. Because of their advantage in age, education, experience, and facility with the language, such teachers experience little difficulty in displaying the sharpness of their wit and of being rewarded with the resounding laughter of everyone except the misbehaving target. Cheap shots of this sort tend to freeze the environment of the classroom and become counterproductive. Instead of eliciting responses from students and of training them to treat things less seriously, sarcasm and mockery tend to frighten the sensitive and inhibit both their responses and their inclinations to try in the face of conspicuous failure. Children who are laughed with may respond as anticipated; children laughed at tend to freeze.

8. *Good discipline needs to be applied in ways that fit the individual or the group involved.* Whereas one child can be instantly diverted from deviant behavior by a slightly raised eyebrow or a mildly surprised expression, another may require more direct, more explicit, or more radical forms of intervention. The instructions of the young mother to the kindergarten teacher in the story about the first day of school seem especially apropos here:

Claude is a very sensitive child. Do not speak in loud tones to him. If you should see him doing anything naughty, merely slap the boy next to him and Claude will discontinue what he is doing.

Some children learn early how to develop thick skins so that many things do not bother them. They bounce back from reprimand in an almost irrepressible manner. To avoid inflicting unnecessary agony upon others who blush and die a thousand deaths when publicly mortified, the knowledgeable teacher will admonish in private.

9. *Good discipline may require a good thunderstorm occasionally rather than a constant drizzle.* If one has ever been exposed to a pick, pick, pick teacher (and very likely we all have), he knows how wearing it can be. If the circumstances are sufficiently traumatic, a thunderstorm can be a very effective device. If a teacher generally makes use of the first eight elements listed in this module and has a good relationship with his students, the traffic will bear the rare storm. Thunderstorms should be used sparingly, however. Once the storm has occurred and the problem made very clear, the issue should be dropped.

In this context, it may be helpful to reflect upon the necessity for divorcing personal rage, vengeance, or retribution upon particular pupils from the action taken. Under normal circumstances, the rage revealed in the storm is simulated and under control of the performing teacher. It can be dissipated as readily as it is generated and, in vanishing, leaves no insuperable barrier to good relationships between the teacher and the deviant student. As a dramatic device, it is set aside when the effect has been gained and is preserved until needed next.

10. *Any technique used too often may lose its effectiveness.* All effective teachers arrange the techniques they use in a hierarchical pattern. They use each in a selective fashion in accordance with the apparent gravity of the deviation

exhibited. Too quick a recourse to the "big gun" for a minor kind of offense confuses students and deprives the teacher of an effective weapon in his repertoire. Too frequent a utilization of the same "big gun" dissipates its aura and tends to diminish its impact.

Factors to Consider in Handling Specific Situations

Obviously, when a problem situation arises, the teacher does not stop and tick off the list of things he must consider before he responds to the problem. In the process of being educated as a teacher, one looks at and studies in various areas; when he finally becomes a teacher, somehow the parts finally come together into an integrated pattern of functioning with children. At least the following six items need to be considered when one copes with a situation.

1. *What are the teacher's values?* Consider, for example, the situation in which a child has done an arithmetic problem on the board and has made an error. Another student ridicules him. Will the teacher deal with the error in the arithmetic problem or with the problem of the ridicule? Which area he treats first and the manner in which he deals with it tells one a great deal about a teacher. A good practice to help you look at your own values is for you to prescribe what action you might take in given classroom situations and then analyze what that behavior reveals to you about the values to which you give first priority. The most astounding revelation of the present decade to many veteran teachers has been the growing acceptability of different cultural values and the inevitability of their emergence in the classrooms. In the earlier years of their teaching career when uniformity was the shibboleth, all students were expected to learn and treasure identical values. Transgressions were evaluated by the degree from the accepted value standard by which they deviated. Regularity of school attendance, conservative use of materials and equipment, and zealous application to mastery of cognitive knowledge were expected of all students. As the research of psychologists and sociologists revealed more about behavior patterns of subgroups within our society, the opportunity for abandoning the rigid single standard of teacher responses in the classroom became possible. It became legitimate and commendable to take into consideration the ethnic and racial environment of students who appeared to be deviating before responding with disciplinary action and to recognize that the values which motivate the teacher may differ from those surrounding the student.

Unless the teacher is aware of the value patterns in his own life, he will not be able to apply judicious attention to the behavior of the students in his classroom. In addition, though, he must also be aware of the various value patterns in the lives of his students and, as he establishes ground rules for pupil behavior, he must exercise care that the resulting regulations do not call for transgressions against the family or subgroup value system.

2. *Which specific individual is affected?* As indicated earlier, different individuals need to be handled in quite different ways. One child might be terribly embarrassed and repressed by a disapproving expression, but another might grin in a friendly, knowing manner and merely stop doing what he was doing. It is important to really know your children so that the effective technique can be applied in the right kind of situation on the appropriate child.

The master teacher is one who, among many other things, knows his students well enough to be able to select the most effective teacher behavior. The journeyman teacher will wield the broad brush on his canvas and affect some in a positive fashion. The skillful teacher will use adroitly a variety of brushes, large and small, thick or petite, to bring about the precise effect he seeks. Such finesse cannot be achieved without considerable study and great sensitivity.

3. *What is the nature of this particular group of students?* Once in a junior high school in a seventh grade, a youngster who had collected money from each of the students came up ten cents short when it was time to turn in the money. One youngster just said, "We know Bob didn't swipe it. Any of us could have lost a dime. Come on, anybody with a penny, shell out." In almost less time than it took to say, the problem was very simply taken care of. In an eighth grade which met later that same day, the response very likely would have been, "He lost it; let him make it up." And the class probably would have accepted that. There is a tremendous difference in groups, and if teachers are going to operate effectively, they must know about the nature of each group.

In some groups, like that seventh grade, a teacher can be much more permissive than in other groups because the students respond quickly and easily to the signals given. Their group self-control seems to be much more highly developed, and the forms of deviation to which they are susceptible are much more simple to defuse. In many cases, in a sensitive group of this sort, students exercise a considerable amount of peer control by overtly discouraging the mischievous from their deviant behavior.

Groups that remain hostile, that never quite develop the esprit of the cohesive classes, require closer attention, quicker responses from the teacher, and more leadership efforts to bring about cooperative behavior. These are the groups which are inclined to seize upon the opportunity provided by the tardiness of the teacher in arriving at the class, or by the kindness, consideration, and softness of the teacher, to create havoc whenever possible. They appear to resist the development of group self-control and, consequently, must be worked with more zealously if success is to be forthcoming.

4. *What skill does the teacher involved have in handling this particular kind of problem?* Each individual has areas in which he is comfortable and effective and areas in which he is not. The important thing is to know which is which. If a teacher is not comfortable in a given area, he is not likely to be of much help if he tries to handle it. In some schools, teachers have worked out a kind of buddy system so as to capitalize on each other's strengths. If one teacher is excellent at working with children who have hygiene and grooming problems but cannot manage to talk with youngsters about things in any way connected with sex, he concentrates on the hygiene and grooming problems while his buddy who does not fear talking about sex takes on problems of that sort. What is important is not who provides it, but that the children receive the needed help. Ideally, the child's own teacher should provide the assistance needed. Since each of us may be somewhat less than perfect in the range of skills he possesses, the intent of this reminder is to assure you that seeking help from your experienced confreres is not an admission of weakness any more than his requesting your help can be considered an exploitation of your youth and inexperience.

5. *Has this situation occurred before?* Unless the situation that arises is simply horrendous, the humane thing to do with a first occurrence is to assume a lack

of understanding. Go through the whole process and make certain that the student understands what is involved. Should it be a repeat performance, then one would go at it differently, depending upon the individuals and the situation involved.

Sometimes the repetition is simply a capitulation to a habit, or the reappearance of a stubborn pattern which one needs more time to extinguish. In such cases, the treatment can be brief and gentle. When the deviation is looked upon by the student, in retrospect, as a mistake and he expresses a desire to meet the challenge successfully the next time, little more can be expected of any student other than that he strive in the future to avoid making the same error in judgment.

Sometimes, though, the repetition of the misbehavior is intentional, or premeditated, or callous. Then the teacher's work is cut out for him. He must go all the way back to the building of a bridge between himself and the student to permit the flow of communication and to gradually establish the basis for self-control. When progress is very slow in this area or when the bridge does not appear strong enough to support the kind of message needed, the young teacher should solicit help from someone more experienced.

6. *What are the age characteristics of the individual involved?* In the fourth grade, a swain who is madly in love with the little blonde may throw his boots at her, a fairly normal act at that age. If a junior in high school exhibits the same behavior, he may have a real problem. One day, a sixth-grade teacher, pushed to the wall because of her unrealistic expectations, had the good sense to stop the activity and to read aloud to the entire class the list of normal characteristics listed by scholars for sixth-grade children. Randy, grinning, said, "Well, I guess we're perfectly normal." The tension was gone, and the class resumed its regular activities. One does not need to read the characteristics aloud to children, but one certainly needs to know what is reasonable to expect of given groups.

It is not uncommon for teachers to lose sight of characteristics normal for children at a given age and, consequently, to expect too much of their students. Students who are large for their age are particularly likely to be victims of unreasonable expectations. A ten-year-old who is as big as a fifteen-year-old is still a ten-year-old. Yet, teachers sometimes forget this fact and expect him to behave as a fifteen-year-old and to penalize him when he does not. Bright students also suffer when their usually precocious responses mislead the teacher into expecting behavior from them which is mature beyond their years.

It must be recognized that the lists of pupil characteristics enumerated by scholars and researchers can be used only as a general guide. Like all averages, they may apply in all specifics to no one particular child. Each child is an individual entity, evolving and developing in accordance to his own schedule and at his individual pace. Even so, some of the characteristics are applicable to all members of some groups so that one can establish general expectations and spot general trouble signs. As long as they remember the possibility for deviations and respect individual differences, teachers can rely upon these general lists of characteristics to supply informative guidance.

Some Tips and Techniques Related to Discipline

There are two main problems to consider when presenting tips and techniques related to discipline: how to avoid writing them as recipes, and how to separate those ideas associated with discipline from those associated with classroom management. For convenience in this presentation, the areas of discipline and classroom management are presented in separate modules. However, you should keep in mind that classroom management is closely related to the entire area of discipline. Remember, too, that what might work well for a given teacher in a particular situation and with a specific child may make absolutely no sense in another situation or with another child. Therefore there are no recipes. Now let's consider a few suggestions which have helped some beginners to find their own ways of perfecting their skills in securing and maintaining well-disciplined classes.

1. *Simple Proximity.* Often the mere presence of the teacher in the classroom is sufficient to discourage many kinds of misconduct. Only the very brazen, or the most powerfully driven, are bold enough to misbehave overtly when the threat of apprehension is imminent. Therefore, the alert teacher makes it a practice to move in the direction of incipient misbehavior as soon as he sees it begin to develop.

When a class is in session, the movement of the teacher down the aisle, or across the room toward the student who is engaging in unacceptable activity, will almost always cause the student to stop that activity. If pupils misbehave while you are teaching, often you can avoid interruptions and correct the misconduct by the simple expedient of continuing to teach while moving closer to the student involved. Usually by the time the teacher has reached him, the culprit will have abandoned his misbehavior without the teacher having to take any special corrective action.

Sometimes teachers become so absorbed in what they are teaching, or so intent on their interaction with a particular student, that they become oblivious to the rest of the class. In such circumstances, playful or mischievous children who are not greatly interested in what is going on may feel free to engage in other unapproved activities. When such lapses occur, you can usually restabilize the situation by the moving technique we have described or by establishing eye contact with the miscreants.

The importance of eye contact should not be underestimated. Eye contact supplies teachers with much of the information he needs for guiding his own behavior. Good eye contact alerts the teacher to the learning climate in the room. By this medium he spots signs of boredom, drowsiness, fatigue, and inattention. He also uses it, as we have seen, to bring pupils back to the proper path. When an intensified glare does not bring a misbehaving pupil into line, moving toward him may do the trick.

2. *Use any opportunity to let a child know you genuinely care about him.* There are many ways in which you can let children know you care: a smile of welcome; a voiceless thank you when a child comes in during a reading group and finally remembers to close the door without slamming it enthusiastically; a "Your paper looks nice" in passing; a book you brought from the library because you have a youngster who is especially interested in the topic; public praise for the child who had the social presence to do something gracious for an unexpected guest in the room. The list is endless.

3. *Expect something positive rather than suspect something negative.* We should all build on the positive. This does not mean that we should ignore the negative but that we should always stress the positive. In a room with five rows of children, for example, if four rows are not ready for an activity when they

should be, praise can be showered on the one row that is ready. By the time you have finished praising the first row, another one will become ready. With individual misbehavior, a "I was surprised at what happened a little whole ago. That's not like you. Is there something I can help with?" will go a great deal further than a growl. With the best intentions, we often negatively reinforce the very behavior we are trying to get rid of.

4. *Make it possible for the child to do what is expected of him.* Sometimes children daydream and become oblivious to the class discussion. When this happens, a simple "Johnny," followed by a pause which allows him to respond to his name and to tune in, "which would you be more interested in working on, the chart or the mural?" will recapture him at least for the moment. The key to this tactic is to give name first and then ask a question the child can answer. If you're not sure he can answer, ask the question in a way that makes it all right if he doesn't know. ". . . do you happen to know . . .?" There are a variety of ways. The important thing is to get Johnny back in the group without a fuss.

5. *Provide psychological space for children.* Give pupils room in which to maneuver. For instance, if a child has agreed to get certain information from outside the classroom, ask him if he has had "an opportunity" or "chance" to find it, rather than, "Did you remember to get . . . ?" Nobody likes being embarrassed. If a child is treated in this way, he will learn to deal this way with other people.

If a teacher says, "I have a story to read today which I think you might like," he should know that he is offering students the choice of not liking it. If he does not intend to offer the choice, then that part of the statement should not be spoken. Everyone then must pay attention to the story which is read. If there is the choice and it turns out that students are not liking it, the story or the activity should be changed. There is nothing moral about liking or not liking a particular story or book and perhaps nothing to be gained by continuing to read a story that is not being appreciated. Although the chances are good that few students will pay close enough attention to the words the teacher uses to be able to hold him to the literal meanings of those words, all too often teachers delude themselves in their planning and activities because they fail to pay more attention to the literal meaning of what they say. If they say *interesting* and mean *interesting,* then they must plan and strive for *interesting.* They cannot claim success if their efforts or their selections were dull, boring, pedestrian, or barely tolerable.

In this context of psychological space, whenever you have been forced to use some drastic form of retribution such as detention or punitive assignments to obtain your goal, it helps to maintain the bridge of communication if you can effect a "private peace conference" as soon as possible. The purpose of the conference, of course, is to indicate that completion of the punishment assignment has cleared the air as far as you are concerned and that you intend to start with a clean slate for the offender. Even if you receive a sullen reaction temporarily, it is desirable that you indicate your willingness to meet the punished student more than halfway and to arrange for some privilege for him, such as passing out papers or being hall monitor at recess, to confirm your intention.

6. *Allow for error in yourself as well as in the children.* Many children are afraid to be wrong at considerable cost to their learning to think well. They have been so convinced of the error of wayward behavior that their capacity for guilt feelings is great. To them, *wrong* has become the opposite of *right* and *failure* the

opposite of *success*. Both bring shame and disgrace and are to be avoided at all costs. Somewhere along the line, these children perhaps have been exposed to teachers who, although well meaning, have succeeded in inhibiting some of the more sensitive from taking any kind of risk lest the effort be marked as failure. Responses to questions in class are swallowed for fear that they may be wrong; new activities are avoided lest they not fit into the realm of the acceptable.

Modifying feelings of guilt and insecurity in children of this sort will take a considerable amount of bridge building and much patience by the teacher. He must encourage students to try their wings at every opportunity, and should demonstrate that incorrect answers are not followed necessarily by negative feelings or grades. In addition, the effective teacher often demonstrates that he himself is capable of mistake and error. The example of the teacher's admitting to error can go a long way in helping children learn to cope with error in themselves. Children need help in looking at what happened and why, with an eye to preventing a reoccurrence, but it can be done in an easy, constructive way.

7. *Be willing to apologize when you are wrong.* If you have been wrong in public, apologize in public. If your error was public but you feel that the child involved would be embarrassed, do your apologizing in private. To be effective, your apology should be given without embarrassment. This enables the child to realize that the world will not collapse if he makes an error. Never, never make a child apologize unless he really means it and wants to. If he is made to apologize and doesn't mean it, he has added a flat lie to whatever error he has already committed. Many children, when they are helped to become aware of what is involved, will very genuinely apologize.

8. *Compliment whenever possible.* No matter how limited any student in the class may be, the concerned and discerning teacher can find something about which to compliment him. The important thing is to be sure that the compliment is sincere and deserved. For this reason, teachers should keep their expectations realistic. If on a ten-word spelling test, for example, a student got only four words correct, one would not ordinarily compliment him. But if a teacher recognizes that in past tests this student's highest grade had been only three and that the score of four represents the result of study and effort, a compliment to the student could be perfectly sincere and deserved and, no doubt, really appreciated.

Children generally respond very positively to compliments. Even though some can be driven through fear to try harder, many others yield to discouragement and despair when their best and most sincere efforts constantly end in disappointment and failure. The effort of the teacher should be to keep the spark of hope alive for as long as possible so that the pupils will continue to try. Nothing is gained if a child is humiliated into hopelessness. Everything within reason becomes possible if a child is complimented and is encouraged to try again and to continue trying until his efforts meet with success.

9. *Call the battles yourself.* If a student has become the class clown and will go to almost any lengths to cause a disturbance, watch for points in the lesson at which you can direct a joke toward that student or provide an opportunity for him to respond in his predictable way at a time when he will not disrupt the lesson. Although the clown is not easy to live with, his clowning is most often a bid for needed attention in the only way that the student seems to have at his command at that time. Try to remember that the demand indicates a need. Learn-

ing to provide attention on your terms can gradually tone down the clowning and meet some of the individual needs involved.

Also, examine your own teaching behavior to make sure that you have indeed been showering as much attention and affection on this child as you have on the other students. If it turns out that you are really dealing with the typical class clown, recognize that the problem may be more deep-seated than you are equipped to handle and that you may need additional specialized help. Work with the student, though, on a one-to-one basis for awhile to gain whatever insights you can into the motivating causes for his behavior. Your intention, as always, should be to build a bridge of communication that will facilitate interaction. If genuine bonds of friendship can be forged, disruptive behavior can be restrained because of the obligations imposed by the relationship. Some needs may be met by providing opportunities for leadership, going on errands, erasing the blackboard, and collecting papers. The major error to avoid is the settling in of a feeling of repugnance toward this child who has problems because he continues to be such a disconcerting influence in the class. If, by providing under controlled circumstances upon occasion a stage and spotlight for the histrionic antics of this attention seeker, a truce can be maintained so as to permit orderly classrooms, the price enacted may be small indeed.

10. *Provide a helping hand at a crucial time.* When a child says, "I won't do it," he may really mean, "I'm afraid to try because I am afraid I can't do it." The child may not be deliberately dissembling; he may, in fact, not know that he is afraid or that he is unwilling to risk finding out for sure that he is not as bright as the world expects him to be. All he feels sure of at the moment of the indignant response is that he does not intend to expose himself to hurt.

The terrible danger in this kind of situation is that the teacher who has troubles of his own may respond in rage and cause a modest issue to become a huge confrontation. Frequently, the teacher is concerned by the domino effect this defiance may have upon other potential rebels. Therefore, he intends to set the record straight so that other students will not feel free to imitate this negative behavior. In doing so, he may overreact.

When faced by situations in which pupils say, "I won't," many effective teachers try to reduce the size of the problem by taking steps toward starving off a confrontation. What these steps should be depends upon the verbal responses of the child or the state of panic to which the child has been reduced. Sometimes a short conciliatory statement will do. It might defuse the situation to say, "Very well; if you feel like doing it later, let me know. If you need help to do it, group A will be happy to work with you." If the situation has approached or reached a traumatic polarization of positions, many teachers try to remove the child from the classroom until tension can be dissipated. Subsequently, in private conference the whole situation can be reviewed. Under all circumstances, since the teacher is the adult and the trained professional, it is his responsibility to see to it that emotions are kept under control until the difficulty is resolved. Children are generally appreciative of being given a way out of the problem into which they have boxed themselves. So total, however, are some of their conclusions, values, and compulsions that even though staring into the jaws of destruction, they may be forced by some inner guide to maintain their position. They may not be able to verbalize how they feel, but their actions reveal their convictions.

11. *Sometimes it is appropriate to use forceful restraint.* General conversation about the law pertaining to restraints upon teachers concerning the laying of hands upon children leads to erroneous conclusions. The spirit of the law concerns the protection of the child from impetuous or injurious attacks by adults. It does not extend to the restraining of the child from physically injuring himself or others in his vicinity. This kind of restraint is protective, not punitive; therefore it should not include shaking or hitting. It is most effective with smaller and younger children and imprudent to use with other and stronger students, even if the teacher is strong enough to carry it off. An example of this kind of discipline might apply to the child who loses his temper and starts to pummel another child or to lift an implement with which to strike another. An appropriate technique would be to lead the attacking child away from the scene, firmly but gently, set him in another part of the room, and maintain a restraining hand upon his shoulder until the atmosphere has cleared.

12. *Use planned ignoring when appropriate.* The problem is to learn when to ignore an incident and when not to. The relatively inexperienced teacher tends to believe that he has to do something about everything or things will get out of hand. There are times, however, when just "not seeing" is the best thing you can do. If that turns out to be not the right decision, you'll find out very promptly.

13. *Have fun and laugh with the children.* Shared laughter is wonderful social glue. In addition, if a child is lacking in the ability to see fun in things, he needs help now. If you don't have a sense of humor, please go find another profession. Teaching will drive you up the wall.

14. *Avoid penalizing the entire group for the offense of one.* Penalizing the entire group is a waste of the group's time, can be embarrassing to the individual as well as to the group, and is just not fair. There may be some situations in which penalizing the group for the offense of one is necessary for some reason, but such situations should be very few. Only once in twenty-three years has the author knowingly done it. The situation was one in which the problem would never have been resolved once the students left the room. The teacher acknowledged to the students that it was unfair but indicated that no other way seemed apparent. It was resolved, but it meant keeping the entire class for a short time after the end of the period.

In addition to the resentment that mass punishment generates in students, there are other factors which should serve to steer the teacher away from this response. Principals are almost notorious for their negative reaction to this kind of discipline, because they are left in such an awkward position by stellar students who complain that they have been victimized. Parents' reactions are even more negative as a rule than that of the principal, especially if their child has had to miss the bus or a dental appointment because of being detained for an offense which someone else committed. The necessity to identify the culprit takes on a different complexion after twenty-four hours away from the difficulty. In addition, justifying your rationale to someone who was incommoded by the mass reaction is virtually impossible.

15. *Avoid confrontations.* In a confrontation, either the child or the teacher will have to lose face. In part, this type of situation is related to the problem of psychological space discussed earlier. However, in these cases, the method by which the incident is handled is much more important than the substance of the disagreement. For instance, suppose you see a child in the act of cheating on a

test. If you are absolutely certain that he is cheating, you don't ask him if he is cheating. If he is sufficiently driven to cheat, he will quite likely lie about it. Let him know that you observed him in the act, but do it in a nice way, such as, "I'm sorry about what happened during the test. That's not like you. Can you come in after three o'clock so we can talk about it?" Unless you are absolutely certain, never, never accuse. A child is defenseless against such an accusation. You can indicate what you thought you saw and give the child an opportunity to respond. Whatever his response, you should accept it. In the absence of evidence, you have no right to go further. There are many pitfalls in this confrontation area. It is most important to try to keep from making flat accusations or statements on which you cannot follow through. Probably everyone who has taught has gotten into this kind of bind at least once, but try to learn from it, and do not repeat it.

For new teachers, the problem with cheating may be the trauma associated with it in their minds. Actually, it may be profitable to look upon cheating as a positive sign, as a sign that the student still cares. The terrible time arrives when a student cares so little about whether he passes or fails that he does not bother to cheat, even when the opportunity is given to him. Such a child has abandoned all hope for success and has accustomed himself to failure.

One question the new teacher should address to himself when pupils cheat concerns the stress being placed upon cognitive memory. Is too much emphasis being placed upon the student's ability to recall facts? Other questions the teacher might ask himself concern the penalties for failing, both from the pupils' and the teacher's point of view. Has the teacher created a climate surrounding mastery of knowledge that equates inability to score well with stupidity or disaster? Has the student been led to believe that he will lose his self-respect if his score is below the norm established for the test? Does the student have the capacity to cope with the quality of the material presented for his mastery, or is he doomed to failure because the test is too difficult for him? Above all, are the expectations of the rest of the student's world, of his parents, and of his friends such that a low grade would call into question the image that he has so carefully built up in the past? When the stakes are high, cheating may seem justified. If the teacher has created a competitive classroom climate that is based upon norms for the grade or the time of the year, it may be wishful thinking for that teacher to expect test behavior that is free from attempts to cheat.

16. *Have, ready for use, an effective technique for attracting the attention of the pupils in a classroom.* The most common attention-getting technique utilized by new teachers is to raise the voice. Under normal circumstances, the raised voice is effective just as is the conspicuous entrance of the teacher to the classroom to assume his position facing the group. These acts signal the beginning of classwork and the cessation of all other activity.

Upon occasion, the noise is so great and the hubbub of activity so hectic that neither the teacher's entrance nor his raised voice suffices to bring about the desired result. More often than not, such a situation ensues after an extraordinary happening in society in general or in the more immediate world of the school playground or principal's office. Resorting to shouting so as to be heard over the din proves to be counterproductive because conversations increase in volume to be heard over the shouting.

The best deterrent to the development of uncontrolled activity is to be on hand in the classroom when the students enter. When physical presence of the teacher, alone, does not suffice, his "sixth sense" of awareness must be called upon to function overtime. Sometimes, the problem of hubbub arises gradually because, although present, the teacher is preoccupied with other things or is so completely engrossed with some children that he becomes oblivious of the actions of the rest. When something happens to cause him to become aware, the situation may have progressed far beyond the norm and be approaching the uncontrolled. Under these circumstances, the effective teacher heads off the problem by walking toward the misbehaving group and issuing instructions.

When the noise and confusion have already generated a head of steam by the time the teacher enters, more dramatic actions are required. Some teachers accustom their students to respond to summer camp techniques used to command the attention of the group—raising the right hand, or both hands and "flashing the finger signal," opening and closing the fingers. Other teachers have found that by taking the most conspicuous position available, facing the students, and silently mouthing directions or instruction, they can capitalize upon the *ripple* effect. As the students not engaged in the hubbub become aware of the actions of the teacher, they will solicit silence from their nearest companions so that they can hear what the teacher is saying. As the volume of students' chatter subsides, the teacher increases his volume until he has everyone's attention.

17. *Encourage students to seek the reasons behind what they are required or requested to do.* When school policies or classroom procedures are well formulated, knowing the background of the policy often insures that students will honor them in daily practice.

A crucial aspect of discipline is a sensitivity to the social consequences of one's actions and a deliberate orientation of one's behavior toward the promotion of the social good. Unfortunately, classroom discipline is frequently pitched at the level of irrational conformity, in which the child respects certain standards not because of their desirability but simply because of mechanical adherence to a rule. True discipline is based on an understanding of what constitutes appropriate behavior and why, and on a positive valuing of such behavior as an integral part of the self, rather than on mere conformity to external standards.

When policies or class regulations have been poorly made or when the needs of students have changed while the rules have remained constant, excessive turmoil can be expected. It is easy at such times to turn your class into a debating session and for you to find yourself engaged in public argument with your students. On many occasions teachers have been trapped into public argument in the classroom about such things as a grade on a paper, a homework assignment, or the scheduling of a test. It is generally a mistake to take the bait under the delusion that the rationales presented to one objecting student will be a good learning opportunity for the others. Debating such matters tends to create opposition where none existed before, to alienate the student who has been overruled, and to solidify into an opposition group students who previously were neutral. The drive for the student to save face may embolden him to take liberties that he would not have taken had the argument occurred in private. The impulse of the teacher to also save face can lead him into committing himself publicly to a course of action which he would never have espoused had the forum for discussion been less exposed.

It is commendable to create the atmosphere of class discussion on serious items, but the skillful teacher avoids being jockeyed into the vulnerable spot of having to defend his position. Instead, he conducts this discussion similar to all others, eliciting supporting opinion, giving the opposition a chance, calling for time deferment to facilitate the collection of further data, scheduling time for further talk, and speaking in private to those with the most intense feelings on the topic. The positive effects that the skillful teacher seeks are the realization of each student that he can succeed and that rules which unnecessarily impede him may be changed if cause can be shown. The negative effects he strives to avoid are being forced to fall back upon his status position to enforce a bad rule, using the bludgeon of bad grades to coerce opposers to conform, or taking unfair advantage of his opponent in the argument because of the latter's inability to express himself. Winning a battle only to lose the war is not a productive approach in any classroom.

18. *When misbehavior begins to assume large proportions, it may be wise to isolate the offender from the group until the situation has been resolved.* This situation is probably the most traumatic for the preservice teacher to contemplate because it seems to be so loaded with pitfalls and so many opportunities for error. But, although it is true that some occasions may be distressing, it must be remembered that they are not the usual mode of classroom action and should be kept in perspective.

The major thought to be kept in mind pertaining to incidents of exceptional misbehavior is that all of the facilities, routines, and organizational designs are theoretically implemented to support the action taken. You may learn from the experienced teacher, for example, that the principal does not appreciate teachers who send students from the class. What they intend to say is that when a serious case arises, no teacher should hesitate to have recourse to the authority of the school leader, but that not every or even many of the cases which arise in normal circumstances should reach these proportions. Errors will be made, and indeed are expected, early in a teacher's career when newcomers are not thoroughly familiar with the hierarchy of seriousness. Administrative dissatisfactions generally do not set in until errors of judgment persist long after the learning period should be over, indicating that the teacher is unable to exercise appropriate control or is unwilling to expend the effort and judgment necessary to attend to the offending conduct.

Generally, each school will have established routines to follow when student behavior calls for exclusion from the classroom. Some will require that no child be sent to the principal's office without sending another child to accompany him. Other schools will require that the teacher send no student without supplying him with a note, explaining the cause for his banishment. In general, however, it is prudent to remove an excited or aroused student from a volatile situation even if all the specifications are not followed to the letter to prevent the situation from becoming worse and also to provide the student, the class, and the teacher an opportunity to think over the whole situation before official action is taken.

The ultimate nightmare may materialize upon occasion when some larger than usual child has become disruptive and responds with "I won't" when you direct him to go to the principal's office. Prudence dictates in such a situation, as with the petulant child who refuses to respond, that a messenger be dispatched to request a visit by the principal to your room. If the principal cannot be found, send the messenger for one of the more experienced teachers who will help to resolve the situation.

At the beginning of this module, it was indicated that the ideas involved in good discipline are fairly simple. It was our intention to predispose you to *catch your students being good*. The problem is that light, positive, and effective ideas are not easy to implement. If you know your children well, if you understand the basic ideas involved in good discipline, if you watch carefully to see what your classroom behavior and planning do to the students and then modify your behavior and planning accordingly, you will be well started on your way toward good classroom discipline.

SUGGESTED READING

Collier, Calhoun C., Robert W. Houston, Robert R. Schmatz, and William J. Walsh. *Modern Elementary Education: Teaching and Learning.* New York: Macmillan Publishing Co., Inc., 1976.

Gnagy, William J. *Maintaining Discipline in Classroom Instruction.* New York: Macmillan Publishing Co., Inc., 1975.

Gnagy, William J. *The Psychology of Discipline in the Classroom.* New York: Macmillan Publishing Co., Inc., 1968.

Jarolimek, John, and Clifford D. Foster. *Teaching and Learning in the Elementary School.* New York: Macmillan Publishing Co., Inc., 1976.

Kounin, Jacob S. *Discipline and Group Management.* New York: Holt, Rinehart & Winston, Inc., 1970.

McDonald, Blanche, and Leslie Nelson. *Successful Classroom Control.* Dubuque, Iowa: William C. Brown Company, Publishers, 1959.

Madsen, Charles H., Jr., and Clifford K. Madsen. *Teaching Discipline: Behavioral Principles Toward a Positive Approach.* Boston: Allyn & Bacon, Inc., 1970.

Meacham, Merle L., and Allen E. Wilson. *Changing Classroom Behavior: A Manual for Precision Teaching.* Scranton, Pa.: Intext, Inc., 1970.

Rubin, Louis J. *Facts and Feelings in the Classroom.* New York: Walker, 1973.

Schuster, Albert H., and Milton E. Ploghoft. *The Emerging Elementary Curriculum: Methods and Procedures.* Columbus, Ohio: Charles E. Merrill Publishers, 1970.

Sylvester, Robert. *Common Sense in Classroom Relations.* West Nyack, N.Y.: Parker Publishing Co., Inc., 1966.

POST TEST

1. In a short paragraph, describe how timing functions in relation to the sort of pupil misbehavior that is part of the growing up experience.

_____

_____

_____

_____

_____

_____

_____

_____

2. Describe what is meant by making "the punishment fit the crime."

_____

_____

_____

_____

_____

_____

_____

3. In a sentence, describe what research has shown about the effect on students of repressive action in the classroom.

_____

_____

4. Cite at least three signals you could establish as standard operating procedure in your classroom for gaining attention when students are noisy.

_____

_____

_____

5. Describe how you might behave so as to recapture the attention of a day-dreamer, without causing a fuss.

_____

_____

_____

6. Cite three of the five actions listed in this module for you to take to help control behavior by your proximity.

_____

_____

_____

7. Write a short paragraph about the "laying on of hands" method of controlling student behavior. In your answer, specify what the intent of the law is and the latitude permitted.

_____

_____

_____

_____

_____

_____

8. Describe in two sentences how teachers improperly exploit their position to the detriment of class climate in their attempts at humor.

_____

_____

_____

_____

_____

_____

_____

9. What is offered in this module as the single best preventative to misbehavior in the classroom?

_____

_____

10. Describe the role played by mutual respect in establishing good classroom control.

_____

_____

_____

_____

_____

11. Should you force a child to apologize? Why? Why not?

_____

_____

_____

_____

12. Specify three things you can do in handling the class clown.

_____

_____

_____

_____

_____

_____

13. What simple response might a teacher make to a child who says, "I won't do it!" so as to avoid a real confrontation?

_____

_____

14. Why is it unwise to penalize the entire group for the offense of one? Cite five reasons for your explanation.

_____

_____

_____

_____

_____

15. In the event of cheating, (a) what should your action be toward the child? and (b) toward yourself as a teacher?

_____

_____

_____

_____

_____

_____

_____

_____

_____

_____

_____

16. When students begin to debate about the policies or rules of the school, (a) what action should you take? and (b) what should you avoid?

_____

_____

_____

_____

_____

_____

_____

17. Should you ever send an offender to the principal? Why? Why not?

_____

_____

_____

_____

18. Is seeking help from experienced confreres a sign of weakness? Why? Why not?

_____

_____

_____

19. Give at least two situations that might permit a teacher to change the time for an announced test.

_____

_____

_____

_____

20. Explain why it is productive even though time-consuming to include the entire class in establishing the class rules.

_____

_____

_____

_____

21. What is meant by the compromise position between consistency and fairness?

_____

_____

_____

_____

_____

_____

_____

_____

22. Specify when the thunderstorm technique can be more effective than the drizzle technique.

_____

_____

_____

_____

_____

_____

23. Explain why the "big gun" should be used sparingly.

_____

_____

_____

_____

24. Name three ways in which you can establish the "catch them being good" climate in the classroom.

_____

_____

_____

25. Explain why discipline by recipe is not possible.

_____

_____

_____

_____

_____

_____

Control and Management

Joseph F. Callahan

Jersey City State College

module 6

Need for Skill in Controlling / Goals of Control / Definition of Control / Role of Interest / Place of Group Unity / Self-Discipline / General Suggestions Regarding Climate / Specific Techniques / Trouble Spots / When a Problem Develops / Causes of Discipline Problems / Teaching Appropriate Behavior / Children with Problems

RATIONALE

In preservice teacher education classes, it is interesting to note the feelings of insecurity expressed by the students related to the management and control of public school classes. Very few students seem to feel insecure about methodology. Apparently, they have sat through hundreds of class sessions without becoming aware of the myriad methodological problems faced by their teachers. All they seem to remember of their teachers' teaching methods is that someone stood up there and taught. They do not appear to worry about their mastery of their teaching content areas either or about their ability to adjust their vocabulary to the level of the children. Nor do they seem to have misgivings about how bright, scholarly, current or well read they are. Generally they evidence little doubt about their capacity for making classes interesting, evidently visualizing themselves as achieving where others have failed. They appear confident that they can catch the imagination of the students, that their students will like them, and that they will be able to establish the intellectual climate so necessary to achieve proper rapport with their students.

But they are worried about their ability to establish and maintain control in their classes. They seem to have little faith in their ability to manage the group, to control an obstreperous class, or to handle difficult children.

In this module, we will focus on some of the ways to respond in the important situations that you may have to face in the future. Our aim is to dissipate some of the fears about management and control which may haunt you. Of course, it will not be possible to discuss a major portion of the varieties of control problems which you could face, but we hope to help you become aware of some of the ways of working with students that have proved successful for others. You will have to adapt these guidelines or principles to make your own so that you can apply them in your own way to the classroom groups you will teach. As you become skillful in applying these principles, you will become comfortable with your students and your students with you.

SPECIFIC OBJECTIVES

Upon the completion of your study of this module, you should be able to do the following:

1. Describe why individualization of instruction will eliminate most control problems.
2. Cite the goals for controlling a classroom.
3. Define control.
4. Point out the differences between control in the traditional classroom and control in the contemporary classroom.
5. Cite some of the elements of good control.

6. Describe the meaning of climate in the classroom.
7. Explain the role of interest in maintaining control.
8. Describe the role of group unity in establishing control.
9. Cite six of the nine suggestions given for developing group unity.
10. Describe the role of self-discipline in developing control.
11. List the twelve suggestions given for establishing rapport with your class.
12. Describe what class standards are, and explain how to establish them.
13. Mention the six procedures established by effective teachers for getting classes started on time.
14. Describe the role of furniture in maintaining control.
15. Explain how illumination and ventilation can affect control.
16. Write a paragraph defending your position on the use of cumulative records to learn about past history of students.
17. Describe four ways in which seatwork can be used to contribute positively to successful control.
18. Explain why sitting at the teacher's desk can interfere with control.
19. Cite the three things a teacher might do when he detects an incipient control problem.
20. Name eight of the twelve specific techniques described for responding which will help to insure maintenance of control.
21. List three ways for getting the attention of a noisy class other than trying to outshout them.
22. Describe the "choreography of the dare."
23. Describe the major defect resulting from inexperience which contributes to loss of control.
24. Explain how a desire for popularity can contribute to loss of control.
25. Cite six of the eight things that good planners do so as to limit loss of control.
26. Compare learning to control one's action to the act of learning kickball.
27. Explain why the docile, conforming child needs the attention of the teacher even though he does not disrupt the class with raucous behavior.

MODULE TEXT

Need for Skill in Controlling

The realization that the teaching situation in schools is fundamentally artificial comes as a jolt to most beginning teachers. But if it were not so, there would be little need to discuss classroom control in a module such as this.

In general, when a single child works with a single adult on a topic of interest to the child, there is no problem of control. Then the two converse naturally, fluently, and informatively without conflict. But when we organize for formal instruction in a school, trouble begins. Instead of just one captivated child, the teacher faces twenty-five or more children together. Instead of interesting items generated from the child's own concerns, the topics for instruction are remote matters selected by unknown adults. The wonder is not that every classroom contains within it the seeds of disruption, but that the majority of teachers reach such a high level of classroom control and management with such apparent ease. Perhaps at some distant time in the future when the present trend towards individualization of instruction becomes a reality in every school, the factor of control may cease to be of significant importance. When that time arrives, instruction will take into consideration the differences in children, and so provide for their individual needs and interests that the artificiality now connected with classroom audiences, compelled to follow a curriculum laid out for them willy-nilly, will become a thing of the past.

Until that day, though, both experienced and beginning teachers must master the problems of establishing and maintaining control. To state it bluntly, mastery of the techniques which contribute to your ability to manage your class skillfully becomes a matter for survival. Learn as much as you can through reading and study. Practice your techniques every time the opportunity presents itself. Observe skilled professional teachers in the act of controlling and managing as often as you can. Attempt to resolve in your own mind the course of action you would follow if the misbehavior that you see were to occur in your classroom, and then contrast your conclusions with the action taken by the teacher observed. In short, try in every way you can to become knowledgeable and expert at classroom management and control. It is important.

Goals of Control

Control in the classroom refers, among other things, to the creation of a classroom atmosphere free from disruptions. Ideal control will result in complete attention to the instruction at hand. Although at times it may be necessary for the teacher to exert outside influence to control the class, the main goal of effective control is to produce self-disciplined citizens who assume independent responsibility for their own behavior.

Good discipline promotes efficient learning. It helps to develop positive attitudes and provides for a two-way exchange between students and teacher. By his treatment of students and his humanitarian attitudes, the skillful teacher elicits respect. In turn, he makes it evident that he respects the students. As a result, each is able to see the intrinsic worth of the other, and each benefits from the contribution that the other makes to the learning experience.

Without adequate control, no class can be a success. Good control makes successful teaching possible. In effect, then, disciplinary measures are helpful and valuable teaching tools that may make the difference between successful or unsuccessful instruction.

Definition of Control

But what is good control? In years past, control connoted repression of physical activity, punishment, or rigid rules of student behavior. It was basically autocratic rather than democratic. This concept of control justified the imposition of rules and regulations without consultation with those who would be governed by them and the utilization of punishments and rewards that were only remotely related to the larger goals of education. The immediate goal of paying attention, for example, was sought by teachers and prescribed by supervisors often at the expense of the greater goals of student self-control, peer cooperation, and the exercise of good judgment.

Many modern theorists no longer hold these notions concerning the definition of control. Instead, they emphasize providing leadership in helping pupils to establish self-control. In this new milieu, the student is expected to control himself because he wishes to do so or sees the wisdom of doing so, and the class group is expected to give its complete attention to the task at hand with very little interference from adult authority. Such behavior is learned behavior and, if this type of control is to succeed, the teacher sees to it that every child learns it. When children catch the spirit of this type of control, it will give them the intrinsic motivation necessary for a learning environment. Theoretically at least, it will also eliminate the necessity for leveling penalties on offenders who callously disregard the learning rights of others.

This type of control is based upon an understanding of children and of the developmental stages they pass through. It embraces the democratic processes connected with group discussion plus incisive teacher-leader action when conditions require directive behavior. Prerequisites for its success are sound judgment on the part of the teacher and a feel for the critical moment, both of which one must develop over a period of time. Teachers can facilitate their mastery of these prerequisites by gathering as much specific information about each member of the class group as the office files can yield and by the observation of as much student interaction in small and large group situations as time permits. Becoming sensitive to the internal and external forces that motivate student actions will help to support one's judgments even though it must be understood that decisions arrived at will not always be scientifically accurate. Mastery of the processes and techniques will not eliminate the existence of all classroom problems, but it should help in the creation and maintenance of a healthy classroom climate.

The climate in any classroom is the consequence of this impact of the many personalities involved in the structure of the class. It consists of the spirit that emerges after the group has begun to operate. This spirit surrounds everyone in the room and conditions the kind of interaction that will take place. Every individual in the class brings with him a multitude of characteristics when he joins the class and, consequently, he sways the development of the group in one way or another by the facets of his personality which he reveals. The teacher, for example, who displays in this interaction a concern for students, who notices and comments upon George's neatness of appearance, or John's careful writing on homework papers, or Helen's contribution of seed for the class parakeet reveals a humaneness that other teachers may not feel. A teacher's demeanor, gentleness of voice, and comments might well lead his students to respond favorably in return for the confidence he shows in their ability. As for the children in the class, one child who is extremely unstable may so adversely affect the others as to make it necessary to structure activities when he is present in a group much more cautiously than would otherwise be necessary.

The successful teacher is constantly aware of the individual differences among his students. Not only is he conscious of their differences one from another, but also he trains himself to take note of their changes from hour to hour or day to day. What is exciting to one child may be dull to another. What generates enthusiasm on Monday morning may be boring on Friday afternoon. Consequently, a teacher knows that the quest for the most profitable environment becomes never-ending, because he knows that no matter how smooth things are at the moment very shortly the winds of change will blow in new, potentially disrupting variations. He also knows that his desire for the ideal must be tempered by patience and by a recognition of the slow pace of improvement and maturation. Therefore, he focuses regularly on enhancing the physical surroundings, enlivening the intellectual atmosphere, tempering the emotional tone, and loosening the social structure so that the resulting climate will foster the optimum growth for all students.

Role of Interest

Undoubtedly the best prescription for the establishment of classroom control is to make each period highly interesting. Adults as a rule act as though pupils were eager seekers of learning, whereas actually they are but members of a captive audience. Although children can be eager educational consumers when properly stimulated and motivated, no teacher should assume that such positive attitudes will typify any class unless he plans to achieve them and then teaches skillfully. In spite of the fact that students stand to profit from their classroom instruction, it is up to the teacher to create the interest necessary if classes are to be productive.

In the traditional schools of former days, teachers paid less attention to the motivational role of interest. To them, interest was irrelevant or even undesirable. Although the children undoubtedly desired freedom, it was the job of teachers to make sure they did not get it. To maintain this kind of control, the child was threatened with the promise of failing grades, or physically thrashed, or denied promotion. Recent research has pointed to the lack of economy of this kind of control. It requires much costly supervision to make it work, and in the end results in very little permanent improvement in the pupils' behavior. Marching in line when moving about the school, enforced sitting still in rows, and insistence upon uniform quiet for each class evidently have little carry-over value as demonstrated by the pandemonium that ensues as soon as the supervision is removed. Seemingly, teacher-dominated children lack the opportunity to master either group or self-control and hence never learn to discipline themselves.

In the world of the 1970s, the action of forces outside of the school focuses great attention upon the need for interesting, peppy classes. By the time children are eligible for admission to kindergarten, they have already been exposed to more theatrical and dramatic presentations through television than many of their teachers have seen in their lifetime. As a consequence, the modern teacher is almost coerced into becoming a showman of sorts so as to remain competitive.

Place of Group Unity

The modern theory of control encourages teachers to develop self-directed children. It emphasizes freedom for the child to make his own decisions rather than strict group conformity to inflexible rules of behavior. In this view, control is not something to be imposed on the pupils but, for the most part, is an achievement of each individual. Many laymen confuse this modern approach with license and caricature the contemporary school as a place in which children do just as they please with no regard for others. But such is not the case. It is freedom and liberty that teachers attempt to cultivate, while rejecting chaos and anarchy as both repulsive and unproductive. The group activities are designed to elicit discussion and cooperative effort. In these enterprises, the children are expected not only to contribute their thinking but also to accept responsibility for the success of the undertaking. One of the purposes in freeing the child to make choices as to his course of action is to bring him face to face with genuine responsibility. For example, if a committee of children has accepted responsibility for building a pen for the class rabbit which is to arrive on Friday, the pen must be ready or the entire class will have to forfeit, at least temporarily, the presence of the expected guest.

When a group decision is reached, the individual child is not free to decide whether or not he will abide by the decision. In a well-disciplined classroom, many decisions will be made by the entire group in a democratic manner. In this process, each child will be encouraged to present evidence and to express opinions. When the decision is reached, however, either by common consent or by vote, each child will be obligated to live by the agreement until new agreements have been reached. The teacher's role is to provide areas of choice in which decisions may be made by the entire group, to arrange and to guide democratic processes, and then to share responsibility for translating the decision into action. Children must learn that the privilege of making group decisions is accompanied by responsibility for making the decisions work, as our example of the classroom rabbit points out.

In situations in which no choice is permissible, students must learn to do as the teacher or principal or parent directs. The second grader, for example, is not permitted an option about how to leave the school building when a fire drill is announced. He must learn that in many areas of living, at specified times, there is no option except to obey. As the fifth-grade student must cross at the corner where the crossing guard is stationed and not in-between, so must the adult park his car where the signs indicate that parking is permitted and avoid driving the wrong way on a one-way street.

Although it seems desirable to allow each student as much freedom of choice as possible, certain natural tendencies must be controlled. Primary-grade children, for example, are normally inclined to be active. Yet they must learn to control their activity in the classroom. Older students may have no intrinsic interest in some subjects but, because learning is hierarchical, it will be necessary to require them to study some things they might not choose if left to their own inclinations.

The following suggestions indicate some of the ways to develop group unity:

1. Plan with children in such a way that they are responsible as a group for putting their plans into action.
2. Share leadership in such ways that group leadership rather than individual domination results and is valued.
3. Provide such socially useful work experience that group pride in accomplishment is achieved.
4. Share curriculum experiences with other groups of children and adults in such ways that your group, rather than the individual child, achieves recognition.
5. Guide children in the decoration and care of their classroom so that they, as a group, are proud of their school home.

6. Utilize trips, games, choral reading, and assembly programs in ways that foster group cooperation.
7. Use committee work to extend social group feeling.
8. Plan and use with the children evaluation techniques that help them improve group socialization rather than promote destructive competition.
9. Teach children to want each member of the class to do well because the group is proud of his successes.[1]

Self-Discipline

This achievement of group unity is a tall order that few beginners are able to fill. Until you master the artistry, you should search for techniques and suggestions that will result in a properly disciplined classroom in which rules are reasonable and in which they are so well accepted by the children that violations are comparatively rare.

It is important to remember that there will be individual differences in self-control abilities, just as there will be differences in the ability to learn at certain rates of speed. A person is not completely disciplined until he can control himself from within and intelligently accept the role of obedience to appropriate outside authority. To help the child reach this point of development, the teacher must give him the room to participate in judgment making, but only the room commensurate with his age and development and only in those situations in which there is a reasonable expectancy that he can make an acceptable decision. The teacher must assume his share of responsibility for the action ultimately taken by the children and must establish at the outset the boundaries within which they will be forced to work. Most children will need help in making choices and facing the consequences of their actions.[2] The pupil who tries hard but whose conduct is not completely up to standards set by the teacher and the pupils may benefit far more from understanding than from punishment. The teacher must help such a child with analyzing mistakes and with replanning that promises to lead to more satisfying results. Once freedom is given within the guidelines, however, it should not be withdrawn unless the welfare of the child demands it. It is not subject to the whim of the teacher. A group decision, such as going outside to play instead of doing calisthenics in the room during the recess period, can be changed by edict of the teacher when really necessary, such as if rain should start, for instance, so as to protect the health of the children.

General Suggestions Regarding Climate

Teachers largely control opportunities for children to create for themselves the kind of school world that has in it little fear and tension and much security. If children learn only to stay out of the teacher's way and to hide their problems, then there is little hope of the school's contributing constructively to their emotional

[1] James B. Burr, Lowry W. Harding, and Leland B. Jacobs, *Student Teaching in the Elementary School,* 2nd Ed. (New York: Appleton-Century-Crofts, 1958), p. 211.
[2] Robert F. Biehler, *Psychology Applied to Teaching,* 2nd Ed. (Boston: Houghton Mifflin Company, 1974), p. 699.

adjustment. The following suggestions may be helpful to you in establishing the necessary rapport and classroom climate with the children whom you teach:

1. Be friendly, but not familiar. Children prefer you to be a sympathetic, kindly adult. They may respond to a teacher's manner, his gestures, his facial expressions, and his silences as much as they do to his words. Operate on the assumption, until convinced otherwise, that each student wants to do the right thing and to succeed.

2. Take into account with each class the separate maturational level of each student and the group level possible with such a composite of students. It is an error to assume that all children aged ten will reveal identical characteristics and that all groups of twelve-year-olds will function at the same level of maturity. Make every effort to match the educational activities you plan to use with the maturity and ability levels so that tasks that are too difficult do not infect the group with feelings of panic. Many students give up very easily, or they become seriously disorganized, or they undergo severe feelings of guilt when they are not able to live up to standards prescribed by the teacher.

3. Strive for consistency of professional behavior in yourself so that students can develop a system for responding to you. Strictness followed by laxity tends to confuse children and to retard their progress toward relaxed self-control.

4. Remind yourself daily that as a professional worker you are obligated to keep considerations extraneous to student learning out of your classroom behavior. Even when you do not feel chipper you must reveal the positive aspects of your temperament and guard against communicating negative attitudes or effects. The problems of your personal world and the worries connected with your career world should be controlled so as not to influence the learning efforts of students who have no control over your life. The most successful teacher in this regard merits the nickname of "the happy schizophrenic." When he enters his classroom, he leaves his own troubles behind and, in a positive frame of mind, he assumes the worries of all his students. He likes schoolwork and cultivates his interest in it and in his students. He is conscious of the moods of his students and seeks for their cause so he can help to dissipate them as he has dissipated his own. His emphasis is on the "can do" part of learning. He radiates the confidence that will infect all of his students to that positive point of view. His sense of humor permits him to treat many potential problems with a light touch and to turn slights aside instead of internalizing and magnifying them. The classroom is made into a friendly place, a nice place to be, and where things are happening.

5. Create an atmosphere in which each student feels free to be himself and free to let you see him be himself. He does not feel compelled to do things contrary to his nature, cheat to get high grades, or disown his friends, so as to secure your attention or to hold your esteem. With many students, you may have to work hard to fend off the development of guilt feelings and fears of failure which crop up to inhibit their freedom and joy. Your job will be to work with each child in such a way that his energies are released and his peace of mind is strengthened.

6. Take time to listen to children's questions, problems, joys, and hopes so you may contribute as needed and when requested. Treat their confidences clinically and confidentially, and try to insure an equal opportunity for each child to your private ear and solicitude. Recognize, of course, that with some your problem will consist of getting them to talk; with others, the problem will be to "turn them off." Every child has a tendency to feel secure once he has established an un-

assailable position as a member of the group. This feeling of security will continue as long as his sense of belonging is not made to depend upon some single factor, such as his intelligence, his racial characteristics, his family's social position in the community, or his physical attractiveness. He belongs because, as he is, he is important and valued by those with whom he lives and learns.

7. Demonstrate that you genuinely enjoy being with your students and your class, rather than that you just tolerate or endure them because it is part of your job. This demonstration should come about very naturally. If you have to work too hard at it, because your general feeling is one of distaste, you might reexamine yourself to make sure that you have not selected the wrong career. Each student should know that he can see you before school in the morning or after school in the afternoon to receive extra help with lessons or with personal problems.

8. Carefully avoid setting up odious comparisons between the work or the behavior of one child or group and that of others. Most children are extremely vulnerable to the taunts, sarcasms, and jibes of the others, but they are, at the same time, often more than willing to indulge in the "pecking" destruction of someone less fortunate than they.

9. Praise generously to accentuate the positiveness of the climate while you concentrate on maintaining your perspective regarding success. The child who gets three right out of ten on a weekly test can be legitimately praised for improvement if his usual score is only one or two right, but under normal conditions claiming a tremendous breakthrough for such a child might communicate a lack of sincerity.

10. Above all, keep patient with children's regressions. Expect and look for improvement but recognize that backsliding sets in quickly and often without apparent cause.

11. Assign many of the routine administrative tasks to students. Such jobs, for example, as distributing materials, collecting money, recording pupils' absences, or graphing achievements may be easily delegated to pupils. Not only does the delegation give the leader time to attend to other important matters, but also the experience of participating has value in itself for the student. The most skillful teachers arrange monitor jobs for almost all their students so that none get overlooked. Sometimes the same jobs are assigned to a team of two students to make for continuity in case of absence. In these cases, one student functions in the morning session and the other in the afternoon. This gives more students a share in the functioning of the class and a feeling that the class is theirs. The development of this social feeling is, after all, one of the ultimate objectives of all teaching.

12. Plan such matters as returning test papers or marking of daily assignments so as to minimize confusion. It is best to arrange papers for easy distribution, by rows, by aisles, or by cluster groupings rather than to return them haphazardly with all the movement, chatter, and confusion that accompanies random procedures.

Specific Techniques

Setting Classroom Standards. Although the teacher must strive continually to understand children as individuals and to keep himself aware of their differences, one from another, his daily direct contact with them will be primarily through the group. One-to-one relations with any child will probably be brief and certainly less frequent than relations with him as a member of the class. Even in group-work situations, however, the teacher must conceive his role primarily as that of coordinating the efforts of individuals.

As our earlier discussion of group unity should have made clear, good group work does not just happen. It has to be planned for, nurtured, encouraged, and developed. It thrives best in an atmosphere in which an insightful teacher works with children in creative ways to foster mastery of the skills he is teaching. It becomes possible only if the teacher has command of some of the multitude of techniques that have been perfected for managing classroom situations.

One of these techniques is the cooperative development of classroom standards. The group is first led to recognize that

a. To protect life and limb of all students, in times of emergency, such as during a fire drill or during a bomb scare, no deviation from the standard operating procedure can be tolerated. The established regulations must be followed as decreed.

b. When administrative decisions have not been issued, class discussions can be permitted about the need for regulations and the form they should follow. The standard once settled upon, although limiting to the freedom of everyone, will nevertheless become the governor of the actions of all members of the group. Having established this base, an effective teacher may then help his class evolve a *Chart of Specific Classroom Standards* which will be posted in a conspicuous place in the classroom.[3]

Classroom Standards
1. We know that there is a place for everything, and everything should be in its place.
2. We respect the rights of others by
   a. treating their belongings with care.
   b. never going through their desks.
3. We laugh *with* people and not *at* people.
4. We share our things, especially when they help the whole group.
5. We realize that a good sport
   a. puts up (with inconveniences).
   b. owns up (if wrong).
   c. shuts up (if his talk injures others).
6. We follow the voice rule by
   a. having "no voice" when someone else is talking.
   b. having a quiet voice during work periods, art periods, and committee meetings.
   c. having a loud voice on the playground only.
7. We never criticize the clothes, appearance, home, family, race, nationality, or religion of other boys and girls.
8. We may criticize the way they *do* or *do not* follow our classroom standards.
9. We know that when the teacher says "My turn," it means "Stop, look, and listen."

Standards such as these are simple and clear. Because they have been arrived at through discussion in a democratic fashion, they invite children to show their

[3] Blanche McDonald and Leslie Nelson, *Successful Classroom Control* (Dubuque, Iowa: William C. Brown Company, Publishers, 1959), p. 8.

loyalty and responsibility to the group of which they are a part and to view the standards as their own doing.

It is important that only a few classroom standards be made at any one time to avoid overwhelming the children. As more are needed, new standards can be added. However the timing of the introduction of new standards is important. The teacher should make sure that the previous standards are fairly well in hand before additions are discussed. For example, at the beginning of the school year, perhaps only the crucial and most disturbing parts of the school day, the beginning, after recess, or at dismissal time, should merit attention as special standards. When the year has been well started and patterns of behavior have been established for critical moments during the day, the focus may shift to other important aspects of classroom life. Gradually, standards such as the following can be added to the list.

10. How to exit from the classroom:
    Keep our hands to ourselves.
    Control volume of voice while enroute to the playground.
    Keep the rules of polite society in mind about letting others go ahead.
11. "The Rule of 30":
    When one person acts alone, he may not need to exercise great care. (A student whistles in the hallway.)
    When 30 people, or a large number, try to do the same thing at the same time, many problems can result. (All students in the class whistle.)
    Consequently, we shall exercise greater self-control when participating with a group or with the entire class.
12. Any additional standard may be spelled out.

A basic consideration in carrying out this procedure is that class standards cannot be legislated by some higher authority if group self-control is the objective; nor can they be established by making critical comments about student action or by casting aspersions upon the values of the families of the children contributing to the chaos. Such actions merely arouse hostilities and encourage lack of student cooperation. Success is more likely to follow if the reasonableness and workability of the standards have been established through the democratic process and implementation encouraged rather than mandated by authoritarian fiat. Whenever there are transgressions against the group-adopted standards, a private conference should ensue. Together, the teacher and the offending pupils should analyze the nature of the misconduct, examine why the offending conduct is not permitted, and agree upon procedures for the future when similar circumstances may prompt additional deviations. Should it turn out that a particular regulation tempts transgression because it has been poorly devised, or is ambiguous, or imposes a greater burden on some students than on others, the discussion should be opened to the entire class for reconsideration and, perhaps, change.

Starting on Time. Good planning provides for getting class started without delay. Unprepared teachers and confused teachers, who do not organize their work, contribute greatly to their own failure to achieve by not opening the class with dispatch. Each new day in the class can develop into a time of buzzing and moving confusion and noisy, aimless activity, or downright mischief unless the teacher plans such confusion out of existence.

The first five minutes of the period set the tone for any class. Ineffective teachers are inclined to squander these minutes and often are doomed to spend the rest of the period and sometimes the rest of the day trying to regain control. They permit students to cluster about them, to make requests, and to delay their taking action until the noise swells to drown out the sound of the starting bell or the voice of the teacher. Effective teachers, on the other hand, establish some or all of the following procedures to insure starting with control:

1. After recess, or whenever students are returning to the classroom from special periods for music or physical education, these teachers stand by the door to indicate that a change of behavior may now be necessary. The loud conversation, the playful tagging, and the potential fighting and arguing are screened out at the door, since they will not be conducive to the achievement of the instructional goals of the upcoming period.

2. The materials to be used during this class have been prepared, collected, and arranged for easy distribution. The return of the class triggers the distribution of materials routine, inaugurated in the early days of the school year, with the monitors for the week discharging their responsibilities.

3. Row monitors or small group captains who respond for the entire group are used to eliminate disruptive behavior during roll taking. Work assignments for the period are written on the board before the students enter so they will have something to begin to work on at once. Ditto sheets, containing instructions for simple tasks described so adequately as to require no oral explanation, also encourage a businesslike atmosphere. The situation that effective teachers try to avoid is keeping the entire class sitting idly by while they call roll or while assignments are put on the board. Students who have questions to ask are expected to be seated and to raise their hand until the teacher calls their name or reaches their desk to respond to the question.

4. Effective teachers make sure they are in their classrooms before the students arrive. Teachers who dawdle elsewhere encourage tardiness among the students and alienate fellow faculty members in adjacent rooms who may be forced to quell rising disturbances. Punctuality at the beginning of the day is not something to be treated lightly. Wise teachers anticipate transportation problems and allow themselves enough time to provide for error and for unexpected delays.

5. Procedures have been established for sharpening the pencil, leaving the room for the lavatory and returning, running an errand to other parts of the building, or being excused to leave for the day. For collecting papers and assignments, the most expeditious procedure often used is for the last student in each row to walk forward, collecting as he goes. Passing papers up a row often causes confusion, noise, and delay. In addition, there are also established procedures for emergencies, for when the teacher must leave the room, when a substitute teacher takes over the class, or when a child becomes sick and needs attention from the teacher.

6. Goals exist for each sequence of instruction as well as for activities which will help move the class toward the goals. Beginning teachers sometimes make the error of underplanning and find themselves with embarrassing "dead time" on their hands. Experienced teachers use a special "tickler file" which contains interesting, highly motivating things to do when only a few minutes are available before beginning something new or dismissing for the day.

The Classroom. No matter what the appearance of the room in which your class will meet, you should set about to exploit all its potential and, by dint of your effort, make it as positive an educative force as your imagination, energy, and time will permit. As you work within the space limitations imposed upon you, you will need to settle upon how best to organize the seating, how to get the most open space for interest centers, activity areas, room library, and science corner. At the same time, you must attend to the functional problem of storage of materials and equipment so they are available when needed but not bottlenecks when not needed.

COLOR AND AESTHETICS. Even though the room has limitations, it should be tastefully and colorfully decorated, at least in those areas in which you are free to work; its appearance should encourage children in their learning and inspire happy living and working together. Cleanliness and orderliness must be maintained, chalkboards must be erased regularly, and housekeeping chores such as dusting and cleaning attended to scrupulously. Students organized into committees or functioning as monitors should assist in replacing equipment that has been used, in preserving materials that must be stored, and in rearranging desks and chairs that have been moved.

Your use of color in your classroom decorations will present opportunities for learning. Children should be encouraged by the variety, intensity, and harmony of your displays to employ similar good taste in their own creative expressions. As you decorate, keep in mind the size and maturity of your students. One teacher, who instructed the student cameraman to "Just look straight through the lens and photograph what you see," when he filmed the class play, neglected to consider this warning. The student happened to be one of the smallest boys in the room. The actors were performing on a low stage, one foot off the floor. When the finished film revealed only shoes, legs, and knees, the teacher was forced to concede that that was indeed all the cameraman could see by looking straight through the lens. Photographs, decorative pictures, and student products, which are hung on the walls or bulletin board, should be at a height compatible with the size of the potential viewers. They should also be changed after a reasonable length of time so that they are seasonal and timely.

FURNITURE. The goal which movable furniture serves is flexibility. If the flow of instruction is always going to be from the teacher to the pupil with the old-style desks arranged one behind the other in rows, it makes good enough sense to provide aisles for movement. But in classes where the method of instruction is going to change from time to time, where pupil participation in planning is expected, and where student interaction is permitted, the desks should be arranged so as to facilitate the accomplishment of the planned goal. In such classes, the teacher's desk will be placed where it contributes both aesthetically and functionally to the appearance of the room. The best plan is to locate it in an inconspicuous place in the room so that it does not consume valuable floor space.

ILLUMINATION AND VENTILATION. As you focus on seating arrangements, you will become aware, perhaps for the first time, of the need for adequate illumination, ventilation, and acoustics. Often classroom control problems result from conditions in the classroom environment about which teachers are oblivious. Children, for example, sometimes erupt for seemingly trifling reasons, because they are suffering from headache or eye strain caused by the glare of sunlight flooding the room in which shades are unattended. In effectively run classes, students are not made to sit facing directly into strong light, or requested to copy material from a blackboard which reflects a glare.

In matters of ventilation, the same kind of awareness and sensitivity must be exercised. No child works well in a room that is hot, stuffy, or malodorous, so the effective teacher keeps on the alert for signs and possible causes of restlessness or fatigue. One test that experienced teachers use is to step outside periodically for a moment and back in again. The change will make the need for ventilation quite evident if the need exists.

SEATING ARRANGEMENTS. In seating children in the classroom, some thought should be given to the compatability of their neighbors. Some children have a bad effect upon others, and care must be taken in locating them so as to keep their disruptive impact to a minimum. Each child should be seated where he will be able both to give and to receive intellectual stimulation from his peers, and where he can sometimes be a leader in thinking, planning, and doing, and sometimes a follower. Cronies have to be observed, lest they sacrifice learning for friendship. Experience with the group will enable you to use the student desire to be seated near a buddy as an incentive. Good friends can earn the right to work closely with each other by being good class citizens. Experience will also sharpen your ability to detect potential malefactors and place them where they will be least disruptive.

RECORDS AND FILES. Of considerable importance in perfecting management skills is getting to know well each student as soon as possible. From the cumulative records, which follow each child through the grades, the teacher should learn to put a face with each name and also to associate the revealing comments of previous teachers with each face. Some teachers refuse to use the cumulative file in this fashion and choose to form no preconceived notions about the members of their classroom. These teachers fear that reading the files will cause them to discriminate against certain children, to perpetuate erroneous past judgments made about them, or to brand pupils despite the fact that they have outgrown the errors recorded. Although such teachers' motives—to receive each child into a room free from bias —may be commendable the practice appears suspect. Anyone so sensitive to the problem as to consider acting in this fashion is probably sensitive enough to treat each child in a mature and unprejudicial fashion after the classes get started. In addition, the files often provide considerable objective data such as standardized test results, health records, and the like. Because of teacher neglect of the cumulative files, in some classrooms children with hearing or visual limitations have been forced to sit through a considerable part of the year before the new teacher discovers the student's disability. Cumulative records for the discerning teacher have the capacity for bringing deficiencies to light even before the school year begins, as well as alerting the teacher to student interests, needs, strengths, weaknesses, and plans for the future. If the records on file are used professionally, they sound an alert for the effective teacher. The value and use of the information he gleans will depend upon his judgment and the avenues of communication which he will open up between himself and each child. His actions will depend upon personal conclusions, based primarily upon his own observations, although he might not have observed as closely or in some particular areas if his attention had not been attracted by the comments of a previous teacher.

Perhaps, the most sensible resolution to the conflict of use or nonuse of records is to insert the caution that records should be used with discrimination.

SEATWORK. Material that is issued to students for independent work at their desks is often referred to as seatwork. Usually the material is prepared by the teacher for a specific purpose, such as allowing children to practice a new skill which they have been taught. Often the seatwork may be of a commercial variety, reproduced from master sheets purchased from a supplier for distribution in the classroom. Sometimes, workbooks are used for this purpose as are selections "cannibalized" from discarded texts.

Seatwork has many purposes. It can be used to provide meaningful practice, it can contribute to mastery of independent skills as students assume responsibility for preparation of long term assignments, and it can be used to individualize assignments. Capable students who can handle the reading can proceed independently toward their goal at a more rapid rate than the rest of the class and eliminate the marking time waste of a single cadence march for everyone. Also, seatwork can supply the guidance needed so that some students can function on their own while the teacher is conferring with or attending to other students who need special assistance. The teacher in this situation will want to be certain that students who are working independently at their desks understand what they are doing and can proceed with the minimum of wasted effort. This procedure recognizes the existence of individual differences in that it permits more advanced students to work with materials that challenge their ability.

Sometimes seatwork is used as busy work or to relieve the teacher of active participation with the class. In such classes, seatwork does a disservice to the pupils. Perhaps the best criterion by which to judge the effective use of seatwork is the degree to which it suits the individual pupil's needs.

The Teaching Position. To teach, one must be active; teaching is not a passive activity. It requires alertness, attentiveness, and energetic output. Even though some teachers may have sufficient personal magnetism to teach while seated at the desk, the majority of effective teachers find that they are most successful when they stand or move about.

By circulating about the room, teachers can learn much about the students, their individual characteristics, and their learning styles. As a teacher circulates, he can discover potential leaders, help potential isolates, and prod potential non-achievers. Circulation is especially necessary when the class is working in committees. It allows one to keep in touch with the progress of the various clusters of students, to be available when help is needed, and to put an end to beginnings which augur no good for the work of the group.

The most tempting time for a teacher to allow himself to relax while teaching comes while pupils are taking a test or studying at their seats. Yet, these are the two occasions which produce some of the most traumatic kinds of disturbances. By sitting at his desk, the teacher almost invites cheating from the student who is unprepared for a test, or who is being pressured to obtain high grades, or who wishes to avoid work by copying the homework of a friend who sits closeby. Often teachers who try to save time by grading papers during these quiet times find that they have created problems for themselves. By moving about the class, they can eliminate a considerable number of the most bothersome kinds of problems.

Trouble Spots

Obviously, there are certain times when the need for control is more crucial than others. Of course, there are some types of teaching that require teachers to sit down with the children; class discussion, conducting a reading group, or reading pupils a story are examples. As a rule, you would be wise to do most of your teaching while on your feet.

It takes little perceptivity to conclude that additional care must be exercised when the class is doing any of the following:

a. About to change activities.
b. About to change groupings.
c. Engaged in committee work.
d. In the process of entering the room.
e. Preparing to leave the room.
f. Returning from recess, lunch, or assembly.
g. Distributing or collecting some items.

Any time when there is to be a change from the normal procedure or a loosening of the reins requires extra care.

To engage the class in any change in the ongoing activities without anticipating the move and preparing the students for the new is liable to end in disruption and confusion. As in all other teaching situations, preparation and planning make up the oil that keeps things running smoothly. To be effective, teachers must train themselves to be sensitive and alert to the many clues provided by the class environment. An increase in volume of a small group discussion, a sudden quiet, sudden motions, vigorous gestures, or a heightening of activity put him on guard. He may do nothing more than stay alert but, by becoming ready to take action if it is needed, he reveals professional expertise.

When a Problem Develops

What should a teacher do when he detects an incipient control problem? Circumstances may require different behavior at different times but generally he (a) moves in the direction of the disturbance; or (b) calls all activity to a halt for a general reminder; or (c) changes groupings or activities.

The major error to avoid at a time like this is to delay action until the disturbance gets out of hand, although sometimes controlled blindness and deafness are the virtues to be cultivated to forestall the exercise of premature interference. Among the specific techniques that may prove useful are the following:

1. Use facial expressions and hand gestures to discourage the strengthening of disruptive forces. Often, for example, when the teacher moves toward the group or person who is creating a disturbance and registers disapproval, disappointment, or puzzlement, the offending activity is discontinued. If it is not, the teacher may call for the attention of the entire class to review the class standards for behavior in groups. Or if this fails to bring about the desired behavior, he may decide to modify the groupings so as to remove the disturbing elements from the disrupting groups.

2. Let the students work. Students learn by doing; if the teacher does all the doing, they so often fail to learn. Effective teachers resist the tendency to grab and hold onto center stage. They diversify their methods; they do not just lecture or question. They analyze the interests of the students and capitalize on the natural motivation.

3. Encourage the efforts of students no matter how halting, limited, or unsatis-

factory they may be. Success for the students can come only from expending energy. As long as students are making some effort, there is hope for a happy ending. Sometimes, an open prod may elicit effort from particular types of students who are prone to expend only a limited amount of energy on their schoolwork. Generally, though, negative action by the teacher tends to produce more harm than good, affecting adversely even students who have been cooperative and positive.

4. Help the student who makes a pest of himself in his quest for attention. Creating opportunities for the class clown to assume a position of significance as a monitor, a messenger, or as a respondent to questions so that he can receive some of the reassurance and attention he needs may help solve his personality problem and your control problem.

5. Avoid trying to outshout a noisy class. Shouting only tends to add more clatter to the confusion. Instead, before you speak, bring the class back under control by the use of some attention-getting device, such as a dramatic gesture, the sounding of a bell, the closing of a window, or the raising of a shade. One of the dramatic devices that sometimes works well is to hand a note that says, "Please stand up," to one child after another after you get the attention of each. Soon, even the rowdiest children will stop their noise to find out what is going on. Such devices should not be overused, however, or they lose their effectiveness. In well-run classes, one should not have to use them often.

6. Give the signal for dismissing the class yourself. It should be your signal, not the bell, or the clock, or the action of the rest of the school, that releases the pupils. Of course, you should not hold the class beyond the appointed time, so finish your lessons and take care of tomorrow's assignments, paper collections, announcements, cleaning up, storing equipment, and housekeeping details in plenty of time. Then, when the bell sounds, insist that all students look to you for permission to go. No one should be allowed to get up and run just because the bell has rung.

7. Make skillful use of your voice in teaching and managing. Avoid monotony by varying the pitch and tempo, and capture attention by utilizing dramatic inflections, meaningful pauses, and change of volume. Some teachers tend to let their voices rise in pitch and especially in volume when they become displeased with behavior. This tendency is most unfortunate. A "quiet begets quiet" approach is usually much more effective. Other teachers talk too much. They forget that it is usually more constructive to get many participants into the act than to continue to talk even though what they say may seem important.

8. Establish effective routines. To announce directions daily, or to have to repeat directions several times at one sitting is both wasteful of time and ineffective. Activities that will be repeated several times during the year should merit serious attention when first introduced so all can learn the process. Then after a specified length of time, they should be so routinized that the announcement of the activity should be all that is needed to stimulate the appropriate student action. When dictation is given, or spelling words are read out, or students are requested to record the next day's assignment, the teacher should pause until all are ready to begin. He should then begin his action while students respond in the way they have been taught, waiting for the second reading if they are unable to retain the whole message after the first reading. Such routine procedure eliminates much confusion.

9. Control the mode in which pupils answer questions. Choral answers should

be allowed only when the teacher seeks them and requests them. Generally, because of the anonymity they provide to the responders and the limited feedback that they provide the teacher, choral answers serve little purpose and may lead to confusion. As a rule, asking the question first and then calling upon a specific pupil is much preferable. If more participation is desired, one can follow up by asking other pupils to comment or react.

10. Reprove students in private. Making issues public often does more harm than good. At times, teachers resort to public reprimands for individual pupils because a) they wish to let the whole group know how they feel about a particular action by publicly scolding a single individual or small group for some specific misconduct, or b) they hope to elicit a change of behavior by lecturing to a mainstream group.

In spite of the potential for the "ripple" effect inherent in public reprimand, the audience aspect of this kind of technique tends to militate against its effectiveness. Most often, the students who do not need the public reprimand are the ones who pay attention to what is being said, but the others at whom it is directed do not. Additionally, if the same public admonition is repeated a number of times, it gets to be something of a joke to callous pupils.

11. Provide an opportunity for the guilty student "to get off the hook." The most effective teachers never make it necessary for a chastised student to save face by destroying himself. They try hard to avoid the type of confrontation one author describes as the "choreography of the dare." According to this account, the behavior of teacher and student in such stressful moments resembles the prescribed ritual of partners in a tribal dance. The scenario he describes might read as follows:

TEACHER: "Joe, you're too loud."
TEACHER: (again) "Joe, you're too loud."
TEACHER: (again) "O.K. That's it! If you can't be quiet, why don't you leave the room and collect yourself."

The first dilemma could begin at this point. If the student is conscious of his position with his peers, he may refuse to go or may respond, "Make me!" If the teacher is conscious of the people watching his behavior, he may respond with "O.K. I'll make you" and trouble results. The other dilemma begins if Joe rises, moves toward the door, and mumbles as he moves.

TEACHER: "What did you say?"

In this case, the student either has to lie about what he has said or tell the truth and force the teacher to send him to the principal.[4]

12. Keep your emotions under control. Action in anger verges on unprofessional behavior. It often results in counterproductive decisions. On the other hand, simulated anger, which can be dropped as soon as the provocation has been removed, can often be used effectively. Since the personality of the teacher is the most important single factor in determining the quality of living that goes on in a classroom, each teacher must be sensitive to the covert as well as overt messages that students pick up about the teacher's feeling for them. Consequently, since

[4] Fritz Redl, "Aggression in the Classroom," from Richard R. Heidenreich, *Urban Education* (Arlington, Va.: College Readings, Inc., 1971), p. 166.

children always expect some affection from their teachers, one should be careful to avoid being so cold and reserved that they never see that you genuinely like them. When students face disconcerting problems or dilemmas, or have had frustrating experiences, your discreet show of affection will be security-giving in its effects. Of course, you cannot substitute for parents in love relationships. Therefore, you should avoid demonstrative forms of response and endearing terms. You should also keep yourself from such racial, religious, national, or class prejudices as will affect your relations with children in the public school situation.

Causes of Discipline Problems

In analyzing the discipline problems which are disruptive of the learning environment in the classroom, we find that they can be grouped under four headings: 1) those caused by the situation; 2) those caused by inexperience; 3) those caused by the teacher; and 4) those caused by children with problems.

Situation-caused Problems. The coincidence of a number of unfavorable factors over which no one has control are the causes for situational problems. A poor community environment, too many students in a classroom, too few books, too warm or too cold a room, or too many rainy days in succession can cause trouble for even the most skilled teacher. Special diligence and increased energy are required for keeping the lid on at times such as these.

Problems Caused by Inexperience. Inexperience often inhibits beginning teachers from being aware of the darkening sky until the cloudburst occurs. Often they are so preoccupied with their plans for the lesson and so absorbed in the topic of the moment that they do not read the many little clues that are exhibited to indicate that all is not well. Through experience, new teachers will develop the capacity both for becoming immersed in the topic of the moment and simultaneously for being sharply aware of the happenings about them. Then they will read the puzzled frown as a request for more explanation, the doodling with a pencil as a waning of interest, and the shifting of body positions at the desk, or the smothered yawn as a request for a change of activity and pace. At the outset though, these danger signs may not even register because the effort in concentration is required for "what comes next." So by the time the neophyte teacher notices it, the misbehavior may have become so pronounced that the task of settling the group is multiplied many times.

Inexperience is also the cause of a considerable amount of inept teaching. Problems caused by this sort of inexperience fall under the heading of teacher-caused problems.

Teacher-caused Discipline Problems. POPULARITY. A subtle but very understandable impediment to the utilization of good management techniques that is traceable to the teacher is the desire for popularity. All of us, teachers and students alike, need to be loved. The more insecure we feel, the greater may be our need for reassuring feedback of affection from our students. Teachers and parents often refrain from acting as they think they should for fear of alienating their children.

To allow this need for affection to deter our exercise of sound control techniques, however, is generally a mistake. It often compounds minor errors and leads to magnified disruptive problems in behavior. Besides, students like a teacher who has standards and who exacts compliance from them. They want him to be fair and consistent so that they can know what kind of response is expected of them. They depend upon his being friendly, approachable, and available although exhibiting the reserve of an adult, not the familiarity of a chum.

The effective teacher makes an effort to like all of his students. He is aware of the fact that the students who need his help most may perhaps be the hardest to like. But he does not play favorites. He does not display preference for the more gifted or more talented students who endear themselves easily, but treats all with equal respect, kindness, sympathy, and affection. He does not make concessions so as to be popular.

CONSISTENCY. Although it is understandable that every teacher wants to be liked and desires to have the good will of his class, it is a fact that children like to know their boundaries and need to have those boundaries remain consistent. The teacher who is reluctant to correct the first child who is misbehaving will probably be reluctant to correct the second and the third child who do the same thing. When finally he is forced by the situation to acknowledge that something must be done and pulls up short the nearest participant in the misbehavior, he runs the risk of creating a confused enemy. Five others have done exactly the same thing without reprimand. Does a child demand further evidence to convince him that the teacher is unfair when only one is punished for behavior engaged in by many? The applicable generalization to remember here is that if the children know of the limitations in any situation, and if the teacher consistently observes these limitations and dispenses correction fairly and justly, the teacher will win respect and cooperation.

DULLNESS. Other causes for shaky control are dull teachers and boring, ill-conceived lessons. If the teacher is dull, students will feel dull. Those who are lively by nature will turn to other outlets to give vent to their excess energy. A helpful practice in this area is to tape record yourself teaching a lesson, and then listen to the playback. Are you interested and excited enough to give your full attention to the recording or do you find yourself dull, also? Remember that children who are interested in what they are doing will find little or no time for misbehavior.

POOR PLANNING. Still another cause of failure to maintain control is frequently the absence of adequate teacher planning. The effective teacher has a plan for each day and follows it. His plans build one upon another. Consequently, there is a continuity in learning from day to day: the work for tomorrow becomes possible because of the work done today; the satisfactions that derive from accomplishment of objectives and advancement toward established goals provide the motivation for continued learning. In addition, good daily planning eliminates wandering on the part of the teacher and prevents useless activities and aimless discussion. It gives purpose to questioning and maps out methods for presentation of material and activities by which to clinch the learning. Effective planners do the following:

1. Generally provide a variety of learning activities. Rarely do effective teachers use an entire period for group activity, for they realize that students are prone to restlessness if a change of pace is not available. No one method is considered best among their repertory; they use a varied assortment.

2. Assign homework that flows out of the lesson of the day. It has purpose, is instructional, and is regulated as to the time it will take a student to complete.
3. Arrange for some activity daily in which even the less gifted students can experience success.
4. Build into their plans opportunities to reteach concepts that were apparently not understood when first presented.
5. Schedule times for summarizing the day's learnings by both the teacher and the students.
6. Give pupils instruction in how to study so that homework assignments can be effectively completed.
7. Rely upon pretests or other procedures to ascertain readiness for additional work. They avoid taking for granted that students understand concepts.
8. Schedule the use of the lecture method sparingly.

Teaching Appropriate Behavior

If trouble does appear, what can be done to help children improve their classroom behavior? You can discuss. You can interpret. You can explain. Above all, you plan and reveal your concern, your interest, and your desire. Children do not naturally manage good behavior immediately any more than they do reading or spelling or kickball. You have to be modest with your expectations and patient in your search for success while you wait for them to master the fine points of acceptable behavior. You must not ignore misbehavior or let children repeat errors. Therefore, you interpret, explain, and teach the logical reasons for good behavior. Teaching apropriate behavior to children is very different from conditioning a dog to respond to cues. Because of the humanity, the intelligence, the personality and the will involved, there must be humanness and gentility, respect and decency if children are to see outcomes and reasons and so learn to think about choices and make defensible decisions. It takes time for a child to learn how to hold in and how to refrain, just as it takes time as well to learn to explain, to hold forth, and to defend. The change over from infancy and early childhood when nothing was held back—not noise, or movement, or gastrointestinal happenings—takes time. As not interrupting is a learned reaction, so are nonhitting and not taking. Furthermore, things which might seem to be daily routine to a teacher may be of paramount importance to the child. Alice may be only one of forty children doing a folk dance for a PTA program, but to herself she is a key figure on whom all eyes are focused and whose every tiny mistake will be noted by all. Unless teachers take time to teach good behavior, they can expect bad behavior.

Children with Problems

No child is "good" or "bad." Each behaves in a way that he feels promises to be most satisfying to him. Sometimes his behavior may be distressing to the teacher, as when it disrupts the work of the group, and sometimes it may give evidence that the child is not making growth in the appropriate direction. The modern teacher, though, as we have seen, instead of condemning the child, searches for the underlying causes for the misbehavior so as to offer assistance. If the primary cause turns out to be an undesirable home situation, or an unwholesome neighborhood, or membership in a minority group, the concerned teacher strives to provide one kind of support. If the major cause of the misbehavior is found to be the rigid school curriculum, relationships with particular members of the class group, or a personality conflict with the teacher, then the teacher provides another kind of support. For causes that stem from the child's deficiencies, or physical disabilities, or pecularities, the teacher applies yet another kind of support. In many cases, he finds that the basic difficulty is a combination of all three of these conditions.

It is the rare child who is not having some difficulty with the problems of living. The greater part of the experiences which influence student behavior in school has taken place outside the school. Some children have already become the victims of seriously miseducative experiences even before they start school. It is not sensible to expect that these children will always respond normally to the school program, no matter how wisely and carefully it has been planned. There can be no set rules or procedures for handling such children except that we must treat the offense, help the child, and avoid identifying the child with the offense and excluding him from the group. How much freedom one can allow a deviant behaver depends upon the relationship that the teacher is able to establish with that pupil and the degree of negative influence his behavior is imposing upon the entire group.

Teachers should not concern themselves only with the pupils with visible problems. Sometimes, the most docile, the most compliant, and the most conforming students are those who have the most serious and deep-seated problems.

The child who appears to have no problems whatsoever and behaves habitually in the most conventional manner may have learned that it is better for him to conceal his problems, and has become expert in so doing. The effective teacher strives to learn by observation and examination of the records as much as possible about such students as he continually searches for a way to be of help. He definitely does not cross them off his concern list merely because they do not disrupt the class or cause overt problems.

Symptoms are important only as they furnish clues to serious difficulties. The effective teacher tries to keep acts of aggression and withdrawal in perspective. He recognizes that temper tantrums, hitting, name-calling, and destruction of property are common forms of aggressive behavior and that daydreaming, inattentiveness, extreme forgetfulness, and truancy may be forms of withdrawal. His search will be for the causation of these manifestations as well as of cheating, stealing, and defiance. Often, it may be best to take no action. But when a student repeatedly annoys the group by shouting out of turn, or continually acts in an aggressive manner toward the teacher, or deliberately hurts smaller children, his behavior must be checked. In such cases, the teacher must act first in the interests of protecting the whole group by restraining or excluding the offending student temporarily, and then continue to work on an individual basis with the offender to find and to eliminate the cause for the offending symptom. If the difficulty seems serious, he, of course, should seek professional psychological or medical help.

A Final Comment. Not all students will respond as you expect them to respond when you apply remedies that strike you as sound to tense situations. Not every problem will melt away the second time you apply your remedy as quickly as it melted previously. But as the passage of time brings with it variations in the types and perhaps in severity of the control problems which will confront you, time will also expose you to a maturing process. Through the application of the techniques you have read about in this module, you will enrich your knowledge and sharpen your skills in controlling, and become more adept at spontaneously handling situations as they arise.

SUGGESTED READING

Biehler, Robert F. *Psychology Applied to Teaching.* Boston: Houghton Mifflin Company, 1971.

Collier, Calhoun C., Robert W. Houston, Robert R. Schmatz, and William J. Walsh. *Modern Elementary Education: Teaching and Learning* New York: Macmillan Publishing Co., Inc., 1976.

Dreikurs, Rudolf, Bernice Bronia Grunwald, and Floyd Pepper. *Maintaining Sanity in the Classroom* New York: Harper and Row, Publishers, 1971.

Gnagy, William J. *Maintaining Discipline in Classroom Instruction* New York: Macmillan Publishing Co., Inc., 1975.

Hass, Glen, Kimball Wiles, Joyce Cooper, and Dan Michalak. *Readings in Elementary Teaching* Boston: Allyn & Bacon, Inc., 1971.

Jarolimek, John, and Clifford D. Foster. *Teaching and Learning in the Elementary School* New York: Macmillan Publishing Co., Inc., 1976.

Johnson, Lois V., and Mary A. Bany. *Classroom Management* New York: Macmillan Publishing Co., Inc., 1970.

Joyce, Bruce, and Marsha Weil. *Models of Teaching* Englewood Cliffs, N.J.: Prentice-Hall, Inc., 1972.

Kounin, Jacob S. *Discipline and Group Management* New York: Holt, Rinehart & Winston, Inc., 1970.

Meacham, Merle L., and Allen E. Wiesen. *Changing Classroom Behavior: A Manual for Precision Teaching* Scranton, Pa.: Intext, Inc., 1970.

Neisworth, John R., Stanley L. Deno, and Joseph R. Jenkins. *Student Motivation and Classroom Management* Lemont, Pa.: Behavior Techniques, Inc., 1969.

O'Leary, K. Daniel, and Susan G. O'Leary. *Classroom Management* New York: Pergamon Press, Inc., 1972.

Schmuck, Richard, and Patricia Schmuck. *Group Processes in the Classroom* Dubuque, Iowa: William C. Brown Company, Publishers, 1971.

Smith, William I. *Guidelines to Classroom Behavior* New York: Book Lab, Inc., 1970.

POST TEST

1. Cite four goals of classroom control.

_____

_____

_____

_____

2. Contrast control in the traditional classroom with control in the contemporary classroom.

_____

_____

_____

_____

_____

_____

_____

_____

_____

3. Cite five of the seven elements of good control.

_____

_____

_____

_____

4. Write a short paragraph describing classroom climate and the structure of a class.

_____

_____

_____

_____

_____

5. Why are interesting and peppy classes much more important in the 1970s than ever before?

_____

_____

_____

_____

6. List six of the nine suggestions given for developing group unity.

_____

_____

_____

_____

_____

_____

7. Describe how monitors can contribute to maintenance of control.

_____

_____

_____

_____

_____

_____

8. Describe the recommended procedure for returning test papers or homework assignments.

_____

_____

_____

_____

9. What is meant by "permitting the student to feel free to let you see him be himself"?

_____

_____

_____

_____

_____

10. Explain the meaning of the nickname for the teacher, "the happy schizophrenic."

_____

_____

_____

_____

11. List eight of the twelve suggestions for establishing rapport in your class.

_____

_____

_____

_____

_____

_____

_____

_____

12. What is the purpose of compiling classroom standards through participatory democratic action?

_____

_____

13. List the six procedures for starting class on time.

_____

_____

_____

_____

_____

14. Write a short paragraph on how classroom furniture can be used to facilitate control.

_____

_____

_____

15. Explain how ventilation and illumination can affect control.

_____

_____

_____

16. Write a paragraph defending your position on the use of cumulative records to learn about the previous history of your students.

_____

_____

17. What is seatwork?

18. Explain why the active, moving teaching posture is recommended over the seated position at the teacher's desk.

19. Name five of the seven occasions listed as trouble spots during which greater vigilance and effort are required to maintain control.

20. Cite the three things a teacher might do when he detects an incipient control problem.

21. Cite eight of the twelve specific techniques described which can be used in the trouble spots of the day to insure maintenance of control.

22. What role should you play when you recognize that you are a participant in the choreography of the dare?

_____

_____

_____

_____

_____

_____

_____

_____

23. Inexperience may lead a teacher to strive for popularity. How can striving for popularity be the cause of lack of control?

_____

_____

_____

_____

_____

_____

_____

24. How can preoccupation with lesson plans for the day contribute to loss of control?

_____

_____

_____

_____

25. Cite six of the eight practices observed by effective planners for limiting erosion of control.

_____

_____

_____

_____

_____

Teaching Language Arts

Edith Nelson

Joseph F. Callahan

Jersey City State College

module 7

Purpose of Language Arts / Listening / Speaking / Reading / Written Expression / Punctuation / Spelling / Grammar

RATIONALE

In general, educators, as Caesar's Gaul, can be divided into three main camps in regard to their views on the language arts. In one camp are those who believe that language arts is a process subject. These are the teachers who weave instruction in the skills involved in listening, speaking, reading, and writing into all of the learning activities of the day and consider them as vital tools for mastering the knowledge that is contained in the curriculum. In the second camp are those who view the language arts as content to be studied in depth, almost as ends in themselves. They work toward mastery in discrete classes devoted to grammar, composition, and literature. In the third camp are those who share both views. These teachers stress the process aspects of the language arts and strive for the refinement of the communication skills but, at the same time, they teach and test for mastery of specific content concerning the structure of the language and of its literature.

Teachers in the elementary grades gravitate toward the first camp. They tend to focus on the language arts as skills to be learned and refined. They strive to interrelate the various components of this curriculum area in the belief that progress in one facet will improve the chance of mastery in every other facet. Even in those schools in which spelling, or reading, or handwriting are separated as discrete entities, the intention is that the skills should be interrelated. Spelling is stressed in all of the subjects studied, just as reading and vocabulary development are often taught using the geography or history textbook.

High school teachers populate the other two camps, moving from one to the other as social conditions influence the educational philosophy of the time. In the second group are those who regard the high school as a preparation for college admission and who emphasize the scholarly content of their subject; these teachers continue with traditional instruction as usual. In the third group are those who have edged closer to utilization of the functional and relevant. Reflecting in their actions the influence of the child-centered philosophers of the 1930s and 1940s, this larger group of teachers attempts to capture the best of both worlds by stressing skill development and content mastery at the same time.

Your success as an elementary school teacher may well hinge upon your ability to help your students achieve competence in language. Should you be lacking in this area, your students may face life with an unfair handicap for which you and your school must accept some responsibility.

This module offers information about each of the component parts of the language arts. Each is treated separately, and lists of techniques and suggested methods are offered to help you visualize yourself in the process of teaching or of planning a lesson. It is expected that you will do the necessary integrating; that you will see why, for example, listening cannot be separated from speaking (even though it is presented here in a discrete section); and that you will recognize how most of the techniques offered under the heading *Reading* are to be adapted when you start to plan a lesson in *Writing*.

SPECIFIC OBJECTIVES

Upon completion of the study of this module, you should be able to do the following:

1. Describe how reading and other language arts are interrelated.
2. Name and cite examples for the three levels of comprehension in reading.
3. Name four methods used in phrase word analysis in teaching reading.
4. Describe three devices or games used with children according to the structural analysis method.
5. Describe the three main camps regarding beliefs about language arts.
6. Cite the six levels of listening, and give an example for each level.
7. Explain the DRA program for reading.
8. Specify two ways the teacher can help a student become aware of his need for improvement in listening.
9. Describe what is meant by half-listening.
10. Name three definite standards that should be developed for listening activities.
11. Name five of the eight factors listed which can influence listening.
12. Describe the three types of speakers among children considered from the point of view of exposure to standard English.
13. Describe three things teachers can do about usage habits.
14. Name in sequence the five definite procedures to employ when teaching oral language.
15. State the main objection that the linguist makes against traditional grammar.
16. Define: 1) phoneme; 2) morpheme; and 3) syntax.
17. Cite three objections that Robert Pooley gives against formal instruction in terminology of grammar.
18. Describe how the teacher communicates punctuation in oral reading.
19. Besides teaching the rules, cite four procedures a teacher can use to provide practice in using proper punctuation.
20. Cite three guidelines a teacher can use in establishing a spelling program.
21. Describe three spelling drills that a teacher might use in the primary grades.
22. Cite three generalizations that students should be taught about forming the plurals of singular words.
23. Cite two generalizations that students can be taught about doubling a final consonant when adding a suffix.
24. Cite an example of a mnemonic device in spelling.
25. List the four steps of a teaching sequence in written expression.
26. Explain four ways to help students develop proper mechanical skills in written composition.
27. List six thinking skills that are used in written expression.
28. Cite eight examples of functional writing that students should perform in the elementary school.
29. List four motivators for writing that a teacher can use in the classroom.

MODULE TEXT

The Purpose of Language Arts

The typical child does not begin to learn his language when he presents himself for admission to school at age five. By that age, most children already have developed an intrinsic knowledge of the structure of oral language. They speak with considerable fluency, use typical sentence patterns in conversation, and reveal an understanding of stress and intonation that many learned foreign speakers never seem to acquire. Furthermore, their understanding of the oral language is quite sufficient to satisfy many of their personal needs.

The introduction to formal language instruction that the school inaugurates is intended to acquaint the children with new forms so that they can use the language more precisely. Basically the plan of the instruction is to apply the children's understanding of the oral language to the written language. In this fashion, the children become aware of the similarities and differences of the two modes, and gradually each child can gain mastery of the more artificial and sophisticated forms of communication.

The beginning school years provide many opportunities for integrating communication skills and correlating language with other learnings. In the kindergarten and first grade, through "showing and telling," children learn to select ideas, to express them in sentences of growing complexity and variety, and to use words accurately and vividly. At the same time they learn to control their use of language, to listen to others with attention, to respond appropriately, to keep to the subject, and to distinguish between fact and fancy. From simple group discussion they learn responsibility in the use of language.

As children mature in language skill learning, they use writing to communicate news or messages to people at a distance, to make records of plans and events, and to express thoughts and emotions creatively. They write letters and notes, simple descriptions and reports, and creative compositions. Each of these writing activities is related to a real purpose and is frequently preceded by reading and speaking.

Speech activities include conversation, discussion, telephoning, making announcements and reports, giving directions and explanations, dramatizations and choral speaking, storytelling, and oral reading. Through these activities, vocabulary, usage, enunciation, and coherent organization of oral communication are improved. Every occasion for speaking presents a need for listening. Additional occasions for refining listening skills are provided by classroom visitors, assembly programs, radio and television programs, phonograph records, and tapes.

Today, the language arts stand in a "special relationship to all studies and activities of the school, as well as to life outside of school, in that the concern is to promote growth in the power to communicate whatever needs to be said or written, and to understand clearly and evaluate critically what others say or write."[1] The problem for each teacher to resolve will be how to take advantage of the maximum benefits of integrated teaching without sacrificing needed instruction and drill in any of the separate skills or areas.

[1] Chester W. Harris, ed., with Marie R. Liba, *Encyclopedia of Educational Research,* 3rd Ed. (New York: Macmillan Publishing Co., Inc., 1960), p. 455.

Listening

The primary function of language is communication. It is true that communication can result through the use of media other than language: a frown can communicate disapproval; a red light, stop; a shrug of the shoulder, indifference; and a smile, happiness. This type of communication is classified as nonverbal. However, language is the most common medium for the communication of ideas, feelings, requests, criticisms, and needs.

A prerequisite to speaking a language with precision is the acquisition of the skill of listening. A baby imitates the sounds he hears. At first these sounds are just a lot of babble; however, as the child grows and listens to the voices around him, he begins to imitate words and expressions. His first utterances which express thoughts are elliptical in nature, but usually he conveys his message successfully because the listeners are so anxious for him to succeed.

Throughout the first four or five years of his experience, the occasions for listening as a way of learning are frequent. The child listens to adult conversations, to voice inflections indicating approval or disapproval, to stories that are read or told to him, to a variety of programs on television and radio, and to the conversation of peer playmates. From all of these listening experiences he learns to understand and to use his language well enough to function efficiently in his environment. Often parents are amazed at the recitation of information that their children have learned through attentive listening. Sometimes they are aghast because their children have learned some language or information of which they disapprove. Because young children are anxious to become an integral part of their adult and peer environment, they listen closely so they can imitate the actions and speech patterns of those with whom they associate. Consequently, after much practice and attentive listening during the first five years of life, children manage to enter formal schooling in possession of a vocabulary of as many as 20,000 words and with speaking patterns that include every part of speech and almost every type of sentence.

Teachers in the very early grades generally pursue a program that encourages children to continue their learning by capitalizing on the method that has so successfully taught them thus far—listening and imitating. To be sure, each child brings with him the limitations of his home environment. His speech patterns, his vocabulary, and his syntax of language reflect the wealth or paucity of his home experiences. However, he will be spending so many hours away from his home environment, and he will become susceptible to influence by his new environment and the experiences available. It therefore becomes the responsibility of the teacher to offer him a wide range of opportunities, designed to furnish practice and improvement of listening skills within a cultivated and controlled environment.

In the primary grades, teachers can help children improve by providing activities that are designed for listening with specific purposes. For instance, children can listen for various sounds on recordings; they can listen to and repeat correct speech patterns; they can listen and retell stories; and they can listen to the information that adults give them when they are on field trips. In general, such listening activities will give practice in acquiring information, following directions, preparing to contribute to discussions, recognizing sequence of events or ideas, differentiating fact from fantasy, and interpreting mood and associating ideas.

In the upper grades, the listening experiences are more sophisticated. At this level, the children should have opportunities to listen to adult-level speeches and panels on radio and television for the purpose of gathering information, or for comparing commentaries of two or more reporters on the same topic; to instructions and directions about the performance of complex and difficult tasks; to panels, discussions, and debates so as to develop skill in recognizing propaganda and bias, proficiency in critical evaluation, and a deeper appreciation for the varied uses of their language; and to oral poetry and drama so as to develop a deeper appreciation for the aesthetic qualities of sounds and words. In addition, the pupils might use the tape recorders to study and improve their own diction and delivery.

At all levels, teachers should stress the importance of listening as a means of learning. They should always set good examples by observing the courtesies of listening, and should insist that the children do likewise. Teachers are frequently the worst offenders in this regard; they are often poor listeners. Frequently, they are so absorbed with grading or evaluating the manners of the speaker or the grammatical constructions contained in student responses that they fail to listen to the ideas that are presented.

Some Facts About Listening. Effective language arts teachers understand and utilize the following general findings of research pertaining to the listening processes, as they plan their learning activities and engage children in language arts experiences:

1. Most children in the intermediate grades have more advanced skills in listening than in reading.
2. Formal or informal listening tests can be designed to help a student become aware of his need for improvement. For example:
   a. Have students close their eyes and listen for sounds during a time interval of several seconds. Check the results of their recall.
   b. Give oral directions once. Have students repeat the directions or perform the task as directed.
   c. Read aloud sentences or a paragraph. Before reading, state the purpose for listening, such as for sequence, number of *a*'s, mood words or phrases, and examples of bias.
3. Listening and speaking are simultaneously reciprocal because one cannot function satisfactorily without the other.
4. Children are easily distracted by people and things in their environment.
5. Children often only "half listen" while waiting for an opportunity to interject their own ideas, or they respond with associations from their own experience rather than react to what is presented.
6. Children who listen attentively, yet still pronounce incorrectly the words they hear, reveal a need to be tested for hearing discrimination.
7. The ability to forget one's self and enter into the thinking of others is a mature process.
8. Definite standards should be developed for listening:
   a. Social courtesy.
   b. Think about what is said.

c. Be ready to respond by asking important questions, by giving comments that are relevant to what was said, or by following the oral directions.
9. There are six levels of listening. When beginning instruction, children should be informed of the level expected of them.
   a. Social—courteous attention to conversation.
   b. Secondary—listening to background music while engaging in other activities.
   c. Aesthetic—listening to music, poetry, or story telling by the teacher for development of aesthetic appreciation.
   d. Critical—listening for usage, speech habits, reasons, meanings, facts, and judgmental information.
   e. Concentrative—listening for directions, sequence, cause and effect, and note-taking.
   f. Creative—listening for association of ideas, visual images, and other stimuli for creative production.[2]

Many teachers seem to feel that teaching is telling. For this reason, during the greater portion of a day students are expected to listen. Teachers should try to use a greater variety of listening situations, such as independent activities, pupil-team learning, and audiovisual approaches. Teachers should vary their oral presentations, modulate their voices effectively, maintain pleasant tones, use good diction and communicate enthusiasm and interest. Above all, teachers must remember to listen carefully to children so as to impress them with the importance of listening.

Speaking

In the developmental sequences of learning, speaking generally follows listening. The exceptions occur most frequently with those children whose intelligence is too low for them to have profited from previous listening, or with those who have physiological limitations or emotional disabilities. Even though speaking seems to be a natural part of a child's development, it must be practiced in a more formal manner to prepare the children for speaker-audience situations. The fact that everyone expresses most of his thoughts through oral language underscores the need for the teaching of speaking to children.

Among primary-grade pupils there are children who have heard and learned good standard speech since they first learned to talk; those who have learned a language that, although it enables them to communicate in their homes and neighborhoods, might cause them difficulty when communicating their ideas to others who use standard English; and those who have been brought up to speak a dialect and must learn an almost new language before they can speak or even understand 'schoolroom English."

When teaching pupils who are not skilled in standard English, it is important that a teacher not show rejection of a child's natural language. If she rejects it, she rejects him and, by implication, his family. A teacher must encourage the child to talk and help him feel that he is accepted. As the child freely converses with his peers and with the teacher, the teacher can listen and take note of substandard usage. Attempts to teach him standard usage can come later.

[2] Paul S. Anderson, *Language Skills in Elementary Education* 2nd Ed. (New York: Macmillan Publishing Co., Inc., 1972), p. 69.

What the Teacher Can Do About Usage Habits. First of all, the teacher must remember not to call specific attention to a usage error until she recognizes that the child feels accepted by the group and appears self-confident; otherwise, by correcting him she might cause him to stop talking. Also, when she does begin to make corrections, she must do so in the proper spirit. If the children persist in saying, "I got," the teacher can direct their attention to proper usage by saying, "I am so glad to hear Mary say 'I have'. It sounds pleasing to my ears." The approval might make others eager to use "I have." There are many drills that can be used in a playful spirit and that can stress correct usage. Plural and singular agreement can be practiced by having the teacher begin a chain question by saying to Mary, "What doesn't Mary like to do?" Mary will reply, "Mary doesn't like to wash dishes." Mary will then ask another child the original question, and that child will reply, and so on. In this way children get practice in saying "doesn't" rather than "don't." Similarly, children can interrogate a puppet, handled by a student, in this type of practice. In the upper-level grades, students might write scripts for a radio presentation entitled, "Aids to English Usage" or they might put on a television quiz show about good usage. With a little imagination, pupils and teachers can create all sorts of dramatic presentations that will help correct improper usage. Probably the most important element in teaching proper usage, however, is the model set by the teacher.

Some Points About Speech Instruction. Speech instruction in the elementary classroom begins with the voice and the words used by the teacher. The teacher's voice is of greatest value when it is calm but firm, well modulated but sufficiently loud to be heard in a busy classroom, and suitably inflected to convey the varied feelings and emotions encountered in oral reading. To discover how you sound to others, tape record your oral presentation of a lesson. By listening to your voice, you can become aware of any qualities about your speaking which need to be improved.

Ear training is important if the children are to improve speech habits. Often children do not pronounce words correctly because they have never heard them correctly pronounced. A poignant example of improper hearing is contained in the anecdote of the boy who frequently threatened people that "Harold would get them" or that "Harold would be displeased with their behavior." His meaning was never clear until he was overheard reciting the Lord's prayer as follows: "Our Father Who art in Heaven, Harold be Thy name."

The teacher must provide activities, exercises, and games which will help children improve their auditory discrimination of sounds in speech. The drill practices that a teacher uses for this purpose usually center around picture-word pronunciation associations. Many games with words can provide both fun and specific practice in pronunciation. Among them are grab bag games in which words that contain the sound or sounds being taught are placed in a paper bag, a treasure chest, or a simulated fishing tank; the teacher lets children take turns in drawing out words and pronouncing them. Another device is to use picture word tests to help a teacher detect specific needs for improvement in individual pupils. As soon as children begin reading, much practice in speech improvement can be given by oral reading.

Oral language practice should be as spontaneous as possible. Language skills are sharpened when children have opportunity to interact verbally with each other.

Expression that is limited to responses to teachers' questions does little for the child's language development. Children need to acquire their skills by actively participating in conversation, questioning, discussing, telling, reporting, announcing, and dramatizing.

Middle-grade students can engage in speaking activities that are more involved with nature topics and with subject matter areas. By fourth grade, most children have reached a level in reading that will enable them to learn library skills that will help them gather information for oral reports. Oral reports about the world news, habits of animals, use of leisure time, family experiences, and customs of various lands, which the children can select according to their individual interests and reading levels, will provide opportunities for the audience pupils to develop better listening skills and for the speaker pupils to strengthen their speaking skills. With these middle-grade children, a teacher can use many varied activities that will give them practice in speaking. Interviewing, survey-reporting, explaining, describing, selling, persuading, debating, and dramatizing are examples of oral presentations which these pupils can handle. Teaching oral language has definite procedures:

1. Emphasis should be placed on a variety of speaking activities: telling, directing, explaining, conversing, discussing, reporting, and acting.
2. Sources for motivational experience include the following:
   a. Pictures, posters, magazines, books.
   b. Trips with parents.
   c. Stories created or retold.
   d. Visual aids.
   e. Class field trips.
   f. Activities in classroom.
3. Assignments should cover a small unit of subject matter, a recent specific happening, and material familiar to the child.
4. Classroom atmosphere should be free and informal, have speaker-audience situation, and have opportunities for sharing experiences.
5. Standards for oral language development agreed upon by students and teacher should be placed on a chart and displayed in the room. These standards might include (a) listening attentively; (b) respecting opinions of others; (c) giving others a chance to talk; (d) not letting talking interfere with work; and (e) any other regulations agreed upon.

Reading

The term *reading-language instruction* reflects the inseparable relationship between children's reading and language development. . . . emphasis on concept development through experiences . . . will directly enhance the child's reading and listening comprehension ability. His control and understanding of language will help him validate decoding through meaning in sentence and story contexts. Expressing his life experiences through oral and written language forms will help him develop an understanding of key components of story organization.[3]

[3] Robert B. Ruddell, *Reading-Language Instruction: Innovative Practices* (Englewood Cliffs, N.J.: Prentice-Hall, Inc., 1974), p. xiii.

As one prepares to teach reading, there are numerous terms, used both in the materials designed for the teacher and those intended for the children, which need clear definitions.

The following paragraphs attempt to define and discuss the more important of these terms. The reader, however, should realize that authorities do not always agree on these definitions and that the discussion does not include all the possible terms or possible definitions. As the terms are defined, ways in which each element may be implemented in instruction will also be suggested.

Reading Comprehension. An oversimplified definition for reading comprehension is "getting meaning from print." In reality, the thinking or comprehension process is complex and defies easy or simple definition. Factors which affect comprehension extend the definition. These factors are one's experiential background and facility with language. Comprehension may also be described as occurring in levels. The first level is literal; the second, interpretive; and the third, utilizational (problem solving).

Classroom activities which help provide experiential background for reading development include discussion of pictures, and presentation of films and slides. Reading related materials to children and the use of models or diagrams may also contribute to broadening each child's experience base.

Facility with language also may be enhanced by working to develop different meanings for the same word. For example:

I set the *table.*
The water *table* is low.
Refer to the *table* on page seven.

Set the pot on the stove.
We learned a new *set* in math.
Mother had her hair *set.*

In the classroom, children enjoy trying to expand their treasure of words by playing word games, using such TV show formats as "Password," "To Tell the Truth," "Who-Where-What," and others suggested by children. Synonyms, antonyms, and homonyms may also be used in the game show format to further enhance language facility.

The study of figurative language is also useful for extending language facility. In practice sessions one can use the literal and imaginative meanings of words to build rich and multiple definitions for words so as to improve effectiveness in writing, speaking, and understanding. Expressions such as *flew into a rage, high as a mountain, give me a lift, fog rolled in,* and others can be given varied meanings through games and stories.

A key to dealing with levels of comprehension is skillful questioning. Literal-level comprehension can be determined by usual questions, such as "What color was the car?" "How fast did the driver go?" or "What was the name of the town in the story?"

The interpretive level of comprehension reflects the child's understanding of his reading. Children's ability to work at this level can be tested by such questions as "What is another possible name or ending for the story?" "If you were Juan, how would you feel?" "Write a telegram giving the most important parts of the story."

The utilization or problem-solving level of comprehension requires the child to use what he has garnered from his reading. Directives for this level would request the child to draw a map of the village in the story, build a model of the adobe hut Juan lives in, or draw a picture to show another ending for the story.

Comprehension cannot be defined simply, but it is the core of the reading process. The study of children's thinking has a specific relationship to the comprehension process in reading-language settings.

Word Analysis. The terms *word analysis* and *word attack* refer to the more or less analytical approach pupils can use to identify words. Included in the scope of these umbrella terms are several specific ways of studying a word. These ways are named *context, configuration, phonics,* and *structure.*

CONTEXT CLUES. Apparently many teachers assume that students automatically use context clues to figure out the meaning of words and so teach the use of context clues only casually. But skill in the use of context clues does not just happen; it must be taught and learned. Basically what reading specialists mean when they speak of using context clues is the identification of unknown words by their setting in the selection to be read. Using context clues is undoubtedly the method most adults use in attacking unknown words. In fact, it is about the only method by which a reader can guess the meaning of words that are strange to him. It is also the only method by which the reader can test the correctness of phonic and structural clues.

One method by which to introduce the use of context clues to unlock meanings is to combine picture clues, supplied by the text, with the beginning of phonic analysis as a basis for a guess. In this method, the pupil guesses the meaning of the word from the accompanying picture and then corroborates the guess by applying his knowledge of phonics. Let us take as an example the sentence, "The young bird was learning to fly," accompanied by a suitable picture. If the pupil does not know the meaning of "young," he might, on checking the picture clue, read "young bird" as "little bird," a perfectly reasonable guess. However, even a beginning knowledge of phonics would tell him that the sounds of "little" do not fit the word "young," so "little" cannot be correct. Similarly, in the same sentence "trying" could well be substituted for "learning," but a beginning phonic knowledge precludes the acceptance of this reading.

CONFIGURATION. Configuration is probably the least reliable method of word analysis listed. It has to do with how the word looks in a line or on a page of print. For example, *car* and *can* appear similar in a line of print, but *tar* and *pat* appear quite unlike in a line of print. The reading materials prepared for use by children sometimes encourage utilization of configuration to distinguish between and among words.

PHONIC ANALYSIS. Phonic analysis deals with the relationship between symbols (graphemes) and sounds (phonemes) in reading. In the word *chin, ch* (consonant digraph) is a grapheme, and the sound it represents (as in *ch*urch, *ch*ild, *ch*ick) is a phoneme. The *n* in *chin* is also a grapheme, and the sound it represents is a phoneme. The vowel *i* also is a grapheme, represented by a sound (phoneme).

The usual and traditional approach to the teaching of phonic analysis is to include both visual and auditory activities for the teaching of consonants, such as initial consonants (*c* in *can, p* in *put, d* in *down*), digraphs (*ch* in *child, sh* in *ship, th* in *they*), blends (*br* in *broom, sl* in *slant, gl* in *gleam*), and long sounds, short sounds, and diphthongs in the teaching of vowels. These examples, of course, are only introductory groups of the phonic elements one must deal with in reading-language instruction.[4]

Some examples of phonic analysis instructional activities follow.

1. *Yes* and *No* Cards. In this activity, after the teacher has passed out *yes* and *no* cards and announced a key word, the teacher pronounces a group of words, and the children indicate by holding up the *yes* card or *no* card which of the words have the same vowel sound as the key word.

2. Riddles. Riddles may be used to teach pupils sounds and symbols used in phonic analysis. In the following example, for instance, the answer must begin with the same blend heard in the word *fly:*

   I am red, white, and blue.
   I have stars and stripes.
   What am I?

3. Silly sentences having many words with the same initial sound, such as "Big Bear batted Billy's ball." Children may be asked to build their own or to work in concert with the class while the teacher records the sentences on the board.

4. Commercially prepared games which emphasize phonics elements, such as Phonics Lotto, Bingo, and others.

STRUCTURAL ANALYSIS. The instructional procedures for teaching structural analysis are essentially the same as those for phonic analysis. The processes are taught concurrently, because they are interdependent.

In structional analysis, some of the elements to be taught are contractions, compound words, prefixes, suffixes, and syllabication. Teaching devices and methods appropriate for structural analysis are as follows:

1. Word Wheels—prefix or suffix in center, possible root words around rim, such as *dis* surrounded by *count, arm,* or *obey.*

2. Word-Making—give children words. Each child finds a partner word to use which will make his word a compound word, such as *back* and *yard,* and *play* and *ground.*

3. Syllable Sale—children hold up number cards to indicate how many syllables in a displayed word.

Teachers who are working or planning to work with these word analysis activities should certainly become familiar with terms, generalizations, and examples.

A general principle to guide one in word analysis instruction is that isolating elements (phonic and structural) should be avoided; each element should be taught in a language context.

---

[4] Arthur W. Heilman, *Principles and Practices of Teaching Reading* 3rd ed. (Columbus, Ohio: Charles E. Merrill Publishers, 1972).

Phonetics and Phonics. Phonetics and phonics are terms which are often confused. *Phonetics* is the science of speech sounds in actual oral language. Linguists, who are scholars in oral sounds of languages, have determined that the English language has forty-four to forty-six sounds. Each sound is called a phoneme. For example, in the word *sit* there are three sound phonemes. The phonetic analysis of the word is /s/ /i/ /t/. The application of phonetic analysis to the pronunciation of a word is called *phonics*. In applying this science of sound to the actual pronunciation of words, the teacher stresses single sounds or combinations of sounds. For example, the /i/ /t/ sounds which form the word *it* might be used by the teacher to show the children this specific combination in words that substitute other sounds for the initial sound of /s/ as in /s/ + *it;* /b/ + *it;* and /f/ + *it*. Phonics is often used in teaching reading and spelling.

Ordinarily, in the primary grades, teachers use the phonics method for teaching initial consonant sounds and blends, vowel sounds and blends, variant sounds of *c, g, s, z, ed,* and *t,* and the recognition of syllables. In fourth, fifth and sixth grades, teachers stress certain generalizations about the sounds of letters such as the "soft" sound of *g, c, ch.* They help the children learn how to use diacritical marks and syllabication through the dictionary skills. At all times, teachers must be alert to pupils' careless pronunciation, such as "gimme" for "give me," "wed" for "red," and "negstor" for "next door."

Some guidelines for use of phonics include the following:

1. Avoid simultaneous introduction of several phonemes for a single grapheme. The "hard" sound of *g* as in the word *great* should not be introduced at the same time as the "soft" sound of *g* in the word *gem,* for example.
2. Use word families for provision of more springboards for potential vocabulary enlargement (bake, make, lake).
3. Present auditory discrimination before visual.
4. Combine auditory and visual in a contextual situation for the mastery of the graphemes and phonemes.

Reading Skills Development Through the Elementary School. At the second-grade level, children begin to develop independence in word recognition. They begin to personalize the experiences they get from books, and to understand that reading can help them solve problems and satisfy their curiosity. Growth in reading skills, however, varies among children, and teachers must provide many different materials, worksheets, and games that will meet the specific needs of many individuals. As children develop in their thinking abilities, the teacher should provide reading exercises that will help them find main ideas, discover logical sequences, make judgments, make inferences, perceive relationships, and understand related values.

Intermediate teachers should help children practice the skills of speed reading, skimming, locating information, and graph interpreting. Probably the most important motivation for normal children who have a delayed pattern of achievement in reading is the provision of a purpose for reading. If a child wants to make an airplane, to find out how to care for a pet, or to discover why clouds form, then he may begin to read with self-purpose. Until children are self-motivating, teachers should attempt to stimulate the desire to read. At this time, a flexible program with varied materials is a "must," both to satisfy the differences in pupil ability and taste and to arouse interest in reading.

LANGUAGE EXPERIENCE METHOD. The language experience method is one approach of teaching reading that utilizes speaking, writing, listening, and reading. This approach is sometimes thought to be appropriate only for beginning reading. It is, however, effective in remedial settings and for extending reading approaches at any instructional level.

Roach Van Allen has long been a most effective spokesman for the language experience method. As Van Allen conceives it, the language experience approach can be best summarized as follows:[5]

What a child thinks about, he can talk about.
What a child talks about, he can write about.
What a child writes, he can read.
The child can read what he writes and what other people write.

For this approach to succeed, the teacher must see to it that the classroom environment provides several conditions.

The classroom environment must stimulate thinking. The teacher must provide activities which result in experiences worthy of a child's thinking time. These activities may be real, such as trips, cooking, building, sculpting, or experimenting, or they may be provocative, vicarious experiences, such as reading to children, or watching TV, movies, and slides.

Time must be available for the children to talk about—explore orally—these experiences. In this talking time, children try out effective language. In a group experience, other children's use of language is also heard and observed.

Sometimes a child or a group of children write or compose stories or anecdotes. When the story teller has not mastered mechanics (handwriting and spelling), the teacher, an aide, or an older child may act as secretary and record the story. As the child records or sees recorded what he has said, the relationship between spoken and written language is being demonstrated.

When the experience has been encoded (written), the child can decode (read) it in response to teacher questioning about the experience. He can also read what other children have encoded about the same experience.

What are some activities which teachers may provide to elicit talk-write-read responses from children?

1. Read to children. After discussing and reacting to the story they have heard, children may make up a conversation with one of the story characters; a group of questions to ask the author about the story; a chapter to follow the final one provided by the author; or a summary in the form of a fairytale or fable.
2. Use photography. Children may write a biography, a humorous incident, or several possible captions for a picture. For this purpose, children may bring photographs from home of themselves, of their family, or of their pets. The teacher or children may take pictures in the classroom. The

[5] Roach Van Allen and Dorris Lee, *Learning to Read Through Experience* (New York: Appleton-Century-Croft 1963), p. 5–7.

photographs resulting from this activity might be used as part of a class log, as illustrations for news stories in a class or a school newspaper, or for some similar class project.

3. Provide Trips. Plan trips to points of interest in the school neighborhood, within the school building, or to a zoo or circus or park or floral gardens. A movie or play might result, or maybe a chart telling what to look for, and a summary of events, or a detailed account of one facet of the trip.

Numerous advantages may be cited for the language experience approach to reading-language instruction. The first, utilization of speaking, writing, reading, and listening, has been emphasized in earlier discussion. A second important advantage is that this approach uses the child's own natural language patterns. Using this approach also promotes an understanding of encoding (writing) and decoding (reading) as a part of the same language process.

So as to ensure that the language experience approach meets its potential value in reading-language instruction, the teacher must be sure certain steps are taken. Wilson and Hall summarize them as follows:[6]

Develop a system of record-keeping with regard to each child's mastery of specific skills.
Be well informed about skills needed by individual children.
Have in readiness supplementary reading materials and selections from children's literature to help capitalize on the interest revealed.
Provide time for small groups to hear each other's stories and for group interaction through language discussion.

Another vital part of the language experience method is the development of individual or group *word banks*. As word banks are discussed, the implications for their use in spoken and written language, as well as for reading should be very evident.

A word bank is just what the name implies. It can be developed through the process of selecting words from both group and individual stories. These words, when written on cards, are accumulated to form a resource for use in storywriting. They become the child's sight vocabulary and serve as a reserve list for developing particular word analysis skills. As the word banks grow, they may also be alphabetized and categorized as color words, naming words, or prefix words. The words from the word bank may also be used in reinforcement games such as "Scrabble," "Password," "Twenty Questions," and "What Is It?"

DIRECTED READING ACTIVITY. In reading instruction literature, the Directed Reading Activity is usually referred to simply as a DRA. The DRA is a plan for teaching a selection of reading matter. It is a viable way to present material for reading in content areas, such as social studies or science, as well as being the plan used in the Teachers' Guides for basal reader selections. Basically, the DRA has four steps: Establishing Background, Guided Silent Reading, Skill Development, and Application–Extension activities.

Establishing Background: Establishing Background refers to instructional time spent surveying what the students know about the topic, developing any further concepts needed to read the selection meaningfully, and setting a purpose for

---

[6] Robert M. Wilson and Maryanne Hall, *Reading and the Elementary School Child* (New York: Van Nostrand Reinhold Company, 1972), p. 63.

reading the particular selection. For example, for a selection to be read about life in America during the Revolutionary War, the following specifics might well make up this establishing background part of the DRA. Students who have read *Johnny Tremain* by Esther Forbes might share what the story tells about houses, cooking, games, and the like. Students who have visited reconstructions at Sturbridge Village or Colonial Williamsburg, or have seen films of them, can tell what they know about Colonial life. The teacher can use pictures and articles from travel sections of newspapers, magazines, and advertising brochures to stimulate discussion in which children can air opinions and raise questions. Such activities should give pupils some understanding of the background of the selection and what further they can gain from reading the selection, thus furnishing the children with both a reason and a purpose for reading. The children may realize that their purpose for reading a selection will be to answer questions raised or to verify opinions given during the discussion. During these activities, the teacher should also give emphasis to vocabulary which will be needed in reading the selection. In this period of developing readiness for reading the selection, the teacher should utilize any related material that children may know from television shows, movies, comic books, and library books.

Guided Silent Reading: The Guided Silent Reading facet of a DRA is a must. During this time, the student reads silently to fulfill his purpose for reading. The teacher's role consists of observing, giving needed help with word identification, and clarifying puzzling concepts. Are word analysis skills applied during this phase of a DRA? Yes, if they can be elicited easily enough so as not to destroy meaning. No, if they become so laborious as to detract from the purpose for reading. The teacher should note word analysis needs which may serve as a basis for future skill lessons.

Skill Development: The Skill Development step of the DRA may consist of a large variety of student activities. Among them are activities designed to check whether the children's purposes in reading the piece were achieved: Were the students' questions answered? Were their opinions expressed, verified, or refuted? Oral rereading (ORR) for specific purposes, such as reading aloud "the paragraph that supports your opinion," or reading aloud "the sentence that answered your question," is often especially useful. So are many of the activities previously discussed in the Comprehension and Word Analysis sections of this module.

Application-Extension: Application-Extension activities give the student an opportunity to do something with the concepts he has gained from reading the selection. Perhaps his reading has made him ready to read other books on the same or related topics, such as *The American Revolution* by Bruce Bliven, Jr., *The Great Declaration* by Henry Steele Commager, or *Yankee Doodle Dandy* by Earl Schenk Miers. As a result of the additional reading, the student may wish to summarize his findings by making a chart, by developing an outline, or by making an oral report. Frequently the art media furnish appropriate means to apply what has been gleaned from reading and also extend children's understanding. A mural, a diorama, or a collage may make a perfect follow-up for one's reading. Similarly, a more technical way of demonstrating and applying what one has learned might be to make a map or build a model. These activities also lead students into the purpose phase of the DRA of the next lesson, thus preparing for moving forward into another reading selection. Guidebooks for basal readers are usually rich resources for activities appropriate to the final DRA step.

By now you have undoubtedly gathered that the DRA approach is a rather traditional plan for teaching children to read, but, used as suggested, it may be a meaningful and dynamic experience for both students and teacher.

Written Expression

Writing requires the child to express his ideas in the encoded graphemic form of the language. This is not an easy thing to do. To write the letters of language requires of the child much muscular coordination, so the primary teacher must provide the beginning writer with examples of writing and much time for practice.

She introduces writing to children by placing her examples of written words on the board. At first, she writes her name, the date, some individual children's names, and then she begins to write sentences which the children dictate to her. As the children tell about an experience, retell a story, or compose a story, the teacher writes sentences on the board. Children are usually delighted to discover that what they say can materialize as written words.

The teacher provides classroom opportunities for the child to write about what he has seen, heard, and experienced in school and in his outside world. Often group compositions provide an opportunity for children to "think together." As the children think together and contribute their ideas, the teacher writes them on the board in proper sentence form and tries to help them notice the logical sequence of the ideas or events in the story. She also draws their attention to the mark that shows the end of the sentence. The teacher stresses the patterning of sentences. With this procedure, she is beginning to teach written composition.

Gradually the children will begin to want to write their own stories. Their first attempts will, of course, contain many errors. A teacher must remember that content should be stressed first and form, second. She can provide lists of the words that a child might use in his writing; she can also help individuals with the spelling of words that they want to use for writing their ideas. It is important that the teacher encourage the child to write and not stifle spontaneity by negative commentary. She should promote the idea that a first writing is always a rough draft, which one changes and corrects until it is about the way one wants, and then copies it over neatly for a final production. Teachers should always show approval for the children's efforts by displaying the final copies or keeping them in a classroom folder for written work.

Sequence for Teaching Written Composition. The first step in teaching written composition is to supply motivation. In the primary grades, motivation may be provided from experiences the children have; from pictures they look at, from stories they read or hear, from field trips they take, from situations in the classroom, from television shows, and from their imaginations. Teachers should furnish many motivational opportunities in the classroom, such as a bulletin board with picture stimulators, or a box with titles or first lines for stories, or with cards bearing such a line as "If you were . . . what might happen?" or a mailbox for letters. A writer's corner in the classroom which contains writing equipment and varied motivational materials has been successful for many teachers. Included in the corner should be word cards or lists of words that are ordinarily used in written work, plus seasonal words, color words, action words, and other words which might be needed for specific topics. These may prevent incorrect spelling. Often teachers require each child to keep a folder containing words most often used in the classroom activities; this folder can facilitate his writing. Other words that might be included in the folder are days of the week, months, kinds of weather, smells, tastes, rooms in a house, and buildings in the community.

The second step in the teaching sequence of written composition is that of skills development. Regardless of the tendency of some, if not many, teachers to develop these skills as isolated concepts of grammar, capitalization, spelling, usage, and vocabulary development, these skills must be learned and used in a context specific to the process of writing.

In speaking, one can communicate his ideas by using effective modulations of voice, proper pauses, facial expressions, and gestures. If he notices perplexity on the faces in his audience, he can state his idea in another way. Not so for the writer. He has only the correctly spelled words, the patterns of the sentences, and the punctuation to help convey his message. Therefore, a teacher is obligated to stress the proper mechanical skills of composing, so that the writer in trying to communicate will be knowledgeable about the tools he will require for success.

On a bulletin board, in the writing corner, or in some other clearly visible place, there should be reminder charts. At the early levels, a reminder chart should probably have only a few statements or questions on it, such as: Have I used a capital letter to begin each sentence? Is there an end mark after each sentence? Is my paper neat? Is my name on the paper? As the children progress through their schooling and learn more writing skills, these new skills can be put on the reminder list. The teacher should keep the list to no more than eight skills at a time, however. Skills of which the students need to be reminded will be evident in their writing. When marking papers, it is best to draw attention only to the skills on the current reminder list. By changing the list in whole or in part from time to time one can get adequate coverage. However, beware of trying to cover too many skills; slow-learning pupils can cope with only one or two at a time. It is important also that the children understand why what they have written is in error and how to correct all the errors on their papers before they return the corrected papers to the teacher.

Challenge your students to be language detectives as you encourage them to proofread their own writing; let them be detectives for each other's writing; have them play detectives for some written language you give to them for discovery of any errors contained in the copy. There are many light and playful ways to place stress upon the mechanical skills, so avoid overuse of red marks. Red marks discourage and confuse pupils.

The third step in teaching writing is that of refinement. If it is at all possible, this step should be taken in private conference with each student. Monotonous style, overuse of simple sentences, illogical relationships, lack of sequence, improper usage, improper agreement, and other transgressions of refined communications should be discussed in a manner that is appropriate to the student's personality. Students respond well to definite, specific types of approaches made by the teacher. The teacher should be aware of these idiosyncrasies and act appropriately.

The fourth step consists of using the student's writing for a utilitarian or commendatory purpose. If a report is well written, have the student read it to the class. If stories are well written, place them in a classroom folder for others to read, or let the student read his story to another group or class of students. If letters are well written, mail them, and then show interest in any replies that the writer receives. If plays are written well, use them in a class production. There are many ways that teachers can encourage their students not only to write, but also to write well.

Functional writing must be taught for the benefit of all students. Creative writing can be encouraged, but with the realization that the number of artists will probably be few. It should be remembered that any artist must use the disciplines basic to his art. Through the mastery of the basic skills, the creative artist-in-training can project his subjective, personal qualities more effectively. In writing creatively, the student artist will draw upon his learned definition of words to produce his personal, subjective connotation of those words; although he may use his own literary form, it will generally resemble those forms which he has encountered in the classroom under the direction and guidance of teachers of literature and composition.

The teaching of functional writing may be performed in any situation in which there is a need for it. Examples of functional or utilitarian writing are writing business letters, friendly notes, and letters of thanks and sympathy; filling in application and business forms; writing factual reports; writing summaries; outlining; note-taking; and making biographical diaries.

In this type of writing, the child works with more utilitarian, realistic, and intellectual purpose. In comparison with creative writing, functional writing requires a more intellectual approach in which one uses the literal meaning of words and the standard forms of English, because other people are involved in realistic and practical interpretation of his written expression. The reader of functional writing must be able to understand the ideas of the writer who has presented them.

All acts of writing help children develop their thinking skills. As the child writes, he is also strengthening his thinking skills by classifying ideas, selecting ideas, arranging events or reasons in sequence, persuading others, substantiating opinions, and similar mental activities.

Punctuation

In the primary grades, teachers are primarily concerned with motivating children to express freely their ideas, emotions, and attitudes without the restrictions of mechanical standards. However, the teacher must remember that she is the model for the children. Therefore, she must always use standard punctuation in the sentences she writes on the board. In addition, she should frequently call attention to the capital letters and the end marks as standard procedures. In oral reading, she emphasizes the pauses, junctures, and voice modulations as indicators of the punctuation that is necessary for the proper communication of ideas. Throughout the elementary grades, teachers must utilize the standard punctuation so that children will be able to communicate their ideas eventually in acceptable written expression. The following lists contain the minimum essentials for an effective program in punctuation in any elementary school:

Primary grades:

1. Periods.
    a. End of sentence—usually stressed in reading and in first writing.

    b. After abbreviations of titles of persons and initials in proper names—
taught as an aspect of spelling.
2. Question mark at the end of a question.
3. Commas (in letter writing).
    a. Parts of date.
    b. Parts of address.
    c. After salutation of friendly letter.
    d. After complimentary close.

Intermediate grades:

1. Commas.
    a. To set off direct quotations.
    b. To separate words in series.
    c. To set off introductory clauses.
    d. To set off appositives.
    e. Before the conjunction in a compound sentence.
    f. To set off parenthetical expressions.
    g. To set off nonrestrictive clauses.
2. Colon.
    a. After salutation in business letter.
    b. Before a long series or a list.
    c. To separate hour from minutes.
    d. To denote examples.
3. Apostrophe.
    a. Possessives.
    b. Contractions.
    c. Plurals of figures and letters.

In addition to specifically teaching the rules of punctuation, a teacher should provide exercises and easy-access reminders for continual reinforcement of proper application of the rules. Some suggested exercises might include the following:

1. Reproduction of unpunctuated passages from a textbook or reader. The child is informed about the number of sentences included. These exercises can be made self-correcting simply by putting the title of the book and the page reference at the end of the exercise.
2. Reproduce parts of letters lacking punctuation for heading, salutation, and complimentary close.
3. Create charts and bulletin board displays with proper punctuation. The children should help make these.
4. Produce classroom dramas using characters such as "Double Dot Colon" or "Fishtail Comma" to help make punctuation come alive. Each character should behave in a manner consistent with its name so that its function can be visualized.
5. Enact a "What's My Line?" TV program. A guest on the program represents a punctuation mark. The master of ceremonies states that the guest does four things (or any number representative of his function). The audience must name all functions in order to identify the guest.

6. Read aloud a passage from a reader or a book with proper pauses and oral inflections. Have pupils write proper punctuation marks in an unpunctuated copy of the passage.
7. Encourage functional writing. Check punctuation with students after they have written letters to pen pals, thank-you notes, requests for information, notes to sick friends, and invitations to parties.
8. Have pupils place punctuation in an unpunctuated news item or sports item.

As a teacher you will compile many more ideas for helping the children learn to use punctuation properly. Primarily your task is to be sure you teach it and reinforce the learning whenever the opportunity occurs.

Spelling

If you think about the spelling process, you will recognize its similarity to that of oral reading. Recognition of letters and sounds is important in both processes. So is the sequence of letters and sound from left to right. Although some individuals use the sight or visual associations in reading rather than the sound method, spelling involves more effort than mere visualization; it requires a child to gain a clear impression of the different letter elements in correct sequence. This process takes a longer time, better visual memory, and more discrimination than simple visual association can provide. The many phonetic inconsistencies in the spelling of words in our language complicate the process and make spelling difficult for many children and adults. When one considers the varied pronunciations of graphic forms such as *ough, ea, aid, eau,* plus the various phonetic soundings of the vowels, plus the presence of silent letters, one wonders that anyone ever successfully accomplishes the task of learning to spell correctly.

In spite of the complexities of English spelling, we, as teachers, cannot afford to let down our standards and give it up as a hopeless venture, even though we may sympathize with Isabel Smythe when she says.[7]

Soliloquy on Phonics and Spelling
This year—I firmly made a vow—
I'm going to learn to spell.
I've studied phonics very hard.
Results will surely tell. . . .

"I thought I heard a distant cough
But when I listened, it shut ough."
Oh, dear, I think my spelling's awf.
I guess I meant i heard a coff.

"To bake a pizza—take some dough
And let it rise, but very slough."
That doesn't look just right, I noe.
I guess on that I stubbed my tow.

"My father says down in the slough
The very largest soybeans grough."

[7] Paul S. Anderson, op. cit., p. 361.

> Perhaps he means "The obvious cloo
> To better crops, is soil that's nue."

> "Cheap meat is often very tough.
> We seldom like to eat the stough."
> I'm all confused—this spelling's ruff.
> I guess I've studied long enuph.

In setting up a spelling program, teachers should consider the following guidelines:

1. Use a list of basic words for mastery. This list should include the words that commonly occur in the everyday activities of the children you are teaching.
2. Have each child record the words that he misspells, and frequently check on his progress toward mastery of them.
3. Use worksheets for those who require letter-sound association practice with syllabication of the words.
4. Use praise for improvement in a child's work.

Method. The usual method for teaching spelling, whether using basic group lists, individual lists, or a combination of the two is the test-study-test plan, using three to five days for its completion. The first stage in this plan is a diagnostic test to ascertain the extent of study that is needed. On the days for study, teachers can follow varied procedures with children who need help, such as the following:

1. Go over those words which a majority missed (a) by noting phonetics of words; (b) by noting similarities to words already learned; and (c) by using the words in sentences.
2. Give instruction to small groups who missed the same words.
3. Give specific help to individuals who demonstrate real need.
4. Have children who need drill do worksheets or textbook exercises.
5. Have children who have spelled most or all of the words correctly write sentences or a story in which they use the words.

The study period is followed by another test (on a different day) to determine the need for further study and testing.

Each child should keep a record of the words he has misspelled on his tests and in his compositions. Teachers should see to it that the children study these words and are ready to display mastery of them after sufficient advance notice. Copies of the list of misspelled words can be sent home to parents so that they can give their children additional help. Often, pupils who have mastered the spelling of the troublesome words can be of great help to the child who is having difficulty.

For years and years, people have successfully used mnemonic devices, such as *i* before *e* except after *c* or when sounded like *a* as in *neighbor* or *weigh,* to help them remember by association. Teachers should try to help children understand the use of mnemonic devices so they can make up their own associations to aid them in the memorizing of words correctly spelled. Teachers should also remember that review and testing of words previously learned should be practiced, because only through repeated use will children spell words properly.

Some drills that can be used for spelling practice in the primary grades include the following:

1. Flash cards—followed by children writing the word.
2. Rhyming words that begin with different consonants or blends. Children write the words.

   Example:
   Rhyme the word *cat* with new words that begin with an *m;* an *h;* an *s;* an *r;* a *th.*

3. Opposite meanings—high:low; fat:thin. Children write the opposites.
4. Have children generalize about final *e* words. Ask them to think about what happens when: *ride* becomes *riding; bake* becomes *baking.*
5. Have children generalize about the endings that make plurals. Use sentences to demonstrate:

   I have one box. I have two box*es.*
   We have a cat. We have two cat*s.*
   I have a penny. I have two penn*ies.*

In using a generalization, be sure that the child knows enough words that are examples for that generalization, and consider only one category of generalization at a time. Some primary level examples for generalizing purposes are as follows:

1. Forming plurals of nouns by adding *s.*
2. Forming plurals of nouns ending in *s, x, sh, ch,* by using *es.*
3. Forming plurals by changing *y* to *i* and adding *es.*
4. Forming plurals by changing the singular form.
5. Forming singular possessives by adding *'s.*
6. Using an apostrophe in a contraction.
7. Using a period after an abbreviation.
8. Using root words for making new words by adding suffixes and following the generalizations already learned.

More generalizations for helping children spell with more accuracy can be added for the intermediate grades, because children at this grade level can usually make generalizations with more mature judgment.

1. One-syllable words that end in a consonant preceded by a short vowel usually double the consonant before a suffix which begins with a vowel.

   Examples:
   hot + *er* becomes *hotter.*
   tap + *ing* becomes *tapping.*

2. A word of more than one syllable that ends in a consonant preceded by a short vowel doubles the consonant before a suffix beginning with a vowel providing the accent is on the last syllable.

Examples:
forgét + *ing* becomes *forgetting.*
occúr + *ence* becomes *occurrence.*

3. The letter *i* comes before the letter *e* except after the letter *c* or when the combined letters have the sound of the letter *a*.

Examples:
believe, relieve, receive, neighbor, weigh.

4. Proper nouns and adjectives formed from proper nouns should be capitalized.

Examples:
Spain—Spanish.
England—English.

There are some learners who do not form generalizations with ease. If a capable student spells poorly but wants to spell correctly, a teacher should create a more detailed procedure for him to follow that uses a look-say-look-write repetitious plan.

There are many commercial materials, games, and drills available which can help children learn to spell.

Grammar

With so much criticism and commentary about the type of grammar that should be taught in schools today, some teachers of the language arts have become confused about what standard grammar is. Some critics (many of them parents) believe that there are only two levels of English: standard and substandard, and that the standard forms are those used in the "King's pure English." Parents clamor that the schools today do not include the teaching of grammar in their curricula. If one were to ask these parents to define grammar, some might reply that it is the parts of speech, syntax, sentence structure, and paragraph organization; others would insist that grammar is the way our language is used. Probably there are as many different understandings for the term *grammar* as there are critics and, therefore, teachers of the English language can expect criticism whether they decide to teach traditional or structural grammar, or generative grammar or tagnemics. Some language authorities have taken a strong stand in opposition to formal instruction in the terminology of grammar in the elementary school. Robert C. Pooley, for example, expresses his opposition in statements summarized below:[8]

1. The first consideration in learning is the question of time. Time used for learning terminology takes away from time available for the practice of the skills of writing and speaking English.

---

[8] Robert C. Pooley, *Teaching English Grammar* (New York: Appleton-Century-Crofts, 1957), pp. 126–28.

2. All evidence of research studies shows that formal grammar has very slight effect on the usage habits of children. A child reflects his background and experience; the knowledge of grammar terminology alone will not change his habits.
3. Formal grammar has little or no effect upon the skills of composition in the elementary school.
4. Grammatical terminology, when not particularly connected with a skill regularly used by the child, is easily confused and forgotten. It should not be taught until the seventh year of school.

In textbooks or course syllabuses, however, there is an emphasis upon either old or new grammatical concepts. Elementary teachers are, therefore, obligated to teach these concepts even though some authorities feel there is little or no merit in doing so. Faced with this necessity, teachers have tried to find more meaningful ways in which to present the concepts.

In the primary grades, the teacher who elicits and records contributions to a story that the whole class is composing is, of course, beginning the concept of sentence sense; she writes sentences on the board with proper capitalization and punctuation, which she points out as the essential signals for beginning and ending a sentence. As the children begin to read, once more the teacher stresses sentence sense by helping them to use voice modulations, and pauses, appropriately. When the skill of writing is introduced, the teacher helps each child become aware of a sentence as a group of words that expresses a complete or sensible thought or feeling. In this process, the child, through inductive methods used by the teacher, gradually comes to understand the four functions of sentences: telling, asking, commanding, and exclaiming. Up to this point, there is no distinction between the traditional and the "new" grammar. A sentence is a sentence.

Both traditional grammar and new grammar share labels in common for at least four parts of speech: nouns, verbs, adjectives, and pronouns. The functions of these parts of speech are the same in both grammars. A noun names a person, place, thing, or idea; a verb shows action; an adjective tells about a noun; a pronoun replaces a noun. A primary teacher is free to use the term *noun* as she helps the children label pictures of persons, places, things, and ideas, regardless of which type of grammar is favored in her school program. When a teacher asks a child to describe "the boy" or "the house," and the child replies, "the little boy" or "the red house," she is teaching the grammar concept of adjectives in any system of grammar. This is true also about the functions of verbs and pronouns. The list of prepositions (fifty or so) and the conjunctions (connectors) must be memorized in both the "old" and the "new" grammars. The adverbs answer where, how, when, and why in both grammars. In both, interjections are learned as words that express strong feelings. Actually, there is little difference in the terminology and the function of the parts of speech in the two systems, at least not enough to disturb the new teacher who has fully mastered the fundamentals of the English language.

Primary children have little difficulty in identifying the subject of a sentence. They respond quickly when the teacher asks, "In this story, who ran down the street?" They are used to who and what questions. The predicate involves many words not included in the specific action word or words, so it presents more involved identifications. Nevertheless, children soon learn through practice and exercises, in which they must furnish subjects and predicates in sentences, that the predicate is that part which tells about the subject.

Specific diagramming of sentences has been abandoned in most classrooms, except when it is used by the teacher to present a visual analysis for those who need to "see" the picture.

There are some differences though between the traditional and the new grammars. The old was based upon rules which originated from the Latin language rules. These rules often do not explain the syntactical aspects of modern English. Actually, the contention of the linguists is that language analysis should pertain to the spoken form of the language, according to its sounds, structure, and syntax. These scholars of linguistics have determined that the smallest unit of sound is a phoneme and that the English language has forty-four to forty-six phonemes which must be learned. They have identified twelve suprasegmental phonemes that affect sound through pitch, stress, and juncture (pause). They maintain that words are made up of phonemes, and that if a phoneme or a group of phonemes has meaning, it is called a morpheme. *Ar* has two phonemes (the sound of *a* and the sound of *r*), but does not have lexical meaning; therefore it is not a morpheme. *At* has 2 phonemes; it has lexical meaning, so therefore it is a morpheme. Sometimes a single *s* is classified as a morpheme, because it has the meaning of plural.

Example:

cat	+	s	becomes
(morpheme)		plural	cats
		morpheme	(two morphemes)
cat	+	's	becomes
(morpheme)		Possessive	cat's
		morpheme	(two morphemes)

This type of grammar is based solely on morphology (structure) of words and syntactical relationship of words within a sentence pattern. Proponents of this kind of grammar maintain that by understanding the sounds, the morphology, and the twenty-six transformations which occur in words and sentence patterns, a person can explain every grammatical form in our language. They identify changes in the morphology of a word or in the patterns of sentences as transformations of the original language structure. In the example given, the first word *cats* is a plural transformation; the second *cat's* is a possessive transformation. The comparative and superlative forms of adjectives and adverbs are classified as morphological transformations. There are also sentence pattern transformations, such as changing a telling sentence to an asking sentence, changing an active sentence to a passive sentence, and combining two or more simple sentences into a single complex or compound sentence. There is much technical terminology in the new approach, because it is more scientific in its description of our language as it is spoken.

During the past decade, this new grammar has been introduced into many school language arts programs. It has gradually been modified; many of the technical, scientific aspects have been eliminated so that now it is more functional and more manageable for students and teachers.

Even though the debate about the inclusion or exclusion of grammatical terminology in a language arts program continues, teachers of elementary children recognize that they must continue to help students speak, listen to, read, and write their language. They continue to stress the following:

1. Sentence forms.
2. Paragraph organization.
3. Vocabulary development.
4. Standard usage.
5. Punctuation.

6. Spelling.
7. Reading skills.
8. Aesthetic forms.
9. Critical thinking.
10. Values clarification.

Teachers have an obligation to understand the concepts of the "old" and the "new" grammars and the relationships between them. Schools are experimenting with various programs of grammar. For teachers to effectively meet the needs of the children who are being exposed to these varied programs and also to cope with the program in the school where they are hired, they must have substantial knowledge about all current trends in grammar.

A Final Comment. The role of the language arts teacher is not simple. It has many facets, requires alertness of the teacher on many fronts, and is vital to the future success and happiness of every child. The effort required and the rewards are great. The broadness of the field creates interest, and the crucial nature of the content provides the vital motivation.

With your study of this module, you have moved one step closer to your goal. Continue your progress toward competency in this area by reading generously from the books listed under selected readings.

SUGGESTED READING

Burrows, Alvina T., Dianne Munson, and Russell Stauffer. *New Horizons in the Language Arts*. New York: Harper and Row, Publishers, 1972.

Dallman, Martha, John DeBoer, et al. *The Teaching of Reading*. New York: Holt, Rinehart & Winston, Inc., 1974.

De Stafano, Johanna, and Sharon E. Fox, eds. *Language and the Language Arts*. Boston: Little, Brown and Company, 1974.

Goodman, Kenneth, ed. *Miscue Analysis*. Urbana, Ill.: National Council of Teachers of English, 1973.

Heilman, Arthur W. *Principles and Practices of Teaching Reading,* 3rd ed. Columbus, Ohio: Charles E. Merrill Publishers, 1972.

King, Martha, and Robert and Patricia Cianciolo, eds. *A Forum for Focus*. Urbana, Ill.: National Council of Teachers of English, 1973.

McDonald, Blanche, Leslie Nelson, Mary Louise Reilly, and Ronald L. Brown. *Methods That Teach*. 3rd ed. Dubuque, Iowa: William C. Brown Company, Publishers, 1972.

Moffett, James. *A Student-Centered Language Arts Curriculum, Grades K-6: A Handbook for Teachers*. Boston: Houghton Mifflin Company, 1968.

Rubin, Dorothy. *Teaching Elementary Language Arts*. New York: Holt, Rinehart & Winston, Inc., 1975.

Smith, E. Brooks, and Kenneth and Robert Meredith. *Language and Thinking in the Elementary School*. New York: Holt, Rinehart & Winston, Inc., 1970.

Veatch, Jeannette, Florence Sawicki, et al. *Key Words to Reading: The Language Experience Approach Begins*. Columbus, Ohio: Charles E. Merrill Publishers, 1973.

Wilson, Robert M., and Maryanne Hall. *Reading and the Elementary School Child*. New York: Van Nostrand Reinhold Company, 1972.

POST TEST

1. Describe the three main camps regarding beliefs about language arts.

_____

_____

_____

_____

_____

_____

_____

_____

_____

2. In the four basic areas of language arts, which areas involve the process of encoding? Which involve decoding?

_____

_____

3. What are the four methods commonly used in phrase word analysis?

_____

4. Name the three levels of comprehension, and cite two examples of questions used for each level.

_____

_____

_____

_____

_____

5. Describe three teaching devices which a teacher can use for the structural analysis method in teaching reading.

_____

_____

_____

_____

_____

6. What do the letters DRA mean? What are the four steps in DRA?

_____

_____

_____

_____

_____

7. List the six levels of listening, and give one example of purpose for each level.

_____

_____

_____

_____

_____

_____

8. Describe two procedures a teacher might follow to help a student become aware that he has a need for improvement in listening.

_____

_____

_____

_____

9. Cite three standards for listening activities.

_____

_____

_____

10. Explain the relationship of the terms *phoneme, morpheme,* and *syntax,* which are concepts included in the "new" grammar.

_____

_____

_____

_____

_____

11. How does a teacher stress proper punctuation in the teaching of oral reading?

_____

_____

12. What are four procedures a teacher might use for giving practice and encouraging proper punctuation?

_____

_____

_____

_____

_____

13. What are three guidelines a teacher might follow for developing a spelling program?

_____

_____

_____

_____

14. What is a mnemonic device? Give an example for spelling.

_____

_____

_____

15. State two generalizations about doubling a consonant before adding a suffix that begins with a vowel.

_____

_____

_____

_____

16. What are the four steps in the sequence of teaching written expression?

_____

_____

17. List four motivators for writing that a teacher might use in her classroom.

_____

_____

18. List five thinking skills that children have to use in written expression.

_____

_____

19. Describe three guidelines a teacher might follow for changing children's improper usage habits.

_____

_____

_____

_____

_____

_____

_____

_____

Teaching Science

Shirley Auerbach

Bank Street College of Education

module 8

Preparing to Teach Science / Recent Developments in Science Education / Planning Science Learning / Questioning / Demonstrations / Experimenting / Correlated, Informal, and Incidental Experiences / Small Group Activities Around Concepts / From Science Corner to Science Center / Science and Reading / Audiovisual Materials / Using the Environment / Sharing Science / Evaluation

RATIONALE

This module deals with the importance of including science learning in the elementary school program. It introduces the possibilities and opportunities for exploring science and proposes a combination of formal and informal activities which build on the spontaneous, natural interests of children. Contrasting modern and traditional approaches, the module describes various ways to implement a worthwhile program. However, it utilizes parts of the actual content of a science program only by way of example or illustration, since it is not a substitute for the appropriate curricula, textbooks, materials, and supplies.

By working through the text of the module, the beginning teacher should be able to appreciate the role of science in the total elementary school program and acquire insight into his or her task as guide to the new interests, richer concepts, and expanded information on the part of the pupils. Since the module serves as an introduction to the entire area, it should be supplemented with an examination of a few detailed curricula and textbooks. Skimming through some of these materials should provide a quick overview of typical facets of science as they are presently being treated. The module offers the reader criteria for determining how traditional or modern the materials are. A fruitful approach to study would involve reading through the module first, then consulting the other materials, and finally returning to the module for further clarification.

Have you ever squeezed a melon to judge its ripeness? When dressing this morning, did you consider the color, texture, and weight of the garments you selected? Did you ever decide to take an umbrella because "it looked like rain"? Without reflecting on it, in each of these cases, you were "doing" science. As a matter of fact, from our very beginnings, we all engage in actions that can be labeled scientific. When we respond to our internal and external environment, trying to satisfy our needs, and solve our problems, we are "scientists." We are acquiring and using both knowledge and practical activity, the basic components of science.

All this takes place, of course, long before we begin to systematize or organize the conscious, factual aspect of experience. In important respects, many people may never proceed very far along the road of understanding and interpreting the phenomena of nature. The choice we all make, however, is not between behaving scientifically and behaving unscientifically, but between more adequate or less adequate scientific behavior. We observe, classify, enumerate, generalize, hypothesize, and infer without using the technical terminology. We expect events to occur because of clues remembered from previous events, and we try to achieve results by controlling or influencing objects, actions, and people. Therefore, we trust elevators, bridges, and automobiles to move or support us. We rely on thermometers, rulers, and scales. We cook, we put ice cream in the freezer, and we flick switches for lights, television, and washing machines. We may watch birds feed or fly, admire sunrise and sunset, and enjoy trees, rocks, clouds, and waves. Everywhere and in almost every activity, science can help us enrich our understanding and appreciation, in the way we describe, analyze, explain, and participate in the world we live in.

Think back about the way you were introduced to science as a child. Did you always seem to be asking why? At present, you can distinguish between the two meanings children give to that question, one being "Please tell me what is happening," and the other, "Please tell me what is making it happen." At an early age the child may often intend the first, but then we see that he moves on to the second. Again thinking back, were you answered patiently or abruptly, fully or partially? Were you satisfied quickly or did you generate a series of follow-up questions? These initial experiences sometimes determine our patterns of curiosity and inquiry for many years. Afterwards came your exposure to science lessons in elementary school. Apply the same criteria and you may recall the positive and negative experiences, the pleasant memories or inhibiting reactions of those situations. Perhaps unconsciously, the attitudes toward science that were acquired at that time may still influence your present feelings.

As an adult, you have come to understand the crucial role of science in our society. You know how vital it is with regard to health, industry, communication, transportation, and much more—in fact, to every facet of living, from physical survival to the advanced reaches of human thought. You may be aware that more scientific data have been accumulated in this century than in all past history, and that more than 75 per cent of all scientists who have ever lived were born in this century. Of course, no single individual can hope to master more than a tiny part of the contents of the "knowledge explosion." But the feeling that there is so much to know can spur us on to become lifelong learners of science and hence better informed teachers of science. Above all, we can recognize in science the achievements of human cooperation, the successes in attacking problems, and the hope for an even more meaningful future.

Fundamental to this perspective in teaching science is building on the curiosity of children, on their readiness to inquire, explore, and discover. A major purpose will have been accomplished if this module stimulates each reader to become more sensitive to the myriad riches of everyday experience as a source of endless discoveries of scientific description, analysis, and explanation. Responding to the beauties, wonders, comforts, and contributions of science ourselves, we can inspire enthusiasm and pleasure in the children for whom we are responsible. As an accompaniment to their joy in learning may come a reduction of fear before the unknown and a challenge to mythology and superstition. Actively engaged in investigation, encouraged and helped by knowledgeable and alert teachers, the children may acquire that balance of self-confidence and questioning that can guide them throughout school and later life.

SPECIFIC OBJECTIVES

As a result of working through this module, you should be able to do the following:

1. State the main purposes of teaching science in the elementary school.
2. Identify the four aspects of science teaching.
   a. Outline the major differences between traditional and modern approaches to teaching content.

    b. Explain the importance of concept formation.

    c. Describe the processes involved in engaging in scientific activity.

    d. Present the two facets of scientific attitude.

3. Trace briefly the development of modern science curricula, and describe in detail one modern approach.

4. Specify the content and significance of the following components of science planning:

    a. Program—concepts and content.

    b. Preplanning.

    c. Building lesson plans.

    d. The art of questioning.

    e. Performing demonstrations.

    f. Conducting experiments.

5. Offer examples of correlated, informal, and incidental science experiences.

6. List the science learning opportunities in many parts of the environment.

7. Enumerate ways of sharing science activities.

8. Describe evaluation, its forms, purposes, and importance.

MODULE TEXT

Preparing to Teach Science

What images does the word *science* conjure in your mind? Do you picture difficult formulas, endless facts, bubbling test tubes, flashing lights, or solemn-faced men in stiff lab coats? Do you think of abstract laws of nature or of lifeless planets revolving in distant orbits? Even if you were to accumulate a working knowledge of these innumerable facts and vast, comprehensive theories, a problem would remain: how would you as a teacher convey your understandings to children? What kind of facts would you choose to teach and how deep would the concepts have to be? How difficult would such teaching be? The point would be to find an approach that is meaningful to children, one that would not necessarily begin with, but would lead toward a definition of science. Only after many concrete, personal experiences would youngsters come to understand and appreciate science as the "systematized branch of knowledge dealing with objects, forces, and phenomena of the physical universe."

Consider the process of development through which one has to live so as to comprehend logical structure, explanatory laws, and empirical verification of hypotheses. How do we help this process along? First, we can view science as an activity which originates in human needs and interests and constantly serves these. Its activity centers around people who are busy finding out about their environment and about themselves as part of it, people doing things to understand and to act upon the natural world. What people have learned, how they have gone about learning it, and what they have done with this knowledge are the actual story of science. One important example of the way this knowledge has been applied is the growth of technology, which is a major cornerstone of our culture and our society.

When we examine the findings of science on a mature level, we learn about the disciplines, such as astronomy, physics, chemistry, geology, and biology into which the data and theories. are organized. Such categorization may be appropriate for adolescents and adults. Helping younger children approach the role of science in our society is more meaningful if we look at the problems which science is called upon to solve. Today, for example, some prominent areas for problem solving include health; materials for clothing, housing, and transportation; information processing; and energy. Sensitive to problems in these and similar areas and alert to the opportunities to introduce and develop them, the teacher initiates and facilitates the process by which children learn to recognize the problems. We know that skills in solving problems can be best appreciated by those who have tried the methods of science. By gathering and arranging relevant facts and by formulating and testing possible solutions, all of us, at any age, can learn science.

Being prepared to teach science to elementary school children, then, need not be a cause for anxiety or concern. Knowing the children, their backgrounds, and interests come first as the basis for deciding what to include in the science program and how to deal with it. We begin with the need of all children to explore, manipulate, and discover the what, how, and why of the world around them. A science program tries to meet this need by including four interrelated aspects: content, concepts, process, and attitude.

Content: the Traditional Approach. Familiar to most of us is the fact that content formerly occupied the central, almost exclusive, place in the elementary school science curriculum. In its narrow meaning, content refers to the facts which children are expected to learn, such as names, numbers, and similar specific bits of information, such as, "The third planet from the sun in our solar system is the earth. The earth is about 93 million miles from the sun and has a diameter of about 8,000 miles." In the traditional program, teacher and textbooks were the major sources of information and the dispensers of knowledge, and the lecture and a study-type of reading were the most common procedures. Questioning was strictly fact-based and teacher-initiated, and data were the uniform body of facts everyone was expected to master. The children were therefore required to memorize the information, frequently after copying it into notebooks. Content learning was evaluated simply by having pupils recall or recognize the information, at a certain age, by means of a paper-and-pencil test. Achievement was measured by the grade each child received.

Many factors contributed to this aproach to the learning of science. Belief was widespread that such content was easy to teach, and often the inexperienced teacher who was insecure in science was urged to adopt this fact accumulation procedure. In many instances, having been subjected to this kind of experience themselves, these teachers knew no other way. Preparation of teachers consisted of acquiring as extensive a mass of information as possible so as to play the role of expert. A simple way of organizing the curriculum was to select from the total several content areas for focus. Some typical study areas were matter—its states and changes; magnetism and electricity; motion and force; light, heat, and sound; earth and its resources; man and biological communities; the solar system; and weather. These subject areas appear in modern programs also, but they are approached quite differently. Specific topics traditionally were developed according to different grade levels. When topics were assigned as a whole to a single level, the approach was called the block method. When the same topics were examined from different points of view and at varying depths in different grade levels, the approach was called the spiral method. Regardless of the method, however, the traditional approach to science as content failed many pupils. It generated the attitude that science was difficult for most children, and that it was interesting mainly to those with educational or vocational aspirations in the area.

Content: the Modern Approach. By way of contrast, in the modern approach, content is given far less emphasis. Isolated facts, unrelated to unifying concepts or to meaningful application, have little significance or value. What is useful for teacher background may not be appropriate for children. The facts about the earth and the sun quoted previously are relevant teacher knowledge for activities concerning weather. The effect that the earth's distance has on the radiant energy it receives from the sun is part of the necessary information for explaining changes in temperature. But contrast the information with content for pupils. As the children observe sunlight, or feel its effects on various objects, such as automobiles, sidewalks, fences, the walls of buildings, their own clothing, and tables in the sun and in the shade, or as they learn to read thermometers, they acquire many facts. This is their content, which becomes their property as they use the facts to answer various questions. Children's activities naturally direct them to concepts: the sun heats and lights the earth; some things get hotter than others; and so on. Clearly the factual content of their activities is different from the conventional approach to content, since the emphasis is different.

One result of drawing on previous experiences is that a spiral approach is most likely to occur. Sensory experience, manipulating materials, questioning for purposes of problem solving, observing and interpreting data, generalizing from results, stating and applying concepts—these are also characteristic of the modern approach. In treating content as intertwined with concept formation and experiencing various processes, this approach, unlike the traditional one, regards content as richer and as broader in meaning when facts are related to children's activities and experiences. Learning the content of science is no longer a matter of consulting the authority—teacher or textbook—for a finite body of information, but an adventure in which children and teacher participate.

Concepts. Learning concepts is a second aspect of the elementary school science curriculum. These scientific ideas or principles of nature enable pupils to understand, to explain, and to predict a broad range of natural phenomena. Concepts learned from one experience should help in dealing with other experiences. In a familiar example, children observing a burning candle may acquire concepts regarding burning, temperature, heat, light, color, change, hardness, phases of matter, and energy. The concepts selected for learning depend on both the teacher and the pupils. Two concrete examples dealing with concept formation appear later in this module. The first one appears in connection with planning science activities and deals with the concept of change. The second illustration, concerned with form and function, appears in connection with small group activities.

Many science curricula are organized around major concepts, which serve as organizing centers for long-range planning. While this framework is useful and necessary, the schedule should be flexible enough to make the most of the unusual and unexpected. Besides its structural purpose, concept learning also helps pupils expect order and predictability in natural phenomena. Encouraged to state concepts in their own terms and to apply them thoughtfully and consistently, children acquire skills that are important for both living and learning.

Process. A third aspect of the elementary school science curriculum, process, refers to activities which must be performed so as to solve the problems on which science works. Process depends first of all on the nature of the problem. If we are interested in finding out how heavy certain objects are, we weigh them. If we wanted to fit the objects into a container, we would measure their sizes. Not all processes are used in any one investigation, and the order listed is not necessarily the way in which a scientific activity proceeds. Major processes are as follows:

1. Observing: Using their senses, children gather information about the problem under investigation. Encouraged to investigate by means of putting things together, taking them apart, pushing, and pulling, children use their muscles as well as other parts of their bodies. They report what their senses indicate and may extend what they learn from their senses by using instruments such as magnifying glasses and mirrors.
2. Classifying: When things are collected, they need separating according to similarities and differences. Organizing, categorizing, and grouping things or events can yield useful results. Children should be encouraged to use their own basis for classification, recognizing that the same set of objects may be classified in different ways. For example, a group of buttons may be classified according to size or color or both. A rock collection may be organized on the basis of size, color, or texture, as long as the classification has significance for the child.
3. Formulating questions: Observing and classifying serve as the starting point for identifying problems. Children are encouraged to ask questions, the most significant ones for investigation being those that they originate. Sometimes arising from previous experiences or from inferences, questions may lead to predictions which must be tested. A special treatment of questioning appears later in the module.
4. Predicting: For children, predicting becomes an exciting game of formulating expected results, proposing explanations, and testing them. Using their past experience, children focus their thinking on a problem. Checking results helps them evaluate their predictions. They learn that the reliability of prediction depends on the accuracy of previous observations and upon drawing correct inferences. Children can make their predicting more scientific by successfully finding patterns in nature.
5. Experimenting: Most commonly identified with modern science, experimenting is a way of finding out, a technique for selecting materials, arranging conditions, and providing a control. It can be distinguished from an experience, in which materials and events are observed in the natural world. As a procedure to gather data and test predictions, experimenting starts with questions, goes on to identify and isolate the variables, and leads toward reasonable conclusions. A good experiment yields a qualified answer and often raises many other questions. Children can be encouraged to devise their own experiments or to become involved in planning experiments conducted by the group.

6. Measuring: Essentially, measuring is the comparison form of observation, an object being compared with a standard. The instrument may be an arbitrary standard such as the span of a person's hand or strips of paper cut to the height of a growing plant. Examples of an accepted standard include a meter, a clock, and a thermometer. Children may be helped to develop measurement skills through planned instruction so as to understand the concept of a unit of measurement. Many concrete experiences with direct and indirect measurement lead pupils through stages in acquiring the skills. Measuring the circumference of a child's head by means of a tape measure, and comparing the mass of an apple to gram-calibrated masses on a two-pan balance are two examples of direct measurement. Observing the rotation of the hands of a clock while ice is being melted in different ways, and watching a column of mercury change its length as a result of a temperature change in the bulb of the thermometer are two examples of indirect measurement, readily performed in the classroom.

7. Interpreting: On the simplest level, interpreting continues such processes as comparing sizes, textures, and weights, distinguishing differences in temperature, and identifying sounds, odors, and colors. Noticing such changes as those in size, shape, and position, the observer goes on to judge the validity and usefulness of the data. On the most advanced level, this process involves determining which data are significant and which are not, and which data have been accurately gathered. The teacher helps the children reach levels of interpretation appropriate for their stage of development.

8. Inferring: Drawing conclusions from a set of related observations requires reasoning and judgment. In a simple example, children roll various balls down a ramp that is set at different angles. One possible inference might be that the speed acquired by any ball rolling down a specific ramp depends only on the angle the ramp makes with the table, and not on the size of the ball used. Alternative inferences can be formulated by the children, and then tested and explored further.

9. Communicating: Recording, describing, and reporting observations, experimental procedures, and conclusions contribute greatly to each individual's understanding. Written statements, experience charts, diagrams, tables, graphs, maps, drawings, photographs, tape recordings, and collections of objects are all valuable outcomes of data gathering.

10. Formulating models: Constructing a physical or conceptual representation of what investigators believe to be reality in nature can make the abstract more concrete, enable students to study interrelationships of objects and concepts, or help them to make predictions. A model of the solar system, consisting of a group of clay spheres, a drawing of circles on paper, or many pages of words, numbers, and equations might serve as an aid to learning. A model is useful when the explanations it generates are consistent with the laws of nature, or when it continues to produce valid predictions. When it fails, it must be revised or replaced. Approached imaginatively, the process of model making and model testing can be enjoyed at different ages.

11. Generalizing: Children should be encouraged to generalize regularly and in their own words about their own observations, experiences, and experi-

ments. They can engage in careful, critical thinking with help from the teacher. Throughout all the activities listed and described as part of process, each individual will achieve on a different level. As each child explores a problem, the teacher observes the pupil's success in performing the necessary problem-solving processes, and provides assistance and encouragement.

Attitude. Another aspect of the elementary school science curriculum is attitude. Attitude refers to the child's feelings about science and toward himself or herself as a problem solver. A science program elicits a good attitude when children eagerly pursue activities leading toward the solution of problems which they want to solve. Overt discipline problems, boredom, and inactivity are minimized or eliminated. As an exciting pursuit, rather than a forced mastery of mainly verbal information, the modern science approach may stimulate the acquisition of concepts and processes that will prove useful for a lifetime.

A positive attitude toward science may help overcome irrational myths and superstitions. Not only does this benefit the child, but, continued and deepened later on, such understanding and behavior aid the adult in successfully coping with the problems of society. Clearly, the integration of content, concept, process, and attitude makes science teaching a significant contribution and makes science learning a vital part of everyone's education.

Recent Developments in Science Education

A twenty-three-inch sphere, weighing eighteen pounds, shot into the atmosphere, made "ripples" which have not stopped. Not only was a new era in science launched in October 1957 when Sputnik I, the first man-made satellite, was put into orbit around the earth, but the impact on American education was also historic, as the demand immediately arose for vigorous emphasis on teaching science. The demand coincided with an already existing drive to revise science curricula in line with a new understanding of the child's intellectual development, and became a national movement productive of many new programs. Two important figures associated with the new approach are Jean Piaget and Jerome Bruner. Perhaps the best-known results of the projects are the science and mathematics curricula for the secondary schools, but there have also been significant changes on the elementary school level.

Embodied in the most influential projects of the early 1960s is the modern approach to teaching elementary science. By familiarizing himself or herself with these concepts of teaching, the beginning teacher may choose to incorporate some of the emphases, materials, or lessons into his or her own science program. Although each project stressed different aspects of current science teaching philosophy, they were all produced by teams consisting of scientists, elementary school teachers, and education specialists. In workshops, they wrote objectives and rationales, produced printed matter for pupils and for teacher guides, and included laboratory experiences, multimedia materials, and evaluative instruments. Summer institutes that focused on techniques and goals trained hundreds of teachers, who then pilot-tested the programs with thousands of children and worked closely with the writers to revise and expand the material. Funded by the National Science

Foundation, this movement was the greatest effort in the history of science teaching.

All project designers agreed that children should learn through first-hand experiences what science is about and what scientists really do. The purpose was to provide cognitive stimulation necessary to development, and the goal was to prepare scientifically literate people, able to cope with situations generated by an ever-changing, complex, technological society. Three examples of these curriculum projects, briefly treated here, are the Elementary Science Study, Science—A Process Approach, and the Science Curriculum Improvement Study.

The Elementary Science Study (ESS). For the Elementary Science Study (ESS), more than fifty units have been written dealing with such topics as bones, ice cubes, pendulums, growing seeds, batteries and bulbs, clay boats, light and shadows, and whistles and strings. Most units can be used over a wide range of grades, the choice being left to the teacher. Children are encouraged to do what they want with the materials, so that they may, for example, decide to design, build, and play their own musical instruments. The units lead to many open-ended activities, which for the most part can be implemented with a small amount of inexpensive, readily available materials. As in all first-hand, discovery-oriented science, children doing ESS make measurements, classify, observe, and infer. The children, however, develop these process skills informally and as needed. The activity is planned to involve the pupils deeply, but mastery of specific concepts is not stressed. Evaluation of student achievement is informed, and the program's success depends considerably on the teacher's ability to run a somewhat unstructured program.

Science—A Process Approach (SAPA). In contrast, the program called Science —A Process Approach (SAPA) builds on structure. Based on Robert Gagne's theories, this curriculum is constructed on the idea of hierarchical skills. Children must master certain simple behavioral skills and acts before they can move on to higher behavioral acts. In an elaborately outlined series of behavioral sequences, the curriculum uses a spiral approach. Since, as the title indicates, process skills are primary, concepts and content are employed mainly in developing the former component. For the inexperienced teacher, the published program offers the advantage of describing in great detail the lessons to be taught. Besides supplying all materials, it also provides a package of evaluative instruments.

Science Curriculum Improvement Study (SCIS).. The third project, the Science Curriculum Improvement Study (SCIS), is a sequential, articulated program based on the structure of science as viewed by contemporary scientists. Geared to the elementary school child's intellectual growth, the scientific concepts are mastered through extensive direct contact with natural phenomena. Three types of lessons have been developed for this program. *Exploration* lessons give the child a variety of experiences with materials and equipment. *Invention* lessons introduce new ideas that help the child derive meanings from his or her exploratory experiences. *Discovery* lessons help the child find applications for these ideas. SCIS also offers the teacher a complete curriculum package, although, unlike SAPA, it provides opportunity for open-ended investigations by the children.

From the three examples it can be seen that a modern science curriculum may be organized around content areas, conceptual schemes, process skills, or self-contained and unsequenced units. Although all aspects may be covered, emphasis will be different according to the program selected. Important in all programs is that the children become involved in activity directed toward solving problems. The teacher functions as a learning facilitator, not as a dispenser of facts. He helps pupils learn to consult him as one familiar with sources of information. He values the posing of questions as well as the giving of answers in guiding the children. He does not impose closure prematurely since he understands that learning is cumulative. He encourages speculative, original thinking and refrains from insisting that evidence be interpreted only in conformity with accepted authority. Scientific learning is approached in many meaningful ways in which inquiry, exploration, and discovery are all present.

Planning Science Learning

By the time a science book or article is published, some of it is out-of-date. Change is rapid and constant. Yet, we cannot conclude that no one can write or teach science. Sometimes the new material is just an addition to the already known and accepted. Or the new material requires slight modification of the old. Or it demands a thorough overhaul or complete replacement of the old. But only if we have a framework in which to place the new discoveries and have criteria by which to evaluate them can we accurately understand and appreciate them. In the same way, the teacher adopts a program of science teaching, but remains alert to revise it as a regular, ongoing procedure. The teacher is guided by the available or required curricula and textbooks and by the children being taught. No one way of scheduling applies to all levels and circumstances. The constants include the logical sequence of science concepts, the themes planned in other curriculum areas for which the elementary school teacher is also responsible, and the changing seasons and special days. The variables are pupil background, maturity, interest, and unusual or unexpected events. (Eclipses are unusual, whereas windstorms may be unexpected.) As in all planning, the science program should have a basic structure, yet be treated with flexibility and imagination.

How concepts, content, process, and attitude are interrelated can be illustrated around the concept of change. For the elementary school child, one possible approach to a sequence of learning through different grades is as follows: Concept I: All things change. Content: Weather changes. Seasons change. Living things change as the seasons change. Water and wind can make changes in the environment. People control their environment by making changes.

Concept II: Many kinds of change occur. Content: Evaporation and condensation, filtering and straining, and separating substances from suspension, by allowing them to stand, produce physical changes. Rusting, burning, bleaching, and souring cause chemical changes. Washing dishes or clothes uses both physical and chemical changes. Tiny living things, such as bacteria, yeasts, and molds, make changes in food. Processes naturally include formulating questions, predicting, experimenting, observing, measuring, classifying, inferring, and generalizing. Attitudes involve overcoming fear before the phenomena of change, recognizing regularities and explanations, and gaining confidence in our ability to predict, adjust to, or control, many changes.

Pre-Planning. Before planning the science learning experience comes the stage of *preplanning*. Preferably with the children playing a role, the teacher considers these questions:

1. What should the children learn? Specific objectives of each lesson include (a) the processes the children will perform more proficiently at the end of the lesson; (b) new science concepts they will understand and apply to other situations; (c) information they will acquire; and (d) scientific appreciations and attitudes they will gain.
2. What methods and materials will be needed to achieve the objectives? Activities must involve the children, and supplies and equipment must be usable and ready.
3. How can the lesson start? Motivating children by catching their interest is most effective when a problem is posed (verbally or visually), a common experience is recalled, or a puzzling phenomenon is demonstrated. Good motivation is short, clear, and appropriate.

Lesson Plans. Although plans should be written according to school requirements, the best plans reflect the teacher's needs. Drawing on the preplanning and serving as a complete reference for the progress of the lesson, good plans include these features:

1. Objectives for the children to achieve; these determine content and procedure and are basic for evaluating strengths and shortcomings.
2. Aims and purposes; children must understand the reason for the activity. These clarify the meaning and value of each experience.
3. Motivation: the interest-grabbing start.
4. Development: the body of pupil activities and the key questions which direct the lesson. (Discussion of techniques and questioning appears later.)
5. Materials, preparations, and equipment: essential for demonstrations and experiments.
6. Conclusion: providing ways to summarize the most important results, in discoveries, facts, and concepts learned, to pose new problems for exploration, and to yield an evaluation of the achievement of aims and objectives.

Questioning

Good questions are vital to good teaching in all curriculum areas, but in science, questions are very special. Scientists begin their research by raising questions. This procedure can also serve as a starting point for children's investigations. Problems posed as questions give purpose and direction to activity. By arranging for situations which provoke questions, the teacher encourages and cultivates the natural questioning attitude of children. Pupils come to feel that school is the place to ask questions, that their questions are important, and that questions often stimulate exciting explorations. The teacher's questions serve as a model for the children as they develop skill in formulating their own.

Drawing on pupil experience, questions may lead to closer observation, suggest trips and surveys, encourage experimentation, help children group and classify, lead to measurement and collection of data, require children to predict, and challenge them to propose explanations. The art of questioning also involves eliciting a variety of contributions and making them form a chain. Effective starters include Where have you seen . . . ? How many kinds . . . ? How can we find out . . . ? Where can we find . . . ? How many ways can we (do) . . . ? How can we be sure that . . . ? What would happen if . . . ?

Pursuing the responses, the teacher involves as many pupils as possible in adding, agreeing or disagreeing, and offering reasons. Teacher-pupil and pupil-pupil interaction, based on mutual respect, leads to cooperative learning. The teacher never forgets to ask the children, "What questions do you have?" and "What do you think?" The procedure of building on the responses leads to more explorations and fresh discoveries. Since all the answers in science are found by people and are limited by the means available at any one time, all answers are subject to change. For example, a very few years ago, we did not know exactly what the moon's surface was like. We are still not sure about the earth's magnetism or whether life exists on Mars. Facts may be ephemeral, but knowing methods of inquiry remains valuable all our lives. As an endless quest rather than a finite body of information, questioning and discussion make science in the classroom an adventure for children and teacher.

Demonstrations

If a picture is worth a thousand words, how much more is a demonstration worth! Carefully planned and rehearsed, a science demonstration is an experience in direct observation of an event, performed in front of a class by the teacher, a child, a group of children, or the teacher plus assistants. It serves one or more of the following purposes:

1. Provides a problem situation which may serve as motivation for the lesson.
2. Illustrates, verifies, or explains information or concepts previously investigated by the children.
3. Provides a basis of experience for further learning.
4. Produces a positive attitudinal change—for example, proves that science is fun.
5. Inculcates principles of safety.

A good demonstration is completely visible to the entire class. It works best when the demonstration is large, when a nondistracting background is used, and when the materials are simple. Even though the actual demonstration may present a puzzling phenomenon, the elements and procedure should be clearly understood. Questions, rather than explanations, should be used to achieve comprehension. Sometimes relying on the element of surprise, the demonstration should be short, should have pupil participation, and should provide guided practice in observation.

Experimenting

Scientists are often identified as the people who try to discover nature's secrets by experimenting. Guided by the principle, "Let's find out," children can be intrigued by the components of surprise and discovery. To develop necessary patterns of thinking and working, the teacher stimulates children to raise problems. An experiment is preferably a cooperatively developed activity with appropriate materials set up to find an answer to a specific problem. As one problem is attacked, additional problems emerge. A real experiment includes some doubt about its outcome, with the experimenter predicting a certain result as the most probable, but being uncertain about it.

Appropriate experiments can be used on any elementary grade level. For example, kindergarten children may observe what happens when they experiment with dropping certain materials (clay, sand, water, or wooden blocks) from a constant height into a pan on the floor. Fifth-grade children may experiment with a battery, two bulbs, and wires, to discover which way of making the bulbs light makes them burn more brightly.

Some guidelines for experimentation are as follows:

1. Start with problems drawn from science handbooks, children's experiences, class trips, provocative materials, or previous experiments.
2. Involve children in designing experiments, deciding on and gathering appropriate materials. Before proceeding, the teacher should check the pupils' comprehension of the way the experiment relates to the initiating problem. Manipulating the materials and working at their own pace, the pupils may perform the experiment individually, by groups working at the same time, or by one group in the class. The more difficult experiments should be tried first by the teacher.
3. Cultivate scientific methods such as the following:
   a. Use a control to provide a basis for accurate comparison. For example, when children try to find out why yeast is used in breadmaking, they make one dough with yeast and one without.
   b. Test one variable at a time to arrive at a more valid conclusion. For example, when children try to find out what a plant needs to live, they deprive it of either sunlight or water, but not both at the same time.
   c. Compare results achieved by different children. They can investigate whether this is caused by variations in techniques used, in materials, in observational skills, or in ability to report observations.
   d. Communicate results by recording, reporting, and deriving generalizations from the greatest number of experiments and observations. The teacher guides the pupils rather than telling them what they see.
4. Use experiments which do not work as an opportunity to solve a real problem. In the sense that what happens is the result of natural forces and components, every experiment works. But why a particular one is not working as expected is the starting point for science learning, in which the children are urged to propose various theories, and then to test them. By adhering to the requirements of a valid experiment, teacher and children share a meaningful appreciation of the problem being explored and tested.

Correlated, Informal, and Incidental Experiences

Besides planning the experiences of a formal science curriculum, the alert teacher takes advantage of the many opportunities for science activities throughout the day. From the endless variety available, only a few examples are suggested here, all of them usable even with the very youngest pupils.

Mathematics—Apples brought in for snacks or for ducking at Halloween are counted, or if cut into halves or quarters, the seeds are counted. Then, classifying by size, color, shape, and variety adds a science dimension.

Language Arts—While talking over plans for a trip, the teacher and class must take into account the weather. Here is a springboard for observations throughout the month or semester. The calendar is covered with symbols for sun, rain, and snow. Someone describes the excitement of snow and making snowmen. Which lasts longer, the one made by the class for indoors, or the one for outdoors? Why does this happen?

Art—The class has made mobiles. What makes them move? What are air currents? What is wind? At another time, it is discovered that paints and paste are drying up. What's wrong? Using a series of jars, half of them covered and half uncovered, the class experiments to find out what happens and figures out why. Working directly with jars of water, the class pursues the problems of evaporation.

Music—Making their own instruments, the children are led to an entire range of questions: What is musical sound? What vibrations are created? How do longer and shorter strings sound? What experiments can they do with volume, pitch, and resonance?

Social studies—Part of the environment is the building. To find out how it gets warm, the class visits the boiler room. In an older building, the experience involves seeing furnace, boiler, and coal. In a more recent one, it involves oil and electricity. Discussion of water and steam leads to an experiment in the room, using an electric hot plate and a pot of water. From there, it is natural to go on to condensation and the cycle of rain.

The class may make a model of the community to demonstrate the interdependence of people, goods, and services. The need to set up traffic lights and street lights raises the problem of electrification. What can we use?

Transportation through the community brings up the question of wheels, and how and why they help. From pulleys to levers and other devices, the discussion moves to many science activities.

Cooking—Hard apples turn to mushy ones when we cook them. The gelatine and water mixtures turn into firm gelatine in the refrigerator. What makes solids turn to liquids, and liquids turn to solids? Small corn kernels pop into fluffy popcorn. What helped? When we put sugar into water, what happens? Which substances can be thoroughly mixed, and which cannot? Understanding cooking processes, problems, precautions, and results has science learning as its outcome.

General classroom experiences include the following:

1. Tacks spill out of the box. How do we gather them quickly? Magnets come to the rescue, and we go on to explore many other facets of magnets.
2. Water is spilled on the table. A sponge is used to wipe it up. What else can we use? Which does it more efficiently, drawing paper, paper towels, or tissues? Why? What are the many properties of water?
3. Some of the party balloons have burst. What was inside? Where did the air come from? When it is let out of the balloon and the balloon flies across the room, what are we observing? From action and reaction, we go on to the question of rockets.

4. While the plants were being put on the table to decorate it for snack time, part of a stem broke off. What do we do with it? What will happen if we put it into water? Over a period of time, we observe the growth of roots. Are there other ways of growing plants?

5. While we are watching a film, someone's hand gets in front of the projector. After discussion of the film, we go on to explore the subject of shadows, light and dark, daytime and nighttime. How are shadows made? What happens when the light source is closer or further away?

In all instances, what starts as a spontaneous response to an immediate experience can be developed as a science activity, which grows out of the children's need to find out. Not always is an experiment necessary. Certainly every scientist does not rush to his laboratory every time a problem arises. But one must take advantage of those teachable moments. The science curriculum is not complete if it encompasses only this potpourri of experiences. But the informal situations, taken together with the planned science topics, give teacher and children a rich, meaningful approach to the many concepts they can be helped to grasp.

Small Group Activities Around Concepts

Assume the class has become interested in the concept of form and function. Isn't it possible to explore the relationship of form to function by using a variety of experiences that different groups of children may engage in simultaneously? Those who enjoy dissection would be cutting up a chicken to determine how internal organs are placed in relation to each other, and would be devising their own explanations of reasons why the chicken is designed as it is. Another group might be trying to reconstruct Swedish angel chimes, without prior knowledge of their structure. They might figure out that the circular disk revolves around the top and rests on a tall cylinder which serves as a natural support column because of its shape. Or those who enjoy collecting things could gather an egg shell, a turtle shell, a fireman's hat, a construction worker's hat, and a model of a human skull as evidence of the sturdy shapes which offer protection to the softer contents they cover.

Then comes the greater learning, when all the activities and observations are discussed in a class sharing of experiences relating to form and function. Not only does this present the cognitive aspects of the concept, but it also demonstrates the way in which scientists generally reach and extend their knowledge, through interaction with other scientists in the field, building on the accumulated knowledge of many who worked concurrently on similar problems.

From Science Corner to Science Center

Children are interested in themselves and in their immediate environment. Therefore, the science program should make use of the total classroom setting. Early childhood materials (paints, paper, clay, blocks, toys, musical instruments, wood, and tools) are a natural. Living and growing things, such as plants on the tables at snack time and pets in the room, given proper housing and feeding, are always valuable. Upper-grade children can certainly make use of these materials, plus others they can bring, such as spools, leaves, plastic containers, shoeboxes, and small animals. Skillful use of such materials and objects has always been a feature of science corners. Although the science area serves as one focal point for activity, science learning should not be limited to one corner. Instead, the classroom itself can become a science center.

Science and Reading

From the environment and their response to it, children become familiar with objects and sensory impressions, which are the basis of enriched speaking and writing vocabularies. As new experiences introduce new science words, speaking, reading, and writing abilities can improve. For example, planning a class garden may involve consulting instructions for sowing and caring for plants, and include names of common seeds, vegetables, flowers, and gardening tools. Pupil experiments, observations, or generalizations may provide the content for experience charts, with the children developing skill first in dictating, and then in reading and writing reports, and making charts, tables, and graphs, especially if these are the results of their own measurements. Titles, captions, labels, and descriptive text are part of preparing science exhibits, and all involve reading and writing skills.

If children are to have an opportunity to select reading materials, they must be supplied with a variety of suitable books and other references. Many texts (rather than one), and encyclopedias and trade books with diverse content, levels, and styles can make the program individualized to meet the needs of different children. The teacher must also provide help with the effective use of reference materials. Just as reading skills are essential for progress in science learning, so do experiences in science provide rich opportunities for reading.

Audiovisual Materials

Modern school children are surrounded by various media. The multisensory approach, so readily available for science learning, requires wise and careful selection by the teacher from a wealth of resources. Television, motion pictures, filmstrips, transparencies, radio, tape recordings, records, magazines, newspapers, charts, models, chalkboard drawings, felt board, and bulletin board—all have something to offer to sight and sound, all can be integrated with instruction, all are effective when they contribute specifically to topics being studied. Selection based on appropriateness and availability is crucial. The teacher provides the material, plans its scope and place, and at no time treats it as a substitute for the teaching-learning process. Children should be involved as active participants. When they are adequately prepared for the concepts and vocabulary, pupils learn more effectively, using audiovisual materials. It need hardly be pointed out that the resources are not to be used to overwhelm the children.

As an introduction to a new unit, these materials can arouse interest and curiosity, or help pupils formulate problems they will try to solve. During exploration of a topic, the materials can supply information, reinforce knowledge and skills, stimulate research, or encourage follow-up activities. At the end of a unit, the aids can provide review. Possibilities are always present for combining learning and pleasure.

Using the Environment

We may not have the vision of the poet who can "see a world in a grain of sand," but we can learn much from the immediate environment. Directly available are the school building with its human use of nature's resources (brick, glass, lumber, and steel); the schoolyard, exposed to sun, wind, and rain; the school garden of living plants in a natural environment of soil, sunlight, air and water; and the trees announcing the changing seasons. Neighborhood trips to see real buildings under construction or real machines at work are also part of the program, in the same way as exploring an ocean front, a bay, a waterfall, a lake, a river, or a swamp. Sparrows and gulls, squirrels and insects, streets, parks, and beaches abound in innumerable varieties of living things. The continuous natural processes of building up and tearing down, as in erosion of soil, rusting of iron, and decaying of leaves, are everywhere. Especially pupils in the very early grades can use frequent trips in and around the schoolyard as their local laboratory. Adopting particular trees for observation is a simple, yet illuminating experience.

When suitably selected, a more elaborately planned trip to an aquarium, museum, planetarium, botanic garden, arboretum, or zoo provides enriching experiences. Preliminary discussion prepares for observation, and follow-up discussion may lead to reports or displays created by the children. Through their own guided activities they use the resources of the total environment, both those planned for science learning and those planned for many different uses.

Sharing Science

Scattered throughout this module are references to the ways in which children share their science learning—individual reports, group reports, class reports, or exhibits made available to other classes. Occasionally, a school will encourage the development of projects to be shared most widely by means of a science fair. Here are some suggestions for making the activity meaningful, rewarding, and pleasurable.

Have the pupils begin work on the project early enough to avoid pressure in completing it. Have them select a project in which they are especially interested and for which they have the necessary skills. To make the project their own, some aspect should be entirely original. The necessary materials should be readily obtainable, preferably at little or no cost. During the activity, complete notes should be kept so that any data can be presented in full detail.

A good exhibit tells a story which others can understand. It should be arranged so that viewers can see all parts clearly and read the labels easily at a distance. If the project is a working model, it should operate without special attention or danger of breakage. It should fit into the available space, yet be sturdy enough to withstand moving. In addition to being accident-proof, the exhibit should be safe from souvenir collectors. Well-motivated and properly executed projects for science fairs can be an ideal means of sharing science learning in an exciting and enjoyable way.

Evaluation

In a well-planned, well-taught lesson everything goes smoothly. The children engage in activities with enthusiasm. Is the lesson a success? To find out whether the objectives were achieved, there must be some sort of evaluation. This may take many forms, such as a written exam given to an entire class, a series of verbal questions posed to a small group, or asking a child to demonstrate a skill or solve a problem. Regardless of the form used, the skillful teacher can also use the evaluative instrument to identify any weakness in the teaching procedure. It is important that evaluation not be used as a club. Children should not be motivated to learn science so as to do well on a test or to get high grades in science. Instead, it is a tool by which a teacher can see whether he provided effective teaching-learning experiences.

When elementary school science stressed content, evaluation was a relatively simple matter. Objective exams (multiple-choice, true-false, completion, and matching) could easily be constructed to demonstrate the degree to which a child had memorized the required information. The degree to which a child had grasped a concept was far more difficult to determine. The following questions might have appeared on a content-oriented evaluative device:

1. Rolling friction is less than sliding friction. True or False?
2. We can decrease friction by making surfaces smoother. True or False?
3. A substance put between two surfaces to reduce friction is called a _____.
4. To pick up a pencil with our fingers, there must be enough _____ between the pencil and our fingers.

To place a greater emphasis on the understanding of concepts, the test could be rewritten as follows:

1. In A, a book is pulled across the floor. In B, the same book is placed on round pencils and pulled. Draw the rubber band as it will look when pulling the book in B.
2. On which of the following surfaces would it be easy to slide a carton of groceries?

cement _____	waxed floor _____
sand _____	soft dirt _____
ice _____	sand paper _____

3. Explain how oiling the wheels of your bicycle helps it to work better.
4. Write a story describing what your day would be like if there were no friction.
5. Write a story describing what your day would be like if all friction became ten times as great.

Evaluation works best when it is an integral part of the science activities rather than an added thorn at the end. It should serve to reveal the child's thought processes rather than serve as an opportunity for the child to receive reward or punishment for producing or not producing the "right answer."

Process, sometimes the most important aspect of a science program, is the most difficult to evaluate. The teacher has to gauge the child's ability to deal with situations in a meaningful way. Clearly, this evaluation can work only as part of the children's activities. Even a single topic or portion of the curriculum can be used to evaluate success with such significant objectives as stating problems, selecting exploration and discovering procedures, manipulating materials, recording and interpreting data, generalizing from results, and stating new concepts and applying them.

Regarding long-term goals, we evaluate whether the children have increased their interest in science and their awareness of their environment. We check whether the pupils engage in science activities on their own, in their hobbies, games, reading choices, or program selections. We note whether they demonstrate keener observation, seek answers to their own questions, distinguish fact from fancy, and begin to expect order and predictability in natural phenomena. The children's enthusiasm, sense of satisfaction in their own achievement, and their smiles are indications to the teacher who evaluates the process of learning sensitively and continuously.

A Final Comment. Within the past few years, adults who have left science and technology to "other people to worry about" have suddenly been confronted with problems of pollution (air, water, and noise), problems of energy and food shortage and of conservation in general, and problems of disease—all involving frightening events, grim predictions, and somber decisions. At the same time, all of us are impelled to marvel at human ingenuity, inventiveness, and power to manipulate the environment through humanity's ever-increasing knowledge and skill. How do we prepare our children to engage in meaningful activities which build their self-confidence and overcome any fears of incomprehensible dangers and disasters? Certainly sources of strength must be their growing understanding of natural phenomena and their ability to recognize and solve problems.

Another source of strength must be a responsiveness to the beauty of this world. In the words of Rachel Carson, "If a child is to keep alive his inborn sense of wonder, without any such gift from the fairies, he needs the companionship of at least one adult who can share it, rediscovering with him the joy, excitement and mystery of the world in which we live."[1]

Perhaps you, the teacher, can be just such an adult. And it is possible if you view your role not as a fountainhead of factual information, but as an interested partner in the exploration of the surrounding world.

SUGGESTED READING

Goldberg, Lazer. *Children and Science.* New York: Charles Scribner's Sons, 1970.
Hawkins, David. "ESI Elementary Science Activities Project," *Science Education* **48** (Feb. 1964), 77–78.

[1] Rachel Carson, *The Sense of Wonder* (New York: Harper and Row, Publishers, 1965), p. 45.

Karplus, Robert. "The Science Curriculum Improvement Study," *Journal of Research in Science Teaching* **2** (1964), 293–303.

Livermore, Arthur H. "AAAS Commission on Science Education: Elementary Science Program," *Journal of Chemical Education* **43** (May 1966), 270–72.

National Science Foundation. *Course Content Improvement Projects.* Washington: U.S. Government Printing Office, n.d. (Annual publication).

Schwab, Joseph J., and Paul F. Brandwein. *The Teaching of Science.* Cambridge, Mass.: Harvard University Press, 1962.

Stone, George K. *Science Projects You Can Do.* Englewood Cliffs, N.J.: Prentice-Hall, Inc., 1970.

———. *More Science Projects You Can Do.* Englewood Cliffs, N.J.: Prentice-Hall, Inc., 1970.

POST TEST

Select the most adequate or appropriate statement. For your own benefit, formulate the reasons why you believe it to be the best and why the other statements are inaccurate or inadequate.

1. One main reason for teaching elementary school science is to
   a. help pupils win prizes for projects in science fairs.
   b. encourage youngsters to plan careers as scientists.
   c. explore the riches of the natural environment.
   d. achieve high scores on science tests.

2. The elementary school science curriculum has
   a. undergone extensive changes in the past decade and a half.
   b. remained virtually unchanged for some time so that it is very easy to teach.
   c. become a less important part of the total school program.
   d. become more technical than it used to be.

3. In the traditional approach to elementary school science,
   a. emphasis was placed on extensive pupil activities and numerous trips.
   b. teacher and textbook were accepted as authorities.
   c. demonstrations and experiments were the central core.
   d. pupil-initiated questions serve as the basis for the program's sequence.

4. In the modern approach to elementary school science,
   a. audiovisual materials are used exclusively.
   b. the teacher becomes the chief source of up-to-date information.
   c. children are encouraged to experiment without teacher guidance.
   d. problem solving is a central feature.

5. The content of science
   a. is regarded as unimportant nowadays because of new discoveries.
   b. is difficult to organize systematically.
   c. does not lend itself to any simple evaluation or testing.
   d. consists of facts and information accumulated through empirical investigation.

6. Concepts in science
   a. are formulated as both principles and theories.
   b. are beyond the intellectual level of most elementary school children.
   c. must be accepted by the layman without challenge.
   d. refer to the confidence of scientists about the future.

7. The processes of science
   a. include formulating problems, selecting procedures, reporting data, and generalizing.
   b. are the easiest aspect to observe and evaluate.
   c. work mainly because they repeat familiar routines.
   d. answer questions so definitively that further exploration becomes unnecessary.

8. A positive scientific attitude
   a. can begin with having children regard science as fun.
   b. is less useful for adults than for children.
   c. makes it unnecessary to know much specific content.
   d. is important only for those who plan for science careers.

9. In science teaching, lesson plans
   a. can be taken directly from teacher guides and standard textbooks.
   b. are less important than casual, incidental opportunities.
   c. combine organization and sequence with flexibility and imagination.
   d. can dispense with motivation.

10. Questioning in science
    a. is effective when the teacher initiates most questions.
    b. is far less important than good visual demonstrations.
    c. is crucial for developing all four aspects of the program.
    d. should be drawn largely from published materials for accuracy.

11. A good science demonstration
    a. may take the entire time allotment for science for one day.
    b. is short and appropriate to the topic.
    c. should be performed by the teacher, with some occasional assistance from pupils.
    d. can be performed only at the end of a unit.

12. Experiments
    a. are mainly intended to supplement a good text.
    b. can be used to lead to further experiments.
    c. are the starting points for scientific investigation.
    d. are good only if they work as predicted or anticipated.

13. Correlating science activities with other curriculum areas
    a. offers many rich possibilities in the elementary school.
    b. depends on suggestions derived from textbook questions.
    c. is somewhat too far-fetched to allow for successful teaching.
    d. can be appreciated largely in the upper grades.

14. Informal science experiences
  a. can interfere with the regularly planned work.
  b. tend to confuse children as being irrelevant and meaningless.
  c. provide many teachable moments.
  d. require much less teacher background than the formal program.

15. In science teaching, audiovisual materials
  a. have been successfully used to replace teachers.
  b. have been developed in a few, limited areas.
  c. should be previewed by the teacher for suitability and proper integration.
  d. are quite elaborate and expensive.

16. In the science program, reading
  a. works best when textbooks, encyclopedias, trade books, and other reading materials are varied in content and style.
  b. works best when these materials are uniform for each grade level.
  c. should be handled primarily by the reading specialist because of its difficulty.
  d. is likely to develop as an adolescent interest.

17. Using the environment for science activities
  a. involves mainly planned trips to museums and zoos.
  b. means community experiences off the school grounds.
  c. entails exploring the most immediate places as well as the more distant ones.
  d. refers primarily to caring for a school garden.

18. Sharing science
  a. includes individual, group, and class reports, projects, and exhibits.
  b. means having all pupils cooperate on a single project at a time.
  c. refers to bringing in materials and supplies from home.
  d. consists of dividing responsibility for different processes among various pupils.

19. Evaluation in science
  a. should consist entirely of objective tests in order to be strictly scientific.
  b. should come only at the conclusion of pupil activities.
  c. should be an integral part of all activities.
  d. can handle only content and concepts and omit process and attitude.

20. The best science program is one
  a. with the latest information organized for quick mastery of content.
  b. which unites teacher and children in cooperative inquiry, exploration, and discovery.
  c. which helps all pupils memorize the most facts and concepts.
  d. which inspires the most pupils to become scientists.

Teaching Social Studies

Janet M. Leonard

Jersey City State College

module 9

The New Social Studies / Concept Development / Concept Development in the Curriculum / Social Studies in the Primary Grades / Social Studies in the Intermediate Grades / Social Studies in the Upper Grades / Unit Planning / Community Studies / Value Seeking in the Classroom / Dramatics / Evaluation

RATIONALE

The teaching of social studies in the elementary school is a challenging experience, which demands that the teacher be able to integrate broad bodies of knowledge in a coherent and meaningful manner. Even as the mode and content of teaching other skills, such as mathematics and science, have changed in the past few years, the teaching of social studies has also developed new content and objectives. To impart social studies effectively, the teacher must be aware of these revisions and be able to utilize them in the classroom. In this module, we shall examine some of these facets that make up the elementary school social studies curriculum.

SPECIFIC OBJECTIVES

Specifically, it is expected that at the end of your study of this module, you will be able to do the following:

1. Explain briefly, but clearly, the "new" social studies.
2. Show the significance of concept development to elementary social studies.
3. Characterize the social studies programs of the primary grades, the intermediate grades, and the upper grades.
4. Describe the process for planning units.
5. Describe the purpose of the various types of community studies and how to conduct them.
6. Explain the use of value clarification in elementary school social studies classes.
7. Describe the use of dramatics in elementary school social studies classes.
8. Show the role of evaluation in the elementary school social studies curriculum.

MODULE TEXT

The New Social Studies

Essentially, the "new" social studies involves many disciplines—history, geography, economics, sociology, political science, anthropology, and archaeology. Newer approaches also include thrusts into psychology and value clarification. The traditional manner of learning the history of one country and, at the same time, studying the geography of another has long been obsolete. Even before current revisions were made, it was understood that the history of a people is directly affected by their environment. The natural integration of both history and geography was but one step towards a broader and richer approach to the study of man.

The focal point of social studies curriculum today is man, individually and in groups. Since man is a social being living in time, social studies views him in his present, past, and future. It analyzes the situations that affect him, studies his reactions to them, and offers some proposals for his future. The problems of war, poverty, famine, and racial injustice are viewed from their economic, sociological, political, historical, and geographic roots.

The fact that the study of man is the focal point of social studies drastically alters the pedagogical method employed. The fourth-grade teacher, who has a unit such as "Deserts of the World," cannot say she is teaching deserts; rather she is teaching children about people who live on deserts or who are associated with deserts. This shift in emphasis may appear minor, but it is actually radical. How many textbooks, filmstrips, and curricula of the past presented material that was completely removed from the life and history of the people who were being studied! As a result, children often learned only sterile material that might have been factually correct, but failed to present an accurate view of the people being studied. Formerly, the fourth-grader studying "Deserts of the World" might have been able to locate them on maps, explain their climatic and geographic conditions, but be removed intellectually and emotionally from the human problems of drought, poverty, and illiteracy which often affect the lives of people who live on deserts.

A broad but essential objective of the new social studies is to develop attitudes of respect for all peoples and cultures. This respect stems from an understanding of needs and problems that people encounter and from a study of the alternatives open to them; therefore, the teacher is careful to formulate questions that stress similarities among people as well as their differences. A child who can relate the needs of others to needs similar to those he experiences will explore social studies in more realistic and human terms.

As with all knowledge, social studies begins with the individual child's understanding of himself and of his social environment. The children's realizations that there are basic human needs which are essential for the development of a full, human life is a starting point for their transfer of that knowledge to people far removed from their geographic, cultural, and economic milieu. Basic human needs include the following: food, clothing, shelter, recreation, human love (family, friends), education, health, government, and a seeking of goals beyond oneself (ideals, humanistic endeavors, and religious beliefs).

Such a listing is intended to indicate the spectrum of human needs which, although not all-inclusive and subject to individual choices, is broad enough to include all peoples. When children understand that they must have adequate, nourishing food to develop sound bodies, then they can more easily realize the effects of drought and famine among people who live in the sub-Sahara. In a society such as the United States where family breakdown is prevalent, the child can be brought to an appreciation that human love, expressed by concerning oneself for another and working for the other's good, is manifested by family and friends in spite of societal tensions. The basic familial characteristics, which consist of care and concern for the other, may then be studied in various cultures throughout the world. The transfer of other human needs, such as education and government, may also be made in a similar manner. Having explored and discussed the meaning of education in a technological society, children should be able to appreciate the fact that much of their education involves the formal schooling necessary for living in a highly industrialized society. From this knowledge, children can begin to study the meaning of education in societies that are different, yet similar, to their own.

To ensure that the individual's rights are protected and that society is structured for the common good, mankind has formulated modes of government. Although the modes of governing and lawmaking differ, the children will be able to understand the basic rationale for all government, whether republican, monarchial, tribal, or other. They will realize that laws, whether they are made for an entire country or for (and by) an individual family, or class, or team, are essentially designed for the common good. Part of the curriculum will be designed to help children develop the ability to analyze the validity and purpose of specific laws and governments.

Health is an essential component for full human development. The need for health reflects other human needs, such as those for food or recreation. The understanding of the existence of such needs does not mean that the child has a utopian view of the world. Most children realize very early in life that inequalities exist in many areas, including that of health. They learn that one must have the necessary sustenance to maintain health or that, if health is impaired, medical facilities must be available. Ten-year-old Johnny knows his family doctor will help him recover from a sudden and severe illness. Johnny needs to ask himself what other children do if they live in an area where there is no doctor or professional medical help.

The realization that part of human development is the ability to extend oneself to other humans or to worthwhile causes is essential to the educative process. Children need to realize that Martin Luther King fighting for civil rights, Solzhenitsyn suffering for his beliefs, and Cesar Chavez championing the plight of the migrant worker are but a few examples of individuals who have courageously extended and risked their lives for the benefit of others. Such ability to transcend self may manifest itself in various ways. The children will understand that they have ideals and goals which emanate from humanitarian or religious motives.

In addition to the basic human needs, the teacher should be aware of pressures in our rapidly changing society that have bearing on the classroom. Among these new societal pressures are the growing disparity between rich and poor nations and the demand for racial and sexual equality. The political and social implications of the civil rights movement and the women's liberation movement cannot be ignored in the classroom; indeed, if social studies is to be relevant and effective, these pressures must be viewed as vital forces that possess positive, integrative qualities.

Concept Development

It has already been indicated that the purpose of social studies is to study man and his relation to his fellow man in his physical and cultural environment. Such investigation results from various factors, among which are the following:

1. The teacher presents to the class an aspect of social behavior.
2. The children investigate the behavior and gather data concerning it.
3. The children formulate a concept based upon the data gathered.
4. The children test their concepts against others dealing with the same kind of behavior.
5. The children alter their first concepts and prepare to continue their investigation.

The process of examining data, making a rational hypothesis, and testing the hypothesis against other hypotheses help the child develop higher powers of observation, reason, and judgment. These qualities are essential to the rational development of the human being and are basic to the full growth of human qualities of compassion, understanding, and tolerance.

The question of what to teach is of primary importance. The amount of materials in the social studies, whether it be history, geography, or the other disciplines, is of such abundance that both the teacher and the child may be overwhelmed. If one's emphasis in social studies is the teaching of factual material, the road is as endless as the multifacts that inundate the society. The purpose of social studies is not to teach facts, but concepts. Factual knowledge is limited in scope and is subject to anachronism; concepts, however, can embody broad segments of factual knowledge and are constantly subject to revision in definition and interpretation. Concepts such as "community," "nation," and "freedom" allow for gathering and testing factual material, but they can be adapted as new facts are presented. Thus, a sixth-grade study of Greek democracy will reveal the fact that early Greek government was determined by privileged males, to the exclusion of others, notably women and slaves. Yet, the concept of "democracy" as practiced in the present-day United States traces many of its roots to ancient Greece. The fact that women now have a voice in government in contrast to their early exclusion does not abrogate the concept of democracy but, rather, alters and expands it.

The problem of the social studies curriculum is, therefore, the selection of concepts that will be taught, and the ordering of those concepts so that they elicit responses that will further the child's human development.

Concept Development in the Curriculum

The following concepts are often listed for development in elementary school curricula:[1]

Grades K–1
   (a) Each person is similar to other people on earth.
   (b) Each person needs other people.
   (c) People live in different environments and use their environments in their daily lives.
   (d) People need rules for the individual and common good.

---

[1] Concepts adapted from *The Social Science: Concepts and Values* (New York: Harcourt Brace Jovanovich, Inc., 1970), Level IV, pp. T16–T17.

Grade 2

    (a) Family members are similar because of hereditary and environment.

    (b) Different environments in the world affect the way families live.

    (c) Families rely on their environment to secure their daily needs.

    (d) Families need laws for their own and others' welfare.

Grade 3

    (a) Individuals and groups relating to each other in a specific environment form a community.

    (b) Communities adapt to their environment.

    (c) Communities use the resources of their environment to secure their needs.

    (d) The culture of the community is reflected by the way it uses its resources.

    (e) Communities need leadership and rules so as to promote the welfare of the members.

Grade 4

    (a) Man learns social behavior from other individuals and from groups.

    (b) Man uses his environment to procure his basic necessities.

    (c) Man cooperates with other people so as to use basic resources.

    (d) Man's peaceful relations with other individuals and groups require societal controls designed for the good of all.

Grade 5

    (a) Biological and cultural factors help people adapt to their environment.

    (b) People living in different environments possess cultures which have many similarities.

    (c) The way man uses his resources is shaped by his environment.

    (d) The economic life of a people reflects the choices it makes and also reflects its environment.

    (e) The government that a people has reflects the degree of participation of people in it.

Grade 6

    (a) Peoples of the earth vary from each other because of biological and cultural differences.

    (b) The values possessed by people interacting with each other form the pattern of social systems.

    (c) Maps reflect alterations in political organizations.

    (d) From a people's cultural values come the society's economic systems.

    (e) Government that has stability and laws that are based on the common good help improve a people's quality of life.

Although content and curricula vary throughout the elementary social studies program, it is appropriate to discuss general themes and approaches to the study. The following descriptive comments for grades K–6 are not meant to be proscriptive but, rather, to be catalysts of productive teaching. The points emphasized for one level do not negate another, but are meant to stimulate pupil and teacher thinking in various social studies areas.

Social Studies in the Primary Grades

During the first three years of school (K–2), the social studies curriculum should help children become aware of their own identities, and foster a sense of pride and individual worth. At the same time, socialization should be encouraged so that the children learn to appreciate their classmates and the adults who form part of their daily lives. Because the young child's perceptions are mainly confined to the immediate, the now, learning is centered upon those aspects of life that are present and tangible. The study of family, community helpers, and, later, the community itself provides the children opportunities to explore their immediate world.

The importance of having children examine their immediate, real world cannot be overemphasized. A unit on the family should center on the actual families of the individual kindergarten or first-grade pupils. The children are encouraged to bring in pictures of their families, to discuss the various members, and to portray activities which the family does together. Of what value is it for a child whose family consists of one parent to have the traditional stereotype of upper middle-class, suburban parents with two children portrayed as the best if not the only, model of family structure? The reality is that children in today's classroom very often have families that do not fit the antiseptic poster image of father going to work, briefcase in hand, waving good-bye to aproned mother and two clean, attentive children playing in a well-tended garden. The image is not the reality for countless thousands of children. Inner-city youngsters whose homes are tenements and middle-class children whose mothers are the breadwinners are only a few for whom the traditional image cannot apply. A teacher who fails to integrate the child's real family situation into a unit on family commits a serious omission. A child, who views the artificial prototype and who knows that his family does not reflect the given image, will have a flawed understanding of the meaning of family. Worse, the very purpose of the unit, the development of the child's sense of dignity and of worth may easily be marred. The end result may be the child's developing attitudes of personal inferiority stemming from a sense that his family is "not as it should be." On the other hand, if the teacher takes a broader view and portrays family as those relations with whom the child lives and who have concern and love for him, this early and crucial study may become a major lever for the child's acceptance of himself, of his family, and the families of his classmates.

The same positive approach should be employed when studying community helpers, people with whom the child comes into frequent contact. Again, it is necessary to enlarge the range of vision. Company-made posters of policemen, firemen, and doctors are only representations that can stultify a child's mind if they are not complemented by more real and tangible examples. Under the teacher's guidance, the children should assume that their parents do help the community. Initiating the children to simple interview techniques can guide them to ask their parents the following question: How do your jobs help the community? The answer, later written in story form, will reveal myriad contributions from truckdrivers, secretaries, gasoline station operators, architects, housewives, and engineers. As classmates share their interviews, all the children will realize that, whatever the occupation, their parents are truly community helpers.

As the study of community helpers expands into study of the community, the teacher will again concentrate on the real life that the child experiences. Walking tours, using cameras and tape recorders, help provide a rich experience. The children are encouraged to discuss the advantages of living in their community, to interview various people concerning needs of the community, to visit stores, parks, museums, and public buildings. Mapping is begun, probably with the school as the central point. Each child is encouraged to draw his house, placing it in relation to the school, and discussing types of transportation used to get from home to school. Personal reactions and aesthetic experiences are also encouraged so that children may reveal their likes or dislikes about the community environment.

The many activities accompanying social studies units can provide opportunities for individual expression through integration with all other subject matter. Language arts, mathematics, music, drama, and science combine to enrich the children's understanding of their world. Roleplaying, a popular technique, gives children a feeling for the problems and needs of others as well as for their own needs. It can also be an aid in helping to create situations for problem solving of future events. For instance, having studied the community and talked with its mayor, the child might dramatize what he or she would do if, as an adult, he or she were elected mayor. Such dramatizations help the children project into the future and help them learn how to identify goals. Role playing, whether of present, past, or future situations, can help children broaden their capacity to identify problems and to formulate solutions. During such activities, the alert teacher will avoid the tendency to categorize students; therefore, in role playing medical services, a girl may be the doctor, and a boy, the nurse; the slow reader may well act as the future mayor, and the child who dislikes school may play the part of future teacher. Such freedom of choice reinforces the children's hopes that their futures are not already predetermined because of sex, race, or even academic ability. To have social studies rooted in the actual world of the children and to give them opportunities to expand their awareness and involvement in that world are goals worthy of the primary grade teacher.

Social Studies in the Intermediate Grades

Studies have shown that children in the intermediate grades have developed the ability to better understand the concepts of space and time. They are able to grasp the idea of the past and can, therefore, begin a study of history. The exploration of family and nationality that was initiated in the primary grades is now broadened so that the children study people removed from them in both time and geographic distance. The need for multisensory and interdisciplinary activities remains essential. The utilization of other disciplines, such as language arts, music, science, and art, add substance and excitement to the social studies program. Carefully selected movies and filmstrips visually help the child understand the history and culture of the people being studied. By constantly relating the way of life of others to that of their own lives, the children come to realize that people are more alike than they are different; yet, they appreciate that there are differences and that these differences add richness and variety to human life.

The social studies teacher at the intermediate level needs to employ various techniques, among which is the "hands on" approach. Such tactile experiences allow the child to handle artifacts from other countries and to use the inquiry approach concerning people being studied. For example, if fourth-graders who are studying Mexico can examine and touch objects made by Mexican people, they can be involved in making rational deductions concerning the products of Mexico and the life style of the people who live there. Some agencies, such as the Children's Lending Department of the Newark Museum in New Jersey, provide teachers with many objects from countries around the world. These objects are intended for use in the classroom and they are designed to be touched and examined by the children. Such material can be of much assistance in helping the child appreciate other cultures. In an era in which films and television have possibly resulted in a surfeit of visual stimuli, exploration by way of tactile experience should not be overlooked. The alert teacher will be aware that handling of artifacts, though important, is only one aspect of a good social studies program. She will complement what might become a stereotyped view of a people by careful selection of audiovisual material that portrays the people's adaptation to, and progress in, a technical, industrial world.

Social Studies in the Upper Grades

Social studies at the upper elementary level continues to employ the multimedia, multisensory approach that was utilized at the younger level. However, more in-depth, critical, and investigative study is possible because of the child's perceptual growth. The teacher will continue to approach social studies from the focal point of the people who are being studied. She will initiate the study from the point of *now,* discussing the people's problems and contributions as they exist at the present moment. Having stimulated the child's awareness of the *now* dimension, the teacher will encourage study of those past events that helped create the present situation. From the *now* is developed the concept of the *past,* and from both these concepts the aspect of the *future* is approached. Time lines for understanding the concepts of relationship and change are more effectively initiated by a *now–past–now–future* approach than by a *past–now–future* introduction. Such an approach lends relevance and meaning to a topic. For example, a fifth-grade class studying the Civil War will spend some time, however brief, at the beginning of the unit examining some of the basic issues that still affect the country today and were causal issues of the war. Thus, the children will explore the meaning of states' rights today; the reasons for the civil rights movement as it relates to the historic racial injustice stemming from slavery; the economic and industrial patterns of life in the North and in the South. These and other pertinent issues will help the child to realize that people's lives are still influenced by many of the powerful movements that once divided the country. Such a mode of introduction need be neither lengthy nor superficial. The teacher's objective is to help the children understand that many solutions for many problems are often complex, that people of good will and intelligence often differ as to those solutions, and that just peace can only come through the free cooperation of all parties involved. With this understanding as a base, the class is ready to look at those past events that gird the Civil War period.

Although there are various ways of studying history, one highly effective method is the choosing of topics of interest for research by small groups. Such research will utilize classroom, library, and community materials. The topics will be designed and chosen by the groups, who will then research the material, report their findings to the rest of the class, and present a project that visually aids the class's understanding of the topic. The class studying the Civil War might divide into research teams to explore such topics as the reasons why the South developed slavery to a greater extent than did the North; what life on a plantation would have been like; how the abolitionist movement started and its influence before the Civil War; the way of life for many Southerners after the Civil War; the geographic locations of the battles and the manner of fighting in those days; and the problems that Lincoln and Lee faced and why they chose different answers to those problems. Such topics and others of the children's choosing are designed to help small groups of children work together on a meaningful problem which they will share with the class as a whole. The visual aid which each group makes and explains will help further develop understanding of the problem. The aid may be demonstrated in various ways, including map work, original skits, simulated news shows, or reconstruction of a newspaper of the period.

Although the study of the past will consume most of the time devoted to the unit, the teacher will provide an opportunity for the children to examine the now and future aspects of the topic before the study is concluded. She will encourage the children to once again consider current aspects of life in the United States that have some bearing on the Civil War period and to project what they believe will be the situation in the future.

Unit Planning

To plan for in-depth learning, the teacher needs to organize content, materials, and activities around a given topic. Such organization is termed a unit. Units are of relatively long duration and require an intrinsic correlation of one learning experience with another. A unit integrates social studies with other curriculum areas, such as music, mathematics, science, and language arts. The concept of the unit is based on the idea that children will be motivated to learn material that they have helped select and design. Having consulted with her students, the teacher can begin to organize their areas of interest into unit form. Such organization facilitates the weekly and daily planning of classroom activities.

As the teacher assists the children in choosing a topic they wish to study in-depth, certain criteria should be observed. Some of these criteria are (1) the usefulness of the topic in relation to the children's abilities and to the available resources; (2) the societal importance of the topic; (3) the potential the topic offers to expand the children's previous knowledge; and (4) the relationship the topic has to the current needs which society experiences.

When planning a unit, a teacher should consider the following questions:

1. What social studies area or unit of work am I planning to teach? How much time am I expected to devote to the teaching of the material?
2. What objectives do I have for this unit of study? Why did I choose them? (Socioeconomic conditions and differentiation of pupil ability are but two of the factors in choosing objectives.)
3. What specific content am I asked to teach? What are the major problems which I wish my class to realize about the area being studied? What are the key concepts I wish them to learn?
4. How will I incorporate two basic concepts of social studies—relationship and change?

5. How will I incorporate current events into the topic being studied? How will I use maps and globes?
6. What kinds of activities have I planned for my students to do in this unit? Do these activities include language arts, dramatics, art, mathematics, and science?
7. Is a field trip possible? If my class is studying the community, can I take them on a walking tour of their neighborhood? How will I plan a walking tour?
8. What kinds of audiovisual aids will be used? Be specific; if it is a question of a film, give the name, date of showing, and where it will be obtained. List some of the questions to be asked when showing the film or filmstrip.
9. What kinds of community resources are available, such as persons who would speak to the class, places to visit, and material which can be brought to the class?
10. What kinds of materials will I gather for this study? What kind of picture file material will I procure?
11. What bibliography, for teacher and pupils, is available to me? How do I plan to use the various resource books with the students?
12. How do I plan to evaluate the topic or area which I taught?

Such unit planning helps the teacher develop a broad perspective of the topic to be studied. She can then organize the class into committees or other smaller study groups. In addition, she will more clearly perceive the objectives, procedures, and activities that will be incorporated.

Community Studies

So as to appreciate their community and to see its relation to their lives and to the surrounding environment, children need to study their community. Such study, often done in second grade, should not be confined to only that level. Older children can give much insight into the problems of the community, integrating their investigations with other learning activities. A study of supermarkets in the community may provide mathematics lessons in unit pricing, comparative shopping, shipping rates, and profit margins. Through interviews with storeowners children can come to some conclusions about the economic stability of their community. Graphs can be made, showing which commodities stores sell, how long the stores have been in business, what businesses have closed, and which ones have moved. Talks with local officials, bank managers, and corporation executives can help the class make some projections concerning the community's immediate and long-range future.

To prepare a class study of their community, the teacher must be aware of its history, present status, and possible future. The local library or historical society will usually provide a basic history of the area. Having read available material concerning the community's past, the teacher can, with the help of her class, choose appropriate landmarks that the children may visit. A tour may then be planned.

An example of such a tour was one taken by senior college students who are practice teaching in Nutley, New Jersey. The local history of the town provided a wealth of material and described the town's development from an early Indian settlement, a later Dutch farming area, and finally to a colonial American region strongly committed to the War of Independence. Two houses of the Dutch period are preserved in their original form by the community. The importance of the past is apparent in the community's concern for the houses' preservation. The present-day utilization of them is shown in the many current civic needs which they meet. They are projected to serve as social gathering centers for senior citizens and for teenagers; currently, they serve as meeting places for various civic and youth groups. The local tavern is the original that existed in pre-Revolutionary days, and its interior is filled with memorabilia of all the wars in which the United States has been engaged. An early church provides much information concerning the town's past, and the cemetery provides an opportunity for visitors to do tombstone rubbings. The local museum contains materials depicting the town's and the entire area's history. The curator gears the tour to meet the needs of the various groups who visit.

The presence of industry, large and small shopping areas, and companies such as Hoffman-LaRoche and International Telephone and Telegraph provide various means of investigating the present and future development of Nutley.

Through interviews with business and cultural leaders, students begin to make some projections concerning the future of the community. Use of cameras, video-tape, and tape recorders help the students to depict their walk audiovisually. Such audiovisual aids, combined with written notes, can be used for later in-depth analysis in the classroom.

A Neighborhood Walk. College seniors, who student-teach in Jersey City, New Jersey, took a community walk in preparation for a later one to be taken with their children. The walk began at their inner-city school location, extended east through a business area, and culminated in a magnificent view of the Hudson River, Statue of Liberty, and New York skyline. The themes of the walk included ecology, architecture, and people. The main emphasis was "beauty." The theme of beauty was chosen so that students would realize that even in older, industrial, inner-city environments beauty can be found.

The following format was given to the student teachers, who used cameras, videotape, and tape recorders during the walk:

1. Use a notebook to record your trip.
2. Before starting, list ten or more things you think you will see on the walk.
3. What do you think you will see that is beautiful? During the walk, jot down or draw anything that you think is beautiful.
4. On the map, X marks the spot of the treasure. What is the treasure for you?
5. During the walk, you will see an edifice made of copper presented by friends of the United States. Make a map of its location and how you got there. Sketch whatever part of the scene you wish.
6. Divide the group into three teams for the walking tour. Each team is to choose one of the following interest groups:
   A. Ecology: Find as many ecological problems that you can (photograph, draw, or bring them back to school).
   B. Architecture: Find as many different styles of buildings that you can. (photograph, draw, or otherwise describe).

C. People: What do you guess about some of the different people you see (socioeconomic level and cultural background)? Try to talk with some of the people.

Table 9–1 shows a list, compiled by the faculty of the Bank Street School in New York City, that provides a helpful guide for the teacher. As indicated previously, trips are useful in many areas of the social studies to develop children's understanding of history, geography, sociology, and economics.

Table 9-1 The Use of Trips in the Social Studies Curriculum

GEOGRAPHY AND SCIENCE	HISTORIC	SOCIOLOGICAL
soil	home of a famous person	an ethnic neighborhood
rocks	home of a period	a newspaper
elevation	site of an event	a church or synagogue
shapes	famous building	settlement house
vegetation	historic reproductions	foreign restaurant
water	objects, documents, and	food store
animal life	displays	housing project
distance	museums	a social agency
directions	graveyards	a festival
weather		a labor union
sun		
ecology		

COMMUNITY (WORK PROCESS, PRODUCTION, AND DISTRIBUTION)		COMMUNICATION
store	food	newspaper stands, plant
factories	clothing	radio station
markets	machines	TV station
farms	building material	telegraph office wires
		telephone company

SHELTER		COMMUNITY SERVICES	
houses	housing projects	police station	electricity
schools	construction	firehouse	wires
churches	materials (lumber, coal)	post office, mailbox	
stores		sanitation plant	
community		water supply, pipes	
services			

SOURCES		TRANSPORTATION	
parks	bus	rides	
schoolyard	subway	terminals and stations	
street	train	factories	
bodies of water	car	garages	
museums	trucks	airports	
weather bureau	planes	bridges	
zoo	boats	tunnels	
		roads	
		harbors and piers	

Value Seeking in the Classroom

An intrinsic aspect of the social studies curriculum is value clarification. From their study of man and his total environment, children realize that choices must be made that will affect their lives and those of others. Such choices are based on the development of the cognitive and affective faculties. A third grade studying a local factory may ascertain that the factory causes environmental pollution; however, the study may also reveal that the factory employs many people who would otherwise not be working. To close the factory would stop the pollution, but would also create another problem, possible unemployment. Choices must be made and alternative solutions found; these choices reflect the values affirmed. Every unit of study has the potential to assist in the development of value clarification. The choices reflect balance in the relation of individual rights to the rights of society at large. The intrinsic values cited in the Declaration of Independence concerning the equality of mankind, the rights of the individual to life, liberty, and the pursuit of happiness provide a solid framework for value clarification.

There are many techniques that can be utilized in teaching value clarification. A popular one is the use of group discussion concerning a situation in which the ending is left for the class to complete. In giving endings to such problem situations, children can discuss the reasons for their choices and can learn how to accept others' choices, which may differ from theirs. The teacher carefully avoids imposing her values but, rather, creates an atmosphere in which the opinions of all are respected. In defending their choices, children will use their power of critical judgment. Eventually, their choices will reflect an awareness of the rights of the individual and also the rights of all other peoples. Value clarification is a long-range learning activity; however, it is well worth the teacher's time and effort as it is an essential part of learning to live in society.

There are various activities that help children become aware of their own value choices. Upper-grade children can list the ten persons, places, or things they consider most valued to them personally. After each, they can indicate whether the item listed requires having money, whether they can have it when they are adults, whether their enjoyment is alone or with others, and when was the last time they acted on the value. For instance, a boy who lists movies as value will be aware that money is required to see a movie; a girl who states that reading good library books is a value might realize that it has been a long time since she last read one. If a value is a reality in one's life, it must be acted upon or it becomes merely a wish, not a choice.

Younger children can draw a fallout shelter, putting into it their most valued things (including people). They can also draw their coat of arms or write their biography. Drawing five pictures that show something they do not have but wish to have is also useful for developing children's awareness of their values. The teacher should always remember that these activities are personal and that the child's privacy and choices should be respected.

Dramatics

Classroom plays can be highly effective learning experiences. They help develop children's creativity and provide vicarious experiences which enable them to better understand the people they are studying. By closely studying a given topic and analyzing reasons why people act as they do, children can begin to formulate dialogue that is appropriate to the play. One fifth-grade class' study of the American Revolution provides an example of this kind of drama. The teacher first read to the class a letter written by George Hewes, a colonist who had participated in the Boston Tea Party. The letter, found in *The Spirit of Seventy-Six,* edited by Henry S. Commager and Richard B. Morris, gave a graphic and detailed description of one eyewitness account. Hewes' letter provided the children with a primary source of history and illustrated for them the difference between such primary materials and other secondary sources.

Having read and discussed the account, the children listed the people described in the letter who would become the characters in the class play. The list included George Hewes; Governor Hutchinson; Boston citizens opposed to the tea tax; a blacksmith who provided assistance to the rebels; a ship's captain and English seamen; and Bostonians who wanted to save some tea for home use. These and other people became the subject of much discussion as the class tried to analyze how each of them must have felt about the tea tax. The children probed the feelings, the problems, and the decisions which confronted the various people so they could meaningfully portray them in the play.

Hewes' letter enabled the class to develop a logical sequence and change of scenery for the play. Such locations as the church, the governor's mansion, the blacksmith's shop, the wharf, and the captain's cabin lent themselves to setting and prop arrangements the children wished to make. The project integrated art, language arts, and social studies as the children developed and wrote the script.

When the play was presented for other fifth-grade classes, time was allowed for group discussion of the meaning and significance of the Boston Tea Party. Through discussion, the children realized that Hewes' letter was only one man's view of the occurrence and that it revealed the author's own opinions in a highly biased manner. Both players and audience discussed the possible feelings that people who did not share Hewes' view may have had. Some of the questions were: How do you think King George felt when he heard the news? Do you think the owners of the tea thought Hewes was patriotic? Why or why not? How might Indians have felt when they heard of the white men's disguise? From such discussion, the children planned to write more plays based on materials they would find which reflected points of view differing from that of Hewes. Such plays helped stimulate creativity in writing and in set design, and fostered group interaction. These plays, although sometimes brief skits, also helped develop critical thinking, awareness of historical sources, and empathy for the various people whose lives were affected by such events as the Boston Tea Party.

Evaluation

The purposes of evaluation are to determine the progress that the child has made during the topic or unit being studied and to plan changes that will improve instruction in the future. Although the evaluative techniques reflect the objectives that were selected at the beginning of the study, evaluation itself should be on going throughout the teaching-learning process. Evaluation should be made after a single learning experience, after group work of a particular topic, and at the termination of long-range study involving the work of a month or of a semester. Questions the teacher should ask herself in evaluation include the following:

Was the class interested in the topic? Were the discussions stimulating, involving many children? Did the various committees cooperate among themselves and with each other? Did the children listen to each other? Did they develop their ability to articulate their own ideas? Did individual children continue their study of interest in the topic beyond what was required? Has the individual child evidenced ability to perform tasks involving skills such as map making, map interpretation, data gathering, and library research?

Children can also evaluate their own learning by means of checklists they have developed. One such checklist was used by sixth-graders to assess the value of art projects they made in relation to group study of Greece and Rome. The list included the following questions: Was the project accurate and complete? Was the project neat? Did the project help in the understanding of the report? Did the project show a comparison of Greece and Rome? Did the project and report reflect the cooperative effort of all members of the group?

Tests, whether made by a teacher or by a company, should be designed to reflect the real learning that has been acquired. Objective tests can be helpful but should not be the only criteria of progress. Essays, individual or group writing of material, and oral and written explanation of research are techniques that allow children opportunity to reveal what they have learned.

SUGGESTED READING

Beyer, Barry. *Inquiry in the Social Studies Classroom.* Columbus, Ohio: Charles E. Merrill Publishers, 1971.

Chapin, June R., and Richard R. Gross. *Teaching Social Studies Skills.* Boston: Little, Brown and Company, 1973.

Fraser, Dorothy McClure. *Social Studies Curriculum Development.* 39th Yearbook. Washington, D.C.: National Council for the Social Studies, 1969.

Jarolmich, John. *Social Studies in Elementary Education.* New York: Macmillan Publishing Co., Inc., 1962.

Keller, Clair W. *Involving Students in the New Social Studies.* Boston: Little, Brown and Company, 1974.

Metcalf, Lawrence E., ed. *Values Education.* 41st Yearbook. Washington, D.C.: National Council for the Social Studies, 1971.

Shaftel, Fannie R., and George Shaftel. *Role Playing for Social Values.* Englewood Cliffs, N.J.: Prentice-Hall, Inc., 1967.

Simon, Sidney B., Leland W. Howe, and Howard Kerschenbaum. *Values Clarification.* New York: Hart Publishing Company, Inc., 1972.

POST TEST

1. What disciplines are included in the new social studies?

_____

_____

_____

2. What seems to be the focal point of today's social studies curriculum?

_____

_____

3. In the elementary school curriculum, what is the starting point for the social studies?

_____

4. According to this module, what is the basic understanding about the rationale for government that all pupils should acquire?

_____

_____

5. List the five steps for developing social studies concepts presented in this module.

_____

_____

_____

_____

_____

6. This module states that the purpose of the social studies curriculum is not to teach facts. What then is the social studies curriculum supposed to teach?

_____

7. When can history be first introduced into a child's program?

_____

8. Intermediate grade pupils should have opportunities to learn by the hands-on approach. What is this approach?

_____

_____

9. At what level does this module recommend that one begin the study of the family?

_____

10. What types of activities might be used to make community study interesting and meaningful at the earliest teaching level?

_____

_____

_____

11. This module recommends that you depart from the strict chronological method of teaching history in the elementary grades. What approach does it recommend?

_____

_____

12. The module lists four criteria to consider when choosing a topic for a unit. What are they?

_____

_____

_____

13. The module lists twelve questions to consider when planning a unit. List five of them.

_____

_____

_____

_____

_____

_____

14. What is the purpose of community study in elementary schools?

_____

_____

15. How do open-ended stories contribute to value clarification?

_____

_____

16. In using value clarification techniques, there is one thing that you must be sure *not* to do. What is it?

_____

17. What are two purposes of evaluation in social studies teaching?

_____

_____

18. What procedure does this module suggest so pupils can evaluate their own learning?

_____

19. This module recommends the use of dramatics in the teaching of elementary school social studies. How does it recommend that you carry out this method?

_____

_____

Teaching Mathematics

Thomas C. McCain

Freeport Union Free School

module 10

The New Mathematics—Was It Really? / Readiness As a Factor / Number Facts and Drill / Problem Solving / Organizing for Instruction / The Future—More New Math?

RATIONALE

The over-all goal of elementary school education has not changed significantly since the days of Ichabod Crane and the hickory stick. We must receive children at a given age—four, five, or six years old—and transform them from illiterate beings to young students who can express their ideas orally and in written form; understand and interpret the ideas of others presented in those two modalities; perform the basic arithmetic functions with whole numbers, decimals, and common fractions; and provide them with an understanding that knowledge is divided into several categories, including literature, science, and the social sciences. In addition to establishing these goals, society has placed upon us something of a time limit; we must accomplish this simplistic objective in approximately a half dozen years.

In the area of mathematics, elementary school educators are charged with the responsibility of providing youngsters with an operational understanding of numeration, approximately 150 number facts commonly referred to as the "tables," and twelve potential applications of the basic operations. Students must be helped to master adding, subtracting, multiplying, and dividing with whole numbers, common fractions, and decimals. As the teaching of "arithmetic" gave way to the teaching of "elementary mathematics" in American schools, several concepts, including developing a vocabulary in geometry, understanding the basic operations of equations, and such impressive terms as "expanded notation," associative, and commutative properties, were added to the fundamental expectations. However, mathematicians and secondary school teachers would agree that the fundamental responsibility of the elementary schools has remained the same: provide young students with the fundamental skills necessary to learn higher mathematics.

SPECIFIC OBJECTIVES

After you have studied and learned the information contained in this module, you will be able to do the following:

1. Explain the meaning of readiness.
2. State the most significant factor in providing drill exercises.
3. Describe four forms of drill used for reinforcing concepts learned in mathematics.
4. Explain the value of learning about problem solving for the student.
5. List four ways that a teacher can provide practical experiences in the classroom for problem-solving learning.
6. Describe three ways for a teacher to determine the functional learning level of a student.
7. Explain why grouping and instructional plans should have a definite relationship.

8. State the four divisions of a lesson plan.
9. State the four guidelines regarding mathematical homework.
10. Give four reasons why teacher-made tests are often the poorest measurement of pupil progress.
11. Describe at least three of the five functions that the evaluation of pupil progress serves.
12. Explain what use a teacher should make of standardized test results.
13. List the four steps that a good teacher should take when a majority of the students fail an end-of-the-unit test.
14. Explain the specific value in using paraprofessionals.
15. Name at least three currently significant innovative programs for mathematics.
16. State the primary goal of American education in the area of elementary mathematics.
17. Distinguish between CAI and CMI.

MODULE TEXT

The New Mathematics—Was It Really?

In the late 1950s, two events, seemingly unrelated, proved to have an enormous impact on the teaching of mathematics in the elementary schools. The Russians challenged the security of innumerable Americans by being the first to launch a grapefruit-sized satellite into orbit around the earth. As an immediate reaction to that event, national leaders determined that the science-mathematics emphasis in Russian schools was directly responsible for that nation's victory in the race to space. With the entire nation in a mood of readiness for change, Congressional leaders provided funds directly for the teaching of science and mathematics, political leaders began demanding that more attention be given to these instructional areas, and educators initiated a thorough evaluation of teaching techniques in the two chosen areas. The result, insofar as it affected elementary schools was the birth of "The New Math."

Teachers across the country were admonished that they should present a new vocabulary to their pupils, begin teaching in a deductive rather than inductive mode, and that they should (redundant as it may seem) be sure that their students became completely familiar with the 150 number facts and the four arithmetic operations as applied to whole numbers, common fractions, and decimals.

The second event was the publication of a brief treatise on the philosophy of education, as it evolved during a meeting of thirty-five scientists, scholars, and educators, brought to Woods Hole on Cape Cod by the National Academy of Sciences. Jerome S. Bruner of Harvard University, writing for the committee, said in part:

We begin with the hypothesis that any subject can be taught effectively in some intellectually honest form to any child at any stage of development. It is a bold hypothesis and an essential one in thinking about the nature of a curriculum. No evidence exists to contradict it; considerable evidence is being amassed that supports it.[1]

Bruner's book, and this statement more particularly, were to the teaching of mathematics in the elementary schools what the battles of Lexington and Concord were to life in the United States in the late eighteenth century. To the typical New England farmer, the battles of Lexington and Concord required a reevaluation of his political stance and allegiance to the King, a fresh look at his opinion of the colonies as a permanent home, and the difficult decision as to whether his support of the war would be direct or indirect, if at all.

Likewise for the elementary school teacher of the 1960s, Bruner's "shot heard 'round the world" caused great consternation in some circles, a universal reevaluation as to whether the mathematics curriculum in the elementary schools was relevant, whether age-old principles were appropriate, and whether the "tried and true" techniques were as true as they were tried. However, the unrelenting expectation remained: teach facts and operations using whole numbers, decimals, and fractions.

Readiness As a Factor

All children come to every teacher with a specific level of readiness. That is, they arrive with the capability of intellectualizing a specific concept or skill, which the teacher is prepared to present to the student. Although the term *readiness* is most often associated with preschool or primary grade activities, it is undeniable that there must also be a readiness for boys and girls to learn the effect of multiplying a number by its reciprocal as a step in dividing one common fraction by another.

Numbers are abstractions, designed to represent a condition in the physical world. This concept of numeration is perhaps the first to be presented by primary grade teachers, and the clearest example of the need of readiness for learning a skill. While many youngsters can recite in rote manner the numbers in sequence (and often in two or more languages), there is often little correlation between their sing-song recitation and actual counting of objects. The alert teacher will begin with "oneness" as a concept, and present it with the aid of concrete materials so that each student can identify one crayon, one picture, and one flower. After a careful progression through several numerals, the young student may be ready to identify the relative differences between numbers and the relationships that exist among them.

Similarly, a student will be more fully capable of grasping the intent of moving a decimal to the right in the divisor when he can understand that he is actually multiplying that divisor by a power of ten, and by multiplying the dividend by that same power of ten he is retaining the relativity that exists between the two numbers. This action makes it possible for him to perform the operation within the confines of number facts that he already knows, making it unnecessary to learn the 1.2

---

[1] Jerome S. Bruner, *The Process of Education* (Cambridge, Mass.: Harvard University Press, 1961), p. 33.

times table if he already knows the 12 table. The adept sixth-grade teacher will recognize (or develop) the readiness for learning this skill, seize upon that readiness, and present the skill to those students who are ready for it. As a result, the students can perform the operation with a full understanding of the process involved, rather than basing their performance on a collection of steps that have been learned in a rote manner without any apparent understanding of the mathematical principles involved.

How then is readiness measured? Put in its most fundamental terms, the answer would best be presented in a single word: developmentally. Since the teacher has an intimate knowledge of the functions of mathematics as presented by the grade level in question, as well as those preceding and following, she should have an equally clear understanding of the correlative and subordinate skills and concepts that are included in each of the curriculum goals. She then must decide whether to take an active or passive role in the quest for readiness. If she chooses the passive role, she must constantly observe students and remain ever alert to some indications of a readiness for skill development. In the more preferred active stance, the teacher organizes activities which may appear to the students to represent immediate ends in and of themselves, but which fit into an over-all approach to the teaching of mathematics and represent readiness levels in the assimilation of specific skills.

For example, within the earliest years of their elementary school careers, all children will learn to combine whole numbers by addition. When the introduction of multiplication as a concept becomes part of the instructional goal for a given period, the teacher may construct a series of situations in which repetitive addition will provide the answers to given situations. At some point during these instances of repetitive addition, students will show a readiness to learn the short cut called multiplication. How satisfying it would be to a student so introduced to the multiplication fact 3×7 when it becomes a shorthand to $3 + 3 + 3 + 3 + 3 + 3 + 3 = 21$.

Readiness then is not a term restricted to the exclusive use of teachers of five- and six-year-old children. Used in its broadest sense, it is a term which explains the developmental sequence of lead-up activities as they relate to the introduction of major skills presented at all levels of education.

Number Facts and Drill

Depending upon how one presents them, there are anywhere from 162 number facts to more than three times that number. If nine addition–subtraction tables are presented, ranging from $0 + 0$ to $9 + 9$, and a similar number of multiplication–addition tables are used, each student must commit to memory 162 facts. If four separate sets of tables, ranging from $0 + 0$ through $12 + 12$, are to be committed to memory, there are then exactly four gross or 576 number facts which must become nearly autonomic in the stimulus–response relationship. On the sheer weight of numbers, then, it would appear worthwhile to consider the presentation of number facts in a combined mode; that is, the addition–subtraction fact as one family, and the multiplication–division fact as another. In this manner, the addition fact $3 + 5 = 8$ can be interpolated so as to mean $3 + n = 8$, or $8 - 3 = n$. A student who has thoroughly internalized the relationships that exist between 3, 5, and 8 will recognize them in whatever sequence they are presented. A similar case can be presented for the relationships that exist between 3, 9, and 27.

Whether there be 162 number facts or 576, each must be committed to memory, and there is no better technique than repetitive drill, whether that drill be provided by oral stimulus, worksheets, flash cards, computer assistance, or with the use of tape recordings, records, or other painless means of repeating the stimulus until the desired response is immediate.

Drill Exercises. Drill, as a method of reinforcing concepts learned in specific lessons, is as fundamental to the teaching of mathematics as shooting baskets is to playing basketball, finger exercises are to playing the piano, or oral practice is to the learning of a foreign language. Drill exercises should be tailored, however, to meet the needs of individual students. All too often, well-intending teachers have individualized their instruction by providing more capable students with double or triple portions of drill assignments and less capable students with abbreviated drill exercises. These attempts at individualization may have resulted in keeping students busily engaged for equivalent periods of time, but they may well have represented the antithesis of the instructional needs for both groups.

Although no specific amount of drill can be prescribed for students in general, the teacher who is armed with a variety of alternatives will find a more willing audience than if the identical mode were assigned consistently. To this end, a tape recorder can be put to excellent use so the classroom teacher can record number facts without answers in a series of ten, or fifteen, or perhaps fifty items. Following that recording, students can be instructed to correct their own answers by listening to the next section of the tape on which the teacher can record the answers to the various number facts. Such check tests can be recorded on cassette-type, magnetic tape equipment and made available in learning stations in classrooms. With proper instruction, even six- and seven-year-old students can be trained to load, play, rewind, and eject cassettes, thereby making this lesson a self-directed one. The technique can become less obtrusive to classroom management if the tape player device is used in conjunction with earphones so as to make it possible for an individual student or a group of students to be following tape-recorded instructions while others are working independently in other areas of the classroom, or under the direct supervision of a classroom teacher.

Flash cards are perhaps the oldest of all visual aids and, at the same time, most adaptable to the reinforcement type of drill procedures necessary to firmly establish number facts for students. Virtually all teachers and potential teachers can establish two or three techniques for their use, and the variety of applications is limited only to the extent of one's creativity. A version of the popular child's card game, "War," can be played, for example, wherein each player displays one flash card at a time and the opponent or opponents announce the answer to the factor represented. The successful respondent then adds the card to his own pile, and the possession of the card becomes proof that he "owns" that fact as his. In another version, each player will present a card, announce the answer to the example on the card, and the correct answer that represents the highest number is the winner of the "trick"; the original presenter of that card adds all cards involved in that trick to his pile.

Students, encouraged to construct their own flash cards, can make them of such size that they fit easily into a pocket, so that the "difficult" facts can be reviewed whenever the student thinks of them.

When it is feasible, there is often an advantage to bringing older students without a clear command of number facts into a setting where younger students are learning them. As the older students take command of the situation and "tutor" their younger counterparts, they often develop a firm understanding of facts themselves as they assure their younger partners a firm review of them.

Bingo is a game popular with people of all ages and, by altering the basic rules only slightly, a classroom teacher can provide an entire group of students with a combination of entertainment and review in number facts. Rather than calling out the numbers in the more traditional fashion, the teacher can generate number facts for each call. In this manner, the call "B − 6" can be presented to students as "B 3 + 3, B 5 + 1, B 10 − 4, B 12 ÷ 2", or as any number fact which results in 6. Such a class activity as this can provide rapt attention to the review of number facts, and often has become popular enough with individual classes of middle-grade students as to be selected as the recess activity on a rainy day.

Science can be combined with the introduction of number facts by directing youngsters in the construction of electric answer boards. After appropriate instruction in the development of simple circuits, students can use the combination of bell wire, brass fasteners, batteries, and flashlight bulbs to create their own electric number fact review boards. If appropriately designed, they can be rewired or redirected so as to be useful for science facts, place geography, or other number facts.

A collection of electronic devices is now available for purchase and, although they vary somewhat individually, each provides students with the novelty of reviewing number facts on a calculator-type machine. Although the repetition of facts is advantageous, these mechanical aids provide the added advantage of encouraging youngsters to work for speed as well as for accuracy in their responses. The cost of the machines varies, and it would be advantageous for each school to buy the most sophisticated piece of equipment it can afford to insure widespread use.

Drills need not take the form of row upon row of examples "from the back of the book," but can be provided by a wide variety of class, committee, or individual assignments. Just as the version of Bingo can be an effective class activity for the review of number facts, a version of traditional spelling bees can be an effective form of operational drill if, in each instance, students are asked to perform mental arithmetic and announce the answer to a problem dictated by the teacher under rules which exactly parallel those of spelling bee.

An interesting variation of this approach is found in a game that might be called "Mathematics Baseball." For this game the teacher will prepare a collection of mathematics examples at four levels of difficulty, each intended to be done mentally and without paper or pencil. With the group divided into two teams, each player has his turn "at the bat" and announces a level of difficulty he elects to challenge. The most difficult of the examples would represent a home run; the slightly less difficult, a triple; a third group slightly less difficult might represent a double; and the easiest examples would represent a single. The teacher then reads the example, and the student responds. If he responds correctly, he moves to his base; if he is incorrect, he has struck out. As in real baseball, three outs per side represent an inning, and a game can be any number of innings.

A clear advantage of this type of spelling bee arrangement is that a careful

5	3	2	9
2	8		1
7		6	

8	6	9	16
0	2		
8	4	1	9

Figure 10-1 *Operational Drill Exercise.*

and sensitive teacher can provide examples of sufficient challenge to individual students but also commensurate with their capabilities in mathematics. Additionally, since all students are members of a team, even those who may respond incorrectly to their example are still "in the game" and will not represent the potential control problem that the early dropouts of a spelling bee may represent.

Individuals or small groups of youngsters can solve cross number puzzles of which many are available in the market place. Resembling crossword puzzles in format and playing rules, these games are available in forms that would challenge the most fundamental factors found in a first-grade curriculum to highly complex applications of fractional arithmetic, ratio, and proportion. Cross number puzzles not only provide a wealth of operational drill on one page of activity, but by nature of their construction provide for students' checking of their own work as they justify their "down answers" with their "across answers."

Another very effective means of providing operational drill can be found in Figure 10-1.

By asking the students to study the relationships between the 5, the 2, and the 7 and to presume the same relationship between the 3, the 8, and the missing number, the teacher can provide a challenging collection of operational drill exercises. Once the student discovers that the relationship is an additive one, the third column becomes less challenging and more rewarding in that it is not the sum that is missing but, rather, an addend. Having once entered the 11 and the 4 in the appropriate boxes, a student can presume the same relationship between other numbers with one or more factors missing.

In a similar manner, when the desired drill is in subtraction practice, the missing numbers could represent subtrahend, minuend, or difference. The significant factor in providing drill exercises is that they should be so designed as to encourage students to become actively involved in the process while they are performing the drill, and not designed so as to be completed in a nonthinking manner, thereby short circuiting their intent.

Problem Solving

Perhaps it is because the teaching of computational skills is less difficult than effective teaching of problem-solving techniques; perhaps it is because a typical mathematics basal text includes only approximately one tenth the problem-solving exercises; or perhaps it is that reading levels vary so widely within a particular group of students at the same age level; but for whatever reason or combination of reasons, it is not at all unusual for elementary school pupils to score lower in those portions of standardized tests that measure their ability to solve problems than they do in those portions dealing strictly with computational skills. And yet, it is these problem-solving skills to which students will refer in later years when they make first-hand utilization of their mathematics abilities. It is only in very limited situations where ciphering is the mathematical need of the day. More often the questions which will need answering will fall into the realm of deciding how much monthly payments will be; how one computes 20 per cent less than the regular price; how much a commodity should cost, given the weight and cost per pound; or a host of practical applications for mathematics in daily life. It would follow, therefore, that early exposure to the problem-solving skills would reap positive and long-lasting results for students and teachers alike.

Just as there are many alternatives to providing practice in computational skills, there are many methods through which experience in solving mathematical problems can be expanded. Introduction of a "grocery store" in the classroom can provide experience in computation, making of change, establishing prices of individual items, and additional skills.

Depending upon the instructional level of the students, the teacher may arbitrarily price empty food containers at 2, 5, or 7 so that it would be difficult for any erstwhile shopper to accumulate any number of items that would be worth more than 15 units, thereby controlling the computational practice to addends with a sum of 20 or less. If students were prepared to work on a more highly sophisticated level, however, the teacher could identify a wholesale price for each item and establish a percentage of profit and overhead that must be included in establishing the retail prices, and have a committee of students determine the retail prices prior to "placing them on the shelf." Other experiences involving setting up the grocery store corner in the classroom would include comparative shopping, wherein the students could determine the relative price per ounce of items sold in large, medium, and small sizes; the relative price of name brands versus house brand items found in chain stores; and perhaps some application of the installment buying concept and determinations of principal, interest, and real cost. The assignments for students can range from making change to maintaining the books for the store, and the actual practice can include drill in mathematics of money, weights and measures, percentage, interest, and volume buying.

Students interested in sporting events can obtain valuable and rewarding mathematics experience by producing exact-scale models of playing fields for baseball, hockey, tennis, or lacrosse. Unquestionably the number of multiplication and division examples necessary in generating one scale model or drawing of a playing field would be equivalent to pages of examples "from the back of the book." Such a project can represent an enjoyable endeavor which also leads to language arts activities, charts activities, further mathematics, and recognition that such playing fields must be watered, fertilized, cut, covered, and lined.

Variety in the assignment of operational drill can provide the student with the motivation necessary to elicit maximum participation. It is hoped it will also provide for the maximum effect of the drill involved. Sporting events, vacation travel, weather variations, time estimates, estimating supplies needed for class activities, establishing costs for field trips, and a host of other activities can provide individual students, committees, or class groups with experience in mathematics applications.

Although a wide variety of prepared problem exercises is available through the various publishing houses, a classroom teacher is limited only by her own creativity in the generation of worthwhile activities. How many different approaches could a classroom teacher expect from her students, for example, in determining the number of times the numeral 2 would be used in the pagination of a novel that is 234 pages in length? Or, how many times will a clock ring during a 24-hour period if its chime announces every hour and every half hour? Or, how many different ways, given a blank sheet of paper with the numeral 6 written in the center, can students express the value 6 by way of arithmetic computation?

In summary, we have said that although "new math" was introduced to the American elementary schools more than a decade ago, there was very little new in it. The goal of public elementary mathematics education in the United States remained unchanged: encourage youngsters to learn the basic number facts, and enable them to perform four basic arithmetic operations with whole numbers, common fractions, and decimals.

Practice and drill remain the most appropriate technique available in assisting students to develop an immediate stimulus-response reaction to the number facts. Monitored, directed practice represents the most effective technique in assisting youngsters to internalize concepts in basic arithmetic operations. These practice assignments should be tailored to the individual needs of students, should be imaginatively presented, and should avoid the form of stereotyped practice exercises commonly provided in many textbooks.

The successful solution of problems is the ultimate goal of all mathematics instruction, and it should be included in the basic program of mathematics teaching at the elementary level. As in the need for providing drill in arithmetic operations, the format of the practice sessions may be limited solely by the creativity of the teacher.

Organizing for Instruction

Essentially, organizing for instruction in mathematics divides itself into four phases: establishing the functional level of students, determining appropriate instructional goals for them, developing and providing instruction designed to meet those goals, and evaluating pupil progress. This last step, of course, provides a full cycle in that the evaluation not only measures the efficacy of the instruction provided, but establishes the new functional level for students.

Assessment of Needs. The identification of functional level or assessment of needs for a group of students may be carried out in a variety of ways. Several formal, standardized inventories are available in the market place, many of them tailored to the instructional sequence of specific textbook series. Teachers who have a firm knowledge of the developmental process in the teaching of mathematics may develop their own inventory and apply it to pupils, or they may simply establish activity centers within their classroom and make careful observations of students who display various strengths and weaknesses as they visit the centers. The latter technique is particularly appropriate in the preschool years and in instructional settings for younger students.

One very effective method of ascertaining the level of knowledge regarding basic number facts would be to provide a record, tape recording, or other technique of reciting number facts for students as they write answers on a sheet of paper. This exercise not only provides for the immediate identification of fundamental skills which are present or lacking for individual students as well as for classes, but can give the classroom teacher a valid basis on which to judge the work study habits of his or her class.

Among the commercially prepared materials that are appropriate in this area are a variety of criterion-testing measures which break the mathematics curriculum into a number of identifiable and measurable subskills represented in sets of items presented in a pretest mode. Since these items are most often carefully standardized and field tested, they can, by using fewer than a dozen items, help to determine a student's mastery of specific mathematic skills. Armed with profiles generated from such a pretest, the classroom teacher can establish long-term and short-term goals to organize the classroom instruction and to measure achievement against the goals originally established. Although some of the materials generated for this purpose are extremely costly, and would best be used if adopted on a school-wide level, others available can be used by individual teachers in establishing instructional groups and objectives for individual classes.

Other standardized assessment devices that may be used by specially trained personnel within the school can provide in a short time clear estimates of the instructional level of individual students as compared to the statistical "average student" who is represented in most nationally normed performance measures.

The final needs assessment technique to be discussed may indeed be the first utilized by a classroom teacher, perhaps even before she meets her students. Since virtually all school districts use standardized tests to assess pupil progress, a careful study of the results of the most recent such examination can provide a relatively accurate prototype of the group and of individuals within the group concerning their computational skills, problem-solving capabilities, and mastery of basic arithmetic concepts. This review might give a classroom teacher valuable assistance in the development of long-range goals for the academic year.

Instructional Goals. Once the needs assessment has been completed, it becomes appropriate to compare pupil performance levels with the adopted curriculum of the school or school district which they attend. Typically, a class-size group of pupils will present themselves as being beyond expectations in some areas, performing on a par with expectations in others, and falling more or less below the school or school district's expectations for students of their age group in a third set of instructional areas. The decision to provide additional instruction in the weaker areas, to provide additional growth in the areas of strength, or to plan for growth in all areas should reflect school or school district policy insofar as it is possible.

Classroom teachers have no choice as to whether they group for instruction. The largest of groups has been established for them by the administrators of the school in that they are assigned "a class" which has been brought together based on some criterion such as age, years in school, performance level, geography, or gender. However, each of the members of this class represents a unique set of backgrounds, of experiences, and skills and needs and, therefore, might be considered to be a group of one ready for appropriate instruction. The presumptions that all students brought together in a class are in need of the identical mode, level, and variety of instruction is fallacious. Virtually every class must be subdivided in some manner so as to make instruction more applicable to the needs of the students in the group. Teachers might select from among ability grouping, interest grouping, long-term or short-term grouping arrangements, specific skill grouping, individualized instruction, or independent study. While making these decisions, however, each teacher must keep in mind the need for balance between academic freedom of teachers, which broadly interpreted means that the professional classroom teacher should make the determination as to what skills, concepts, or materials are taught to students in her charge, and the professional responsibility of teaching faculty to appropriately present the curriculum developed for the local community by representative citizens and professionals in that community. Beginning teachers would be wise to thoroughly peruse curriculum materials, syllabus publications, and statements of philosophy generated by local boards of education, building administrators, or department chairmen. Other sources of valuable information would include veteran teachers, school administrators, and, when they are available, State Department of Education Guidelines.

The keys to success in grouping for instruction lie in a classroom teacher's ability to define the purposes for which the groups have been developed and to determine the length of time for which the groups are to remain intact. There was a time in the history of the profession when teachers were required, almost as moral obligations, to have three groups for reading instruction (one high, one average, and one low) and two groups (and only in extreme circumstances more or less than two) for instruction in mathematics. Although professional administrators and teacher trainers supported this concept for decades, researchers discovered that in many instances students in the average group were able to outperform the mean level, represented by those assigned to the highest performing group, and that in some instances pupils assigned to the lowest instructional level had specific skills that were equal to or surpassed those of pupils assigned to the top group. It was as an outgrowth of these studies that organizational patterns were developed and promoted, providing for short-term groups brought together for instruction of specific skills. While the amount of record keeping in such instructional patterns is great, successful short-term grouping systems have been developed borrowing the data processing techniques developed in industry. It is now possible for groups that have 150 or more pupils at a particular instructional level to be grouped and regrouped on a semi-monthly schedule, based upon specific skill need and commonality of instructional level.

It is commonly believed that however the groups are organized they are or soon become artificial in structure. The only truly tailored program of grouping takes the form of individualized teaching, in which students work at their own rate of speed and are brought together only when two or more of them are in need of instruction in the same skill at the same time. Although this mode of instruction may at first appear impossible, some very interesting research in this regard has been done at the University of Wisconsin under the title of Individually Guided Education (IGE).

In the IGE arrangement, students are pretested to determine their grasp of a given number of fundamental mathematical skills. Using a base number of 120 to 150 students, a team of five to seven teachers reviews the data collected by way of the pretest, and determines instructional grouping based upon specific skill needs of students in that group. Students and teachers are then assigned to each other for approximately two-week periods, and careful direction is provided to teachers regarding the specific skill needs of the students in their groups, sources of teaching materials for that skill or group of skills, informal measurement devices which can be used to identify students who have mastered the skills prior to the end of the period set aside, and a collection of teaching materials which have been successfully used for teaching the skills assigned to the various groups for the given period of time.

At the end of the number of days or weeks set aside by the team for this period of instruction, post test measures are then administered to all students, most commonly by way of single sheet evaluations which appear to students to be simply "one more ditto sheet." Once scored, the performance level of individual pupils is compared to the criterion of mastery as established by the school or school district, and students are judged as having mastered the skill or as needing further instruction in that skill. The cycle continues again with the team establishing new instructional objectives, new groups, and a new period of time during which the instruction will take place.

While the introduction of this very formal grouping pattern may seem ominous to the reader, it represents a workable and highly appropriate technique for assuring that instruction provided to individual youngsters is appropriate to their instructional need, and does not represent redundancy or a level of difficulty not commensurate with pupil capabilities.[2]

Planning for the Group. Once the instructional goal has been established for a group, specific lesson plans must be developed to guide the teacher and students through the acquisition of the skill or concept identified. Generally, effective lesson plans begin by identifying the skill or concept to be mastered and contain a section directed at establishing a level of readiness among pupils, a section devoted to the presentation of the skill or concept, and a review section containing directions for students. The practice may take the form of written or oral class work, interplay with machines, or homework.

Just a word about homework. Any classroom teacher with instructional responsibilities for students of any age level who has given any amount of homework to be done by pupils outside of the regular instructional day would find upon canvassing the attitudes of parents of her students that in the eyes of some parents students were given too much homework while others believe they were not given enough. Given the dilemma, what is the teacher to do? It would appear that four guidelines should be followed in establishing homework policies within any classroom. First, assignments should be tailored to the needs and strengths of individual students. A performance requirement, for example, that would keep the best student busy for forty minutes might result in tearful hours for a slightly below-average pupil who feels an obligation to complete the assignment. Second, homework assignments in mathematics should be varied. They might include accompanying a parent grocery shopping, determining the dimensions of one's room, reviewing of number facts, carrying out exercises from the textbook, developing story problems, or carrying out measurement activities at the kitchen sink. The variety will not only encourage a more enthusiastic response on the part of the students, but will help parents to accept the concept that homework is not something that children "go and do." The third guideline for mathematics homework is that it be regular. This is not to say that it would be appropriate every night, but for long-term ad-

---

[2] Individually guided education materials are available through Kettering I/D/E/A.

vantages the assignments should not be sporadic. The fourth guideline is that the homework assignment must be possible; that is, it must demand of a student only those skills that he or she has clearly and completely within grasp.

A popular story is told involving an elementary school teacher who determined that for her class to accomplish the academic goals she had set for the year, they would have to receive instruction in a new concept each day. Her lesson plans were well ordered and standard. Each lesson included a review of the homework completed the night before, which served as a measure of the effectiveness of the instruction of that day, and an indication of the readiness of the class to move on to the next concept. Her planned motivational portions and presentation of the new concept section were also amply recorded. Each day, after appropriate class discussion, students were given an assignment which was to be completed at home. The assignment, of course, represented the reinforcement phase of the lesson as homework and provided the basis for the review of the concept during the next morning's class.

After several weeks of this systematic and apparently highly successful mode of teaching, the teacher received from the father of one of her pupils, which read as follows:

Dear Miss Anderson,

Maggie and I have worked on arithmetic about forty minutes a night since school started, and I have taught her all of her lessons so far. Now the math is getting too hard for me to teach Maggie. Can we swap jobs? You teach her the math in school, and I'll correct the papers at home.

Yours truly,

Evaluating Pupil Progress. Measuring pupil growth is important from several points of view. It provides students with an indication of success, it gives the teacher an opportunity to see how the performance of her students compares with the goals that she has set for them, it provides schools and school districts with an over-all evaluation of the teaching of mathematics within their district and of the possible need for further in-service education for their teachers. Perhaps most traditionally, however, evaluating pupil progress makes it possible to report that progress to parents.

Each school has its own mode of evaluating and reporting to parents. The techniques considered appropriate in innovative schools include an opportunity for students' progress to be compared with specific goals set for them rather than arbitrary grade-level expectations developed by a district-wide committee. The evaluation, if it is to serve the functions listed, must be related to the instructional goals set for the period of time that the evaluation covers. One popular basis for evaluating pupil progress is the teacher-made tests. While these tests are often the easiest to administer, they are also often the poorest measure of pupil progress. Classroom teachers have been known to force the individual scores of pupils to approximate the normal curve of distribution, a statistical procedure designed to identify the relative differences between thousands or tens of thousands of numerical events, and most inappropriate for the distribution of two dozen numbers. Classroom teachers have also been known to adopt the practice of utilizing "answer columns" and of scoring individual items, based upon the entry in the column, regardless of the arithmetic operations that are recorded by the student to the left of the response. Other questionable practices of classroom teachers include partial credit, neatness having an effect on the total grade, counting an answer completely wrong if it lacks a label, or using poorly typed or poorly reproduced worksheets.

The essence of appropriate evaluation would seem to depend upon identifying the specific instructional goals and the behavior which would, when carried out on the part of the student, indicate accomplishment of the goals. The standard for percentage of accuracy required for a student to receive credit for having mastered the goal would have been established prior to the test. If these principles are included in the planning phase, it should not be difficult to avoid the pitfalls of the past.

The characteristics of an appropriate worksheet or homemade evaluation device to use in implementing sound evaluation principles are presented differently by as many authors as write about them. Most authors, however, would probably insist upon at least the following four items: The device should (a) accurately measure only those skills which have been taught in the class and not demand mastery of skills not yet presented; (b) be clear in directions to pupils so that there can be no misunderstanding of the function they are to perform; (c) represent good format from the printing point of view, even though it may be handwritten on a spirit duplicator master; and (d) provide students with ample opportunity to display their capabilities in a skill area, and not presume to test capabilities with a single item or a pair of items.

Standardized tests, as described earlier, are becoming more and more popular as public concern for accountability in education becomes more current. Although politicians and school board members may have their own applications for standardized test results, the astute classroom teacher uses them as an effective diagnostic tool to identify specific areas of strength and weakness for individuals or groups of students within her class, and from this diagnosis she can prescribe specific instruction to meet those needs. The criterion tests described earlier can be either of the homemade variety or of the type developed by commercial publishers. In either instance, they can provide classroom teachers with important information, which can be helpful in the regrouping of pupils for instructional purposes.

Application of Principles. Let us assume that having made a diagnosis that a group of students needs instruction in the skill of regrouping in the tens column, a classroom teacher develops a series of lessons, including in her plans appropriate motivational devices, ample opportunity for practice, and homework assignments using this skill. Let us further assume that on the end of the unit quiz (researchers will call it the post test) the majority of the pupils fail to reach that standard established in the class as indication of having mastered the skill. What happens next? Have the students failed or has the teacher? Does the teacher reteach the skill in hopes that the students will develop a prowess next time around, or does she succumb to the pressure of time and the need to "finish the book" and move on to a new skill?

This situation presents several interesting points. It is clear that if the majority of students did not meet the goals toward which the teacher was giving instruction, they have not been taught. Among the possibilities for this lack of success could be the teacher's misreading of their readiness level, or the students' lack of a clear understanding of prerequisite skills. In this instance, perhaps students had no clear understanding of the place value concept of numbers. It might be that the instructional modality selected by the classroom teacher was inappropriate for the students involved, or that other activities going on in the class were distracting to them. Whatever the case, it is hoped that the revelation that students have not achieved the skills established for the unit would come after only a few lessons and not after a unit of several weeks' duration.

At the point of discovery that students have not learned the skills, the teacher must regroup, attempt to identify the reason for the joint failure, develop a new approach to the skill, and make another attempt at teaching it.

The Future—More New Math?

As we described earlier, no fundamental changes have taken place in the responsibilities for teaching mathematics in the American elementary schools. The significant and impressive changes have taken place in the modalities, materials, equipment, and teaching techniques which have been developed since the Sputnik scare of the 1950s. Changes over the past decade have been dramatic, and equally dramatic changes are projected in elementary classrooms for the decade to come.

For several years, computer technology has outstripped the ability of educators to develop sound programmed learning packets which could provide individualized instruction for students. Professional educators are catching up with the engineers, however, and there are currently a limited number of high-quality, computer-assisted instruction programs available to students from the early elementary grades on through traditional high school courses.

Computer-Assisted Instruction (CAI). The computer-assisted instructional method is one which provides a highly individualized program. Although it can be expensive in relation to other modes of teaching, the addition of two or three computer terminals to an elementary school provides simultaneously an opportunity for remediation of students falling behind expectations of individual grade levels, enrichment for youngsters who are capable of performing beyond normal grade level expectations, and practice and drill possibilities for students at all instructional levels. In addition to being highly motivational, a computer-assisted instruction program provides highly individualized, prescriptive practice for each student. After the entry point has been established for the student, the computer provides a series of practices on the appropriate instructional level, taking him upward at small incremental steps, while monitoring and recording each student's progress. If a student answers a question incorrectly, he is given a second try; if he does not get the correct response at that point, he is given the correct answer.

It does not end here, however, because the same or similar question will be presented again in his ensuing program until he achieves mastery. If the level proves to be too difficult for him, his instructional program will automatically move down a level until he is successful. After mastery, the instruction again moves upward in small steps. The very personalized program, starting with the computer's "Hello" greeting by name after the student types his identification, and going through to the immediate tally of correct responses and ending with "Goodbye, John," provides a student with a program "tailored to fit" his particular needs.

The computer-assisted instructional method is one which provides a highly individualized program. Lessons as such do not exist in the computer memory, but are prepared for each student individually on the basis of his or her achievement while he or she is working at the terminal. Diagnosis of students' strengths and weaknesses is enhanced and daily teacher reports can be printed to provide a profile of each student's position in a concept area which represents a specific skill grouping. The computer programming arrangement permits an individual student to advance in some areas while getting extra practice or remedial assistance in other areas of difficulty. The Strands program tailors each student's lesson to his own achievement level, guaranteeing a successful experience and increasing the student's motivation to do well. This represents a vast improvement upon the traditional approach of giving class lessons which were prepared in advance by a classroom teacher without knowledge of individual student performance.

Historically, research on CAI in mathematics has shown that programs which produce more rapid learning of basic combinations and more efficient mastery of basic skills and concepts contain the same sets of basic ingredients. These ingredients are: (1) the drill and practice lesson covering the process to be mastered; (2) drill and practice lessons graded in length and depth of coverage; (3) the exercises graded in difficulty to permit a student to achieve some degree of success; and (4) exercises which are mixed. Studies have shown that daily lessons on which students spend from five to ten minutes in a fast moving, well-planned set of exercises produce the greatest gains in achievement.

Computer-Managed Instruction. Whereas computer-assisted instructional programs are generated so as to provide the instruction by way of a computer, computer-managed instruction becomes a tool for teachers rather than for pupils. In them the computer can be used to provide pretest and post test evaluations, to retain student performance records, and to store in its memory bank information for teachers regarding the source of instructional materials. It is possible, for those select and fortunate districts who have computer services available, to commit enough information to the computer's memory so that a teacher can ask such questions as, "Where can I find material that will help me to provide practice in the skills used in estimating quotient numbers?" or "What publications are there that help in problem solving—time, rate, and speed?" or "What filmstrips are available that help in the teaching of addition of fractions by fractions?" Teachers who have this service available to them are provided, for all intents and purposes, with the result of decades of teaching experience, and a vast body of knowledge upon which they can base their instructional grouping and their lesson plans. Although the initial outlay will deter many school districts from becoming deeply involved with computer-assisted or computer-managed instruction, it is not unrealistic to expect that education, like industry, will find that the computer memory far outstrips that of man and that it can be appropriately put to use in the planning aspect of education.

Personnel Assistance. Paraprofessionals are becoming more popular and better trained than ever before. These extra members of the instructional staff can provide students with additional individualized attention and can free the professional teacher for developing diagnoses and prescriptions for students who work under her charge. A wide variety of organizational patterns have been developed as alternatives to the self-contained classroom in the elementary school, and these alternatives nearly always use paraprofessionals as one of the methods of providing more efficient use of teacher time. Among the more significant organizational innovations in recent years are the Individually Prescribed Instruction programs, developed at the University of Pittsburgh; the Individually Guided Education approach, developed at the University of Wisconsin; and the introduction of learning stations or centers, which has undergone parallel and simultaneous development in Prince George's County, Maryland, and several other highly regarded school districts across the country.

Individually Prescribed Instruction. Individually Prescribed Instruction (IPI), developed by D. Robert Scanlon at the University of Pittsburgh and described in literature as the "Oak Tree Project," provides for a criterion approach to teaching mathematics, reading, and language arts. By using a combination of worksheets, teacher assistance, and flexible scheduling within an elementary school, Dr. Scanlon and his group have developed a technique of instruction whereby youngsters move at their own pace through a given number of exercises, each representing one small incremental step in the development of appropriate mathematic skills. As the child completes a worksheet, he presents it to a teacher assistant who corrects it, and then to a professional teacher who evaluates the performance and prescribes his next lesson.

Individually Guided Education. The Individually Guided Education (IGE) approach is also diagnostic and can be applied to reading, mathematics, science, social studies, or the humanities. As in the case of IPI, IGE schools are prescriptive and diagnostic in their approach to instruction, and bring into the schools additional staff members in the form of teacher assistants. The fundamental difference between IGE and IPI is that IGE schools use small group instruction as their most common instructional mode. These groups of students are brought together only so long as instruction in that skill area continues. Proponents of IGE indicate that while their instruction is individualized, it is not independent. This technique, developed by Dr. Klausmeier at the University of Wisconsin, has been adapted by the I/D/E/A Kettering Foundation and promulgated across the country.

Learning Station Approach. Another technique, generated more commonly at the school district level and containing some of the characteristics of both IGE and IPI, is represented in the learning station approach to elementary school instruction. This approach won popularity with instructional planners in Prince George's County, Maryland. In this technique, learning stations or centers are established in individual classrooms and are comprised of a series of self-directing, short-term lessons, which can be carried out by students with or without the company of other pupils and most often without direct intervention on the part of classroom teachers. Students can be given free choice option in stations that they are to visit; they can be assigned specific stations by classroom teachers or teacher assistants; or they can be directed to a series of centers which will provide reinforcement of skill instruction at various levels.

In all of these organizational patterns and with the awesome array of human and mechanical assistance at her command, the ultimate goal of the elementary school teacher in the area of teaching mathematics will remain the same: She will be required to guide children through the internalization of the basic number facts common to all arithmetic manipulations and to lead them to a proficiency in the four arithmetic operations as applied to whole numbers, common fractions, and decimals.

SUGGESTED READING

Ashlock, Robert B. *Current Research in Elementary School Mathematics*. New York: Macmillan Publishing Co., Inc., 1970.

Brumfiel, Charles, and Eugene Krause. *Elementary Mathematics for Teachers*. Reading, Mass.: Addison-Wesley Publishing Co., Inc., 1969.

Collier, Calhoun C., and Harold H. Lerch. *Teaching Mathematics in the Modern Elementary School*. New York: Macmillan Publishing Co., Inc., 1969.

Copeland, Richard W. *Diagnostic and Learning Activities in Mathematics for Children*. New York: Macmillan Publishing Co., Inc., 1974.

Copeland, Richard W. *How Children Learn Mathematics*. New York: Macmillan Publishing Co., Inc., 1974.

Dwight, Leslie A. *Modern Mathematics for the Elementary Teacher*. New York: Holt, Rinehart & Winston, Inc., 1966.

Fehr, Howard, and Jo McKeely Phillips. *Teaching Modern Mathematics in the Elementary School*. Reading, Mass.: Addison-Wesley Publishing Co., Inc., 1972.

Howes, Virgil. *Individualizing Instruction in Science and Mathematics*. New York: Macmillan Publishing Co., Inc., 1970.

Kane, Robert B., Mary Ann Byrne, and Mary Ann Hater. *Helping Children Read Mathematics*. New York: American Book Company, 1974.

Kelly, John L., and Donald B. Rickert. *Mathematics for Elementary Teachers*. San Francisco: Holden-Day, Inc., Publisher, 1970.

May, Lola June. *Teaching Mathematics in the Elementary School*. New York: Macmillan Publishing Co., Inc., 1974.

National Council of Teachers of Mathematics. *More Topics in Mathematics for Elementary Teachers*. Thirtieth Yearbook. Washington, D.C., 1971.

Spitzer, Herbert F. *What Research Says to the Teacher: Teaching Arithmetic*. Washington, D.C.: Association of Classroom Teachers of the National Educational Association, 1957.

Turner, Ethel M. *Teaching Aids for Elementary Mathematics*. New York: Holt, Rinehart & Winston, Inc., 1966.

Wren, F. Lynwood. *Basic Mathematical Concepts*. New York: McGraw-Hill Book Company, 1973.

POST TEST

1. As a beginning teacher of elementary mathematics, what are four ways for finding the functional level of your students?

_____

_____

_____

_____

_____

_____

_____

_____

_____

_____

2. React positively or negatively. "A child shows readiness for learning a skill in mathematics when he can recite in rapid manner the numbers in sequence."

_____

_____

3. List at least four methods for drill that a teacher might use to help students memorize number facts.

_____

_____

_____

_____

_____

4. What is the significant factor in designing drills?

_____

_____

_____

_____

5. Define the basic purpose for grouping.

_____

_____

6. List the kinds of grouping a teacher might use in the classroom to fulfill this purpose.

_____

_____

_____

7. What four divisions should be included in a lesson plan?

_____

_____

_____

_____

8. What is the value of teaching problem solving? Give three practical experiences that a creative teacher might use to help the students in the classroom.

_____

_____

_____

_____

_____

_____

_____

9. What are four guidelines for homework assignments in math?

_____

_____

_____

_____

10. List three of the five functions that evaluation of pupil progress serves.

_____

_____

_____

_____

_____

11. Give four reasons why teacher-made tests are often a poor measure of pupil progress.

_____

_____

_____

_____

_____

_____

_____

12. How should a teacher make use of the results on a standardized test?

_____

_____

_____

13. When a majority of students in a class fails to show mastery of a skill at the end of a unit, what four steps must a good teacher follow?

_____

_____

_____

_____

14. Explain the major purpose for using paraprofessionals.

_____

_____

_____

15. According to the goal of American education, what is the primary responsibility of the elementary mathematics program?

_____

_____

_____

_____

16. Name three currently significant, organizational, innovative programs for mathematics.

_____

_____

_____

Teaching Values

John C. Turpin

Baldwin-Wallace College

module 11

Definition of Value or Values / Values Education and the Cognitive Area / Values Clarification / The New Approach / The Traditional Approach / Levels of Teaching / Value Rich Areas / Value Clarification Strategies / Future of Values Clarification / Some Other Value Approaches

RATIONALE

In education today, a teacher can not avoid dealing with values. Even if he asserts, as some teachers do, that he does not need to be concerned with values, inadvertently he will find himself dealing with them. Each teacher in his daily classroom efforts communicates value concepts to his students, overtly or covertly. He tends to emphasize certain facts over others by gestures, speech, mannerisms, and voice inflections often without being aware of the effect of his performance. Attentive students or sensitive students, as a consequence, assimilate, also without awareness of the why or how, predispositions toward positive or negative attitudes, depending upon their relationship with their teacher. This module is concerned with the need for elementary teachers to deal consciously with values in their classrooms. Today when youth are tending to reject the culture of the old and are beginning to develop a culture of their own, the need for knowledge about and skill in teaching values is greater than ever before.

Every society is sustained by a core of "universals"—elements of the culture which all people know, believe, use, and do—which represent the society's ideals, standards, and norms. The heart of the universals is the values or the rules by which people order their social existence. As the core of universal elements in the culture of a country grows small relative to the other elements, such as the alternative and the specialized elements, people in general lose some of their feeling of security and certitude about the response expected of them in many areas of living. Smith, Stanley and Shores[1] describe the specialized elements as the values cherished in common by members of a particular group. The alternative elements are described as values practiced by a number of people who have nothing in common except respect for the particular element.

Operational values develop from this core because of personal needs and sometimes they conflict with society's normative values. What people do and what they want are not always consistent with what they believe and profess that they want. For example, the national preoccupation with problems dealing with the racial issue in the 1970s illustrates one of the dilemmas for our culture. Freedom, justice, and equality have always been claimed as democratic ideals by Americans. Yet, lack of freedom, injustice, and great inequalities have existed in this country because personal values about race and religion, bolstered by custom and habit have overridden the patriotic ideals of many of our people.

Unless teachers and the schools remain sensitive to the nuances of this social revolution that is in progress, they run the risk of losing touch, of becoming expendably irrelevant, and of culpably abandoning their charges to the consequences of a culture in flux. Today teachers are beginning to identify clearly and convincingly their own values in the changing world. Teachers, having determined where they stand as adults and as educators, can then help students to meet the challenges and identify clearly and convincingly their own values.

This trend for teachers to deal with values, their own and their students', leads

---

[1] Othanel B. Smith, William O. Stanley, and J. Harlan Shores, *Fundamentals of Curriculum Development* (New York: Harcourt Brace Jovanovich, Inc., 1957), p. 6.

to a basic theme of this module—that what is really needed in education is not more teachers who have a zealous and unyielding dedication to inculcating a fixed set of values, but rather more teachers who have the habit of self-improvement, who are emotionally, socially, and morally committed to helping the young formulate satisfying guides for personal living and social interaction. It is this author's opinion that this type of teacher can help students examine their own values and define them even though the core of universals has diminished in size.

In the recent past, elementary teachers have not dealt in a methodical way with values since values development was an area enshrouded in differences of opinion and controversy in an emerging pluralistic society. Teachers mainly have been concerned with teaching facts, principles, and concepts—the kind of knowledge that could be tested, charted, and reported upon. The common approach used by classroom teachers to values formation has been the incidental system. Course content has been selected in the social sciences, for example, from those aspects of our past which revealed the virtues and perfections of our national leaders, our form of government, and our economic system. From this viewpoint, a good citizen might be defined as one who could recall the positive qualities of George Washington, Thomas Jefferson, and others; who could test high on questions about democracy and the several freedoms outlined in our Bill of Rights. Students were viewed essentially as passive recipients of inherited wisdom, and the curriculum was based on the "tacit assumption that knowledge is automatically transformable into action."[2] The fact that teachers of subject matter might be fostering provincial attitudes in lieu of universal values and an unduly restricted student comprehension of the tentative nature of knowledge was not widely recognized.

Today, on the contrary, values education is beginning to assume some of the proportions of a fad with many people paying attention to it. The danger is great in such a popular movement that concepts, areas, and fundamental values may be introduced prematurely and by practitioners who are lacking in several of the essential skills, so that more confusion is caused than is necessary. Studying about the techniques and strategies in this module should help you prepare to assume a more appropriate role in the future.

SPECIFIC OBJECTIVES

Upon completion of this module, it is expected that you will understand the need for working with values in the elementary classroom, be aware of some strengths and limitations of the values clarification approach, and be aware of some of the other approaches to teaching values which are available.

Specifically, when you have completed the study of this module, you should be able to do the following:

---

[2] William C. Merwin, Donald O. Schneider, and Lester D. Stephens, *Developing Competency in Teaching Secondary Social Studies* (Columbus, Ohio: Charles E. Merrill Publishers, 1974), p. 5.

1. Explain and defend in your own words at least two reasons why it is necessary to deal with values in the elementary school in some overt manner.
2. List all seven components of the values clarification definition of a value, and explain whether you think all are necessary.
3. Give your own definition of values and relate it to other definitions which you have learned through other approaches.
4. Explain the basic assumption and the eight categories of the Lasswell values approach.
5. Explain in your own words the relationship between cognitive and values areas of education.
6. Establish in your own words the need for teachers to grow as individuals by looking at their own values so as to truly help students improve as individuals.
7. Explain the basic assumptions of the values clarification approach and whether you agree with them.
8. Demonstrate that you can develop your own strategies for use in the classroom by developing at least one strategy or values experience which you could use with students in an elementary school. Explain why it could help students with their values.
9. List at least three cautions of which a teacher needs to be aware when deciding whether or not to implement values clarification in the classroom.
10. List at least five approaches for helping individuals grow which implement in some way values education and which the student can study on his own to learn more about the area of values education.

MODULE TEXT

Definition of Value or Values

When one considers values education, it is of first importance to determine what the word means. This can be a complex task since there are numerous definitions of the word *value* or *values* and also extensive approaches which implement some of these definitions.

A review of the literature dealing with the term *value* or *values* has identified a number of somewhat different definitions. A sampling of these definitions shows that a value may be any of the following:

a directive factor in human behavior.[3]

the standards held by individuals or groups.[4]

a subjective appraisal of a situation, proposal, or event.[5]

the total universe of a person's beliefs about the physical world, the social world, and the self.[6]

[3] W. Engbretson, "Values of Children, How They Develop," *Child Health Education* (Feb. 1959).
[4] M. Douglas, *Social Studies* (New York: J. B. Lippincott Co., 1967).
[5] E. Carey, "Value Judgments in Economic Education," *Social Education* (April, 1962).
[6] M. Rokeach and L. Mezel, "Race and Shared Beliefs as Factors in Social Choice," *Science,* 1966, p. 151.

a belief centrally located within one's belief system about how one ought or ought not to behave, or about some end-state of existence worth attaining.[7]

Some writers have prepared more comprehensive descriptions of values. Scriven,[8] for instance, has identified the following different types of values and value claims:

1. "Personal" values which include matters of taste (not opinions), such as "I like strawberry ice cream."
2. Market values and value claims which are described as existing when a group of people "have some common elements in their personal value 'profiles' so that they create a market."
3. "Real values and value claims" or the traditional values of the individual.
4. Implicit values and value claims which encompass those things which we say, but which we do not intend to be taken in a literal fashion. We say, for example, that somebody is intelligent and, obviously, mean it as "purely descriptive" in the context of "tall" or "stout."

Bond describes value[9] as "an assertable belief about the worth, goodness, preferability of an object, event, idea, act, or other phenomenon; by valuation (or valuing), I mean the act of determining the goodness of worth of phenomena; by valuation model (or theory), I mean a system of processes which can be employed deliberately for the purpose of determining value."

Raths and his associates[10] see values as the general guides to behavior which grow and develop out of our personal experiences. As each individual lives through the events of his life, his values evolve and mature and are modified. When the pattern of experiences changes, when conditions impose different restrictions, varied responses, based upon altered sets of values, are called upon for guidance in decision making. Seldom do values function in a pure and abstract form. Because the decisions made by each individual may be mediated by complex and conflicting demands, the judgments arrived at become not so much hard and fast varieties as patterns of behavior in certain sets of circumstances. Those things emerging as right, or desirable, or worthy from the process of internal disputation tend to become our values. Although there can be no universal agreement upon the values arrived at by a total population nor even by a single individual at any given time or place, an environment consensus can be reached about the effective processes which can be utilized to assist the individual to make judgments based upon value sets. The Raths researchers propose the use of seven characteristics (listed later) in evaluating a belief or a feeling to determine if it rates consideration as a value in one's life.

Another comprehensive definition is the one given by Harold D. Lasswell[11] who

[7] R. Beech, "Values Systems, Attitudes, and Interpersonal Attraction" (Michigan State University, unpublished doctoral dissertation, 1967).

[8] M. Scriven, *Values and the Valuing Process* (Orinda, Calif.: Diablo Valley Education Project, June 1971).

[9] D. Bond, "An Analysis of Valuation Strategies in Social Science Education Materials" (University of California, unpublished doctoral dissertation, 1971).

[10] Louis E. Raths, Merrill Harmin, and Sidney B. Simon, *Values and Teaching, Working with Values in the Classroom* (Columbus, Ohio: Charles E. Merrill Publishers, 1966), p. 46.

[11] Harold D. Lasswell and R. Rubenstein, *The Sharing of Power in a Psychiatric Hospital* (New Haven, Conn.: Yale University Press, 1966), p. 84.

defines the social process as "man seeking values through institutions using resources." His work identified what he feels are eight basic value categories, which he claims are common to all cultures and in which every person needs fulfillment to grow as an individual. If the individual is deprived in any of these value categories, that prevents the individual from achieving his potential and can even lead through severe deprivation to mental illness. The eight value categories or needs are affection, respect, skill, enlightenment, power (influence), wealth (meaning goods and services), well-being (mental and physical), and rectitude (responsibility).

These are some of the definitions of a value that are available for the elementary school teacher to consider when deciding to deal with values in the classroom. None of these models is intended to be "the" model for this module since model choice is an individual decision of each teacher. It is suggested that you look over these definitions and write one of your own, which may or may not include the definitions given. Since this module is only an introduction to the values education field, space does not permit an exhaustive treatment of any of these approaches.

A thorough examination and study of some of the volumes in the Suggested Reading list at the end of the module will help you discover how each of the values program designers visualizes his system in operation. In this module, our goal is to cover the field of values in general, so that you may begin to grow in familiarity with the terms used, come to understand some of the concepts involved, and lay the groundwork for further study and effort on your part.

Let us begin our examination of the values area with a consideration of its relationship to the area of cognitive education.

Values Education and the Cognitive Area

One error teachers often make when they define values for themselves consists of treating the cognitive and value areas as if each were a completely separate entity. This conclusion has caused many teachers to deal with only the cognitive area in the classroom, and to ignore the values area, or the opposite.

Because of this problem, some authorities have pointed out that teachers need to learn more about values, value theory, and related areas and to be trained in the ways and means of teaching values to their students.

Concerning the overemphasis of the cognitive approach by so many teachers, Gerald Weinstein and Mario Fantini[12] have identified the traditional emphasis in education as one in which "all instructional roads seem to lead to cognition as the end product." It is their contention that in our educational institutions today, cognitive processes and content are riding the peak of the educational wave. The entire machinery of the school, they believe, including its reward system, reflects only the degree of mastery of cognitive learning. And a change in behavior is commonly interpreted in schools as only a change in cognitive behavior. Their solution is to provide a humanistic education in which values have a major part.

---

[12] Gerald Weinstein and Mario Fantini, eds., *Toward Humanistic Education—A Curriculum of Affect* (New York: Praeger Publishers, Inc., 1970).

The literature, then, suggests the need for teachers to be trained to deal with the cognitive area and also with values education, for all knowledge is related to values. Teachers should not speak of intellectual training as if it were separable from values training. Learning leads to basic values that become the foundation of one's character, and behavior leads to experiences that produce learning and insights, which then modify behavior and reinstate the cycle.

Mager[13] expresses the same concern when he states "a universal objective of instruction" should be simply "the intent to send students away from instruction with at least as favorable an attitude toward the subjects taught as they had when they first arrived." With this background in mind, the prospective elementary school teacher should be ready to examine the strengths and concerns of one approach to values in the classroom which, although by no means the model approach, can be used with elementary school age students. That approach is called values clarification, based largely on the works of Louis E. Raths and his students.

Values Clarification

The values clarification approach to values education is intended to help students clarify their own values rather than force them to accept the values imposed upon them by the teacher. Up through the 1960s most major curriculum development efforts in the elementary schools aimed at developing good citizens through inculcation of selected beliefs, values, and attitudes. However, major problems with this approach developed over the years. Some of the beliefs and values stressed in school conflicted with philosophical positions and deliberate actions of some of the citizens in the community. For example, the value position that restricts the individual behavior for the protection and welfare of others conflicts with that position which restricts the rights of the majority to protect the rights of the individual.

The apparent conflict between admired American values such as brotherhood, cooperation, loyalty, competition, individualism, and the right to one's own beliefs and values has regularly caused major problems in the schools. Teachers giving first allegiance to a belief in a free market place of ideas, for example, can hardly comply with the expectation of the school that they will indoctrinate children to a particular idea or to one way of behaving as compared to others. This fundamental problem has led many educators to disavow attempts to indoctrinate students with particular values and beliefs and instead to advocate instruction that helps students clarify and develop their own beliefs and values in a rationally defensible manner. To understand this currently popular attempt to resolve ambiguity for teachers and pupils, it is necessary to understand some of the basic tenets of the philosophy used. In the Raths system, the following areas are included as vital components: (1) definition of a value, (2) value indicators, (3) the "new" approach to values, (4) the "traditional" approach to values, (5) the three levels of teaching, (6) value rich areas, (7) value strategies, and (8) some strengths and limitations of the approach. The remainder of this part of the module will explain briefly each of these parts.

[13] Robert Mager, *Developing Attitudes Toward Learning* (Palo Alto, Calif.: Fearon Publishers, 1968).

A Specific Definition. The basis of the values clarification approach is contained in Raths' definition of a value, which requires every value upon examination to satisfy each of the following seven criteria: (1) chosen freely, (2) chosen from alternatives, (3) chosen after thoughtful consideration of the consequences of each alternative, (4) prized or cherished so one is happy with the choice, (5) willingness to publicly affirm choice, (6) acted upon so that the person does something with his choice, and (7) acted upon repeatedly, forming some pattern in a person's life. A belief, for example, to merit consideration as a value must have been freely chosen by the believer. Although the environment in which he dwells and the hortatory behavior of those around him may have conditioned his act of choosing, he cannot be compelled to value anything. In the past, people with the same background, as well as members of the same family have regularly made choices which contradicted each other regarding the values they have established and the courses which their lives have followed. Having selected from among alternatives after thoughtful consideration, and cherishing the selection, each family member has used his values as a guide in his life. He has openly professed the position he has taken, has advocated it for others, and has been willing to be associated with it publicly. This delimitation of the meaning of a value places special emphasis upon the process by which values are formed and lives are influenced.

Value Indicators. The obvious question becomes, "but what if my thought, opinion, belief, or aspiration does not meet all seven criteria?" The answer is that it is not then a value but a "value indicator"—an alert to the presence of a value item, but different in some degree or degrees from a value. A value indicator becomes, as one group of students of the writer liked to call it, a "partial value." Raths[14] lists the following eight value indicators:

1. Goals or purposes. A stated purpose may be looked upon as a potential value. If we are not willing to do what is necessary to achieve our goal, it may be that we really don't prize it enough or that we are experiencing only a passing interest.
2. Aspirations. Vague dreams and remote expectations must be rigorously examined before they can qualify as values.
3. Attitudes. We may be for or against some things in only a shallow fashion, not really caring deeply one way or another. Until depth of significance sets in, attitudes remain indicators.
4. Interests. Often interests stop at the point of being passing fancies and never work into values.
5. Feelings. Our responses of hurt or outrage, gladness or sadness may be expressions which can and will be dissipated easily by brief reflection.
6. Beliefs and convictions. A verbal statement that is lacking in careful examination or that will yield to doubts upon mature reflection lacks the depth of a value.
7. Activities. It is not only a question of practicing what one preaches. Also involved are the valuing of what one is doing and the degree to which it represents a pattern in a person's life.

[14] Raths, Harmin and Simon, op. cit., p. 30–33.

8. Worries, problems, obstacles. Whether the worries are casual conversation pieces or represent deeply rooted and greatly prized points of view will determine whether values or merely indicators are present.

When a value indicator reaches a point where it satisfies all seven criteria, it then becomes a value. While it is an indicator, it remains an expression which is headed toward values but has not yet arrived. These indicators are, however, ideal matter for value-clarifying responses. A teacher who listens for students' comments that fall into one or several of these categories and who then responds within the framework of the valuing methodology can do much to advance the clarification of values and also witness significant behavioral changes among his students.

The New Approach

The implementation of the values clarification approach is referred to as the "new approach" to values.[15] It starts with some area of conflict when students are confused or have not as yet accumulated all of the characteristics of a person having values. The teacher involves the students in some activities which require their responding to a problem by encouraging them to make some choices, leading them to examine alternatives, weighing these alternatives in the light of their personal feeling, encouraging students to consider what they prize and cherish, giving them the opportunity to make public affirmation of their choices, and encouraging them to live according to their choices. An example of this procedure might come from a class discussion about the absence of black students in an all-white, suburban school district, or the lack of transportation for the elderly in a community which is spread out and which confines stores and shopping districts to appropriately zoned (but distant) districts. Focusing upon the choices offered for the solution to such a problem and examining the community rationale for the prevailing condition would lead to scrutiny of personal feelings, an examination of the benefits of alternative courses of action, and perhaps a personal ranking in the order of preference of the solutions proposed by others in the discussion. The opportunity to hear how other students resolve the problem, to consider what one values oneself, what he wants of life, what type of person he is, and to hear the response of those who hold contrasting views helps to bring students closer to formulating a personal value system.

In his work with the clarification approach, Harmin[16] has been concerned with developing techniques by which students and teachers can clarify their own values rather than adopt suggested or prescribed values. These researchers are not interested in measuring the values that people have. Their concern is not so much what a person values or says he values as it is with where the person got his idea about values and why he values as he does. It is this process of valuing that they believe is so important because by valuing, students can learn how to determine what they should do with their lives and energy. Many adults in our contemporary affluent society appear to suffer from lack of clear purposes, from indecision about what they are for or against, and from lack of conviction about where they are going.

---

[15] Raths, op. cit., pp. 51–56.
[16] Merrill Harmin, H. Kirschenbaum, and Sidney Simon, *Clarifying Values Through Subject Matter—Applications for the Classroom* (Minneapolis: Winston Press, 1973).

The fact that these adults lack criteria for choosing what to do with their time, their energy, and their very being alarms these value researchers. The methodology they propose is designed to avoid this lack. It is intended to furnish lifelong processes, procedures, and criteria by which one can become more purposeful, more enthusiastic, more positive, and more aware of what is worth striving for.

In the classrooms where value clarification is taking place, there will be much less teacher talk and much more teacher listening to what students say. Questions of the open-ended, divergent kind will replace the closed, convergent, factual type. Discussion will supersede right–wrong kinds of responses. In general, active teachers will respond to a value indicator with a clarifying question or comment, designed to help the student use one or more of the seven valuing processes. If, for example, a teacher suspects that a child doesn't give much consideration to what is important to him, he might try a clarifying response that gets at reprizing and cherishing. Sometimes "the form of the value indicator may suggest the form of the clarifying response." For example, "a thoughtless choice suggests responses that get at choosing, and a fine sounding verbalization suggests responses that get at incorporating choices into behavior."[17]

The Traditional Approach

In contrast to this new approach and less effective, according to the values clarification theory, is the "traditional approach" to values teaching. For years, the methods used by teachers to get students to adopt certain values have been as follows:

1. Set an example. Either by their own behavior or by selecting outstanding examples of virtue among the adult world, living or dead, the teachers drew attention to the practice of values which they looked upon as acceptable.
2. Persuade. By presenting their arguments carefully, teachers hoped to prevail upon students to accept selected sets of values which were approved by segments of the adult population.
3. Limited choice. By eliminating attractive but unacceptable value choices from the options offered to students, teachers attempted to provide practice in judgment making. They offered, for example, two "goods" so that despite the selection made, no conflict with society resulted. Or they stacked the deck and offered choices, one of which was so obnoxious as to leave little doubt about the option exercised.
4. Inspire. Through the use of fable, myth, biography, and history, teachers highlighted and made attractive the values they wished to inculcate.
5. Establish rules and regulations. The intent of these rules was the control of behavior by rewards and punishments until the stage of automatic "correct" response had been reached.
6. Cite religious dogma and historical tradition. Acceptance of values was encouraged on the grounds that holy people or heroic people of the past had practiced them.

[17] Raths, op. cit., p. 82.

ugawithlobbycord

7. Appeal to conscience. By indicating the shame or guilt associated with one way of behavior, teachers cultivated behavior of the opposite sort in accordance with the values they supported.
8. Tell students what to believe. Using their position of esteem gained by superior knowledge, teachers explained their personal values with the expectation that students would accept them without much debate.

A basic assumption of the values clarification approach is that as a "new approach" to values it is much more effective than the traditional approach and should therefore be used by teachers. However, not all teachers are abandoning procedures to which they have been accustomed and adopting the new. Like all other changes in education, modification in teacher behavior is a slow process which will depend upon the judgments of the individual teachers made after a consideration of data.

Levels of Teaching

Value clarification can be done effectively in the classroom by implementing the three levels at which subject matter can be taught: the facts level, concepts level, and the values level. The facts level is confined to an examination or inquiry into the "what" that happened, the events that transpired, the people involved, the materials used, and the sequence of events leading up to or happening as a consequence of any given event. The concepts level extends to the implications of the facts, to the hypotheses that become justified because of the facts, and to the extended ramifications of knowledge which extend the usefulness of the learning for the student. The values level is the level of subject matter that touches the student's choices, because they indicate what he prizes and also determine his actions.

The point is obvious: effective teachers teach at the values level, and that indicates the need for values clarification techniques.

Value Rich Areas

Whenever teachers deal with values, they get into what are called the "value rich areas" or areas in which people in general tend to develop values. The value rich areas, according to Raths,[18] are money, friendship, love and sex, religion and morals, leisure, politics and social organizations, work, family, maturity, and character traits.

Although Raths has identified only ten value rich areas, it appears that there may be more than ten of them. Areas such as education and death, teaching, and the school appear as likely areas with concealed value wealth. For teaching purposes in the elementary school, these areas are sources of feelings, convictions, biases, and confusion for every student, and are fruitful areas for probing, discussing, and clarifying.

[18] Raths, op. cit., p. 260.

Value Clarification Strategies

It seems then that values clarification has become a major approach used by many elementary teachers in the classroom because it stresses the need and the necessity for assessing the values. "Through its processes, values are constantly related to the experiences that shape them and test them. They are not so much hard and fast absolutes as they are the results of hammering out a style of life. Fundamentally, the responding strategy is a way of interacting with a student so that he considers what he has chosen, what he prizes, or what he is doing. It stimulates him to clarify his thinking and behavior and his values by thinking."[19] Obviously, then, the basic method a teacher must use in the classroom in responding to a student in a value-clarifying situation is that of questioning, of challenging, of avoiding moralizing, and of helping the student to look at what he has chosen, or is prizing, or is doing. Teacher dictation, no matter how cleverly done, cannot dissipate value confusion because it does not satisfy the seven criteria for creating a value. If no options for students to exercise judgment are available, students should be so informed and specifically directed by their teacher concerning their behavior. When, however, options are available, the teacher must avoid trying to influence the students to accept particular values. Thus, in matters such as setting a fire in the classroom wastebasket, or using profane language during class when no choice is permissible, the teacher may be clear and forceful in denying choice to students with the understanding that an unwise choice cannot be tolerated by the policies which govern the group behavior; but in matters that are less crucial, when choice is possible, teachers must be willing to give children the freedom to choose, if values are to result.

Value clarification requires that the student look at his own behavior and make decisions from the alternatives for action that exist. Even if he chooses not to examine the alternatives nor to think about the options, the teacher must accept and respect his decision, for the teacher's role is not to dictate but to attempt to set a mood in which the student has an opportunity to modify the direction of his life, if he wants to. This clarification strategy requires many of us educators to change our basic orientation; under these value clarification ground rules, we can no longer try overtly and regularly to sell our intellectual wares so as to persuade the pupils. Stimulating students to clarify their values seems almost a whole new ball game.

The Rank Order. The strategy called rank order and each of the other four strategies presented later in this module can be used by the elementary teacher in any classroom. They can be built into the lesson as part of the plan or introduced with no relationship at all to the topic being taught to the class.

Example: Complete the activity by ranking in order from most important to least important to you the following choices. Begin the order with the selection you number as one.
   1. A shopping center or mall nearby.
   2. Green grass, trees, and flowers in your yard.
   3. A home with all the modern conveniences you desire.

[19] Raths, op. cit., p. 51.

4. Neighbors whom you enjoy and feel comfortable around.
5. Good schools near your home.
6. A church of your faith near your home.
7. An unlimited supply of gas, oil, and electricity.

As you have worked upon this rank order, you should have been struck by some of the benefits it holds out for use in your classroom. It should have become apparent that the participation of any student in this ordering activity would provide the following:

1. A provocation to each student to take stock of his position on the seven statements in the order.
2. An opportunity for each to hear the position taken by his classmates concerning the order.
3. An atmosphere in which each can differ from any of the others and rank the group in accordance with individual preference.
4. Practice in rendering judgments and making choices.
5. Opportunity to practice the courageous act of making a selection and proclaiming it before all the world.

The rank order can be done in groups by writing on the chalkboard or by using an overhead projector to present the rank order to the class. It can be done verbally with younger students. The following are some additional rank orders which may be used in an elementary school classroom. The intent of the entire exercise is for students to simply clarify what they believe.

Would you rather
1. go swimming.
2. ride your bike.
3. go on a sled ride.

Would you rather have a father who
1. is a clown.
2. owns a candy store.
3. owns a toy shop.

Would you rather eat
1. ice cream.
2. chocolate cake.
3. peanut butter cookies.

Would you rather be

Boys	Girls
1. a fireman.	1. a teacher.
2. a policeman.	2. a nurse.
3. an astronaut.	3. a movie star.

These examples were originally developed by Joan Niemits, a prospective elementary teacher at Baldwin-Wallace College, Berea, Ohio.

To enable you to learn to use a rank order, it is suggested that you write some rank orders of your own. You are also referred to the four books on values clarification identified at the beginning of the module for further reading and possible examples.

Values Continuum. A similar activity is the values continuum strategy. You simply write a value continuum line on the blackboard (or use a transparency), explain the strategy, present the issue, and then have students respond by identifying the number location of the position they favor. The issue might be some value-laden topic such as racial integration, religious tolerance, or abortion. The polar positions represented by the numbers 1 and 7 on the continuum line should be identified by opposing statements, such as, "Students in all communities should be bused to bring about integrated schools" or "No busing should be permitted for purposes of integration." In the discussion that ensues, other positions that can be taken and solutions which have been offered or tried are proposed and identified by position on the continuum line. The value of the activity is to point out the number of and the differences among the alternatives possible, each of which carries with it consequences that are distinctive. This strategy is one of the most useful value-clarifying tools because it enables the teacher to keep free of committing himself to a position until all the alternatives have been located, and it helps the students to recognize the possibility of multiple alternative solutions instead of a black-white, either-or situation.

Some value continuums which may be appropriate for students on the elementary level are as follows:

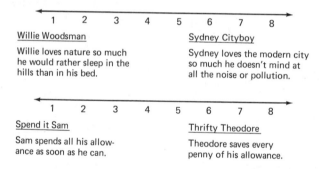

This strategy is used the same as the rank order. It is suggested that you try to write some value continuums of your own. Beware not to use words in your caption so loaded that they force pupils to react to your biases.

Voting. Another effective activity for the elementary student is the voting strategy. To use this strategy, the teacher simply asks students some questions and has them respond by raising their hands high if they agree, holding their hands in front of them if they half agree, and hitting the desk if they disagree. All the other guidelines apply as explained with the other strategies.

An example of a voting strategy, which may work well with elementary students and which you as a prospective elementary teacher might even respond to in your own mind, would be as follows:

Voting List—Elementary
1. How many of you like playing in the snow?
2. How many of you spent some time this weekend doing something you really wanted to do?

3. How many of you would rather receive a puppy or a kitten for Christmas rather than a toy of your choice?
4. How many of you would rather spend Saturday afternoon babysitting for a neighbor's two-year-old instead of watching TV? (Older elementary students)
5. How many of you have certain chores you have to do around the house each day?
6. How many of you get an allowance for these chores? Any allowance at all? No allowance?
7. How many of you just ask your parents for money when you need it? Never ask for money?
8. How many of you would rather ask for money when you need it instead of getting an allowance? Get an allowance?

You may also want to write a voting list of your own.

Proud Whip. Another strategy which may work well with elementary school students is called the proud whip. In this strategy, the teacher asks the students to name something they are proud of in some area and then goes around the room as each student names something. The guidelines given for the ranking technique also apply to this strategy.

An example of some proud whips which you might respond to on your own and which may work well with elementary school students are the following:

1. What have you done this week of which you are proud?
2. What do you have in your desk of which you are proud?

The goal of this activity is the encouragement of growth in positive thinking. Students who are inclined to denigrate themselves, their accomplishments, and their possessions in an activity such as this are faced with the necessity to find something which is mentionable. The process learned in the classroom, it is hoped, can be extended to many facets of everyday life, both inside the classroom and outside the school. Pessimistic habits of thinking are easy for some people to cultivate because the grass they see is always greener in other people's yards. Stimulated to examine their own yard in order to participate in the proud whip activity, and coerced to listen to the recitations of others whose claims may be modest indeed, students who are predisposed toward self-denigration may be encouraged to relax their rigor in evaluating themselves and begin to look more receptively at the positive things that happen in their lives.

These are a sampling of only a few of the many strategies that are available for teachers to use in the elementary school. For further reading, you are referred to the four sources indicated in this module which treat other techniques such as role playing, the contrived incident, the devil's advocate, thought sheets, time diaries, the public interview, and others.

Guidelines for Using Clarification Techniques. The following are some important guidelines which you will need to remember as you use most of these techniques with groups of students, since students will respond verbally with their preferences in most activities. The teacher needs to always create a warm and accepting classroom atmosphere when doing values clarification in the classroom.

First, identify and explain the strategy to let the students know that to begin the technique, you will start with someone and go around the room. You then read the nonverbal communication of the students in the classroom to identify who would like to start the responses. (To identify this nonverbal communication, you simply look at the faces of the students, and those who would like to begin the exercise will tell you so by the way they look at you. Those who do not want to start will also tell you by looking at the floor.) In most classrooms, a student will offer to begin on his or her own.

Next, be sure that students know they can say, "I pass," if they do not want to respond.

Third, be sure that every student participates in the technique by either giving his response or by saying, "I pass." Do not allow students to start saying, "I agree," to a former reply, but inform them that they must give their own response, even though it may be the same as the person's before them. (If you allow students to say, "I agree," a social pressure soon builds up to say the same thing.)

Fourth, when all students have had the opportunity to respond, you simply thank them and proceed with your normal lesson (or you may have a discussion if you desire).

Future of Values Clarification

What is the future of values clarification, and what are some of its strengths and limitations?

Sidney Simon predicts the future of the values clarification work as something that will "grow dramatically in the next few years because of the unrest in schools. Something has to be done for the kids, for they are hurting as much as adults."[20] In Raths' opinion, "Further research will bring a better understanding of values clarification and its implications for education, and this in turn will hopefully lead to better results in the classroom and happier, better integrated, more productive individuals." He goes on to state, "For years, we gave special treatment to those students who suffered from physical disabilities. Later, we learned many approaches to those children whose problems indicated an emotional disturbance. Now we believe similar understandings and practices can be directed to children who have value-related disturbances. These children are often identifiable by idiosyncratic behavior patterns—apathy, flightiness, extreme uncertainty and inconsistency, drift, overconformity, and underachievement. The common malady of these children seems to be confusion of values."[21]

One of the strengths of the clarifying responses as seen by Raths is that they are usually aimed at "just one student at a time, often in brief, informal conversation held in class, in hallways, or anyplace where the teacher comes in contact with the student who says or does something to trigger response . . . The purpose of the clarifying response is to raise questions in the mind of the student, to prod him gently to examine his life, his actions, and his ideas." Under the prodding, some students may find the thoughtful consistency between words and deeds that characterizes values and which results in deepening some of the indicators to the extent

[20] F. Gray, "Everybody Talks About It, But Some Teachers Are Doing Something About Values," *Learning.* (Dec. 1972), pp. 15–18.
[21] Raths, op. cit., p. 7.

of qualifying for the category of values. This clarifying is done by the conscientious teacher in an informal manner, on a consistent basis, and over a period of time. It is performed in a positive and helpful fashion without moralizing, preaching, or dogmatizing. The environment provided for the student during clarification is supportive and nonthreatening; no eyebrows are raised by student responses, no snickers allowed, no shock permitted to register. The mood required is that which emanates from basic and honest respect for students by the teacher. Teachers unable to project this quality will probably be but partially successful.

Another strength of the approach, as seen by proponents, is that each person is expected to wrest his own values from the available array. It is the process of making decisions that is the goal in this pursuit—the contributive something that should serve students well and long after schooling has ceased.

Still another of the basic strengths is that for it to be successful, the teacher needs to create an atmosphere of acceptance and warmth in the classroom, and that type of atmosphere can be a positive one for the growth of the student. Students of the writer have stated that the atmosphere and the "opportunity to look for the first time at my own values was a valuable experience."

Some educators, however, view the values clarification approach with alarm. They fear that it is being accepted by teachers without consideration of its limitations or of the problems caused by its utilization. Such acceptance, they feel, could be fatal. As with any other strategy, one needs to be aware of the limitations of the values clarification approach whenever one considers using it, especially in an elementary classroom. According to John S. Stewart,[22] some problems and inadequacies of the values clarification approach are as follows:

1. Values clarification has almost become a sacred cow, and a well-developed fad. Some teachers become so involved with it that they don't want to look at the limitations of the approach.
2. It is very superficial since it tends to deal with "why" the student believes what he believes rather than with "what" the student values.
3. Values clarification relies too much on peer pressure, and in a society in which what your peers think is very important to the young person, then this may possibly cause more harm than good.
4. When teachers use values clarification, they are supposed to be nonjudgmental, but the methodology of the approach is judgmental, and often contradictory.
5. Values clarification is based on moral relativism. Of the criticisms made against it, probably none is made more frequently or more loudly than the charge that it is inadequate, ineffective, and possibly even dangerous because of its basic moral relativism.

It could be that when a teacher has students clarify their own values without making a value judgment about the correctness of that value, he is as much as saying, "Whatever you believe is all right." And, of course, that may simply not be true. In fact, the student may be clarifying a value which is destructive to himself as an individual. Also, nonverbal messages may be both as important and as destructive as the verbal message given in this area by the teacher.

[22] John S. Stewart, "Clarifying Values Clarification: A Critique," *Phi Delta Kappan,* pp. 684–688 (June, 1975).

Since these criticisms are stated both briefly and in part, the reader is referred to the original source if interested in more detail.

Some Other Values Approaches

Since this module is intended to be only a brief introduction to values education in the elementary school, space has been devoted so far only to material concerning values education in general and values clarification in particular. You may want to be at least aware of other resources which are available to study on your own. Some resources which are valuable for both their use in the elementary classroom and for the growth of the elementary school teacher are the following:

A. The American Institute for Character Education. This is a nonprofit educational institution which, according to its brochure is "dedicated to one basic objective: to provide teachers with those skills, techniques, and materials that will enable them to beneficially influence children and youth." It consists of a newly revised "Character Education Curriculum" with a teacher's guide, posters, activity sheets, and evaluation instruments. They all come packaged in a cardboard box with one entire set for each grade level from first through fifth. Additional information about this approach can be obtained by writing American Institute for Character Education, P.O. Box 12617, San Antonio, Texas, 78212.

B. Another resource is "The Coronado Plan for Preventive Drug Abuse Education," developed by the Coronado Unified School District, Coronado, California. It has been published by Value Education Publications, P.O. Box 947, Campbell, California 95008. Although this appears to be simply a drug abuse program, it is much broader than that and is based on the assumption that most drug abuse programs have done little more than increase the students' information about drugs and, therefore, possibly even drug usage. This approach, which uses values as part of its program, can be used with regular teaching materials. It appears that successful use of this program could prevent not only drug usage but many other types of problems. Materials are available for grade levels ranging from kindergarten through grade twelve. Each grade level section contains an explanation of the philosophy and background of the entire approach.

C. A resource for use with parents is published in a book by Herbert O. Brayer and Zella W. Cleary, entitled, *Valuing in the Family—A Workshop Guide for Parents*. This book incorporates each of the values of the Lasswell approach explained earlier, and gives suggestions to parents on how to help their children develop so they will not need to try to fulfill their needs through drug usage or other unfulfilling means. Teachers in the elementary school could well use this book in helping parents to help their own children as well as in the classroom.

D. A resource which has been developed for the improvement of the individual adult (which includes elementary school teachers) is the Human Values Institute in Denver, Colorado. This is a very positive approach to human growth and self-improvement which incorporates values, some values clarification, much psychology theory, and some analysis of operating principles that either help people to or keep people from succeeding. This approach is a synthesis which appears to have some real value. For more information, the student can write the Human Values Institute, 360 S. Monroe, Suite 430, Denver, Colorado 80209.

E. Another popular and well-researched resource that is directly opposite to values clarification is *The Cognitive-Developmental Approach to Moral Education,* developed by Lawrence Kohlberg, director of Harvard University's Center for Moral Education. Dr. Kohlberg has developed six moral stages which individuals *may* pass through at some time in a normal lifetime. They are very interesting and can contribute to a better understanding of the pupil. A good source to read for an introduction to this approach is "The Cognitive-Developmental Approach to Moral Education," published in the June 1975 issue of *Phi Delta Kappan.*

These are some of the numerous other values approaches which are available for the student. It is the feeling of the author of this module that what is needed is a broad, comprehensive model which incorporates many approaches into a synthesis. Such a composite would form a values education approach which is more valuable than any of those mentioned singly. The author is presently working on such a model.

We hope this module has enabled you to gain an introduction to the values education area, to better understand the values clarification approach, and to become aware of some other approaches which are also available. The quality of the individual person is still the single most important factor in values education. As you strive to help young people to grow and to develop as individuals, there really becomes no limit to the amount of good you can do in students' lives if you don't care who gets the credit for it.

SUGGESTED READING

Brayer, H., and Z. Cleary. *Valuing in the Family—A Workshop Guide for Parents.* San Diego: Pennant Press, 1972.

Carr, G. *Values and Curriculum.* A Report of the Fourth International Curriculum Conference, National Education Association Center for the Study of Instruction, 1970.

Harmin, M., L. Raths, and S. Simon. *Values and Teaching: Working with Values in the Classroom.* Columbus, Ohio: Charles E. Merrill Publishers, 1966.

Harmin, M., H. Kirschenbaum, and S. Simon. *Clarifying Values Through Subject Matter—Applications for the Classroom.* Minneapolis: Winston Press, 1973.

Mager, R., *Developing Attitudes Toward Learning.* Palo Alto, Calif.: Fearon Publishers, 1968.

Massialas, B., and J. Zevin. *Creative Encounters in the Classroom—Teaching and Learning Through Discovery.* New York: John Wiley & Sons, Inc., 1967.

Morrisett, I. *Concepts and Structure in the New Social Science Curricula.* New York: Holt, Rinehart & Winston, Inc., 1967.

Raths, L., M. Harmin, and S. Simon. *Values and Teaching, Working with Values in the Classroom.* Columbus, Ohio: Charles E. Merrill Publishers, 1966.

Scriven, M. *Values and the Valuing Process.* Orinda, Calif.: Diablo Valley Education Project (June 1971).

Shaver, J., and A. Larkins. *Decision Making in a Democracy.* Boston: Houghton Mifflin Company, 1973.

Simon, S., L. Howe, and H. Kirschenbaum, *Values Clarification—A Handbook of Practical Strategies for Teachers and Students.* New York: Hart Publishing Co., 1972.

Simon, S., and H. Kirschenbaum. *Readings in Values Clarification.* Minneapolis: Winston Press, Inc., 1973.

Weinstein, G., and M. Fantini, eds. *Toward Humanistic Education—A Curriculum of Affect*. New York: Praeger Publishers, Inc., 1970.

POST TEST

1. Describe in a paragraph the purpose for emphasizing the formulation of values in the elementary school.

2. Describe value clarification techniques. Why are they used and under what circumstances?

3. Define the term *value indicators*. What significance do they have for the elementary teacher?

4. Name five of the seven qualifications an indicator must satisfy before it can be considered a value.

5. Name five of the eight categories in Lasswell's system for identifying values.

_____

_____

_____

_____

_____

6. Do you think that the schools have stressed the cognitive areas over the value areas in the past? Explain.

_____

_____

_____

_____

7. Name the four value clarification strategies discussed in this module.

_____

_____

8. Scriven identifies four different types of values: personal, market, real, and implicit. What does he mean by real values?

_____

_____

9. Describe what is meant by the "core" of the culture.

_____

_____

_____

_____

10. Distinguish between operational values and normative values.

_____

_____

_____

_____

11. Describe the "incidental system" for teaching values used when cognitive learning was stressed.

_____

_____

_____

12. Does Raths look upon values as hard and fast verities or as evolving and modifiable guides?

_____

_____

13. Describe the kinds of dilemmas posed for elementary teachers by societal expectations apropos values.

_____

_____

_____

_____

_____

_____

14. List at least four of the seven value indicators referred to by Raths.

_____

_____

15. The new approach requires the teacher to involve the students in some "problem" activities. Cite four of the six ways he can do this involving.

_____

_____

_____

_____

16. State four of the ways in which a new approach class will differ from the traditional class.

_____

_____

_____

_____

17. List six of the eight ways by which values have been taught in the traditional classroom.

_____

_____

_____

_____

_____

_____

18. What are the levels of teaching values?

_____

19. Name six of the ten value rich areas listed by Raths.

_____

_____

_____

20. In the Clarification system, does the teacher indoctrinate, or dictate, or subtly communicate the values sought? Explain.

_____

_____

_____

_____

21. Cite three of the four guidelines listed for using clarification techniques.

_____

_____

_____

22. To whom does Raths liken students who suffer from confusion of values?

_____

_____

23. Name three of the five weaknesses of the clarification approach pointed out by Stewart.

_____

_____

_____

_____

_____

Creativity and the Elementary School Teacher

Thomas C. McCain

Freeport Union Free School District

Joseph F. Callahan

Jersey City State College

module 12

Definition of Creativity / Teacher Attitudes and Creativity / Skill for Teaching Creativity / Attitudes of Students in Creative Classrooms / Classroom Organization and Creativity / Roadblocks and Freeways to Creativity / Creativity and the Academics / Creativity in the Special Subject Areas

RATIONALE

Research gives evidence that creativity develops in an environment which values it. In cultures which bestow adulation and heroic characteristics upon the gifted and imaginative in particular fields, human talents are developed in those fields to their highest level. Plato's way of expressing this thought was, "What is honored in a country will be cultivated there." In Renaissance Italy, it was painting and sculpting that captured the attention of creative talent; in eighteenth-century Germany, music in many genres; and in nineteenth-century America, inventions of earth-changing proportions.

No doubt, this intention to honor and cultivate something important was the motivation for one administrator of an elementary school in New Jersey to bring the world to a stop in his school for thirty minutes each day to focus on "reading for pleasure." In this school of modest size, everyone on campus was requested to do nothing during a designated period daily except read. The principal and secretaries in the office, the teachers and students, the ladies in the cafeteria, and the custodians interrupted what they were doing to sit quietly with their books until "reading time" was over. Parents were requested not to telephone; salespeople, not to visit. Those people who inadvertently appeared were invited to pick up a book and join the "leisure legion" which numbered many members of the PTA who had written to indicate they would participate in the activity while at home.

The shibboleth for this creative approach to reading improvement became, "How do you like your book?" People in the school society, who rarely had interacted with each other in the past and then only in a precise and businesslike fashion, were suddenly provided with an opening topic of leisure conversation before the business which sometimes took them into references to other books of a particular author and books by other authors that were as good or better. The tone of the school became friendly and warm; the visitations to the class library, the school library, and the town library considerably more frequent.

The classroom where you teach can become a school-as-usual kind of operation, if you, the teacher, establish such a tone as the goal toward which you strive. It can, however, become a different kind of place, with a different climate, and with different possibilites if you honor and cultivate individuality, independence of thinking, self-confidence in making judgments, willingness to risk and experience failure, and striving for originality in thought. Module 12 will help you in your quest for information about creation in the classroom and supply some of the do's and don't's practiced by teachers who are respected as creative classroom leaders.

SPECIFIC OBJECTIVES

When you have completed the study of this module, you should be able to do the following:

1. List at least six characteristics which make up the creative ability of an individual.
2. Identify the seven skills which Paul Torrance counsels teachers to integrate into their behavior repertoire.
3. Give the specific age levels at which creative imagination tends to peak in boys and girls.
4. Show specific knowledge about the characteristics of a creative classroom atmosphere.
5. List the ways in which teachers supportive of creative thinking try to eliminate the unconscious cultural drift towards conformity.
6. Describe the various kinds of assignments which show creativity in a teacher.
7. Differentiate between divergent and convergent questions.
8. Identify any given specific behavior of a teacher in a classroom as being creative or noncreative.
9. Give five reasons that make testing for creative potential in an individual difficult.
10. Identify specific behaviors of students in a classroom as creative or non-creative acts.
11. Identify the characteristics and specific acts of behavior of a creative teacher which appear in her planning and teaching performance.
12. Describe the concept *brainstorming* as a method for teachers to encourage creativity in students.

MODULE TEXT

For one planning to enter elementary teaching as a career, the term *creativity* represents very much the same kind of dilemma that the term *love* does for a new bride, and the same kind of challenge that the term *spirit* poses for a football coach. Just as the family which abounds in love manifests a number of attitudes, behaviors, and operational characteristics, so does it happen with the football team that enjoys a high level of school spirit. Members of such teams with spirit tend to run faster, hit harder, and scramble more effectively than their opponents who may be somewhat lacking in those characteristics. If a family counselor were to spend significant portions of time with a number of families, he would undoubtedly find it possible to identify those in which love abounds. Similarly, football scouts or rival coaches would find it possible to make rather accurate identifications of those teams in which spirit abounds, after observing only a few practice sessions. The dilemma evolves only after the observers try to discriminate among the functionings in the various organizations they have been visiting. The unexplainable truth is that while the level of spirit in a football team, or love exhibited in a family may vary widely from one situation to another, the activities of the teams with and without spirit may seem very similar to one another, as will the activities of families with and without love. So it is with the elementary school classroom and creativity. While any of a collection of classrooms may be the scenes of proven and successful activities leading toward creativity on the part of students and teachers, the true spirit of creativity may be completely lacking in some, evident to a minor degree in others, and the all-pervasive climate in a third group. The significant difference then does not seem to lie in the actions of the teacher or directly with the behaviors of the pupils. Rather, it seems to depend directly on the intangibles of relationships which exist between and among teachers and pupils in the classroom.

Creativity has become a hallmark of much that is good and desirable. To live creatively, to work creatively, and to think creatively are considered admirable goals by the majority. People view creativity as the ingredient needed to solve problems of pollution, of world overpopulation, of urban blight, and of international strife.

Creativity can be nourished or it can be stifled. Support, understanding, and being valued—all tend to enhance it. Criticism, control, rejection, and insistence on conformity tend to hamper and diminish its development. The concerned teacher accepts as one of his more demanding goals the obligation of seeking creativity and nurturing it in his classroom. Since genuine creativity is inhibited in so many ways in our highly organized and structured culture, the sensitive teacher does all that he can to nurture the creativity he does find at his level of instruction and to avoid activities that inhibit its growth.

Several attitudinal similarities exist among teachers who employ a high level of creativity in their classrooms; others exist within the attitudes of the students in those classrooms, and a third set relate to the activities that are carried out in such instructional settings. This module is divided into six basic areas: (1) definitions of creativity; (2) the attitudes common to teachers who are successfully creative in their classrooms; (3) the attitudes exhibited by pupils; (4) typical patterns of organization in highly creative classrooms; (5) sample activities which tend to typify the more creative approaches to the academics; and (6) a word about creativity and its impact on the teaching of special subjects.

Definition of Creativity

As with almost any other concept dealing with the education of the elementary school child, the concept of creativity is subject to as many definitions as there are speakers on the topic. Carl Rogers, a prominent American psychologist, perceives the creative process as "the emergence in action of a novel relational product, growing out of the uniqueness of the individual on the one hand, and the materials, events, people, or circumstances of his life on the other."[1]

E. Paul Torrance describes creative thinking as "the process of sensing difficulties, problems, gaps in information, missing elements, making guesses or formulating hypotheses about those deficiencies; testing these guesses and revising and retesting them; and finally in communicating the results."[2]

Glen Hass defines creativity in the classroom as "bringing into existence ideas or products new to the individual, but not necessarily new to others." Since the

[1] Carl Rogers, "Toward a Theory of Creativity," *Creativity and Its Cultivation,* ed. by Harold H. Anderson (New York: Harper and Row, Publishers, 1959), p. 71.
[2] E. Paul Torrance, *Rewarding Creative Behavior* (Englewood Cliffs, N.J.: Prentice-Hall, Inc., 1965), p. 8.

goal is the development of creativity within the student, the concern is not with whether or not the individual's discovery is known already to others, but whether the process or the products are new to the student. Hass concludes from his research of researchers on the topic that the two main sources of creativity and, therefore, the two avenues for approaching its development are the utilization of methods of independent thinking and the development of an adequate self-concept and self-expectation.[3]

The work of such researchers alerts us that creative thinking is not a "unitary ability" that can be readily isolated, identified, and indexed. It does not yield conveniently to expression as a C.Q. (Creative Quotient)—a single, quantitative, coded indication of the measure of the ability possessed by an individual as is the I.Q. Instead, it is made up of a multitude of characteristics such as the following, which function when developed in a multitude of ways:

1. Sensitivity. Creative students have the ability to sense and discover gaps in information and to discover the areas most in need of additional data.
2. Fluency. Creative students have the ability to produce a large number of ideas on the topic examined. They are not confined to a limited number of responses.
3. Flexibility. Creative students have the ability to produce a variety of responses to problems, as different as they are numerous.
4. Originality. Creative students have the ability to produce ideas and responses that are off the beaten track, unusual, unique, even bizarre.
5. Elaboration. Creative students have the ability to expand upon ideas and solutions, to flesh out the bare bones of an outline, and to supply the details to the general headings.
6. Redefinition. Creative students have the ability to perceive ideas in ways that are different from the usual and to define proposals in ways other than those intended or previously established.

For our purposes in this module, we shall consider creativity to be the production of ideas and products which are new to the individual, as well as the process involved in the production. We shall consider it as contrasting with conformity in that different points of view or unique ways of viewing problems are cultivated, rather than the reproduction of the responses usually expected.

Teacher Attitudes and Creativity

All mothers and all football coaches, sooner or later, will find it necessary to provide specific direction to those individuals under their control. This may take the form of reprimand, pointing out an error or weakness that needs attention, or insisting that the level of energy demonstrated by the subordinate individual be increased. Similarly, every elementary school classroom teacher will spend a considerable amount of time providing direction, correction, and encouragement to her charges. Just as the emotional resilience of the child and the determination

[3] Glen Hass, "Creativity," *Readings in Secondary Teaching*, ed. by Glen Hass, Kimball Wiles, and Arthur Roberts (Boston: Allyn & Bacon, Inc., 1970), p. 254.

of the football player are direct products of love or team spirit, the response of students to the activities of the teacher depend heavily upon the level of creativity that exists within the classroom. For a student to share a paragraph entitled, "The Things I Fear Most," he must feel completely secure in the knowledge that his teacher will treat the confidentialities he presents in an appropriate manner, and that the reader of his paragraph will respond to the presence of these fears in a supportive, rather than a condemnatory way. A basic characteristic of teachers who are successful in the use of creativity, then, is sincerity as it manifests itself in the form of respect for the rights, privileges, concerns, and attitudes of others ranging from Superintendent of Schools to the youngest of pupils.

An elementary school teacher who is dedicated to the proposition of creativity in the elementary classroom cannot indulge herself in the assumption that there are singular "correct" responses to given situations. The correct mathematics response, by whatever procedure obtained, must be accepted as correct. Also, the response, "He died in prison," must be accepted as appropriate in reply to the question, "What's special about Christopher Columbus?" as is recitation of the fact that he is most often remembered for his voyage of 1492.

That students of elementary school age are wary and flexible is undeniable. It is clear, for instance, that soon after their introduction to formalized education, they learn to read the minds of their questioners and to decide which answer of those which come to their own minds is appropriate for teacher's interpretation of the situation involved. When a ten-year-old student is asked the question, "Who was the most important man in American history?" it is highly likely that he will look first to his knowledge of history, and second to the calendar. If it is October, his answer might be Christopher Columbus. If it is February, however, he might have to rely on the calendar to decide whether his teacher is heading toward a discussion of the Father of the Nation or of President Lincoln. Similarly, by prejudging the direction of the teacher's questioning, a highly talented student often decides whether the "correct answer" is Thomas Edison, Crispus Attucks, Martin Luther King, Jr., or Paul Revere.

This example then describes another of the characteristics of creative teachers. They phrase their questions in such a manner that students know whether there is only one correct answer or whether they are being invited to express their opinions. The thought processes inspired by the question, "Who invented the cotton gin?" are quite different from those inspired by the more open-ended version, "How do you think life on a cotton plantation changed after the introduction of the cotton gin?" While most authorities would agree that there is only one "correct answer" to the first query—Eli Whitney—the second question provides students with an opportunity to express their own opinions, react to the opinions of others, amplify suggestions made by their classmates, and perhaps even go beyond the cause-effect relationship intended by the teacher when she phrased the question. Therefore it would seem best that a teacher defer to the class for decisions concerning the appropriateness or inappropriateness of specific responses.

Another characteristic of a creative teacher is that she removes herself from the role of "center of knowledge" as often as is possible. This results in a situation in which pupils develop what they consider to be valid responses to questions, and in time, the correlative skill of defending their opinions. In a creative classroom, it is often the defense of opinions which typifies a discussion period, rather than the

"Guess what answer I am thinking of" game that takes place in classrooms with less creative teachers at the helm.

A fourth fundamental characteristic of creative classroom teachers is most effectively identified as flexibility. The slogan, "Damn the torpedoes, full speed ahead," might be highly appropriate for the commander of a submarine, but for a classroom teacher to indulge herself in the luxury of continuing in a lesson despite a lack of interest, response, or enthusiasm on the part of her students is both foolhardy and self-centered.

A word of caution must be introduced at this time, however, in that there is a vast difference between the flexibility which allows a classroom teacher to shift directions within a lesson so as to pursue a worthwhile interest, event, or situation, and an approach to classroom teaching which relies on motivation by spontaneous student input rather than on careful planning. Flexibility, when applied to the act of classroom teaching in the elementary school, is defined as the ability to adjust one's planned lessons so as to improve the instructional setting, rather than as the hope for some stimulus on the part of the students which will result in a worthwhile endeavor on the part of the entire class.

Creative teachers in the elementary school are flexible in the positive sense. They have skill, the wisdom, and the fortitude to discard their planned lessons occasionally when it seems that their goals would be better served to capitalize on an international event, a change in weather, or an event causing excitement among the students.

By way of amplification, assume that two teachers of eight-year-olds have planned, on a particular afternoon, to present the concept of wind to their students. Each has developed a carefully prepared lesson plan and, although they vary slightly, the behavioral objective of each is the same: that students will demonstrate an understanding of the invisibility of air, that wind is moving air, and that although neither wind nor air can be seen, the effects of wind are clearly evident. Presume that each teacher's lesson includes a discussion of wind, the showing of a motion picture, and sharing of children's experiences having to do with wind. Also, for the sake of this example, assume that the lesson is presented on a warm, windy day in March.

In the one classroom, the lesson proceeds as planned: motivational discussion, sharing of experiences, screening of the motion picture, discussion of the film, and completion of a writing assignment by each student in which he indicates that he has accomplished the instructional objective for the lesson.

In the other classroom, the teacher notes the students' interest in the fact that it is a bright and windy day and that much of their attention is directed outdoors. She leaves her photographs on her desk, leaves the film in its can, and opens the windows with the comment, "What a beautiful day it is outdoors. Let's let the wind in." Thereupon, all windows are opened and the breeze enters the classroom and begins blowing around papers, maps, charts, and other items within the room. After having the wind blow through the room for a few minutes, the teacher asks for the windows to be closed, and invites children to develop a list of words on the chalkboard which describe the effects of the wind in their room. There is no need now for photographs, motion pictures, or retelling of personal experiences. The entire class has undergone its private demonstration of the effects of wind. After a brief discussion (and a short cleanup period), the teacher gives the written assignment she has planned—"Develop three or four sentences which tell what wind is, what it is made of, what it can do, and anything else you know about wind."

This anecdote is included to impress upon the reader the fact that creative teaching requires meticulous planning. It demands a flexible approach to situations and students. It coexists with effective classroom control (although it cannot guarantee good control, it can become an important tool). It is effective.

Skill for Teaching Creativity

Evidence in abundance exists to demonstrate that many things can be learned in creative ways more economically and effectively than in ways which are more staid, traditional, or authority-centered. One researcher has suggested that all teachers, but especially new teachers, could profit greatly from practicing and exercising on specific skills dealing with creativity on a monthly basis. His schedule for teacher workshops for the school year includes, among others, the topics in the following list, with counsel that participants gradually integrate all of the skills into their behavior repertoire:[4]

1. Recognizing and acknowledging potentialities. This is a difficult skill to perfect because it necessitates that each student be viewed not as he is but as he could be. When he misbehaves, or is aggressively vocal, or exasperatingly curious, the vision of what could be is often dissipated by the impatient teacher responses of the moment.
2. Being respectful of questions and ideas. When students have been motivated to wonder, to puzzle, and to see gaps in knowledge, they are impelled to seek answers. Responding to their questions in such a way as to elicit future inquiries is what requires the finesse.
3. Asking provocative questions. Ninety per cent of the questions asked in the classroom, it has been said, call for reproduction of the textbook information or of teacher delivered data. Exercising the question-asking skill will necessitate formulating questions that call for translation of ideas, for interpretation of ideas, for analysis or synthesis, or evaluation of data.
4. Recognizing and valuing originality. The fact that many creative responses of children are original means that they will sound strange and thus may be received with disinterest. Since the natural tendency is to be suspect of the new, cultivating a tolerance for the unique often requires much practice.
5. Developing elaboration ability. Society needs not only thinkers who produce original ideas, but elaborators who develop unique plans for implementing new ideas. Pursuing creative responses beyond the point of bare identification and halting before the point of excessive elaboration is the goal of practice in this skill area.
6. Unevaluated practice and experimentation. New teachers are often trapped into motivating their classes by offering graded rewards for effort. What are rewards for some become punishments (lack of rewards) for the others

[4] E. Paul Torrance, "Nurture of Creative Talents," *Readings in Secondary Teaching,* ed. by Glen Hass, Kimball Wiles, and Arthur Roberts (Boston: Allyn & Bacon, Inc., 1970), p. 264–271.

who are unsuccessful. Practice in this skill will not only serve to entice students to volunteer who are normally wary of demerits, but also will encourage teachers to depart more often from their restricting tendency to grade.

7. Developing creative readers. In perfecting this skill, the teacher focuses on making reading an active, rather than a passive, process. He learns how to encourage students to be sensitive to the possibilities that are suggested by the reading, to synthesize the unrelated elements into new uses, and to do something with what is read.

Through trial and error with the passage of years, the sensitive and motivated teacher will develop his repertoire of skills to enhance his classroom effectiveness. The beginning teacher, concerned about the creative climate in his classroom, will set about from the outset to accelerate the cultivation of his personal skills, lest he become part of the environment which blocks the creative development of his students.

Attitudes of Students in Creative Classrooms

Given the situation in which it is no longer necessary for them to play "Guess what the teacher is thinking" for great periods of their school day, students who attend classrooms where creative teaching takes place often develop a marked sense of security. This may relate to the fact that their opinions are held in high regard, or that their confidences are not broken, or that the instructional goals set for them are more often realistic in nature. It is true, however, that these students will more often venture their opinion, will be more receptive to suggestions made by others, and will be less inclined to disguise their weaknesses.

Although the studies which have been made may not relate specifically to creative teaching modes within the classroom, there have been some interesting revelations about student behavior and student attendance, which suggest that in schools where teaching is tailored to their needs, where their opinions are given a high degree of respect, and where they have some voice in decision making, student attendance appears to increase and discipline problems decrease. Not surprisingly, these conditions more often exist at the upper elementary and junior high school age level than at the preschool or primary grades.

Numerous studies show that creative imagination reaches a peak during early childhood between the ages of four and five with a decline setting in upon the entrance of school.[5] During the first three grades, there is a gradual rise in creativity, followed by a sharp drop at the beginning of the fourth grade. The next rise during the fifth and sixth grades is followed similarly by a decline at the beginning of the seventh grade.

In the first rise in the early grades, boys are increasingly superior to girls in creative thinking, but by the fourth grade, they appear to capitulate to conformity and fall behind girls. Each of the declines appears to occur at a time of stress and at a transitional stage in education, and is viewed as resulting from man-made

[5] E. Paul Torrance, *Creativity* (Washington, D.C.: National Education Association, 1963), Pamphlet **28**, p. 11.

causes such as the change from the security of the self-contained classroom to the flexibility of the middle or junior high school, rather than as natural phenomena. In Torrance's study, the rise between the seventh and eighth grade was reported as continuing through until the end of the high school years.

Student attitudes make testing for creativity very difficult. Some creative students are alienated by the testing situation and are not motivated to perform in the structured testing situation. The fact that most tests contain time limitations militates against positive creative effort for those who resent the coercive efforts to limit or provoke production. In addition, some creative students lack facility with written communication or with oral presentations and find it difficult to describe their ideas as requested.

I.Q. tests generally do not reveal creative ability and are not good instruments for revealing strength in this area. Tests of this type measure general reasoning, vocabulary ability, number ability, and memory for ideas. According to one researcher, "If we were to identify the children as gifted on the basis of intelligence tests, we would thereby eliminate approximately 70 per cent of the most creative."[6] There is some indication, however, that very creative professional individuals do have high intelligence.

School grades also generally fail to indicate the extent of creative ability among students. Usually, grades are given in school for mastery of information, and "sheer mastery" does not appear to evoke regularly creative performances. Even in industry, among adult subjects, low correlations have been found to exist between academic achievement and creative ability when studies have been made to determine the predictive quality of accomplishment in cognitive areas.

The fact that creative potential is complex enough to involve a spectrum of abilities makes identification by testing extremely difficult. Some of the best known tests which have been devised for this purpose include Flanagan's Ingenuity Test, Guilford's A-C Test of Creative Ability, Burkhart's Divergent Questions Test, Fredrickson's Formulating Hypotheses Test, Mednick's Remote Association Test, and Torrance's Tests of Creative Thinking. Most of these tests, although suffering from inadequate statistical procedures, attempt to measure one or more of the following: fluency, flexibility, originality, elaboration, redefinition, and sensitivity to problems.

Classroom Organization and Creativity

It was stated earlier that no single set of practices or techniques could guarantee a creative atmosphere in an elementary school classroom. It was also implied that while any of several teachers may introduce techniques used successfully by creative teachers, following these suggestions to the letter, so to speak, they may in so doing, violate the entire intent of the technique and introduce the antithesis of creativity into their classrooms.

So it is with this section. The organizational characteristics presented here cannot in themselves guarantee a creative atmosphere, but they are common within those classrooms where creativity is the order of the day.

---

[6] Paul Torrance, *Guiding Creative Talent* (Englewood Cliffs, N.J.: Prentice-Hall, Inc., 1962), pp. 4–5.

The lecture technique, accepted by educators for decades as a highly ineffective and yet very popular instructional mode, is virtually nonexistent in creative class-rooms. It is replaced by group discussions led by the classroom teacher, a trained student, or a committee of individuals. Other popular instructional modalities include learning stations, small group or committee assignments, individualized or independent study, and other situations in which students have some degree of option as to the order in which they will accomplish tasks, the manner in which they will complete assignments, or the group with which they will work.

Creative teachers learn to work effectively in a climate that abounds with the "noise of industry," made up of the combination of students moving about the room, discussing the tasks at hand, making or listening to tape recordings, performing simple science demonstrations or experiments, administering spelling tests, or viewing films. Any or all of these activities may be carried on at once, thus transforming the teacher's role from that of center of attention for the entire class to coordinator of activities. It is important to note in this regard that the creative classroom in which students are allowed to exercise options requires a much higher degree of organization on the part of the classroom teacher than the classroom with the less creative options.

1. Preoccupation with order must be diminished. Compulsive attention to the minutia of control is likely to discourage intellectual "breaking loose" to find new solutions.
2. The role of authority with insistence upon support, evidence, and scientific method is modified. By definition, these tactics can stifle inquiry for children since they elicit no exploration from those students accustomed to accept the "higher word" or to defer to the older "scholars."
3. Sparing use is made of cookbook techniques—filling in of blanks or coloring pictures as directed.
4. The use of force or threat is judiciously controlled. Severe forms of punishment, ridicule, or humiliation are never used.
5. Mistakes are not considered sinful; guilt and badness are not exploited as devices for gaining student compliance. Children are trusted and expected to respond to the "challenge" when confronted with problems with which they are able to deal. They are spared the threat of being confronted with problems with which they are unable to cope.
6. Managerial and administrative conveniences, lock-step procedures, rules and regulations are made subordinate to human considerations. The individual child is treated with trust and respect to encourage the onset of self-respect and self-trust, without which he will not participate in creative activities.
7. Subject matter is offered as a medium for preparing students for future developments, instead of as a look backward or a recitation of historical accomplishments. Arithmetic, science, and social studies are presented as tools to be used in solving future problems, not just as the products of scholars who have devoted their lives to researching their fields.

An additional characteristic of the creative classroom is that students become adept at applying the skill of self-evaluation. As the teacher moves from the role of central judge and evaluator, and students are assigned instructional goals commensurate with their skills and needs, the opportunity for accurate self-evaluation becomes more evident and often becomes the fundamental evaluation of pupil progress. In this manner, the substitution of competition with self for peer group pressure, particularly for those in the preadolescent years, becomes a reality.

In summary then, the classroom of a creative teacher is often typified by the coexistence of several factors: students exercise options, a concerted effort is made to replace teacher evaluation with self-evaluation, a wide variety of activities takes place simultaneously, and the carefully developed plans are upon occasion laid aside so that a classroom teacher may capitalize on an event or condition extant within the classroom.

Roadblocks and Freeways to Creativity

Teachers in creative classrooms do not subscribe to the prevailing misconception that the development of creativity is best left to chance. They obviously are aware that hereditary factors do play a role in the potential development of the talents of any student and that creative talent has flourished among individuals in the past in spite of neglect and abuse. Their efforts, consequently, are directed at controlling the environmental factors that support or inhibit creative thinking. Teaching methods in many modes and educational materials of all sorts are implemented to create the classroom climate supportive of freedom of inquiry.

The pressures in our culture that tend to affect adversely creative activity stem from the peer group, the family, some community agencies, the mass media of communication, and the schools. As a rule, it is the conforming member of any of these groups who is rewarded with recognition and approbation. Nonconforming members are often either criticized, or ostracized, or both. The mass media generally reflect the mores of the majority groups in any area, not the innovative or alternative forms of thought and behavior of the various minorities. In the schools, the mandate to transmit the cultural heritage, the peer ridicule that is inflicted on deviators, the teacher reprimand visited upon those who fail to comply with regulations, and the rewards extended to the docile all contribute to preserve creative activity only for the intrepid or the callous.

Teachers aware of the unconscious cultural propensity towards conformity take the following special steps in their classrooms:

1. Control or abolish the tyranny of peer opinion or group castigation of unusual ideas. Students are helped to see things from varying perspectives, to accept diversity and ambiguity, and to seek different ways to solve problems.
2. Recognize and cultivate a respect for ideas which go beyond the usual. To avoid the exclusion that accompanies membership in the minority group, imaginative teachers frequently group by abilities and interests so that deviating thinkers can experience functioning with kindred souls. Research points out that on such occasions, better socialization and cooperation, a higher level of spontaneity and originality, and less inner hostility are the results.[7]

[7] Hass, op. cit., p. 256.

3. Diminish the fear of failure, and of making an error. By his openness and acceptance of suggestions, the creative teacher encourages a free flow of communication. His control, which is not excessively tight, is made to accommodate diversity of opinion and conflict. Students are encouraged to value creativity by the example of the teacher who demonstrates his respect for it in the encouragement he gives.

Sometimes the success-oriented motive, characteristic of the American culture, may be detrimental to growth in creativity. Creative learning involves experimenting, taking risks, and making and correcting mistakes. If making errors is severely punished, children are prone to give up hope of meeting with success and to stop trying to learn. The creative teacher encourages children to succeed first in ways that are possible and natural for them. Subsequently, he can focus on the use of the resulting growth to motivate his students to higher levels of creative functioning.

4. Eliminate the differences in sex roles between boys and girls. Creative behavior by its very nature requires both sensitivity and independent thinking. In the United States, however, sensitivity and receptiveness are looked upon as acceptable feminine virtues, and independence in thinking is viewed as masculine. Consequently, training in the arts for boys is provided and stressed as well as training in science and mathematics for girls so that the creative talents of all may flourish.

5. Change the stereotype about the mad genius. The fact that creative, divergent-thinking students often perform in ways that are unacceptable to parents and teachers contributes to the belief that unusually gifted students who do not conform to the norm group are mentally unbalanced. Unless all students can be helped to feel secure about themselves, some will be reluctant to attempt creative learning.

6. Provide facts and principles, but rely on students to work out answers through analysis of factors and their relationship. Students learn the methods of independent thinking, of data collection, and of reaching conclusions which they practice repeatedly until they attain skill in their use. Students allowed to accept or reject ideas presented by the teacher in favor of ideas of their own tend to develop in self-determination of goals and self-assessment. They learn to evaluate their creative work on the basis of its merit and not by the value placed upon it by the teacher's grade. Torrance feels that many scholars in the past have been led to an "overemphasis upon the importance of providing a stimulating environment to the neglect of providing a responsive environment, an emphasis upon recall and reproduction to the neglect of problem solving, creative thinking and decision making."[8] In many districts, children in the elementary school were considered to be incapable of creative scientific thought, so science as a subject was not introduced into the curriculum until the high school years, where it was taught as a body of accumulated knowledge to be transmitted by authority. Lately, the picture has begun to change and in many subjects, such as history, science, anthropology, and sociology, students are being taught the thinking skills used by scholars in each of those disciplines.

[8] Torrance, op. cit., p. 5.

7. Equip the classroom with a variety and an abundance of educational materials that evoke curiosity and tempt independent projects. The mechanical autocracy of the clock is diminished to the extent possible to grant students the freedom to explore, investigate, think, feel, and express themselves in class.

Creativity and the Academics

A popular distinction made by elementary school administrators differentiates between the teacher who has had one year of experience fifteen times over and another teacher who has had fifteen valuable years of teaching experience. The creative teacher would seldom carry out the same activities in an identical manner two years in succession. While discarding the less productive aspects of each year's experience, she will often revise the successful experiences to meet the corporate personality of each new class as she receives it, keeping in mind the over-all curricular goals established for her by appropriate authorities at the state, community, or school level.

As mentioned earlier, the key difference between a creative and a noncreative teacher does not lie in the relative amount of output extracted from pupils. Rather, the differentiation is based upon the type of assignments given. In lieu of requiring pupils to do four rows of mixed addition and subtraction practice, for example, the creative teacher might ask them simply to write the numeral 7 in the center of a blank sheet of paper, encircle it, and then rewrite the value in as many different arithmetic statements as possible, hoping to fill the page with restatements of the value 7. Or, the creative teacher might simply request that students carry out 30 minutes of practice in addition and subtraction skills, and be prepared to discuss them with their teacher in the morning. In this instance, students can exercise several options, but the common requirement is that all work for the 30-minute period. Although it is obvious that the quantity of work will vary among students, it should also be clear to the reader that this opportunity to exercise options has a built-in requirement of self-evaluation and possession of a clear understanding by each student of his strengths and relative weaknesses.

The traditional book report, both feared and revered for generations, might also be approached differently by the creative-minded teacher. The assignment, "Do something that shows you have read the book," might bring forth from a group of nine-year-olds descriptive paragraphs, dioramas, puppet shows, selected readings, dramatizations, tape recordings, artwork, or other appropriate responses. Whereas each response would necessarily reflect the book selected and read by the pupil, the variety of products submitted to the teacher can be as vast as the satisfaction enjoyed by students who tailor their own assignments.

As a final example of creative homework assignment, let us look at the typical social studies curriculum as it is presented to seven- and eight-year-olds in America's public schools. By using the vehicle of familiar community helpers, teachers are required to establish the concept that when man comes together in social organizations, he becomes interdependent and exchanges goods and services for the betterment of the group. This, indeed, is a highly abstract concept, and may frequently be given short shrift by insecure classroom teachers.

What better first-hand exposure to the concept of providing services than a homework assignment which requires that each student identify a person whom he admires or a condition near his home which is within his power to correct, provide a service for the selected person or alleviate the problem identified, and be prepared to report his activities to his classmates.

Activities within the classroom of a creative teacher also differ widely from the stereotypic representation. In addition to being known for their "noise of industry," as described earlier, creative teachers exhibit great skill in their questioning technique during discussion periods. Questions are often introduced with such phrases as, "In your opinion," or "According to what you've read," or "What do you think about," or "Why, do you suppose," or "Who can add something?" Also, there is rarely an instance where students do not clearly understand whether they are required to carry out a specific process or to produce a given product.

Students might be seen sharing incomplete pieces of creative writing and appealing to their classmates for suggestions as to plot, title, or names of major characters. Brainstorming might be a popular activity and provide students with an opportunity to present their ideas for consideration by the group. It consists of producing a multiplicity of ideas about some thought or problem which are then explored for as long or as deeply as profitable. For example, the topic could be posed, "What would schools be like in a land controlled by fifth-grade students?" In social studies classes, this activity can also be turned into one known as "Blue-skying." The goal is the same, to evoke creative expressions and provoke to creative thought, but the blue-sky activity may be more extensive than is brainstorming. In the latter, some semblance of normality must be retained and some efforts made to substantiate responses on the basis of feasibility, but in the blue-sky exercise, all restrictions are eliminated. Lack of financial backing, inadequate building facilities, and paucity of trained personnel can all be legitimately ignored in the remedy proposed, since the goal is the exercise of the creative mind rather than the discovery of a workable solution to a problem.

In language arts classes, literary-artistic scrapbooks are profitably encouraged. The goal of the teacher using this activity is to encourage students to look at the world and at pictures of the world discriminatingly and to respond actively to the messages they communicate. Christmas cards, advertisements, and pictures of pastoral or dramatic scenes in popular magazines are used as inspiration for accompanying text. In reacting to the inspiration, the student is permitted to select the aspect of the scene which particularly evokes a response in him. He may attempt to do with words what the photographer or artist has done with camera or brush. He may also choose to develop the reflections to which the contemplation of the picture has moved him. One teacher encouraged his students to assume the posture of novelists as they recorded their verbal inspirations. He urged them to assume that they were beginning to write chapter five or six of their major work and were about to introduce their hero to another exciting experience. The mountains in the picture which they selected to accompany their text, or the countryside, or the people, or the action depicted are presented as the visual record of what they have created with words.

For a specific example of creative classroom teaching in science, let us turn to a concept commonly taught to nine- or ten-year-old students. Because of the abstract nature of the molecular theory, many pupils simply memorize in rote fashion the concept, warm air tends to rise.

Dissatisfied with rote learning in this instance, a creative teacher might attempt a role play, identify three students as warm air molecules, and ask them to stand near the radiator. Clearly, these molecules could not rise on command, nor could the microscopic version thereof. They will remain in the position assigned to them until some heavier (or stronger) cold air molecule causes them to rise. Hence these students would have a clear understanding (particularly if theirs was a strong teacher who could assume the role of cold air molecules and lift his warm air molecules) that warm air tends to rise and cannot rise of its own accord without the assistance of cold air molecules.

If, in the generalization of the newspaper business, one picture is worth a thousand words, so the production of a picture might be worth thousands of words of discussion. This would be particularly true if the picture was an 8mm motion picture based upon the Revolutionary War, researched, written, filmed, and edited by middle- or upper-grade elementary students. In a similar manner, primary elementary youngsters can be trained in the use of simple cameras to prepare slide presentations or collections of photographs representing a topic of common study within the classroom.

In the preceding paragraphs, we have attempted to demonstrate that although the instructional objectives in the curriculum pursued by creative teachers is similar or, in most instances, identical to those pursued by their less creative colleagues, the varied approaches to those curricular goals allow students to react personally, emotionally, and deeply with the subject matter at hand.

An important consideration is that creativity cannot be turned off and on as an electric switch. It must be part of the total curriculum and part of the complete environment of the classroom, rather than something interjected at particular points during the day. It can be fostered by resorting to frequent divergent questions in place of convergent questions. Divergent questions are characterized by flexibility and originality in the production of new ideas; convergent questions are characterized by dependence on reproduction of the already learned and the fitting of old responses to new situations in a more or less mechanical way. As creativity cannot be triggered on cue, neither can it be hastened to fit the prescriptions of the clock. Sometimes it can be fostered in a synergistic fashion by teamwork, but the thought must be kept in mind that many creative people do their productive work in isolation. They do not prosper in group production efforts.

The asking of divergent questions to foster creative thought tends to evoke originality in the quality and diversity in the quantity of responses. Successful teachers have learned in regard to such questioning to extend their wait-time in discussions to permit reflection. When they have become habituated to the short wait-time of the stimulus-response style of convergent questions, learning to wait longer entails considerable practice.

Creativity in the Special Subject Areas

If the organization within a classroom is based upon the principles of creativity, there need be only minor adjustments made so as to include the areas more commonly identified as creative. In most school districts today, an art specialist and a music specialist visit with students on a regular basis. This results, in many classrooms, in an over-all reduction in the amount of art or music instruction provided students inasmuch as classroom teachers rarely provide follow-up activities designed to coincide with the lessons of the specialist. For the creative teacher, however, it is a natural extension of the general mode of operation for students to prepare gifts for their parents at holiday time; to take pride in decorating their room with their own works of art; to organize dramatic presentations for audiences comprised of classmates, other students, or parents; or to make slight alterations in well-established assignments such as, "Do something, using some sort of artwork, that shows you have read the book."

Music may be introduced to the daily classroom activities in a similar manner in that a listening station can be established as part of a social studies endeavor; choral speaking can become a group project; those who are talented and have received instruction in the performing arts may feel more secure in providing entertainment for their classmates; traditional group singing may be approached with enthusiasm, given the basic understanding that no individual will be ridiculed for his frailties.

As with the other specialties, the teaching of physical education has, in many instances, fallen to the staff member trained for exclusive instruction to children. The creative teacher, however, can use physical education principles to great advantage within her classroom. Short bursts of calisthenics tend to provide students an opportunity to dissipate pent-up energy. Rhythmic activities related to topics at hand may range from marching and hopping for primary students to folk and square dancing for preadolescents. Textbooks on the pedagogy of elementary school physical education abound with adaptations of Indian games, jousting, pasttimes of other countries, and adaptations of popular American sports, which do not require fully trained coaches, athletes, or officials.

Although each teacher must evolve her own unique ways of effective teaching, experimental studies show that the following principles or procedures, not previously mentioned in this module, are among those which have positive value in facilitating creative behavior:

1. Create the classroom atmosphere which is generally hopeful and which fosters the impression that difference is good and desirable. Encourage each student to develop a feeling of belonging so that self-revelation rather than self-defense becomes the order of the day.
2. Feature, tolerate, or encourage creative homework assignments. Project work requiring creative research and imaginative responses satisfy many of the criteria concerning effective ways to learn.
3. Exhibit the creative work of students to the class. Call attention of the school to outstanding examples of creativity so that the pattern of acceptability, value, and esteem become associated with imaginative products.
4. Provide clues of increasing complexity or of fragments of a series to encourage anticipation of solutions. As intellectual detectives, encourage students to reconstruct situations or to arrive at conclusions by depending on the fewest number of hints and promptings possible from the teacher.
5. In creative writing exercise, assign some purpose. The assumption that such writing skills are developed by requiring a theme a week has been proved false by a number of studies.
6. Warm-up exercises should be used as an introduction to creative activities. Students can be helped to shift gears for the new activity by participating

in some mind-stretching exercises that create the appropriate conducive climate.

7. In the warm-up, exercise care to avoid giving examples that are too specific or detailed. The provision of such illustrations has the tendency to freeze unduly the thinking of student participants in a particular direction and elicit responses which reflect identical patterned responses.
8. Restrict teacher responses and commentary during these exercises to the noncommittal variety. Values imputed by tone or length of teacher reaction contribute to short circuiting the diversity of responses.
9. "Just for fun" responses should be encouraged by this unevaluated practice. Make originality of response the target with the understanding that no contribution will be downgraded.
10. Critical peer evaluations are not permitted during the exercises. It is recognized by successful teachers that one of the quickest ways to dry up the source of imaginative ideas for many students is to permit fellow students to comment negatively or harshly.

In summary, it should be concluded that the concept of creativity presented in this module is similar to the concepts of apple pie, patriotism, and motherhood. While local mores require that the classroom teacher should be in favor of all three, there is no question but that the quality of apple pies, the levels of active patriotism, and the biological capabilities of potential mothers differ greatly. So it is with creativity. Virtually all elementary school teachers favor the concept to some degree, but only the most bold commit that faith to action. The truly creative classroom teacher is emotionally secure enough to accept the possibility that she will not be the sole center of attraction in judgment making, in decision making, or in evaluating. She must be facile enough to capitalize on events of the moment and turn them into instructional situations. She must be well enough prepared as to be able to shift gears when a lesson is not meeting with success and alter or discard as conditions dictate. She must be sensitive to the needs and interests of her students and constantly aware of the vast chasm which exists between telling and teaching.

SUGGESTED READING

Featherstone, Joseph. *Schools Where Children Learn.* New York: Liveright, 1971.

Koch, Kenneth. *Wishes, Lies, and Dreams: Teaching Children to Write Poetry.* New York: Chelsea House Publishers, 1970.

Mearns, Hughes. *Creative Power: The Education of Youth in the Creative Arts.* New York: Dover Publications, Inc., 1958.

Miel, Alice. *Creativity in Teaching.* Belmont, Calif.: Wadsworth Publishing Co., Inc., 1961.

Parnes, Sidney J., and H. Harding. *A Source Book for Creative Thinking.* New York: Charles Scribner's Sons, 1962.

Read, Donald A., and Walter H. Greene. *Creative Teaching in Health.* New York: Macmillan Publishing Co., Inc., 1975.

Smith, James A. *Creative Teaching of the Language Arts in Elementary School.* Boston: Allyn & Bacon, Inc., 1967.

Smith, James A. *Setting Conditions for Creative Teaching in the Elementary School.* Boston: Allyn & Bacon, Inc., 1966.

Taylor, Calvin. *Climate for Creativity.* New York: Pergamon Press, Inc., 1972.

Torrance, E. Paul. *Guiding Creative Talent.* Englewood Cliffs, N.J.: Prentice-Hall, Inc., 1962.

Torrance, E. Paul, and R. E. Meyers. *Creative Learning and Teaching.* New York: Dodd, Mead & Co., 1970.

POST TEST

1. *Place a check before only the statements that you believe describe creative acts.*

   _____ **a.** Mary has finished her geometry homework, consisting of problems solved using the technique described in her text.

   _____ **b.** Richard designed a new masthead for the classroom newspaper.

   _____ **c.** Billy circulated some definitions for the pig-Latin vocabulary he just added to his secret language.

   _____ **d.** Everyone in the class received a passing grade in the spelling class today.

   _____ **e.** In the writing class, Fred compared his feelings of glee to a "meadow laughing with daisies."

2. *Check only the statements which describe the actions of the creative teacher.*

   _____ **a.** Don't change anything for tomorrow's class; just try harder.

   _____ **b.** Accept suggestions from students about alternate possibilities for homework assignments.

   _____ **c.** Establish a daily routine for the classroom which is efficient and comfortable.

   _____ **d.** Reflect after each day upon a better way to do what was done today.

   _____ **e.** Make a checklist for goals that you wish to accomplish the next day.

3. *Circle the letter of the word or phrase which refers to characteristics of the creative teacher.*

   a. Sincerity.

   b. Requires verbatim responses of text.

   c. Frequently uses probing and divergent questions.

   d. Facilitates learning by accepting single-word responses.

   e. Carefully plans for flexibility.

   f. Keeps free from planning by depending on spontaneous answers from students.

   g. Makes frequent lectures interesting.

   h. Relies upon much group discussion for learning.

   i. Changes plans as opportunities permit.

4. The seven skills in the creative teacher's repertoire that Torrance recommends should be practiced in regularly scheduled workshops are
   a. ability to spot the future trouble maker.
   b. capacity for putting bold and cheeky people in their place.
   c. recognizing and acknowledging potentialities.
   d. being respectful of questions and ideas.
   e. ability to discourage weird responses.
   f. willingness to accept and value original thinking.
   g. eliminate grading aspect from motivation efforts.
   h. cultivation of students' abilities to elaborate.
   i. development of students' abilities to recount what they have read without embellishment.

5. (*Circle T or F.*) Studies reveal that
   a. creative imagination peaks between ages 4 and 5.   T   F
   b. creative imagination declines upon entrance into school.   T   F
   c. creative imagination climbs from K to end of Grade 5.   T   F
   d. creative imagination experiences a sharp drop at beginning of Grade 4.   T   F
   e. the sharp decline in creative imagination at the beginning of Grade 7 is the result of physiological development.   T   F
   f. girls are superior to boys in creative imagination as early as Grade 2.   T   F
   g. boys catch up with girls in creative imagination by Grade 5.   T   F

6. (*Circle one.*) Testing for creativity is
   a. difficult because creative students do not respond positively to the rigid, structured format of the testing situation.
   b. unnecessary because identical strengths are revealed on I.Q. tests.
   c. relatively easy because it is composed of so many facets.
   d. not necessary when grades are available since the high scores will identify the most creative.
   e. easy since creative people are stimulated by the competetive aspect of the testing situation.

7. Six characteristics revealed by the creative student are
   a. stability.   **f.** originality.
   b. persistence.   **g.** fidelity.
   c. sensitivity.   **h.** elaboration.
   d. fluency.   **i.** redefinition.
   e. flexibility.   **j.** pacificity.

8. (*Circle one.*) Creative teachers
   a. do not differ in any way from the noncreative.
   b. do many of the same things as noncreative teachers, but differ mainly in the kind of classroom atmosphere they establish.
   c. are the youngest members of the faculty.
   d. generally become officers in the local professional association.
   e. are strong disciplinarians.

9. (*Circle three.*) In creative classrooms
   a. students are free to ask questions.
   b. discussions are precipitated by open-ended questions.
   c. cheeky students are kept in line by peer pressure.
   d. students who waste time know they will be penalized by low grades.
   e. students learn to anticipate the type of answer which the teacher is seeking.

10. (*Circle two.*) The creative teacher in the classroom functions in a
    a. "center of knowledge" leadership role.
    b. coordinator of learning activities leadership role.
    c. catalyst for action leadership role.
    d. "guess what I am thinking" leadership role.
    e. adult supervisory leadership role.

11. (*Circle two.*) Creative teachers
    a. are flexible in their planning and can make alterations to fit changing conditions.
    b. are firm in their refusal to change plans that have been well thought out beforehand.
    c. depend upon promptings by students at the beginning of each class to trigger their planning.
    d. appear to believe that things can be learned in creative ways more economically and effectively than in traditional ways.
    e. must accustom themselves to survive in an atmosphere that permits almost unlimited student control.

12. (*Circle one.*) Of all the modes of learning used in the creative classroom
    a. the lecture is the most reliable.
    b. the lecture is the most frequently used.
    c. the lecture is the most infrequently used.
    d. the lecture is the most rewarding for the students since it facilitates best the imparting of knowledge to inquiring minds.

13. (*Circle three.*) Creative classroom are
    a. quiet islands of studious application in a buzzing school.
    b. enclaves, buzzing with the noise of industry.
    c. orderly and studious centers controlled by a professional person.
    d. rooms in which students move around, discuss tasks in hand, listen to tape recorders, perform science demonstrations, and view films simultaneously.
    e. areas in a school which require a much higher degree of organization on the part of the classroom teacher.

14. (*Circle one.*) Successful creative teachers, to insure adequate application and sufficient learning, rely upon
    a. threat, force, or detention.
    b. compulsive attention to the minutia of control.
    c. research by students of wisdom of traditional scholars.
    d. Workbooks, lab manuals, numbered pictures to serve as guides for students working on their own.
    e. Trust and expectation that students will respond to challenge.

15. (*Circle one.*) The aim in creative classrooms is to help students develop skills in all of the following except
    a. self-respect.
    b. self-trust.
    c. self-indulgence.
    d. self-evaluation.
    e. self-motivation.
    f. self-revelation.
    g. self-defense.

16. (*Circle two.*) Teachers in creative classrooms must control drift in direction of impeding conservativity by
    a. eliminating tyranny of peer castigations.
    b. cultivating tolerance for unusual responses.
    c. cultivating fear of failure.
    d. reinforcing the success-oriented motivation of our society.
    e. accentuating difference in roles of the sexes.

17. (*Circle five.*) Creative assignments
    a. demand equal output from each student.
    b. clearly define the products for which the student is responsible.
    c. entice the student to become absorbed in responding.
    d. are within the limits of student's ability to cope.
    e. permit student to enjoy the work he does.
    f. permit the student to exercise options.
    g. can be satisfied in a variety of ways with a variety of products.

18. (*Circle two.*) Divergent questions
    a. often start with "In your opinion . . ."
    b. elicit single-word answers.
    c. are good to use in provoking discussions.
    d. require students to anticipate what the teacher has in mind.
    e. encourage students to search for the "right" and to eliminate the "wrong" answer before responding.

19. (*Circle two.*) In brainstorming
    a. the creative mind is encouraged to produce.
    b. responses need not be feasible.
    c. a multitude of ideas is elicited as possible solutions for a problem.
    d. flexibility, fluency, sensitivity, originality, elaboration and redefinition in thinking are practiced.
    e. students are free to debunk the bizarre ideas of the weird thinkers.

20. (*Circle five.*) In general, creative teachers
    a. feature a hopeful classroom atmosphere stressing the feeling of belonging.
    b. comment at length for guidance of other students after each creative response.
    c. feature creative homework assignments.
    d. establish a businesslike tone in the classroom to help induce proper attitude.
    e. exhibit the creative work produced by students.
    f. encourage students to sharpen their critical reaction to efforts of their fellow students.
    g. give clear examples of mind-stretching responses sought so students can follow the pattern.

Post Test Answer Key

Module 1

1. Belief in democracy, equality, progress, and education.

2. Local government.

3. State statutes.

4. Local taxes.

5. Urban.

6. Inequity of fiscal support.

7. To advance religion.

8. To prepare boys for higher education.

9. **a.** 5%   **b.** 70%

10. Reality of human nature and the natural law.

11. No. Sophie was to be Emile's helpmate and was, therefore, inferior to him.

12. Froebel.

13. Horace Mann.

14. He published articles that described poor school conditions and inadequate learning environment.

15. **a.** How can the school get closer relations with the home and community?
    b. How can history, science, and art be taught in a relevant manner?
    c. How can reading, arithmetic, and spelling be integrated with other subjects and be linked to life experiences?
    d. How can adequate attention be given to individual needs?

16. To apply scientific methods to the study of human behavior.

17. In 1957 after Russia launched Sputnik.

18. To change society's values, not to merely transmit them.

19. The innovations focused on skills and subject matter, but ignored basic philosophical questions.

20. Blacks, ethnic minorities, and women.

Module 2

1. a	**6.** b	**11.** c	**16.** e	**21.** a
2. b	**7.** b	**12.** a	**17.** c	**22.** b
3. c	**8.** e	**13.** c	**18.** c	**23.** b
4. d	**9.** d	**14.** c	**19.** a	**24.** c
5. d	**10.** e	**15.** c	**20.** a	**25.** c

Module 3

1. a	**5.** c	**9.** c	**13.** a	**17.** d
2. d	**6.** d	**10.** d	**14.** b	**18.** b
3. c	**7.** b	**11.** b	**15.** a	**19.** c
4. b	**8.** a	**12.** c	**16.** c	**20.** b

Module 4

1. e	**6.** b	**11.** d	**16.** b	**21.** c
2. c	**7.** b	**12.** b	**17.** d	**22.** c
3. c	**8.** a	**13.** a	**18.** e	**23.** c
4. e	**9.** d	**14.** e	**19.** a	**24.** d
5. d	**10.** e	**15.** a	**20.** d	**25.** b

Module 5

1. Timing plays an important role in responding to potentially disruptive behavior. Many actions such as pushing and punching can be ignored as part of growing up experiences until the playful tone exhibited by both parties begins to fade in one or both. Sometimes, incisive action can be deferred until the aggressive child is just about to respond when a passive child is in the

process of rebuking him so that each can experience the growth inherent in the activity.

2. The punishment must be specific for the misbehavior. Persistent failure to do homework should carry a penalty of doing the homework after school. Constant disruptive behavior indicates the need for private conferences after school about the reasons for deviant behavior, the understanding of why such behavior cannot be allowed, and possible solutions for eliminating it. Avoid meaningless punishments such as copying a page of the dictionary because the student was noisy in the halls. Avoid vindictiveness; keep positive.

3. Repressive processes generate tensions that can precipitate misbehavior and become counterproductive.

4. **a.** Extend both arms above the head, and flex the fingers rapidly.
   b. Mouth silently your instructions until the volume of student conversation decreases.
   c. Stand where you can be seen, and clear your throat.
   d. Open a window and divert attention to the cold air.
   e. Place your hands over your ears to simulate blocking out the sound.
   f. Simulate recording of some coded symbol into the grade book.

5. Call the child by name, pause slightly, and then ask the question. If you feel he might not be able to answer, ask the question in a way that makes it all right if he doesn't know. "_____, do you happen to know. . . . ?"

6. **a.** Walk toward the offender.
   b. Stare at the offender.
   c. Shake your head to indicate "No."
   d. Gently place your hand on the offending student's shoulder.
   e. Pick up something from his desk to catch his eye, and continue to teach as you shake your head in negation.

7. The spirit of the law pertaining to child abuse is that the child should be protected against vindictive, malicious, excessive, physically harmful, or brutal acts upon his person. It does not prohibit restraining a child for his own physical good or for the temporary protection of other occupants of the room so long as the restraint is not abusive.

8. When teachers use their age, their superior education and knowledge, and their facility with words to create situations that elicit resounding laughter from everyone except the misbehaver, they do not always achieve the goal they seek. This type of action tends to freeze the environment of the classroom and to inhibit the sensitive child, lest he expose himself to the public ridicule that the sharp-tongued teacher will visit upon him.

9. An interesting, productive, and active lesson is the single best preventative to misbehavior.

10. Positive feelings of mutual respect are as infectious in spreading a supportive esprit as are grumbling tones in the hatching of rebels. Teachers do not humiliate students, and students do not mock each other. Instead, they discuss standards and support the search for self-control.

11. No. If he is forced to apologize and doesn't mean it, he has added a flat lie to the error he has already committed. Usually when you talk with children and help them become aware of what is involved, most of them will genuinely and voluntarily apologize.

12. Watch for opportunities in the lesson when you can direct a joke toward him and thus give him a chance to exhibit his predictable behavior when it won't disrupt. Work on a one-to-one basis to gain insights into the motivating causes of his behavior. Assign leadership or responsibility duties to him.

13. "Very well; if you feel like doing it later, let me know. If you need help to do it, group A will be happy to work with you."

14. a. Waste of group's time.
    b. Embarrassing to individual and to the group.
    c. Isn't fair.
    d. Principal object to this kind of discipline.
    e. Parents' reactions.
    f. Difficulty in justifying your action.

15. a. 1. Don't ask the student if he is cheating; he will probably lie.
       2. In a nice way, let the student know you observed his action; you might say, "I'm sorry about your action during the test. It's not like you. Can you come in after school so we can talk?"
       3. If you're not sure, never accuse.
    b. 1. Ask yourself if you have placed too much stress on cognitive learning.
       2. Ask yourself if you have created a climate in which lack of mastery of knowledge equates with stupidity or disaster.
       3. Ask yourself if the climate in the classroom is too competitive.

16. a. Conduct the discussion properly, eliciting supporting opinion, giving chance to opposition, calling for time deferment to collect further data, and scheduling further talk. Positive effect is that students feel that rules can be changed if cause can be shown.
    b. Avoid being trapped into public argument by taking the bait that this might be a good learning situation.

17. Yes, if a student becomes excited or aroused enough to cause a volatile situation. Always protect the many from any ill effects of the one harmful offender. Be sure to follow the procedures established by the administration regarding this type of action.

18. No. It is prudent to recognize your strengths and your weaknesses. If you feel you might bungle the job, seek help from someone more experienced.

19. a. Administrative plans, such as school assembly or fire drill.
    b. Homework papers indicate a need for better learning of the concepts scheduled for testing.

20. It provides understanding for all of what is involved in the rules and regulations, and it makes the rule, when adopted, that of the student rather than of the teacher.

21. The individual differences that exist among students make it easier for some students than for others to comply with regulations. If being consistent means that everyone gets treated the same way and suffers the same consequences for similar acts of misbehavior, those students who have the most difficulty in complying will not be treated with fairness. Each teacher must find a way to provide some flexibility to meet the extenuating circumstances involved.

22. When a rash of petty acts of misbehavior leads the teacher to a succession of criticisms, it may clear the air to explode so as to set the class off on another mode of responding. A teacher who "picks" at students resembles parents who "get on their backs," and such behavior interferes with the climate which the teacher is trying to create.

23. Too frequent use of the "big gun" familiarizes the students with the consequences so that the potential of inhibiting force is dissipated. In addition, students are alienated by the application of such a heavy measure for a first offense or for a minor infraction.

24. a. Compliment the class as a whole for good behavior whenever you can.
    b. Draw the attention of the misbehavers to the acceptable behavior of particular groups or clusters.
    c. Practice good timing in the administration of disciplinary action. Don't step in until you have to.
    d. Consider the age and developmental level of the class in establishing regulations.
    e. Accentuate the positive.

25. a. Children differ, one from another.
    b. Students respond so differently from one day to the next.
    c. Each teacher varies in his response from one situation to the next and from one day to the next.
    d. Groups develop a corporate personality of their own which may alter the individual responses normally to be expected.

Module 6

1. a. Produce self-disciplined citizens.
   b. Promote efficient learning.
   c. Help develop positive attitudes toward learning.
   d. Make successful teaching possible.

2. In years past, control connoted repression of physical activity, punishment, or rigid rules of student behavior. It was autocratic rather than democratic. In the contemporary classroom, there is emphasis on providing leadership in helping pupils to establish self-control. The student is expected to control himself because he wishes to do so or sees the wisdom of doing so. There is very little interference from adult authority. Democratic processes are practiced in group discussion plus teacher-leader action when conditions require directive behavior.

3. **a.** Understanding of children.
   b. Use of democratic processes.
   c. Use of incisive teacher action.
   d. Sound judgments.
   e. A feel for the critical moment.
   f. Conducive classroom climate.
   g. Awareness of individual differences.

4. Classroom climate consists of the spirit that emerges after the group has begun to operate. This spirit surrounds everyone in the room and conditions the kind of interaction that will take place. Every individual in the class brings with him a multitude of characteristics when he joins the class and, consequently, he sways the development of the group in one way or another by the facets of his personality which he reveals.

5. The action of forces outside of the school through television has exposed the children to more theatrical and dramatic presentations than the teachers have seen in their lifetime. The teacher is forced to be competitive by making classes interesting and peppy.

6. **a.** Plan with children in such a way that they are responsible as a group for putting their plans into action.
   b. Share leadership in such ways that group leadership rather than individual domination results and is valued.
   c. Provide such socially useful work experience that group pride in accomplishment is achieved.
   d. Share curriculum experiences with other groups of children and adults.
   e. Guide children in the decoration and care of their classroom so they have group pride in their school home.
   f. Utilize trips, games, choral reading, and assembly programs in ways that foster group cooperation.
   g. Use committee work to extend social group feeling.
   h. Plan and use with the children evaluation techniques that help them improve group socialization.
   i. Teach children to want each member of the class to do well because the group is proud of his successes.

7. The delegation of routine administrative tasks to monitors gives the teacher time to attend to other important matters. The experience of participating has value for the student by giving him a feeling that he is an important member of the class group. This pride in class unity can contribute to maintenance of control.

8. Arrange papers for easy distribution, by rows or by aisles, or by cluster groupings. This procedure can avoid a lot of movement, chatter, and confusion which often results when papers are returned haphazardly.

9. This occurs when you as teacher create an atmosphere in which the child does not feel compelled to do things contrary to his nature, or cheat to get high grades, or disown his friends, so as to secure your attention or to hold your esteem. The teacher works with each child in such a way that his energies are released and his peace of mind is strengthened.

10. This means that the teacher, when he enters the classroom, leaves his own troubles behind and in a positive frame of mind assumes the worries of all his students. He helps students dissipate their moods as he has his own.

11. **a.** Be friendly but not familiar.
   b. Take into account with each class the separate maturational level of each student and the group level possible with such a composite of students.
   c. Strive for consistency of professional behavior in yourself.
   d. Remind yourself daily that as a professional worker you are obligated to keep considerations extraneous to student learning out of your classroom behavior.
   e. Create an atmosphere in which each student feels free to be himself and free to let you see him be himself.
   f. Take time to listen to children's questions, problems, joys, and hopes so as to be able to contribute as needed and when requested.
   g. Demonstrate that you genuinely enjoy being with your students.
   h. Carefully avoid setting up odious comparisons between the work or the behavior of one child or group and that of other pupils.
   i. Praise generously to accentuate the positiveness of the climate.
   j. Keep patient with children's regressions.
   k. Assign many of the routine administrative tasks to students.
   l. Plan such matters as returning papers so as to minimize confusion.

12. The rules agreed upon then become "our rules" and "rules designed by the class" instead of "his rules" and "rules forced upon the class by the teacher."

13. **a.** After recess, or whenever students are returning to the classroom, teachers stand by the door.
   b. The materials to be used during this class have been prepared, collected, and arranged for easy distribution.
   c. Row monitors or small group captains who respond for the entire group are used to eliminate disruptive behavior during roll taking.
   d. Teachers are in their classrooms before the students arrive.
   e. Procedures have been established for sharpening the pencils, leaving the room for the lavatory and returning, running an errand, or being excused for the rest of the day.
   f. Goals exist for each sequence of instruction as well as for activities which will help move the class toward the goals.

14. The teacher's desk will be placed where it contributes both aesthetically and functionally to the appearance of the room. The desks should be arranged so as to facilitate the accomplishment of the planned goal.

15. Children sometimes erupt for seemingly trifling reasons because they are suffering from headache or eye strain caused by the glare of sunlight or the reflection from a blackboard. No child works well in a room that is hot, stuffy, or malodorous.

16. It is an obligation of a teacher to know about a child's background. A teacher should be aware of student interests, needs, strengths, weaknesses, and plans for the future. A teacher should know about any physical disabilities.

17. Seatwork is material that is issued to students for independent work at their desks.

18. By circulating about the room, teachers can learn much about the students, their individual characteristics, and their learning styles. By moving about, a teacher can have better control over various groups or committees and can be available for helping them. Moving about deters students from cheating, copying homework, or loafing.

19. **a.** Change of activities.
    b. Change of groupings.
    c. Committee work.
    d. Entering the room.
    e. Preparing to leave room.
    f. Returning from recess, lunch, or assembly.
    g. Distributing or collecting some items.

20. **a.** Move in the direction of the disturbance.
    b. Call all activity to a halt for a general reminder.
    c. Change groupings or activities.

21. **a.** Use facial expressions and hand gestures to discourage the strengthening of disruptive forces.
    b. Let the students work.
    c. Encourage the efforts of students no matter how halting, or limited, or unsatisfactory.
    d. Help the student who makes a pest of himself in his quest for attention.
    e. Avoid trying to outshout a noisy class.
    f. Give the signal for dismissing the class yourself.
    g. Make skillful use of your voice in teaching and managing.
    h. Establish effective routines.
    i. Control the mode in which pupils answer questions.
    j. Reprove students in private.
    k. Provide an opportunity for the guilty student "to get off the hook."
    l. Keep your emotions under control.

22. One that avoids confrontation. Never make it necessary for a chastised student to save face by destroying himself. Provide an opportunity for the student "to get off the hook." When it becomes obvious that a student is trying to save face, you as the mature, responsible, professional member in the difficulty, withdraw as gracefully as you can. Avoid pressing the child until he has to commit a flagrant breach of behavior. Request to see him after class, start the class on another activity, or send for an experienced colleague in a nearby room.

23. It often compounds minor errors and leads to magnified disruptive problems in behavior. Students like a teacher who has standards and who exacts compliance from them. They want him to be fair and consistent so that they can know what kind of response is expected of them. They depend upon his being friendly, approachable, and available although exhibiting the reserve of an adult, not the familiarity of a chum.

24. Through preoccupation with lesson plans for the day, an inexperienced teacher will fail to notice happenings about him—the doodling with a pencil, the shifting of body positions, and the smothered yawn—and misbehavior will result.

25. **a.** Provide a variety of learning activities.
    b. Assign homework that flows out of the lesson of the day.
    c. Arrange for some activity daily in which even the less gifted students can experience success.
    d. Build into their plans opportunities to reteach concepts that were apparently not understood when first presented.
    e. Schedule times for summarizing the day's learnings by both the teacher and the students.
    f. Give pupils instruction in how to study so that homework assignments can be effectively completed.
    g. Rely upon pretests or other procedures to ascertain readiness for additional work.
    h. Schedule the use of the lecture method sparingly.

Module 7

1. **a.** Those who believe language arts is a process subject. Instruction in the skills of listening, speaking, reading, and writing is woven into all the subject activities of the day.
   b. Those who believe language arts is a content subject to be studied in depth almost as an end in itself. They instruct toward mastery of grammar, composition, and literature.
   c. Those who share both views. They instruct and test for mastery of specific content concerning the structure of the language and its literature, yet stress the process aspect by striving for refinement of communication skills.

2. Listening and reading: decoding.
   Speaking and writing: encoding.

3. Context clues, phonics, configuration, and structural analysis.

4. Literal: What color was the car? What was the name of the town in the story?
   Interpretive: If you were (*character*), how would you feel? What is another possible ending?
   Utilization: Draw a map of the town. Build a model of the adobe hut.

5. **a.** Word Wheels: prefix or suffix—center of wheel, and root words—around rim of wheel.
   b. Compound word making: Simple words on cards. Children pair off when they find a partner whose word can be used with theirs.
   c. Syllabication: Number cards used to denote number of syllables in displayed word or words.

6. Directed Reading Activity.
   a. Motivation.
   b. Silent Reading.

    c. Skill Development.
    d. Application–Extension.

7. **a.** Social—conversation.
  b. Secondary—background music.
  c. Aesthetic—music and poetry.
  d. Critical—facts, meaning, and errors.
  e. Concentrative—directions and sequence.
  f. Creative—visual images and association of ideas.

8. **a.** Give directions once only. Have student repeat the directions or perform as directed.
  b. Close eyes and listen. List all sounds heard.
  c. Read sentences or a paragraph aloud. Have pupils count incidence of: *and, a,* bias words, and the like.

9. **a.** Social courtesy.
  b. Think about what is said.
  c. Be ready to respond with comments or questions and for participation in discussion.

10. A phoneme is a unit of sound in language. Combinations of phonemes form words which have meaning; these units of meaning are called morphemes. Morphemes can be patterned into sensible thoughts for communication; these pattern arrangements are classified as the syntax of a language.

11. A teacher stresses proper punctuation by voice modulations and pauses that are necessary to convey ideas sensibly.

12. **a.** Have students place punctuation in unpunctuated passages.
  b. Have students perform in a drama which has punctuation names for characters in the play.
  c. Use TV programs as model games.
  d. Have reminder charts visible in the classroom.
  e. Use functional writing such as letters, notes, and the like.

13. **a.** Use a list of basic words that are commonly used by children.
  b. Have each child make a list of words he has misspelled.
  c. Test regularly for diagnostic purposes and for checking on progress.
  d. Use worksheets for those who need letter-sound practice.

14. A mnemonic device helps one remember by association. Example: princi*ple* or princi*pal; pal* refers to the man in office. (Any other correct example is acceptable.)

15. Double the consonant (a) if the word has one syllable and ends in a consonant preceded by a short vowel; and (b) if the word has more than one syllable, has a final consonant preceded by a short vowel, and is accented on the last syllable.

16. Motivation, skills development, refinement, and use.

17. Pictures, writer's corner, stories to finish, letters to write, treasure chests, and fishing game.

18. Selecting, classifying, organizing in sequence, substantiating, synthesizing, and comparing.

19. **a.** Do not call specific attention to usage errors until the child feels accepted and self-confident.
    b. Make corrections in a proper spirit, showing a positive attitude for correct usage by stressing approval of it overtly. Create games for practice of correct usage, so that all children can participate.
    c. Always set a model of proper usage for children to hear and imitate.

Module 8

1. c	**2.** a	**3.** b	**4.** d	**5.** d
6. a	**7.** a	**8.** a	**9.** c	**10.** c
11. b	**12.** b	**13.** a	**14.** c	**15.** c
16. a	**17.** c	**18.** a	**19.** c	**20.** b

Module 9

1. History, geography, economics, political science, sociology, anthropology, and sometimes psychology and value clarification.

2. Man, as an individual and as a member of groups, past, present and future.

3. The child's understanding of himself and of his environment.

4. Governments exist to develop and maintain the common good.

5. Teacher presents an aspect of social behavior.
   Pupils investigate it.
   Pupils formulate concept about it.
   Pupils test the concept.
   Pupils revise concept in view of new data.

6. Concepts.

7. Intermediate grades.

8. Pupils manipulate real materials and consider real problems.

9. Primary level.

10. Walking tours, interviews, visits, mapping, personal reactions, and anything that concentrates on the real lives of children.

11. First the now; then the past.

12. Usefulness in respect to pupils' abilities and the available resources.
    Societal importance.
    Potential for future growth.
    Relationship to societal needs.

13. What social studies area or unit of work am I planning to teach and how much time am I expected to devote to it?
    What objectives do I have for this unit of study?
    What specific content and concepts am I asked to teach?
    How will I incorporate the concepts of relationship and change?
    How will I use current events, maps, and globes?
    What kinds of activities have I planned for my students?
    Is a field trip possible?
    What kinds of audiovisual aids will be used?
    What community resources are available?
    What kinds of materials will I gather for this study?
    What bibliography is available to me and the students?
    How will I evaluate the unit?

14. Children's understanding the relationship of the community to them and to their lives.

15. They give pupils a chance to recognize and appreciate the opinions and ideas of others.

16. A teacher must not impose her own values on children.

17. To determine pupil progress and to develop ways to improve future instruction.

18. Develop and use checklists.

19. Have pupils develop and produce their own playlets from teacher-introduced springboard materials.

Module 10

1. Historically, teachers have used one or more of the following procedures to discover the functional level of their students:
   a. Review of results of standardized tests in central office file.
   b. Observation of students as they use the activity centers in the classroom.
   c. Use of a formal, standardized inventory tailored to the sequence of a specific textbook being used.
   d. Develop their own inventory.

2. Not necessarily. The repetition could result from rote memory instead of from the recollection of mastered concepts.

3. Use of recorded tapes to ask questions and supply answers.
   Use of flash cards.
   Playing of games such as War, Number Bingo, or Mathematics Baseball.
   Construction of electric answer boards.
   Use of calculators.
   Use of cross number puzzles.
   Assignments involving drawing to scale.

4. Drill exercises should be so designed as to encourage students to become actively involved in the thought process while they are performing the drill. They should not foster absent-minded, nonthinking participation which will short circuit the intent of the learning activity.

5. The basic purpose of grouping is to help make instruction more applicable to the needs of the students.

6. Ability grouping, interest grouping, long-term grouping, short term-specific skill mastery grouping, individualized instruction, or independent study.

7. Identification of skill or concept to be taught.
Motivational section.
Presentation of skill or concept.
Drill or practice section.

8. It is these problem-solving skills to which students will refer in later years when they make first-hand utilization of their mathematics abilities.
   a. Set up a grocery store.
   b. Produce scale models of playing fields for sporting events.
   c. Time estimates: travel for field trips, travel to planets.
   d. Clock ticks or clock rings in specified period.
   e. Amount of water used or cost per summer for water on school football field.

9. Assignments should be tailored to the needs and strengths of individual students.
Assignments should be varied.
Assignments should be regular.
Assignments must be performable.

10. It provides students with an indication of their progress.
It helps the teacher to compare performance to the goals established.
It helps schools and districts to ascertain over-all progress.
It provides information for reporting to parents.
It helps districts arrange workshops to meet teacher needs.

11. Teachers have forced individual scores to approximate the normal curve of distribution.
Teachers have used answer columns in a mechanical way.
Teachers have awarded partial credit.
Teachers have included neatness as part of the grade.
Teachers have counted problems wrong if labels were missing.
Teachers have used poorly reproduced test copies.

12. As an effective diagnostic tool, to identify specific areas of strength and weakness, and to guide remedial prescriptive efforts.

13. Identify the reason for joint failure.
Regroup.
Develop a new approach to the skill.
Reteach and retest.

14. Help provide individual attention for students.
Free the teacher for professional activities.
Aid in the change from self-contained classroom.

15. Guide children through the internalization of the basic number facts common to all arithmetic manipulations and lead them to a proficiency in the four basic arithmetic operations with whole numbers, common fractions, and decimals.

16. Individually Prescribed Instruction.
Individually Guided Education.
Learning Stations and Centers.
Computer-Assisted Instruction.
Computer-Managed Instruction.

Module 11

1. Teachers and the schools must remain sensitive to the nuances of the social revolution that is in progress; otherwise, they run the risk of losing touch, of becoming expendably irrelevant, and of abandoning their charges to the consequences of a culture in flux. They must help the young formulate satisfying guides for personal living and social interaction.

2. The values clarification approach is intended to help students clarify their own values rather than force them to accept the values imposed upon them by the teacher. The teacher must give instruction that helps students clarify and develop their own beliefs and values in a rationally defensible manner.

3. A value indicator is an alert to the presence of a value item—a partial value. A teacher can respond to comments of the student which fall into the category of a value indicator within a framework of the valuing methodology. In this way a teacher can do much to advance the clarification of values that might bring about behavioral changes in the student.

4. It must be chosen freely, chosen from alternatives, chosen after thoughtful consideration of consequences, prized or cherished, accompanied by a willingness to publicly affirm choice, acted upon, and repeated action forming a pattern in life.

5. Affection, respect, skill, enlightenment, power (influence) wealth (meaning goods and services), well-being (mental and physical), and rectitude (responsibility).

6. Yes. There has been an emphasis on cognitive learning as indicated by standardized tests, college boards, grading systems which reflect the degree of cognitive mastery or deficiency and, in general, an interpretation of behavior change as one of cognitive change.

7. The rank order, values continuum, voting, and proud whip.

8. Implicit values are indicated in those things which we say, but which we do not intend to be taken in a literal fashion.

9. The core of the culture contains the elements of the culture which all people know, believe, use, and do, and which represent the society's ideals, standards, norms. The heart of the universals in this core is the values or the rules by which people order their social existence.

10. Normative values represent the core of universals in a culture—freedom, justice, and equality as democratic ideals of Americans. Operational values develop because of personal needs. They, therefore, can be in conflict with the professed normative values of the culture.

11. Teachers stressed cognitive learning about the virtues and perfections of our country. They assumed that the knowledge would be automatically transformed into action.

12. As evolving and modifiable guides that will help one make decisions defensibly in complex and demanding situations.

13. Some beliefs and values stressed in school conflict with philosophical positions and deliberate actions of some of the citizens in a community. The value position which restricts the individual behavior for the protection and welfare of others conflicts with that position which restricts the rights of the majority to protect the rights of the individual.

14. Goals or purposes, aspirations, attitudes, interests, feelings, beliefs and convictions, activities; worries, problems, obstacles.

15. Encouraging them to make some choices, lending them to examine alternatives, weighing alternatives in light of personal feeling, encouraging students to consider what they prize, giving students a chance to publicly affirm choices, and encouraging students to live according to choices.

16. There will be less teacher talk, more listening, open-ended questions, discussion instead of right-wrong responses, and use of valuing processes.

17. Set an example, persuade, limited choice (stack the deck), inspire, establish rules and regulations, cite religious dogma and historical tradition, appeal to conscience, and tell students what to believe.

18. Facts level, concepts level, and values level.

19. Money, friendship, love and sex, religion and morals, leisure, politics and social organizations, work, family, maturity, and character traits.

20. A teacher subtly communicates about the values sought by questioning, challenging, avoiding moralizing, and helping the student to look at what he has chosen, or is prizing, or doing.

21. a. Identify and explain the strategy to let students know how to participate.
    b. Be sure students know they can say, "I pass."
    c. Be sure every student participates.
    d. Thank students for their responses. (Discuss if you desire)

22. Children who have patterns of apathy, flightiness, extreme uncertainty, drift, overconformity and underachievement.

23. **a.** Teachers become too involved in it; it becomes a well-developed fad.
    b. It is superficial; it deals with "why" a student believes what he believes rather than with "what" the student values.
    c. It relies too much on peer pressure.
    d. Teachers use a judgmental approach to implement a program in which they are supposed to be nonjudgmental.
    e. It is based on moral relativism.

Module 12

1. b, c, e

2. b, d, e

3. a, c, e, h, i

4. c, d, f, g, h

5. a. T
   b. T
   c. F
   d. T
   e. F
   f. F
   g. F

6. a

7. c, d, e, f, h, i

8. b

9. a, b, e

10. b, c

11. a, d

12. c

13. b, d, e

14. e

15. c

16. a, b

17. c, d, e, f, g

18. a, c

19. a, c

20. a, b, c, e, g

NOTES

NOTES

NOTES

NOTES